AN AMATEUR CYCLIST'S 10,000-MILE
SOLO BIKE TRIP ACROSS AMERICA

SHARING
THE
ROAD

JOHN NITTI

Fedd Books
P.O. Box 341973
Austin, TX 78734

www.thefeddagency.com

Published in association with The Fedd Agency, Inc., a literary agency.

Author Headshot: Judy Walker

ISBN: 978-1-957616-15-5
eISBN: 978-1-957616-16-2

Library of Congress Number: 2022913024

Printed in the United States of America

For Mom, for speaking this book into reality.

For Dad, for being a role model.

"I have learned that the pace of a bike is so different than a car. I see every house, every driveway. I race past dogs that bite at my heels because I am exposed to the world as they are. I say hi to the lady gardening her corner of the globe. I smell every dead animal and it doesn't leave me right away. I see uphills as work. I see downhills as reward. I see other bikers as comrades. I smell the sage and the seaweed and I am with them."

– Jedidiah Jenkins

TABLE OF CONTENTS

PART III | BACK

1

HOOVES ON THE PAVEMENT

ROCKY MOUNTAINS AT THE CONTINENTAL DIVIDE NEAR PEÑASCO AMARILLO
NORTHERN NEW MEXICO
FRIDAY, APRIL 20, 2012

"Road Trippin'" – Red Hot Chili Peppers

Another false summit. I couldn't believe it. Every time I thought I was approaching the top of the pass, the sparsely traveled US-64 would go downhill a little, but then, inevitably, back up—a *lot*. Sure, I'd seen the mountain trick before, but I'd never been fooled like *this*. It didn't make any sense to me. Few things test the patience and morale of a cyclist like a false summit, much less a series of them. The son of a bitch just kept going up and up, like that bewildering, never-ending staircase illusion. It seemed I would never reach the top.

Naturally, I began second-guessing myself: Was I going the right way? *Yes, think so.* Did I make a wrong turn? *No, definitely not—nowhere to turn.* Was my distance calculation off? *Probably.* Will this climb ever *end*? *Not sure, probably* not.

The pedal strokes were becoming overwhelmingly arduous now; I was *really* struggling, wheezing and gasping for breath at the icy alpine air, the wind continuously whistling in my ears. The sun's frighteningly rapid descent wasn't helping matters. I'd been tested on the bike before, but this time I was at my limit—out of energy, out of patience, and almost out of time.

In what seemed a distant memory, I had woken up that Friday morning well-rested after a deep sleep in the snuggled down Taos Inn—an historic hotel with quintessential New Mexican adobe architecture and warm, cozy rooms

1

with plush carpets, low ceilings, and fireplaces—in the enchanting mountain town of Taos. A hearty breakfast burrito and a couple cups of hot coffee in the inn's lobby rejuvenated me before I set out, bound for a much smaller town called Tierra Amarilla via bicycle. It was a beautiful, sunny morning. Just a perfect day. The road was flat and without wind; the sweetly charred Southwest air was a crisp, comfortable temperature; and I was surrounded by mountains in every direction, most with snow-capped peaks.

I knew at some point that day I'd be crossing the Continental Divide, but in the a.m. hours it was the furthest thing from my mind. The sun warmed the exposed skin on my arms, giving me goosebumps. The sky was a crystalline, piercing azure blue. Blood was pumping, legs were alive. My iPod played the Red Hot Chili Peppers; the music just seemed to fit. (And who knows, maybe the chili peppers on the New Mexico welcome sign I'd passed and photographed a few days before had had a subliminal effect.) Despite having a pretty bad cold, I felt great. I remember actually thinking to myself, *Where else would I rather be today? This is incredible.*

By late afternoon, though, it had turned into a very different day. The day had begun down in the valley. But now I was much higher up in the mountains—the snow-capped *Rocky* Mountains—and I wasn't exactly equipped for the situation that was beginning to play out. First of all, I didn't have cold weather gear or an adequate headlight; for what I was about to face, I needed both. My legs were so fatigued and drowned in lactic acid that I actually had to get off the bike and push it up some of the climbs. This is incredibly inefficient, time taxing, and demoralizing, but it was absolutely necessary at the time. My quads and calves were just on empty, and trying to grind out any kind of steep climb hauling eighty-plus pounds of gear on a thirty-pound bicycle was simply out of the question. Hitting false summit after false summit was mentally exhausting, as well, mostly because I couldn't gauge how much farther I had to go.

I'd had to settle for a small lunch that day, too, hours earlier. *Way* too small. It consisted of a smooshed-bread peanut butter sandwich and a few Twizzlers Pull 'n' Peels I'd taken from my bags at an abandoned gas station in Tres Piedras, a dot that made the map, but wasn't really a town. When there was nowhere to eat, I had to resort to the basic food I carried with me. As I ate that lunch, looking at

2

weeds creeping high through cracked concrete beside lonely, aging pumps, I had only a slight idea of how insufficient it would be to power me through that afternoon. From that gas station, a marathon thirty-mile climb began.

As I pushed up each climb, sometimes pedaling and sometimes walking, I wasn't sure if there would be another just around the bend. Over and over again, there was. The sun was quickly dipping toward the horizon, the temperature was dropping at an alarming rate, and, of course, walking and pushing only slowed me down even more—*much* more, actually. At an elevation well over 10,000 feet, the thinner air seemed to have a very noticeable effect, especially because I was already sick.

I carried a tiny one-person tent with me, so my usual backup plan, if all else failed was just to set up camp for the night a little off the road. On this day, though, camping wasn't an option. I didn't have winter camping gear with me or fire-building supplies. It was April, but for all intents and purposes, it was winter. It wasn't snowing, but there was now a good amount of snow on the side of the road, building in accumulation as I climbed, and the air was suddenly frigid, with wind chills that were dangerous to exposed skin. Hypothermia. Frostbite. Exposure. These were starting to become valid concerns. I was biking in shorts and a light windbreaker. Of course, I had mailed my only pair of sweatpants back home to my parents to free up space in my bags. As a result, I was getting so cold that my body was beginning to shut down. Even if I did try to camp, I don't think I would've been physically able to set up the tent because my hands weren't working—I couldn't feel my fingers and could barely get them to move. I had to make it to Tierra Amarilla, and I had to keep my legs moving, no matter how painful it was to pedal.

As the sky approached twilight, one of the few cars I saw on 64 all day slowed down and stopped, which was comforting. It was a relief to talk to someone—a reassuring reminder that I wasn't on some barren ice planet trying to survive on my own. When they lowered the driver-side window, I saw that the couple inside was young and good-looking, probably in their late twenties or early thirties. They were from nearby Pagosa Springs, Colorado. I was out of breath, barely able to speak, but they offered me some water and told me I was only a few miles from the top. The *real* top.

"You better hustle, though," the woman warned.

A few more miles of climbing seemed like a few hundred to me, but at least I knew that there was, in fact, a top now and that I was actually getting to it.

It was another couple of mini-climbs, at times pushing the bike on foot again when I was too tired to stay on, until I was at the actual summit. The *real* one, once and for all. When I got there, the sun was setting. Every minute of daylight I had was so critical, but I still paused for a moment and walked over to an overlook to appreciate the sunset and take a picture. The sunset is one of those rare everyday things we appreciate every time we see it—my sister Annie would say that. *But how often do you get to see it from the top of a mountain?*

I didn't stop for long, though. I wasn't out of the woods yet, by any stretch, so I hastily trudged through the snow from the overlook back to my bike by the road. I knew I had at least twenty miles to go, and now it would be in the dark.

After the next turn to the right, I shifted gears and started to descend. I picked up significant speed, and it was invigorating to finally be able to go so fast—but it was also much, *much* colder. As I started to coast, the wind sapped even more body heat—and there was a lot less of it being generated now that my legs were no longer pumping. On the first couple of switchbacks, it was still light enough to make out the road fairly easily. After that, the sun's twilight remnants were completely gone. The new moon wasn't helping, and in a matter of minutes, I could barely see anything.

My first concern was staying on the road. I wanted to get there as fast as I could, because I was literally on the verge of hypothermia, but I didn't want to run off the road, of course, either. With the hairpin turns the way they were, flying off the narrow road was entirely possible, and I had no idea how much of a drop there would be in the darkness beyond. *Were there cliffs? What about guardrails?* This was the remote Rockies—long, steep drop-offs were certainly likely, and guardrails weren't guaranteed.

The only light I had with me was a mini-headlight about the length of an index finger. I had used it before as a flashlight for camping, but never as a headlight for the bike. Stopping for a moment, I flicked it on and pointed it forward, but *shit*—it barely did anything; it only illuminated a tiny circle of the road if I pointed it straight down. So instead of shining it directly in front of me, I turned it almost straight down to the right, so that it hit the white line on the right side of the road. This was the only way to make it useful; I figured if I could keep the tiny circle of light on the white line, I would stay on the road. It was kind of like a game, but a frustrating one, since the turns were so sharp, and the headlight wasn't fixed to the handlebars. Because I had a handlebar bag, there was no room for it, so I put it in the side pocket of the handlebar bag and kept having to adjust it if it moved, which happened with almost every little bump I went over. I had my left hand on the brake and my right hand on the light.

Coasting fast, I controlled my speed as best I could with one hand. I kept thinking that I *definitely* couldn't afford a flat tire or a crash. After ceasing to pedal for only a few minutes, I had reached the point of an all-out shiver.

And then, after a hairpin turn to the left, an unexpected encounter. If I had been listening to my iPod, I wouldn't have heard them. As dark as it was, I couldn't see them. No, I wasn't as alone up there as I'd thought. The sound was unlike anything I'd ever heard, but somehow it was instantly recognizable. It was the sound of *hooves*—hooves on the pavement.

I started to make out these heavy, galloping shadows in the faint starlight, and realized *I was on a collision course with a herd of elk crossing the road!*

Eyes wide open and adrenaline bursting through my veins, I slammed on the brakes with my barely functional hands, as hard as I could, painfully squeezing them just enough to slow down sufficiently, and breathed a quick sigh of relief as they passed, continuing into the silent, wintry wilderness. Collision averted.

I didn't stop. Not even for a moment. It's strange looking back on it. I had just experienced one of the most incredible, terrifying, exhilarating moments of my life, but I kept going, quietly, as if I had just moved the handlebars slightly to steer around a rock in the road. No pausing to collect myself, no trying to take a photo as they disappeared up the mountain, no calling or texting friends or family. In a different situation, I'm sure I would've at least *stopped* for a minute, but my lack of any type of reaction, I think, was simply due to basic survival instinct: I was cold, and I needed to get somewhere warm—*fast.*

But as desperate and worried as I was, I still kind of enjoyed it in a way—all of it. The dark, the cold, the switchbacks, the elk, the shivering, the snow, the pain in my legs, the freezing wind in my face—and now, for the first time, the *stars*.

As the road began to flatten out, I looked up, no longer needing to worry as much about keeping the tiny circle of light on the white line, and witnessed the most unfathomable sky I had ever seen. It was like a planetarium in a way, but this pristine New Mexico sky was more than just the real thing. It was a perfectly clear night, and the visible star count seemed to be in the millions. Each star seemed to have a unique size and luminosity. Even more striking than the biggest, brightest stars was the endless ocean of faint little ones behind them.

I've always been fascinated by the stars, especially by the fact that we literally look back in time when we look up at them. Because they're so far away, their light takes an almost inconceivable amount of time to reach us—*years* to reach us, even though light can travel around the Earth nearly eight times in just a second. Even the closest star system to our solar system, Alpha Centauri (a triple star system), is 4.37 light-years away—meaning it takes over four years for its light to reach Earth. When we look at Alpha Centauri, we see it as it appeared when its light was emitted over four years ago, not as it is presently. Here's another way to think about it: if a star 1,000 light-years away exploded—the dramatic mark of a star's death known as a supernova—we wouldn't see the supernova until its light reached us 1,000 years after the explosion.

Almost this exact situation may play out, actually. There's been evidence in recent years that the red supergiant star Betelgeuse may be getting ready to explode. Astronomers have noticed it's been dimming more than usual, which could be a sign of its pending demise. Betelgeuse is a very large, bright star about 642 light-years away. You can find it in the night sky by finding the well-known constellation Orion, the hunter. Betelgeuse is the red star that marks Orion's right shoulder, just above the three stars that compose Orion's Belt. The Betelgeuse supernova would be visible during the day and likely brighter in the night sky than the full moon, for months—and because it's 642 light-years away, the actual explosion will have occurred 642 years before we see it, whenever that may be. If it doesn't happen in our lifetimes, I think it's enthralling to imagine our children or grandchildren or great-grandchildren staring up at it in the night sky from a beach bonfire somewhere, witnessing an event, *live,* that occurred during the European Middle Ages, possibly before Europeans even discovered America. It's equally mesmerizing to look at it today, apparently intact, and imagine that it might have *already* exploded hundreds of years ago and is *really* no longer even there.

Most stars, even those that are considered close neighbors of ours in the outer arms of our Milky Way galaxy, are much farther away than 4.37 or 642 or even 1,000 light-years; some are tens of thousands of light-years away and more. So when we look up at a vast night sky, like I did that night in New Mexico, with far too many stars to count or comprehend, we are looking back in time to all different centuries, millennia, and ages simultaneously—sometimes thousands and thousands of years back in time. Some stars visible to the naked eye emitted their light far before there was human civilization on Earth, and it's just showing up now. Light from more distant galaxies was emitted *millions* of years ago—in many cases at least as far back as when the dinosaurs roamed the planet—and it's just arriving now. (The most distant object the naked eye can see is the Andromeda Galaxy, 2.5 million light-years away, but we can see much farther with amateur telescopes or even binoculars.)

I thought about all of this as I coasted down the rest of the mountain, and I felt lucky to be there. I felt fortunate to feel how infinitesimally small we are on an astronomical scale, and to remember how our sun is just another little, white star in some distant planet's night sky. I felt fortunate to see that otherworldly, unfiltered window to our incomprehensibly vast and beautiful universe—with my own two eyes—and to appreciate that cosmic perspective. That perplexing relationship between space and time. No, this wasn't a planetarium, and it sure as hell wasn't the Discovery Channel. My shivering body and numb hands and feet could attest to its authenticity. As Plato said, "Welcome out of the cave, my friend. It's a bit colder out here, but the stars are just beautiful."

What if we *didn't* have the ability to see the night sky? What if we lived on a planet that was always covered in clouds, or whose sun (or suns) never set—or we just couldn't see the stars for some other reason? There would be nothing to pique our interest, to inspire us the way Earth's dazzling night sky has galvanized human beings for millennia. Maybe our concept of "universe" would be limited to just our planet, or our solar system. According to American physicist and futurist Dr. Michio Kaku, a lack of a night sky would likely limit how advanced other intelligent civilizations throughout the universe become. Kaku argues that a civilization born on a cloud-covered world like Venus or Titan would be "stunted," and it would be highly unlikely that they'd ever develop a space program—or the telecommunication and weather satellites that would come with one.[1] So maybe we should feel extremely fortunate when we look up at our night sky. Fortunate that we've been given the chance to wonder. To ponder. To marvel. To *see*.

I felt like I had a zoomed-in view of our night sky, as if those Rocky Mountains were so high that they were tangibly closer to our stellar neighbors and the rest of the Milky Way galaxy. If it hadn't been for my struggle that day, I would have made it to my destination before sunset, as I usually did, and I never would have seen those stars. So, to me, they were Peñasco Amarillo's gift for making it over the pass, for grinding out that never-ending climb. "Okay, now you've earned the right to see this," the mountain said, with a slight nod of approval. "Take a good look—you might not see it again quite like this."

***

So how did I get here, alone in the New Mexico Rockies, on the brink of hypothermia, flying down a dark mountain on a bicycle, and flirting with death by elk trample? I was twenty-four years old, fulfilling a crazy dream of cycling across the United States—and *back*. I started in North Carolina and would eventually bike to Los Angeles, up the coast of California to Portland, Oregon, and then all the way back home to New York City. The seven-month, 216-day journey would take me through thirty-five states and take off about twenty-five pounds. The route I charted for myself was a daunting 10,000 miles, and I was alone.

When I decided I would go through with this trip the year after I graduated college, I had no idea what I was in for. I was in between life stages—having finished college but not started my career yet. I felt I was in this liminal, nomadic space. What better way to acknowledge that than by waking up in a new and strange place every day?

How I viewed the world and others would shift and solidify on this trip. How I viewed America would shift on this trip. I'd travel across all types of terrain that I'd never experienced before, from the swamps of Louisiana to the giant redwood forests of California to the desolate plains of South Dakota. The strange and ever-changing terrain felt like a reflection of my physical and mental state—constantly evolving as I biked over mountains and met kind strangers.

Travel has always been a part of the human story. We are nomadic by nature. We're explorers. For the vast majority of human history, some ninety-eight percent[2] of it, we moved from place to place, anchorless, constantly in search of another home—however temporary. Because we needed to. We *still* have a real need to explore, to travel. Whether for survival, resources, family, power, religion, business, or pleasure, travel takes us from point A to point B, generally for a larger purpose than just arriving. I think that's a big part of what this trip was all about. And I think especially *long* journeys allow us to tap into our nomadic nature to the fullest, with surprising benefits.

* * *

Finally, I could see faint lights in the distance; I was going to make it, at last, to Tierra Amarilla! I was psyched and incredibly relieved, like a lost sailor spotting a lighthouse. When I got there, I knew I had to get inside quickly—but I found that, much like Tres Piedras (my abandoned lunch spot that day), it was hardly a town at all. There was no motel as far as I could tell. No stores, restaurants, *anything*. All I saw were some trailer homes and a few small houses, and nearly all were completely dark.

I was very, very hungry, and the cold had become excruciating. I wasn't sure what to do. Then I saw an elderly couple in a lit driveway getting out of their car down the road to the left. I sped up, pulled into their driveway, and got off my bike before I even said anything.

The two of them were frozen in place beside their car, holding brown paper grocery bags. I don't think they were afraid, but I don't think they quite knew what to make of me, either. Okay, maybe they were a *little* afraid.

I tried to explain my situation. There was so much I wanted to say: "I'm going cross country, trying to make it to California, but there was this herd of elk, I'm really cold, you seem like nice people, can I *please* just come inside . . .?" I was trying to speak, but my face was so numb that my mouth just couldn't form the words right, and I was shivering violently now, to the point that my teeth were chattering, and my nose was running down my face. I must have looked and sounded absolutely ridiculous—the thought of my appearance from their perspective would've cracked me up if I wasn't so desperate.

Barely comprehensible, I asked them if there was a motel nearby. They said no, but that there was a post office down the street, and the first door (into the entryway) was probably open, so I could sleep on the floor with a roof over my head. The door being open wasn't a guarantee, though, and they could tell I wasn't too keen on the idea.

"I can drive you to Chama," the man said. "There's a hotel there."

Chama was a larger town down the road. I managed to explain in broken, muffled words that I didn't want to go farther down the road because I didn't want to cheat. I wanted to go the whole way, from coast to coast, under my own power, and hitching a ride would be cheating.

Finally, I more or less asked them if I could stay the night, even though we had been talking for just a few minutes. The man was friendlier and more sympathetic than the woman. I could tell the woman was a little hesitant to let me into their home. I wasn't used to this, actually—unconditional kindness and hospitality from strangers had become the norm on the trip, incredibly. But, hey, I couldn't blame her, either; I must have looked and sounded literally insane, on a bike in the mountains in the middle of a freezing night, in *shorts*, with all that gear, barely able to speak. They both agreed they would help me, though, and we went inside.

Henry Ulibarri, seventy-seven, a cancer survivor and Marine in the Korean War, and his wife, Mabel, had a fairly large home because their store—which had been established in 1967 and sold everything from building and plumbing materials to hardware and rancher supplies, to groceries, fishing, and hunting supplies, to paints and liquors—was attached to it.

We left the bike and gear in a storage room just off the driveway, where I would later sleep on a couch, and went upstairs, where the living room and kitchen shared one large, toasty-warm space with a high ceiling and an antique wood-fired stove that heated the house, just off the kitchen. The old, cozy log cabin home was adorned with an eclectic collection of little ornaments and trinkets, tchotchkes, and novelties. There were family photos, rifles, dream catchers, Native American blankets, scythes and other tools in one area hanging on the wall, animal skins, an elk bust with antlers, and small statues of the Virgin Mary and Jesus Christ.

I was thrilled to finally be indoors. Based on the home decor and Henry's accent, I knew he was Native American. The nearby Jicarilla Apache Nation Reservation was further evidence. I sat inches from that wood-fired stove and happily thawed for a couple of hours as I told them my story, slowly sipping cups of hot coffee and gratefully gobbling some eggs and toast Mrs. Ulibarri made for me for a very late dinner (it was around 10:00 p.m. or so by the time I finally ate). I had no need or desire to move from that spot; I could've sat there all night. I was extremely fortunate for their hospitality. On this night—the end of what ended up being the second most difficult day of my entire 216-day trip—they had saved me. It was something I'll never forget.

Mabel made the same meal for us for breakfast the next morning before I set out, bound for Dulce (two towns down the road, after Chama), where I decided I would stray from my budget a little and stay at the Best Western Jicarilla Inn and Casino, partly because I was sick and a little beat up. I figured a comfortable hotel bed would do me some good. Since I'd be staying at a hotel with a casino that night, Henry and Mabel asked me if I liked to gamble. Before I could answer, their adult, forty-something daughter or niece, who had stopped by to join us for breakfast (and to get a look at the crazy man on the bike, I guess), chimed in.

"He's already gambled enough . . . with his *life*. And he *won*." She looked at me seriously, with wide, disapproving eyes, like she was my mother.

I finished my eggs, showered, took a picture of Henry and Mabel standing together in their living room to remember them by, collected my belongings, thanked them again, and left. It was another sunny day, back on the road.

PART I
PURPOSE AND PREPARATION

2
NO FEAR

"I Still Haven't Found What I'm Looking For" – U2

On the fifth day of eighth grade, at thirteen years old, I woke up in my Long Island childhood bedroom, with its sports-themed wallpaper and unfinished wooden furniture and turned off my blaring New York Yankees alarm clock. The alarm mimicked a baseball announcer, shouting, *"He leaps...he's got it!"* followed by a fake crowd's roar over and over again, sounding like an archaic video game. It was still mostly dark outside at around 6:00 a.m., so I flicked on the light over my bed.

As my eyes struggled with it, my mind drifted to the typical responsibilities of a new eighth grader. My reminder notepad on my desk read *Follow New Schedule* and *Earth Sci. Quiz Today*. As the clock on my wall ticked in my otherwise silent room, I continued to sit there on the bed, feeling the full brunt of the early Tuesday morning—feeling *groggy*. The summer days of sleeping in were over, and I wasn't quite used to it yet.

Suddenly, a knock on the door broke the silence. It startled me a little. I leapt off the bed and opened it. It was my dad, John J. Nitti, dressed in business clothes (Nitti isn't a common Italian surname, but we have no relation to "The Enforcer" Frank Nitti, Al Capone's right-hand man, as far as we know). At just forty-three years old, Dad was damn big and strong, and occupied most of the door frame, towering over me. The 1980 captain of the Yale football team, which won the Ivy League championship that year, he was a six-foot-two, 230-pound running back who went on to play for both the New York Jets and

New York Giants in the early '80s. Tanned, with blond hair and a blond mustache, people used to say he looked like the Brawny paper towel guy back then. With little body fat and legs like tree trunks, he could run a 4.6-second 40-yard dash and bench press over 400 pounds, making him the strongest running back on the Jets by a good margin. On the Giants, linebackers coach Bill Belichick, who would become the greatest NFL head coach of all time, once bet him that he couldn't beat a defender in practice. Dad did, and is still owed.

Dad could fight, too, and wasn't the type to back down from one if provoked. Our family moved to Pleasanton, California, in the Bay Area, for a year in 1995, when I was in second grade. Shortly after that, Dad noticed a big man with a scar streaking across his face making lewd gestures toward my mom as they dined in downtown Pleasanton with Dad's coworker and his wife at a crowded, upscale Italian restaurant owned by John Madden. Dad calmly removed his watch and his 1980 Ivy League championship ring, placed them on the cloth-covered table, and walked over to the man's table. Just before he got there, though, the man leveraged the sides of his table's booth and swung out at him, landing a heavy front kick to the chest with his spurred cowboy boot. Dad held onto the boot and twisted the man down to the ground, tables and chairs went flying, and they wrestled on the restaurant floor in front of horrified, screaming patrons—some of whom knew my parents from church as the "newcomers from New York." Dad held the man in a sturdy headlock before the man could land any punches with his brass knuckles, rendering him helpless and winning the fight.

Dad stayed in shape long after his NFL days were cut short by multiple injuries, enough to earn a tryout in the Canadian Football League at age forty. So when he stood at my bedroom door at age forty-three, clean-shaven now, but perpetually tanned, and almost as strong, he still filled most of the frame.

"Hey, JM. I'm leaving for California," he whispered, trying not to wake my two sisters, Annie and Cailyn, eleven and nine years old respectively, in the room next door. "I didn't want to wake you, but I saw your light on, so I wanted to say goodbye."

We hugged and said "Love you," as we always did. I wasn't sure what it was, but something felt potently different about *this* goodbye. The hug was a couple of seconds longer than usual. The parting words seemed to be said more slowly, and with more emotion.

As he walked away and rounded the staircase with the hurried pace of someone on their way to the airport to catch a morning flight, he paused on the stairs, looked back, and waved one more time in the darkness. He'd never done that before.

Still under the doorframe of my illuminated room, in my pajamas, I waved back, somehow aware of the potential importance of the moment and locking the image in my mind.

* * *

When Dad got to the gate at JFK, he looked at the silver, red, and blue American Airlines plane through the window, parked under a clear blue sky and scheduled to leave at 8:00 a.m., and thought, *That plane's not making it to California.* He flew routinely, and had never once had that feeling. He'd been known to have strange, unexplainable premonitions from time to time, but this day wasn't just any other. *This* day was September 11, 2001.

Most of his strange premonitions couldn't be proven, so, of course, we were always skeptical and have made light of them over the years, calling him the second coming of Nostradamus—but on *this* day, before he left for the airport, he'd left an envelope with a life insurance policy that was expiring on September 30 on the kitchen counter for my mom. On the front of the envelope, in the darkness of the early morning, he scribbled a note: "If anything happens, mail this check in ASAP." The month before, he'd switched to a larger policy, which had become active, but as long as Mom sent in a check for the old policy before September 30, she'd have both.

You can't exactly tell your boss you missed the meeting because you had "a bad feeling about the plane." Dad had a big presentation to make that afternoon in Sunnyvale in front of a large audience. So he boarded.

The flight began normally. It took off on time, which was important; an 11:00 a.m. landing at SFO would give Dad just enough time to rent a car, drive to his company's headquarters, have lunch, and set up for the 2:00 p.m. presentation.

As I sat in the front row of Mr. Domenick's Earth Science class, taking that quiz, Dad sat in a window seat on the plane, with nobody next to him, eating breakfast as he worked on his laptop. The clear blue skies made for silky-smooth flying. The day was off to a good start. That quickly changed, though, when the pilot got on the PA a little later in the morning.

"We're about to hit *major* turbulence," the captain warned. "Flight attendants get to the back of the plane. Everyone please take your seats and make sure your seatbelts are fastened."

Dad had flown about three million miles on American Airlines alone and had never once heard a pilot refer to turbulence as "major." He looked out the window at the clear blue sky. Something was off.

The flight attendants scurried about the plane. As one passed him, she saw his laptop and snapped, "Turn that off, please."

"Turn off my laptop for turbulence? What's going on?"

She looked at him, almost desperately. "Please just turn it off."

Then, pausing for a moment longer, and appearing to change her mind about something, the flight attendant gathered Dad and the large man sitting behind him closer to her. Speaking much more softly now, so others couldn't hear, she collected herself and said, "Two planes have crashed into the World Trade Center. It is known to be terrorism. We have been told a total of eight planes in the air have terrorists. We've been told we are one of them.

"We don't want to alarm all the passengers. We're asking the two of you to help us. Please don't tip this off, and please don't ask too many questions. We just need you to keep your eye on them and help us, please, as needed."

She then inconspicuously pointed out four young men, seemingly of Middle Eastern descent. Three were in plain sight. Dad slowly leaned over to catch a glimpse of the fourth.

The man sitting behind Dad was the biggest person on the plane, and Dad was second biggest—it was clear why they were chosen, and he felt up to the task.

"What do they have? Guns, a bomb, what?" Dad asked, his mind racing.

"We believe they have some kind of knife."

Okay, at least we have a fighting chance, Dad thought. He was as scared as he'd ever been in his entire life, but he tried to remain calm, reassuring the flight attendant that she'd made the right choice picking him and the big man behind him.

***

Back on the ground, Uncle Kevin, a seasoned NYPD detective in his early forties, called my mom at home. "Give me his flight information," he said hurriedly to his younger sister.

"I—I don't have it," she answered, frantically. "Let me look."

There were reports that one of the planes that hit the towers was an American Airlines flight heading to California.

My mom isn't easily frazzled. She's always sure of herself. Calm and steady. I've always trusted her judgment. Pat McAleese was the second-oldest of five children and the "model student" of the McAleese family (pronounced MAC-a-leese), who all the teachers at Baldwin High School on Long Island adored—especially compared to her seemingly unrelated three brothers, who were often getting into trouble. An accomplished track athlete, she set the New York State high jump record in high school before heading down to Alabama for college to high jump at Auburn. Tall with short dark hair, she was a runway model in the 1980s, who looked a little like Demi Moore. Tough and honest (even brutally so at times), she doesn't hold things back. But she's almost always in a good mood.

Mom's two younger brothers, Uncle John and Uncle Brian, were both New York City firefighters in their mid-to-late thirties. They both worked in Brooklyn—John at Ladder 105/Engine 219 on Dean Street and his younger brother, Brian, at Engine 226 on State Street—and sometimes fought the same fires.

Uncle John was hurt at the time, though, and Uncle Brian was supposed to be off on September 11.

Looking after his little daughter, Kerin, who was watching *Sesame Street*, and unaware of the events unfolding on TV, Uncle John answered the phone casually when Uncle Kevin called him that morning.

"What's going on, Kev?" he answered.

"What's going on? You don't know what's going *on*? Turn on CNN," Uncle Kevin demanded, in his old school New York accent.

***

Back in the air, as the flight attendant continued speaking to Dad and the big man behind him, the rest of the flight attendants were making their way to the back of the plane.

"Why do you all need to get to the back?" Dad quietly asked.

With fear in her eyes, she hesitated. Even more quietly now, she answered, "We have information that flight attendants on other flights had their eyes cut out in front of the passengers. The hijackers yelled, 'Look at us and this will happen to you,' as they did it. That's why we're in the back. Please don't let them bring any of us up there."

Suddenly, the plane began to rock back and forth. With the severity of the "turbulence" and the abrupt descent of the plane, passengers began crying. And screaming. Dad assumed this rocking was part of the crew's plan somehow, but he wasn't sure. *Had they overcome the cockpit, as they did on the other planes?* He could see three of the supposed terrorists, but not the fourth, since he couldn't stand up or lean over far enough in such an unstable environment. Like everyone else, he gripped the armrests tightly, and more thoughts raced through his mind. *Could the fourth have gotten into the cockpit? Was this his failed attempt to fly the plane? Were we headed for a building or crashing into an open field? Or was the pilot rocking the plane so no one could stand and get to the cockpit?* He watched the other three "terrorists" holding on for dear life too.

Now they didn't seem like terrorists. They seemed like everyone else—afraid and confused.

But it still seemed as if the plane were crashing—or, at best, making a desperate emergency landing. With the ground in view below, as the plane descended farther, Dad thought about Mom, us kids, his parents, and the rest of our family and friends. He wondered if there was any possibility of surviving a crash. He wondered what could have possibly made him think they weren't making it to California earlier that morning . . .

But then, with the sound of the wheels coming down, a feeling of immense relief. The plane stopped rocking, slowed down, and finally landed—on a runway, without incident.

Once on the tarmac, the pilot came on the PA again. "We've been forced to land in St. Louis by the FAA. Two planes have crashed into the World Trade Center and all planes throughout the country are grounded. We'll pass on more information once we have it."

A little later, the flight attendant was back.

"Have you been watching them? We're not out of the woods yet. They were trained pilots on the other planes. They can get us back into the air."

Dad was amazed by how much they already knew.

Then she added, "Did you see when the pilot announced the attack? They all nodded to each other."

While other planes sat on the tarmac, Dad's plane was expedited straight to a gate. As the passengers got off, they were swarmed by about fifty MPs. The four "terrorists" were engulfed in a sea of navy blue. Dad put his carry-on and laptop bag down for a moment to reach for his cell phone to call Mom, but a police officer approached him and yelled, "Pick up your bags and get out of here. This airport is evacuated!"

***

As a kid, there was no question who my heroes were. They were my dad, my mom, and my uncles.

Kevin McAleese, or Uncle Kevin, my godfather, was the oldest and toughest of the five McAleese siblings, and the most cerebral. Although he never had a college education, he was very intelligent, subscribing to *Popular Mechanics* and reading up on the latest science and space exploration. With a love of nature and the ocean, he eventually became a scuba diving instructor. He also loved art, creating exquisite pencil and charcoal drawings. But his real passion was fighting crime. (If I said that to Uncle Kevin, he'd probably say, "Passion for fighting crime? What am I, *Batman*?" and start his classic, choking cackle of a laugh that past girlfriends have described as "horrible.") But it was true—he wasn't just a cop for a paycheck—his passion for stopping the bad guys was genuine. He started his NYPD career as a police officer in crime-ridden 1980s New York City, in the middle of the crack epidemic. The 83rd Precinct in Bushwick, where he asked to be transferred to from the much quieter Canarsie, had the highest homicide rate in the city and was actually where the crack epidemic started. He later became an investigator in the NYPD's select Gang Intelligence Unit and did undercover work for the Brooklyn DA's office, including once posing as a Westie (as in the ruthless West Side Irish Mob, not the fluffy West Highland White Terrier) in a money laundering case with a Chinese gangster that owned a chop shop in Brooklyn.

All three uncles had crazy stories working as New York City first responders, but none matched the absurdity of Uncle Kevin's. He would hold court at my grandmother Nana Mac's dining room table at family holiday dinners, doling out one story after the next, leaving his listeners shocked and awed—especially the kids, who usually weren't old enough to hear some of the things he was saying.

The height of the crack epidemic was a tough time to be a cop. And they didn't have tasers back then. So, instead of tasing the bad guys to subdue them, they'd have to wrestle with them. Once, as Uncle Kevin wrestled with a perpetrator on a rooftop in Brooklyn, the man got a hold of him and threw him right off the roof. He fell four stories, literally thinking, *This is it*, on the way down. Luckily, he landed on a tool shed, which cushioned the fall enough to save his life. Not many people can say they were "lucky" to land on a tool shed.

Another time, at a violent riot, he got out of the police car (because he was "young and stupid" and "thought he was Superman," he would later recall), and someone at the riot threw liquid lye, a corrosive alkali that's used for murder and dissolving corpses, directly at him. The lethal chemical substance missed him, but peeled the paint off the police car instantaneously. The attacker ran, and Uncle Kevin chased him back to his apartment. That was a mistake, though, as the attacker had a whole *pot* of lye cooking on his stove and threw even more of it when Uncle Kevin entered the apartment—this time hitting his mark. The lye doused Uncle Kevin's chest, peeling off the top layers of his uniform. Luckily, it was winter, and the thick jacket he was wearing saved him.

Another time, he approached a bodega in Brooklyn that was being held up. A man held his gun upside down as he waived it at the cashier, shouting at him, and then shot the cashier three times, subsequently firing at Uncle Kevin as he entered the store, missing him and shattering the store window behind him. As they ran in parallel aisles toward the back of the bodega, the shooter continued firing at him, exploding chip bags and other groceries on the shelves along the way. When he tried to escape through the back of the store, the shooter was attacked by a Doberman.

And another time, he responded to a call and found a whole family calmly sitting at the table, eating Thanksgiving dinner. All except a man that had his face in his food and a butcher knife in his back. There was an argument, the family explained, about how much dark meat the man had taken on his plate.

When Uncle Kevin was promoted to detective, he brought his shield back home and walked up to Papa Mac, confined to his wheelchair with MS. He placed the shield down on his lap. Papa Mac, his tough-guy dad, who was a decorated Korean War vet and used to smoke cigars while fighting fires in the FDNY, looked down at it and started to cry.

Responding to an armed robbery in Brooklyn in 1985, Uncle Kevin found an innocent bystander lying in the street, shot twice in the diaphragm. The sixteen-year-old kid had been riding his bicycle, and now he was minutes from death, unable to breathe. As he started CPR, Uncle Kevin put cellophane on the wound and applied pressure, creating a seal that allowed the kid to breathe until the ambulance arrived. When CPR is necessary, only about 10% survive. This one survived.

First responders. Real heroes.

***

John McAleese, or Uncle John, was the middle child of the five and the most mischievous as a kid. At thirteen years old, he secretly started driving after he was able to have an extra set of keys made for the family car. When he was caught, he bought a go-kart and started driving *that* around town, including to school each day. In his late teens and twenties, he was John Travolta's doppelgänger and dated lots of girls before he met Aunt Heather—including Taylor Dayne, whose debut hit single "Tell It to My Heart" reached the Top 10 across fourteen international music charts later on in the late '80s.

Unlike his two brothers, he didn't play football or any other sports—he was more into classic cars and rock and roll, channeling these interests to become a self-taught mechanic and skilled drummer. He didn't really care much about school, but high school teachers gave him passing grades for fixing their cars. When Mr. Ratner's butterfly was stuck in his carburetor, for example, Uncle John fixed it and didn't have to go to gym class for the rest of the year.

Of the three brothers, Uncle John was the funniest. He was also a history buff with an uncanny memory. He'd often have me for the day when I was little, so we'd drive around, go to the movies, get "pizza at the place"—which was always better than delivery, he taught me. "Because it steams in the box," he'd say. With his foot on the pedals, he'd let me take the wheel and teach me the basics of driving in empty parking lots.

Papa Mac made Uncle John take all the civil service tests, telling him, "You know what you need to be a firefighter? You need to be a US citizen and have a high school diploma, a clean record, and a driver's license. I think we can achieve that with you."

Since there were so many Johns at Ladder 105/Engine 219, which had been Papa Mac's firehouse, Uncle John's nickname was "Jake." He didn't get it, though, at first, and asked one of the senior guys one day, "Why are they calling me Jake?"

The vet shook his head. "Just be glad they're not calling you asshole, kid."

Uncle John loved the job, the guys, the camaraderie. He loved following in Papa Mac's footsteps. And some of the stories he told, you just can't make up. One of my favorites is a random encounter they had with comedy legend Chris Farley. In the early '90s, Farley was eating a hot dog on the street in Manhattan when Uncle John's rig was passing by. Farley shouted out to them, "Hey guys, can I hop on?"

They decided to let him hop on the back step, and Farley rode with them for four blocks—still holding the hot dog in one hand, hanging on with the other, and smiling from ear to ear, shouting out, "Hey guys—this is great!"

But the job, of course, wasn't always so buoyant. In March 1993, Uncle John was in a building collapse at a warehouse fire and was pinned under rubble for forty-five minutes—with two others, a captain and a chief. The captain wasn't religious, but he asked Uncle John to pray with him. Uncle John was pinned on his back, unable to move or feel his legs, with fire above him and water rising around him, beginning to submerge his shoulders. He thought, *I'm either going to be burned alive or I'm going to drown.* They were rescued, but if they'd been standing just four feet to the left, they would have certainly been killed.

Uncle John was actually in *two* building collapses over the course of his career, which was exceedingly rare. "Guys were superstitious," he'd later recall. "Building collapses kill more firefighters than anything else, so if they survived one, they'd look around and grab a small object—a piece of debris or something, *anything*—and put it in their helmet, to keep. They'd take it with them to other fires. They'd reason, 'What are the odds this'll be in another building collapse?'"

Uncle John was known as "the compassionate one" in the firehouse, with the best bedside manner, so the duty of speaking to dying people in their last moments—a responsibility that all first responders must accept as part of their job description, but that not all actually experience—was often relegated to him. He'd play the part of the stranger's family members who couldn't be there. One middle-aged man was pinned by a subway train after he was pushed onto the tracks—as soon as the train moved, he would die. Uncle John held his hand and talked to him until it went limp.

On a frigid winter night, just after New York's historic blizzard of '96, Ladder 105/Engine 219 responded to a call for an unresponsive infant. The baby had stopped breathing and was beginning to turn blue. When Uncle John ran in and saw the baby, the adults in the room looked to him, expecting him to save the day—to just immediately save the baby's life. But he'd never had to revive a baby before, and there was hardly any time at this point. Certainly no time to wait for more trained paramedics. He started CPR, trying to be gentle yet effective. It wasn't working. The baby was turning a deeper blue. He kept trying. No luck. So he picked up the baby to rush it to the ambulance outside, which had just arrived.

As he started to trudge through the deep snow outside, just after they hit the cold air, the baby's eyes opened up wide and looked straight up at him.

First responders. Real heroes.

* * *

Brian McAleese, or Uncle Brian, was perhaps the most kindhearted of the three brothers—but also the best fighter, ironically. And the most competitive. Like his older brother Kevin, he had a keen interest in science and was a great football player. Like his older brother John, he was a history buff and loved rock and roll—especially the Rolling Stones, Bob Seger, and U2, but *especially* the Stones. When Uncle Brian graduated high school, he went across the US and back in a van with friends—without telling his parents or family where he was going. He returned home five months later, on Thanksgiving morning, sporting a poncho and a full beard.

In a lot of ways, Uncle Brian was like an older brother to me—he was only in his early twenties when I was born. We'd wrestle, he'd tease me and give me "noogies," we'd watch TV—mostly The Discovery Channel or The History Channel. Spending time in the McAleese house as a kid, I got to see a side of him that many, perhaps, did not. Once, there was a massive spider web on the deck outside. As a kid, I was afraid of it in a way, and wanted to get rid of it. But he appreciated nature's beauty, and encouraged me to look at the spider web a different way. Like Uncle John, he'd sometimes have me for the day. We'd drive around and go to the park and go for deli sandwiches, and when I refused to have a sip of his Snapple, he'd say, "What, do I have *cooties*?" in joking disgust, giving me that narrow-eyed look he always gave you. It's funny the random things you remember from being a kid.

Known as "Mac" at Engine 226, he'd often show up to work wearing his FDNY Yankee hat and sunglasses, a cigarette in his mouth and a coffee in his hand. "Like Dean Martin," as other firefighters at 226 have described his appearance. He'd volunteer for the MS Society, and others from 226 would follow his lead. He was also the prank mastermind of the firehouse. One of his favorite pranks was pouring Tabasco sauce on cherry Italian ices and then putting the covers back on and placing them back in the freezer. If a cup of water fell on you as you opened a cabinet door at 226, you knew it was Brian. He'd do the same thing with buckets on the roof.

"He literally had me looking up before I walked into my damn house for years," fellow 226 firefighter Tommy Casatelli recalled (Tommy was a younger guy, who was a Marine in Desert Storm, known at 226 for winning a medal from the city, a very rare distinction, for pulling someone out of a collapsed brownstone after a gas explosion; a large banner still hangs in 226 commemorating the award).

Uncle Brian always wore t-shirts with the names of other firefighters who had died in the line of duty.

Nana Mac, often thinking it was too sad or dark, finally asked him "Why do you wear those shirts all the time? It's so morbid."

He answered, "We have to remember them."

I heard somewhere that people die twice—once when their heart stops beating and again when people stop talking about them.

Greg Fix, or "Fritz," was Uncle Brian's best friend, and the best man at his wedding. Their birthdays were four days apart, and they even looked alike. Fritz was at the McAleese house so much growing up that he was thought of as the fourth brother. Papa Mac liked him, so he basically had the keys to the house; he could stay over as much as he wanted—a privilege bestowed on nobody else. Everybody loved Fritz—he was just that kind of charismatic person—with a big heart, and this unrelenting positive energy.

Fritz and Uncle Brian met in third grade. The McAleeses had just moved from Rosedale, Queens, where the children attended Catholic school. Accustomed to wearing a uniform, Brian continued to wear his to school every day (even though he was now in public school). Fritz and a couple of his friends made fun of him for it and would chase him every day after school. One day, Brian fought back and beat them all up. From that day forward, the two were best friends.

After Fritz graduated from Old Dominion in the late '80s, he came back to New York and started a career as a commodities trader on Wall Street. After a few years, as he looked at his weary reflection in a subway door, he thought, *I can't do this for the rest of my life. I need something else . . . I need to be a firefighter.* Despite scoring well on the FDNY test, he was placed on the waiting list.

In 1994, he moved down to Wilmington, North Carolina, to start a career on the Wilmington Fire Department, where he'd eventually work his way up to battalion chief. He finally received a letter of acceptance from the FDNY, but they didn't give him much time to make a decision—so he stayed in NC. Uncle Brian wasn't happy about his choice—he wanted Fritz to come back up to New York and join Engine 226. They didn't speak for a long nine months, an eternity for them—until Papa Mac died in January 2001.

Other than that nine-month gap, they spoke often and continued to be very close friends, despite the physical distance between them after Fritz's move. The distance, they thought, was only temporary, anyway. It had to be. There was a promise they'd made to each other that they had to keep. As teenagers, they'd made a pact to open up a bar together when they were older and retired from firefighting. An Irish pub combining their two names—called McFritz's Pub. This was their dream.

***

At the St. Louis airport, Dad searched for a cab. There was a line of at least a thousand people waiting for one, though, so he went around the corner and found a limo instead. He handed the driver a hundred-dollar bill.

"Can you get me out of here?"

"Get in. Where are you heading?" she replied.

"Anywhere there's a hotel room."

He called several hotels in the area before finally finding one with vacancy. When he spoke to Mom on the phone, he learned that the towers had collapsed. He'd had so many meetings in those towers. It was an incomprehensible thought.

***

Back in New York, Uncle Brian was called into overtime early that Tuesday morning. As soon as he arrived at Engine 226, over an hour before the first plane hit, he heard firefighter Tommy Casatelli was sick with the flu and was thinking of tapping out for the day.

When he saw Tommy checking the rig, he said, "Wow, you really *don't* look too good . . . but you're not tapping out." He reminded him that he'd have to go to the medical office to get permission to leave, and that it would be a process. Like a big brother, he said to Tommy, "Tuesday day tours are slow. You can rest—Stan, Dave, and I will pick up your slack.

You'll have tomorrow and the next day off to sleep—so you should just suck it up."

Tommy stayed. He didn't want to look weak in Brian's eyes.

"Let me drive," Tommy asked. He had been chauffeur for the first half of his 24-hour shift and was assigned "back up" for the second half (the most physically demanding job in the fire department, the "back up" position backs up the nozzle man as they fight the fire, taking the brunt of the hose pressure as the nozzle man gets all the glory and has all the fun).

Brian's face lit up. He was assigned chauffeur that morning but hated driving. Like most firefighters, he wanted to be on the back step, in the mix (chauffeurs have to stay with the rig, so they don't go into fires with the others), and driving would be easier for Tommy in the condition he was in. So they swapped spots.

About an hour later, on the kitchen TV, someone noticed black smoke billowing from the World Trade Center. The sound was off initially.

Brian said, "We're definitely going," and instructed the others to start loading extra air cylinders onto the rig. They got the call shortly thereafter, when the box went to a fifth alarm.

Firefighters swap positions routinely, and once they swap, there's no swapping back. That's just the way it is in the FDNY. *But* this was an extraordinary moment, and as they were getting ready to pull out of quarters, Brian asked Tommy if he wanted to switch back, knowing a call to the Trade Center was sure to be a career fire for them all. He was psyched—they all were. You have to have that mentality as a firefighter. It was time to go to work. Brian felt lucky that he'd gotten out of driving and would be part of the action at the biggest fire of his life, but felt bad that Tommy would have to sit it out. *He* was supposed to drive, after all. Brian was Tommy's mentor; he had trained him, and he wanted Tommy, his probie, to get the work.

"This is gonna be the job of your career," he said to Tommy as he offered to switch back.

Tommy *did* want to switch back—he wanted to be in the action, not on the street looking up—but he couldn't do it. It would've been selfish. He thought to himself, *You made your bed and now you gotta lie in it.*

One of the most chilling radio recordings from that morning came from Ladder 10/Engine 10, (or "10 and 10," as firefighters call it), a firehouse right across the street from the World Trade Center: "Engine 1-0 to Manhattan. Engine 1-0, World Trade Center, 10-60. Send every available ambulance, *everything you got*, to the World Trade Center, *now*." A "10-60" code is a request for a major emergency response. It's basically a call for "all hands on deck." Another recording lists the responding ladder and engine companies. The list seems never-ending: "Battalion 1-2, Ladder 1-6, Ladder 2, Ladder 1-3, Engine 2-2-1, Engine 2-3, Engine 2-0-9, Engine 2-1-2, Engine 2-7-9, Engine 2-3-0, Engine 2-2-9..."

Lights flashing and sirens blaring, Engine 226 screamed down the streets of Brooklyn—starting on its home State Street—and eventually over the Brooklyn Bridge.

As Tommy drove the rig on the bridge, he said to Lt. Bob Wallace, who had been detailed from Engine 205, in the cab next to him, "It looks like *both* towers are on fire."

Wallace didn't think so at first—the radio traffic was so busy they didn't even know there was a second plane yet. As it turned out, though, the second plane had hit while they were somewhere between Downtown Brooklyn and the bridge. Amid a deafening cacophony of sirens echoing through the concrete canyons of Lower Manhattan, the rig parked at the corner of Church and Vesey streets, at the northeast corner of the World Trade Center complex, and hooked up to the first open hydrant Tommy saw.

As Tommy hooked up, he noticed thousands of papers floating down, but, focused on the task at hand, didn't see an airplane wheel just twenty feet from where he parked. As he got the rig ready to pump water, the other four firefighters—Brian McAleese, Stan Smagala, Dave DeRubbio, and Lt. Bob Wallace—strapped on their bunker gear, gathered extra tools, hoisted extra air cylinders, and threw hose roll ups on their shoulders. They mustered on the side of the rig when they were dressed, and as Lt. Wallace tried to establish comms on the radio, Brian said to Stan and Dave, "This is bad. Let's make sure to go slow and stick together."

As the four firefighters departed, their names could be read on the backs of their black and neon yellow bunker coats: McALEESE, SMAGALA, DERUB-BIO, WALLACE. From the corner of Church and Vesey, the four marched off with laser focus and purpose, calm and under control. They weren't afraid. They knew to conserve energy—climbing with all that equipment would be tremendously taxing.

They made their way toward the South Tower and ascended into the largest and most dangerous high-rise fire in the history of the world. Running up the stairs of the burning Twin Towers that day, as others rushed out, is one of the most courageous things I've ever read about, seen in any film, or just plain heard of—fiction included.

The ability to carry on past unbearably intense heat, scorching flames, poisonous smoke, and unexpected explosions, while ascending structurally compromised buildings, despite the ever-present underlying fear of never seeing their spouses or children again—all to potentially save a perfect stranger—*that* is the courage of a firefighter.

A note was later found, thanking the firefighters from Engine 226 "for helping us down—twice." The note read:

To Engine 226 – Thank you for helping me down (TWICE) in the WTC (2). I feel so bad for my friends and you guys that helped us twice. Love you for helping me.

-Abby and Brian Ingrassia

First responders. Real heroes.

***

As soon as Fritz heard about the attacks, he called Aunt Dawn, Brian's wife, to ask if he was working. She confirmed he was, and that he hadn't called her yet. He tried to console her. "They're busy right now . . . you know, they're just really busy. But he'll call." When no call came, Fritz started driving up from North Carolina.

At 9:59 a.m., less than an hour after being struck by the second hijacked airliner, the temperature of the fire in the South Tower stretched its steel to the point that the exterior walls buckled and the fire floors collapsed, uniformly. This created a pancaking chain reaction, resulting in the entire building unexpectedly collapsing, in just twelve seconds. A skyscraper that had taken eleven years to plan and build had come down in twelve seconds. Witnesses compared the sound of the collapse to the roar of a jet engine. Half an hour later, at 10:28 a.m., the North Tower also collapsed, and suddenly New York's iconic Twin Towers were gone.

Tommy barely survived both collapses, seeking cover in a pre-war building's outer stone vestibule for the first and a smaller vestibule for the second. He suffered lung damage, an eye wound, and neck and back injuries, and was later diagnosed with PTSD. He had tried to leave the rig and enter the South Tower before it fell, but was turned away twice by chiefs at the command center.

Just twenty minutes after the North Tower collapsed, Uncle Kevin's life was inadvertently saved by two firefighters running from One Liberty Plaza, adjacent to the World Trade Center. Unbeknownst to Uncle Kevin, who made his way to Lower Manhattan as soon as he heard about the attacks, a piece of the skyscraper had broken off and was about to crash down near where he and others were standing. As the two firefighters ran at full speed, they rammed right into Uncle Kevin, picking him up, the three of them catapulting through the already-blown-out window of the Burger King on the corner of Liberty and Church, likely saving his life.

From his home on Long Island, Uncle John rushed to the World Trade Center, driving on the grass median of the highway at times. The Brooklyn Bridge was packed with people in business clothes, covered in gray dust—and some in blood. He arrived at around 11:00 a.m., immediately climbing to the top of the pile of debris that was the South Tower to get the lay of the land. The destruction was unfathomably vast. When the sun and cobalt blue sky peeked through the smoke from time to time, the sunlight reflected off other responding firefighters' bunker gear below. They looked like thousands of bioluminescent ants. At the top of the pile of debris, he found the intact body of an office worker, with ballpoint pens still neatly tucked into the breast pocket of his shirt. The body, while intact, was deflated. Flattened. Remembering advice he once received, Uncle John avoided eye contact.

He had once asked a recovery worker of the 1996 TWA Flight 800 crash how he did it. "How did you pull all of those people out, still buckled into their seats at the bottom of the ocean?"

"You can't look at their faces," he advised. "Because that makes it personal."

Uncle John found the 226 rig at the corner of Church and Vesey, at the foot of the pile of debris that was the South Tower. The rig was crushed like an aluminum can, but still connected to the hydrant. The engine was revving, still pumping water. The cab was on fire. He put out the fire with an extinguisher, climbed in, and found the riding list, which had Brian listed as chauffeur ("ECC" was next to his name, which stands for "Engine Company Chauffeur"). Feeling immediately relieved, he looked up at the sky, thanking God. If Brian was driving the rig, he didn't go into the building. That's common knowledge in the FDNY. Standard protocol. Chauffeurs stay with the rig. *He's got to be around somewhere*, John thought.

Late in the day, after Uncle John was relieved from putting out one of the surrounding fires, he got a ride to 226. He saw a young guy on the street, looking down, who looked like Brian. *Finally.* He ran up to him and put his arm around him. The kid looked up, startled. It wasn't him. Moments later, when he saw the captain of Engine 226, Billy Carew, and the look on his face, Uncle John knew the truth.

"They switched," Billy explained. It was a cardinal sin to not update the riding list, but there wasn't time.

* * *

Earlier in the day, after the principal announced the tragedy over the loudspeaker at my middle school, kids were being picked up by their parents left and right. I stayed the full day in school, but my mom was waiting for me at the end of the driveway when the bus pulled up to my house. Moments later, two fighter jets roared right over the front yard, heading west toward the city. We got in the car and drove straight to Nana Mac's. Every FM radio station we tuned to on the car ride played news coverage, and dozens of emergency vehicles whirred by us on the shoulder of the highway as we sat in traffic. It seemed we were at war.

As I sat down inside her old Baldwin house that sunny afternoon, Nana Mac told me, "John Michael, today is a very dark day in our country's history. Probably the darkest."

I couldn't believe it. "Even worse than Pearl Harbor?" I asked.

"Yes, even worse."

The "day of infamy" sixty years ago we'd learned about in school? How could today be worse than that? It was hard to fathom. As it turned out, Nana Mac was right—there ended up being more casualties on September 11, 2001, than on December 7, 1941.

As the afternoon progressed, we still couldn't get in touch with Uncle Brian. Mom had left a voicemail on his cell phone earlier in the day. From his St. Louis hotel room, Dad called the missing persons hotline several times and finally got through. They told him Brian was at the morgue, helping to identify bodies for the FDNY. Dad breathed a sigh of relief, and passed the news along to Mom. It almost seemed too good to be true. *But why hadn't he called?* Surely he would have found a way to call *someone* by now. It wasn't adding up. Then Dad received a call from David Beamer, who he'd worked with a few years prior. David had lost his son Todd Beamer just that morning; Todd was the hero that said "Let's roll" before storming the cockpit of United Flight 93 with other passengers, preventing the hijackers from crashing the plane into the US Capitol. But David heard Brian was missing, and so he called, selflessly, to see if there was news. Dad would later describe it as "the hardest conversation I ever had with anyone in my life."

Later that evening, we learned that the morgue report must not have been true, because Uncle Brian was "officially unaccounted for." As the night wore on, the feeling of panic started to increase in the house. It wasn't looking good. I remember looking up at the clock in Nana Mac's kitchen when it hit me. That awful gut punch feeling. The clock seemed to stop. The involuntary ebb and flow of breathing seemed to stop, too, and so I had to do it manually. Consciously.

Later that night, sitting at the kitchen table, Nana Mac began to feel a sense of grief that words can't describe. That unfathomable pain that no parent should ever have to endure. As the adults spoke in the kitchen, beginning to fear the worst, she said, "I want to hold Brian's head and wash the rubble off his face."

They say nothing can ever prepare you to lose a child. Nana Mac used to tell us this, even before 9/11. There are many forms of loss and grief, all incomparable of course, but losing a child is perhaps the one that's most different. It defies the natural order of things. When Mom saw three silhouetted figures walk through the front door late that night, she thought it was her three brothers, reunited. But the third wasn't Brian—it was his best friend, Fritz.

With flights still grounded indefinitely on the morning of September 12, Dad rented a car and drove from St. Louis back to New York, only stopping for food and gas. Driving well over the speed limit at times, he was never pulled over and made the trip in seventeen hours. As he drove over the Verrazano Bridge, he could see smoke still rising from Lower Manhattan. No one honked or complained in a traffic jam, as six lanes converged into one.

"It seemed we were all in this together as Americans, with a common enemy," he would later say. "And we were solemn."

When he got home, Mom ran downstairs and hugged him for a long time.

"So much had changed since I had last seen her," he'd remember. "So much would never be the same."

On September 12, Uncle John went back to 226. Tommy was there, and was dreading seeing John. He felt he had murdered his brother.

Uncle John greeted the other firefighters that had solemnly gathered around him, his eyes searching the corners of the firehouse. When he finally saw Tommy, the room fell silent as he stepped away from the others and approached him.

Uncle John grabbed him and hugged him.

"It's not your fault . . . it's not your fault. Tommy, I'm glad you're alive."

Tommy tried to get away from him because he didn't want to hear it. But Uncle John held him there.

"I'm sorry my brother's dead, but I'm glad you're alive."

***

Starting on September 12, Fritz, Uncle John, and Uncle Kevin started going daily to dig and look for Uncle Brian. The media called the debris field that covered the WTC campus "Ground Zero"—but the workers who actually went down there every day to search for survivors and to begin the long clean-up process just called it "The Site," or "The Pile." They went to The Site every day for weeks, hoping to find something . . . anything.

The rubble was piled up so high in the early days that the three had to go up to the eighth floor of the American Express building in the World Financial Center just to step out onto it. The wreckage was still burning deep underneath. Workers that knew how to use metal-cutting tools were in very high demand, to search for survivors.

The scene was gruesome and hellish. The smell of death permeated the air, but few human remains were found. Relatively few objects, in general, were found. So much had been pulverized into dust, with the occasional exception of human ears and sometimes limbs, which were found by search dogs. Fritz once found a small, square piece of tile, probably from a bathroom or kitchen, and kept it—since it was the only thing he ever found that was perfectly intact.

When it rained on Friday the fourteenth, the smell of death reached its peak. The morgue said they found the firefighters from 226 and wanted Uncle Kevin, Uncle John, and Fritz to come identify Brian. Of course, that was the call we'd all been dreading. But the next day, the morgue apologized, admitting they'd made a mistake—it was 236 or another engine company. Fritz was relieved. He thought he had come up to New York to save his best friend—his soulmate, as he's referred to Brian—reminding us that soulmates don't necessarily have to be romantic. He'd come to pull him out of the rubble, alive. He visualized pulling him out, over and over. He really believed it would happen. You had to hang on to that hope. The alternative was unbearable.

The three would spend sixteen-hour days at The Site, barely sleeping, getting home around 2:00 a.m. each night. On the rare occasion that someone was recovered, everything stopped. Machinery was cut off. Everyone stood silently, at attention. They would drape the body part in an American flag and carry it to an ambulance nearby. One day, later on in the recovery effort, a younger guy in his twenties recovered a firefighter from 118 Truck, which was iconically photographed as it went over the Brooklyn Bridge on 9/11, but declined to carry him to the ambulance. "McAleese should do it," the guy said, referring to Uncle John. "He's been down here every day, looking for his brother. He should do it." And so he did.

The fact that two brothers—a cop and a firefighter—were down there every day, looking for their third brother, also a firefighter, was noteworthy. New York Giants Head Coach Jim Fassel talked about them in a press conference after meeting them at The Site, saying he'd "never, ever forget those two brothers." Radio deejay Gerry Martire from Q104.3, New York City's classic rock station, played U2's "I Still Haven't Found What I'm Looking For" as a tribute to the brothers' search. A *Newsday* cover story a couple of weeks after the attacks was titled "The Search for Brian McAleese." My mom had taken the cover photo, of Brian holding his four children, at the beach on September 9, 2001.

The thought of Uncle Brian's death was impossible to come to grips with. You couldn't help but hold on to this beyond minuscule chance that some stairwell or part of the building remained intact under the rubble and that he was in there, waiting to be dug out. Your gut knew the reality of the situation, but your heart held on to that chance.

Every day after school, Mom drove us the twenty-five minutes to Nana Mac's house, where the whole family gathered each night. Friends and neighbors dropped off endless trays of food. Uncle Kevin and Uncle John continued digging at The Site by day, coming back covered in light gray dust each night.

This went on for weeks. We would do our homework there, eat dinner there, and wait to hear something.

A week after the attacks, Uncle Kevin went to Engine 226, and found himself in front of Uncle Brian's locker. He forced himself to open it. Inside, he found a wedding photo of Dawn and Brian, surrounded in concentric circles by photos of their four children and then photos of his nine nieces and nephews, of which I was the oldest. His clothes were neatly folded. The wood of the locker meticulously painted. Kevin looked for Papa Mac's fire department retirement ring, but couldn't find it.

"I realized he wouldn't have taken it off," he later said. "It was comforting to know that it was on his finger when he met my dad in heaven that day."

In the weeks that followed, Fritz and Uncle John eventually listened to the FDNY radio recordings. The radios weren't working well that day, but Fritz thought 226 had made it to the upper 70s—maybe to the seventy-seventh or seventy-eighth floor of the South Tower—which was the lowest part of the airplane's impact zone. Radio confirmed they made it at least as high as the fifty-eighth floor.

***

In October 2001, after several harrowing and heartbreaking weeks, New York was finally afforded welcome distractions via The Concert for New York City and the Yankees' World Series games. I attended both, with Dad. As we walked into the Garden on October 20, the Stones were playing, ironically. The song was "Miss You."

We headed to the old Yankee Stadium on October 31, the night after President George W. Bush threw a perfect first pitch to raucous chants of "U-S-A." Bush was planning on throwing the pitch from the base of the mound, but Derek Jeter suggested otherwise as Bush warmed up under the stadium, saying, "You better throw it from the mound. Otherwise, you're gonna get booed. This is Yankee Stadium." He later added, "Don't bounce it. They'll boo you."

The Yankees were down 2-1 in the series after losing the first two games in Arizona, and there was a different kind of electricity in the crisp Bronx air that Halloween night. A tattered American flag recovered from the World Trade Center flew defiantly above Monument Park behind the left field wall.

With the Yankees down 3-1 in the bottom of the ninth, with two outs, Tino Martinez hit an incredibly clutch two-run homer to right-center, sending the game into extra innings. Every fan jumped up and down, literally shaking the stadium. Beer flew through the air.

And then, as the clock struck midnight in the bottom of the tenth, a bell tolled over the public address system, signaling something significant. For the first time in the history of Major League Baseball, the season had been extended to November. The scoreboard read, "Attention Fans: Welcome to November Baseball."

Jeter, my favorite player and the eventual captain of the team, who would end up playing in more postseason games than any player in baseball history, was at the plate. Diamondbacks pitcher Byung-hyun Kim was on the mound. A Yankee fan held up a sign that read, "Mr. November." The FOX cameras focused on it. Calling the game on TV, Joe Buck responded, "Somebody has to be. Somebody *will* be, by the end of the night . . . if only for one day . . ."

On the *very next pitch*, about thirty seconds later, Jeter hit a 3-2 pitch into the right field stands—a walk-off home run to win the game and tie the series. That game was the greatest sporting event I'll ever go to, and one of the best memories I have as a kid with my dad.

***

Uncle Brian was never recovered, so there was no funeral for him. "Homicide" was designated as the cause of death on his death certificate. He was one of 343 firefighters lost on 9/11. Instead of a funeral, there was a memorial service, held on December 7, 2001—the sixtieth anniversary of the Pearl Harbor attacks.

The bagpipes wailed outside St. Christopher's Church on a sunny day in Baldwin, playing "Amazing Grace," the traditional music of a fallen firefighter. The church was the very same church that Uncle Brian and Aunt Dawn were married in just seven years prior. The steps leading to the entrance, the very same steps where the newlyweds ducked under a shower of rice thrown on them by family and friends on a sunnier day, were now packed with firefighters in their Class A uniforms.

In his homily, Monsignor John Bennett told the story of when Brian gave up his Class A uniform so that a retired firefighter in his eighties, who didn't have one, could be buried in it. When Brian brought his Class A's to the funeral home, the undertaker told him that the man had already been dressed in a regular suit. "Sorry, we can't do it," he told Brian.

But there were no gray areas with Brian McAleese—something was either right or it was wrong, and this seemed wrong to him. And *forget* about talking him out of something. He convinced the undertaker to help him undress and redress the dead firefighter himself.

"I wish you could've seen the look on the battalion chief's face at the next uniform inspection," recalled Matt Nelson, a captain at 226, when Brian showed up empty-handed. "The chief was surprised, but no one in Engine 226 was."

Aunt Dawn, Uncle Kevin, Uncle John, and Mayor Giuliani also spoke at the service. Uncle Kevin spoke to the bravery of the firefighters, saying, "They climbed those stairs into the history books."

When Giuliani spoke, he compared 9/11 to the attack on Pearl Harbor, and asked the thousands of people packed into the church—and overflowing out the door onto the street—to stand and applaud. To thank Brian McAleese for his bravery and sacrifice. A deafening thunder came over the church, echoing through its rafters and off its tall stained-glass windows. The roar persisted for minutes.

Uncle Brian's death was a loss on many fronts. In our family alone, he was a father, a husband, a son, an uncle, and a sibling. My mom had lost her little brother. Your siblings are uniquely supposed to be there for every phase of life. For all the ups and downs. From your eighth birthday to your wedding to the passing of your parents. They're kids when you're a kid, they're old when you're old. Except sometimes it doesn't happen like that, like it's supposed to happen.

But it wasn't just family and friends who mourned Uncle Brian—it was strangers and the slightest of acquaintances—that day at the memorial service and even decades later. On the twenty-year anniversary of the attacks, a sixty-two-year-old man our family had never heard of, named Artie Bentley, made his way to Citi Field to watch the Mets host the Yankees—with Uncle Brian's name on his baseball cap. Artie worked at the Key Food supermarket in Brooklyn, near 226, where Brian often shopped. "He was just a very nice guy," he told Reuters on the way to the game.

Ten years after the attacks, Tommy Casatelli named his newborn daughter Abigail Brien, after his mentor. "Brian was everything I wanted to be," he'd later say. "He was handsome, popular, and funny. He was a great fireman and family man." Abigail was born at 4:09 p.m. The address of Engine 226 is 409 State Street. When the nurses placed her on a broken scale, the red numbers on the display started cycling, stopping at "226." Then they disappeared. Tommy was flabbergasted; he wholeheartedly believes it was a sign from Brian, to honor his child and live his life without guilt or sorrow.

If you walk through the 9/11 Museum today, there are quotes on the walls in one section. The one that's most striking to me is from Beverly Eckert, the wife of South Tower victim Sean Paul Rooney, who said, "I didn't want that day to end, terrible as it was. It was still a day that I'd shared with Sean." There's also a photo of Engine 226 parked at the corner of Church and Vesey in the museum, before the towers fell.

When Uncle John met President Bush at an FDNY event, he had Uncle Brian's mass card in his dress cap.

"Who is that?" Bush asked.

"My brother."

"Can I have it?"

Uncle John handed him the card, and the president carefully put it in the breast pocket of his suit jacket, giving it two taps to suggest he'd take good care of it.

***

The last time I saw Uncle Brian was September 9, 2001. It was Sunday, the weekend after Labor Day. Summer was supposed to be over on Long Island, but it felt like the middle of July at Robert Moses Field 5, the beach we always went to. Just a beautiful, perfect day. Uncle Brian was wearing his FDNY Yankee hat that day—I'd never seen it before, but I liked it very much. It was navy blue, with the New York Yankees trademark interlocking "NY" symbol in white in the middle, surrounded on either side by a red "F" and "D." Below that, "Engine 226." I was going to compliment him on it, but for some reason I didn't. As a kid, I was often shy. Now, I wish I had said something. It could've led to a conversation that I'd no doubt remember every word of today. *Why didn't I just say something about the damn hat?* It taught me a painful lesson—if you have something positive to say about someone, even about something as trivial as a hat—just tell them.

The day, though, was idyllic. Uncle Brian loved taking his kids to the beach—building sandcastles with them (and carving out the castle tunnels with a wiffleball bat, as he always did), and teaching his kids to "never turn your back on the ocean." He had recently told Aunt Dawn, "Nobody's got it better than me. Life is complete."

Later in the day, as Dad and Uncle John smoked cigars, facing the descending sun, Uncle Brian and Aunt Dawn packed up their things and four children and left a little early, before everyone else. We thought we'd see them again the following weekend, at their fourth-month-old son Aidan's christening. Uncle Brian looked like a pack mule, carrying a bevy of beach bags and his son, Liam, strapped to his back in a chair backpack. They were leaving early because he had to head into Brooklyn for a 24-hour shift. I wasn't there when they left, so I never had a chance to say goodbye. I saw them from a distance, though, walking toward the parking lot. It would be the last time I'd ever see him.

***

When I was a little kid, Uncle Brian was the first to teach me about the asteroid that ended the reign of the dinosaurs, how the Big Bang suddenly started the universe, and how to flip over a cherry Marino's Italian ice to get to the "good part" first (even though I liked saving it for last), among many other things. It's still hard to believe that the last time we saw him was that Sunday at the beach, all those years ago. But I know that he lived fully. That he loved his family wholeheartedly. And that he made his thirty-six years here count. He didn't wait around for the "good parts." He proactively sought them out, created them. Not everyone is like that. But when I think of him, or 9/11, or the Twin Towers, it reminds me to be *more* like that.

On the ten-year anniversary of 9/11, we went back to Engine 226. I walked upstairs with my parents, sisters, and brother and opened Uncle Brian's locker, as Uncle Kevin had done a week after the attacks. It was still just as he had left it—meticulously painted bright red and light gray, clothes neatly folded. The photos of his four children, encircled by each of his nieces and nephews, including us, were still there. I'd known about the photos. But on the inside of the locker door, I noticed something else. Something we weren't aware of. It was a subtle inscription, almost hidden behind the light gray paint: the words NO FEAR, carved into the wooden door in bold capital letters.

Carved, not inked with a pen or a Sharpie.

Carved, so they would never fade.

It was a perpetual reminder that a brave man once passed this way, and a comforting confirmation that his last moments were not enveloped by fear. They couldn't have been. The interminable message in the wood is eternal proof.

3
BEFORE IT'S TOO LATE

"Learning to Fly" – Tom Petty

Six years after 9/11, as a freshman at Cornell University, a thought came to me as I ate lunch one day in the Risley Dining Room—a dining hall on North Campus that looked like something straight out of *Harry Potter*. Even though I was only a freshman, for some reason I was thinking about what I was going to do after graduation—perhaps for the first time. I thought about Uncle Brian living to only thirty-six years old. I didn't appreciate just how young that is until I got to college. As a thirteen-year-old kid in 2001, thirty-six didn't seem particularly young. Uncle Brian was an adult, nearly triple my age, with four kids. (No matter how old you are, if someone is triple your age, they're old from your perspective—whether it's a fifteen-year-old to a five-year-old or a ninety-nine-year-old to a thirty-three-year-old.) But as I approached my twenties in college, that perspective changed dramatically. Suddenly, thirty-six didn't seem all that far away.

What do I want to do? Career-wise, I had pretty much no idea. I took courses in my main areas of interest—astronomy/astrophysics, environmental science, and business/economics—but I didn't know how anyone could possibly bundle those three things up into any kind of practical job. But I wasn't just thinking about a career. I was thinking about adventure. I was thinking about *life*. What do I want *to do*, when all this structure is gone? The class schedules and finals, the rules and expectations—school had provided that structure for as long as I could remember. After graduation would be the first time I'd really be on my own, to do what *I* wanted to do.

I was very fortunate that my parents were paying my tuition, so I wouldn't have student loans to pay off, as long as I graduated on time. And because of that, I had a golden opportunity—for unconditional, unrestricted freedom. The structure didn't have to continue. It could evaporate, in fact, if I wanted it to. I thought it was too good an opportunity to pass up. Why go straight into a full-time job, where I'd undoubtedly be on the lowest rung of the ladder as a new hire straight out of college? Why not get *out* of the flow, *out* of the structure, right after graduation? *That will be the time*, I thought. But what would getting out of the flow look like? What would I *be* when the structure was gone? What was I going to *do*?

I've always loved travel—even just ordinary road trips, or simply getting on a plane—no matter the destination. So I decided I wanted to do some kind of trip—a *big* trip, right after college. Something to remember. Something significant and tangible to look back on. Something that would slow down time. Before the grind of the real world, with a real job and higher-stakes responsibilities. Before having a family of my own. Before mortgage payments, and endless expenses, and 401(k) contributions, and sales targets, and performance reviews, and morning commutes, and allotted vacation days. Before I was old. Before it was too late.

The first thought that popped into my head, as I ate that lunch at Risley, was a bike trip. But certainly not because I was any kind of cyclist. In fact, I'd never ridden a bike more than about nine miles in a day in my whole life. My dad would do a nine-mile loop as a workout around Dix Hills, my Long Island hometown. I did it a few times, too—and that was the extent of my cycling experience. That and riding bikes around the neighborhood as a younger kid—usually never more than a mile or two at a time. So no, I was definitely *not* a "cyclist," in any shape or form. The reason a bike trip came to mind first was a man named Chris Prior. The Priors were our close family friends; Mom and Michelle Prior were best friends in high school, and Michelle and her husband Chris had four children—two boys and two girls, like our family.

Right after college, Chris biked across North America with his friend; they started on the East Coast, went west and then north into northwestern Canada, and then biked all the way down the Pacific Coast Highway, ending in San Diego. When they ran out of money in Jasper, Alberta, they worked in a restaurant for a couple of weeks and then got back on the road. The whole thing was 6,000 miles and took six months.

When I first heard about this epic journey as a kid, I was awestruck. How could someone *bicycle* all the way to California? That's a *thing*? That's *possible*? Even as a kid, I could tell Chris enjoyed talking about it, that he was reliving good memories. As I got older, I'd ask him about it every once in a while, still amazed by it all. I couldn't imagine a bigger adventure. One time, he quantified the experience in a way that really struck me. He told me the two greatest experiences of his life were:

1. Having a family.
2. The bike trip.

Chris Prior's post-college ride across North America was the first inspiration for my bike trip. The second inspiration was books I'd read and movies I'd seen collectively over the years, most notably a book named *Miles from Nowhere*, by Barbara Savage, which was required reading for a class I took at The Peddie School, a prep school in New Jersey I attended for one year between high school and college. The book was a true story about a California couple who rode their bikes across the US, and then kept going all around the world. I loved it, and the details the pages provided gave me some solid insight as to what it would take to actually pull a trip like it off. The famous running scene from *Forrest Gump* was another motivation.

And the third, and perhaps most compelling, inspiration was 9/11. The day that changed my family. The day that changed the world. Research conducted by the Center for Generational Kinetics has found that 9/11 is a generation-defining moment for millennials like myself—and is the key divider between millennials and the next-younger generation, Gen Z, which was too young to remember it. The day has led to various differences between the generations, the research claims, including different financial habits. 9/11 proved the uncertainty of the world. This, along with the Great Recession of 2008, led to Gen Z's more conservative approach to spending compared to millennials', which has allowed them to accumulate wealth faster and not delay certain adult milestones (such as marriage, children, and home ownership) as much as millennials.[3] Anecdotally, I've noticed that millennials have prioritized *experiences* and travel over saving and buying material things more than other generations, and I think 9/11 has a lot to do with that.

FDNY chaplain Father Mychal Judge, who was the first certified fatality on 9/11, always used to say, "If you want to make God laugh, tell Him your plans for tomorrow." So often we think, *There will be time for that.* But what if there isn't time? It's a chilling question to ask yourself: *If I don't do this thing now, or go to this place now, will I ever get the chance to?* A months-long cross-country trip certainly fit into that category. If I didn't do it right after college, as Chris Prior did, the odds were overwhelmingly probable that I'd never get the chance to again. It was literally a once-in-a-lifetime opportunity.

I kept the bike trip idea to myself that year, as a freshman. It was a far off, distant, fuzzy dream that I didn't think too much about in the new, super-busy, fast-paced life that was college, which was intensified by playing a sport. Football was a full-time job on top of school, and the academic atmosphere at Cornell was unforgiving. I kept the idea on the back burner—it was just a "someday/maybe" type of thing. But it picked up some steam the following year.

As I thought about it more, I decided it was something that I definitely wanted to pursue. And I decided I'd ask my roommates and football teammates, Alex and Mango, to join me.

We'd met on the football team our freshman year—I was a quarterback, Alex was a safety, and Mango was a linebacker.

Alex had a lot going for him. He was easygoing, athletic, smart, humble. Even-keeled, level-headed. Always down for any adventure, big or small. An engineering student who could write code but wasn't nerdy. He was the kind of guy that was good at everything, and curiously good at peculiar things like foosball and ping pong. He was almost impossible to fight with. If he disagreed with you, he'd get his point of view across definitively and with fervor, but then fully listen to yours. He seemed to enjoy debating controversial topics, and was open about discussing personal things. Sometimes the things he *didn't* know would surprise you, though, such as the time he wished me a Happy Halloween one morning in college—on October 13th.

A licensed airplane pilot since early high school, Alex joined the Ithaca Flying Club in college—which meant we could rent out planes for the weekend and fly them pretty much anywhere we wanted. All we had to do was pay for the fuel. We'd fly the single-engine Cessnas around the Ithaca area, too, just for fun sometimes on a nice day, and he'd even let us take control on occasion (briefly, and never for takeoff or landing). My parents hated this, and would quietly protest by leaving newspaper clippings of single-engine plane crashes on my desk at home, but I never had any concerns flying with Alex. That is, until one frigid morning when someone from the airport staff rolled an odd-looking, antiquated contraption in a beat-up, rickety shopping cart over to the plane we were about to fly. It was a *heater*, to warm up the engine before we turned it on. Then there was the time we had to deice a plane ourselves with plastic ice scrapers you'd use to hurriedly clean off your car before you rush to work. If we took a fourth person with us, we'd take half the fuel out of the plane before takeoff so we weren't too heavy. "No big deal," Alex would always say.

One time, on the way back from my family's Super Bowl party, it was snowing in Ithaca, and they weren't letting us land. After a rough flight (we were all nauseous, even Mr. No Big Deal, and Mango was vomiting in the back seat like he'd been poisoned), we had to circle around Ithaca over and over again but were completely out of fuel after thirty-nine minutes. We landed in the snow without incident, but, technically, also without permission (in these situations, it's ultimately the pilot's call). This was one of Alex's favorite flights. "Flying on a sunny day is great," he'll tell you. "But as a pilot, you kind of *want* something to happen sometimes." Fortunately, Alex never had aspirations in commercial aviation.

Mango was an undersized linebacker, but he was tough. Ferocious, even. Head Coach Jim Knowles, who would later coach at Ohio State, once called him "The Manganimal" as we watched film during a team meeting, marveling at a big hit on a special teams play. He was a regular on the "Top 10 Plays of the Day" in those team meetings. A standout running back in high school, he was fast. But he was humble too.

He also might be the most intelligent person I've ever known. Without taking any classes, he taught himself advanced computer programming. You could ask him anything about anything, and I guarantee you he'd have a good answer—even if it wasn't complete. As ruthless as he was on the football field, he was a very introverted, quiet, and kindhearted kid off of it. He had a pet snake named Joe that we used to feed live mice to as we played the snake's favorite song, "Tusk (Live)" by Fleetwood Mac, and a very traditional Halloween costume (he cut two holes in a white sheet and went as a ghost). He enjoyed cooking and wine, neither of which was common in college (especially on the football team) and was so good at making pizza that we turned our apartment into a pizzeria junior year (delivery only)—called "Mango's Pizza Company." We had pizza boxes, menus, flyers to advertise, a receipt printer that printed our logo (a green oval logo with an orange mango as the apostrophe) atop the itemized order, insulated bags to keep the pizza warm in transit, a TracFone, the whole nine yards. Mango was notoriously impossible to get a hold of. He wouldn't pick up his phone and would very rarely return texts or emails. But if you called that TracFone, the damn thing would barely ring once and he'd energetically answer, "Mango's Pizza!" The business did fine for a few weeks, but when I opened the fridge one morning looking for the orange juice and found that it had been gutted and filled to capacity with nothing but sauce, dough, and cheese—I thought maybe we were taking it too far.

One year, we were caught "gorge jumping" (similar to cliff diving, it was a popular student pastime at Cornell in the area's many gorges, but had suddenly become illegal) and sentenced to twenty-five hours of community service by the dean's office. So on Mondays, our only off days from football, we'd go around cleaning the local YMCA with large, very old-fashioned vacuum packs strapped to our backs, looking very much like the Ghostbusters.

One day, Alex and Mango skipped class to attend my "How to Play the Australian Didgeridoo" speech to my public speaking class.

After a massive water balloon fight with our neighbors across the alley senior year that might've "disturbed the peace" just a bit, I left a voicemail for Mango pretending to be the Ithaca Police Department's overzealous Sergeant McDaniels, a character I made up who sounded like *Seinfeld* lawyer Jackie Chiles. It was my best prank call of all time.

Besides the fact that they were my closest friends in college, Alex and Mango were uniquely qualified to embark on a long, outdoor adventure. They had both gotten into hard-core winter camping in upstate New York via a college club over winter breaks, learning how to build lean-tos from scratch and survive for days at a time in freezing temperatures. They'd proven that they could stick to a grueling schedule. I thought they each brought the right skillsets and personalities to the table—as a team of three, I was confident we'd be able to overcome the adversity we were sure to face, and I knew for sure the three of us got along really well, especially as a group. The social dynamics just worked. There was balance.

The concept of forgoing a job after graduation to bicycle across the country sounded okay in my head, after marinating for a year or so, but when I tried to put it into actual spoken words sophomore year, it kind of sounded insane.

The best way to describe my college dorm room sophomore year is a castle closet. The dorms on West Campus were Gothic buildings that looked like old English castles, with rutted stone facades, narrow latticed windows, and doors fit for a fortress. On a gray, blustery day, which was common in Ithaca, South Baker Hall looked haunted. On the top floor of the building, Alex and Mango shared a fairly large, drafty room. I had a single room right next to them, which was nice—other than the fact that it was the size of a closet. Its small patch of carpet next to the desk and bed took about seven seconds to vacuum, and the mirror room across the hall was *literally* a storage closet. We'd throw a cot in there with a mint on the pillow to host visitors.

To formally pitch the bike trip to Alex and Mango, I made a slide show on my laptop and presented it to them in their room, as they sat on bean bags next to the room's bunk beds and foosball table. On a cold winter evening in Ithaca, when there's studying and textbook reading to do, an adventure across the sunny American countryside is especially appealing. I played the slideshow to Tom Petty's "Learning to Fly" and a few other songs. It showed all the places the trip could take us: The Grand Canyon, Yellowstone, the Pacific Coast Highway, Mount Rushmore, and dozens of other places in between.

On one slide, I included a poignant quote from H. Jackson Brown, Jr., that perfectly summed up my pitch:

> Twenty years from now you will be more disappointed by the things that you didn't do than by the ones you did do. So throw off the bowlines. Sail away from the safe harbor. Catch the trade winds in your sails. Explore. Dream. Discover.
>
> – H. Jackson Brown, Jr.

At the end of the presentation, they were pretty much sold.

***

The next step was trying to come up with a route. It was going to be difficult to connect all the places we wanted to see—Yellowstone and Mount Rushmore were in the north, for example, while the Grand Canyon and New Orleans were in the south. After the three of us discussed the things we wanted to see, we had about ten or so other main points of interest. Looking at a map of the country, I realized it wasn't going to be possible to hit all of them, *unless* . . . we biked across the country . . . *and back*. Now saying *that* out loud *really* sounded insane. But if we could somehow pull it off, it might be possible to connect all of those dots. The question was: would there be enough time, before it got too cold?

I started to do the math in my head. I figured it would take us about two or three months to get across and two or three months to get back, including rest days and everything. That was up to six months already. If we biked out to the West Coast through the south in the spring, and then back east through the north in the summer, ending back home in New York . . . it might just work, weather-wise. And we could connect the southern route to the northern route by biking up the Pacific Coast Highway—a major pinpoint on our list. You'd probably have to factor in another month to do that, so now we were at seven months. If we started the trip in February or March, it just might work.

Later, Ranley, my closest friend from high school, agreed to join the trip and offered to drive a small RV as our support vehicle. We didn't have the RV yet, but we planned to buy or rent a small one, splitting the cost as a group. Ranley and I had been co-captains on our high school football team. A built, quick-witted, middle linebacker and wrestler, with a deep, baritone voice and an easygoing personality, Ranley's nickname in high school was "The Haitian Hulk." He was one of those people who got along with everyone—all the different cliques of high school. I was thrilled that he wanted to come along, and having an RV would give us a major advantage—it would mean we wouldn't have to carry all our gear on the bikes, we'd have roadside support, and we'd have a permanent shelter and place to sleep each night. Long-distance cyclists usually call a support vehicle like this a "sag wagon."

The bike trip that I imagined seemed like such a dream. A journey into the unknown. A fulfillment of the American ideal of Manifest Destiny, to see the land between the two great oceans. Land I'd never seen (I'd been to both coasts, but pretty much nowhere in between). When I thought about the trip, I pictured us waking up in a tent in some picturesque, rustic place with pine trees and a mountain stream; cooking breakfast and brewing a fresh pot of coffee as a group outside, in the chill of the crisp morning air; playing classic rock as we broke down camp and packed up the RV, feeling the sun getting higher in the sky and looking forward to the day's ride; hitting the road, enjoying the exercise and the rush of getting the blood pumping again; savoring the forests, mountains, canyons, and streams we'd pass. A great adventure to look forward to after graduation that we'd experience together, as a group—the four of us plus Tucker, Mango's new, slightly psychotic but undeniably adorable runt-of-the-litter Jack Russell Terrier puppy.

We'd hit the beach in Florida for spring break, party on Bourbon Street in New Orleans, cut into some quality steak in Texas, see Arches National Park in Utah and the Grand Canyon in Arizona, gamble a little in Vegas, take a few days off to relax in LA, bike the Pacific Coast Highway and go whale watching in Monterey, eat on Fisherman's Wharf and go to a baseball game in San Francisco, camp out in the Redwoods, go whitewater rafting on the Umpqua River in Oregon, bike up and down the Rockies, explore the wonders of Yellowstone and the great city of Chicago, see the Yankees play in Cleveland, go back to Cornell to stay with friends for a few days and pretend like we were still in college, make a quick early-autumn stop in Boston, and end the trip in Manhattan's Little Italy—with a big party to celebrate with our families and friends. All in one trip.

I didn't want college to end. But I was very excited for this trip.

4
RED LIGHTS

"Red Lights" – Tiësto

The summer after my sophomore year, I decided to tell my family about the bike trip idea when I was home on summer break. As a family, all six of us were eating dinner outside on the backyard patio one evening when I paused for a moment, stopped eating, and put my fork down.

"I have an announcement to make," I said, for the first time in my life.

My parents looked at me seriously, their eyes saying, *Uh oh.*

"After I graduate, I'm going to bike across the country."

There was silence—everyone continued to chew their food. You could hear the clanging of forks and knives on plates and the droning, midsummer buzz of cicadas in the green suburban trees surrounding us, but nothing else. No one uttered a word—until Mom broke the silence a few moments later.

"*What?*" she asked, quizzically.

"Is this because of Chris Prior?" inquired my dad. "Is Dylan going too?" he asked, referring to Chris's son.

"That's awesome!" said my little brother, RJ—the baby of the family at fourteen years old, and the only one excited about the ludicrous idea.

When we went back inside to scrape our plates, my teenage sister, Annie, told me, "You won't do it."

"Okay, we'll see," I responded, feeling the challenge for the first time.

***

If we were going to commit ourselves to this thing, I thought we should do it for a good cause. It would give the trip a greater sense of purpose, and help us get through the harder days. If people could raise money doing forty-mile bike rides, a ride across the country and back had to be worth *something*, right? For me, the obvious beneficiary was the Marty Lyons Foundation, which grants wishes for chronically and terminally ill children aged three to seventeen. It was similar to the Make-A-Wish Foundation in terms of its mission, but unlike Make-A-Wish, it allowed children to receive second wishes in some cases. To date, the foundation has granted over 8,000 wishes for chronically and terminally ill children. My dad had played with Marty on the Jets and had been serving on the board for decades. Since I was a kid, I'd volunteered at events, such as the annual golf outing. The foundation was important to me, and Alex, Mango, and Ranley were immediately on board for making it our trip cause.

I knew that if we were going to pull this thing off, staying on schedule would have to be a priority. So junior year, when Alex, Mango, and I were living just off campus in an apartment above a bar-bristling area of Ithaca called Collegetown, I started mapping out the route with Google Maps, creating a day-by-day itinerary. It was actually fun to do this—it was a great way to procrastinate when I should've been studying at night.

I spoke with the owner of a bike shop, called "The Bike Rack," on the street directly below our apartment, to ask his advice. I thought we should average sixty to seventy miles per day, but wasn't sure about it. Was it too little or too much?

"That's actually about right," the owner, Gary, said, as he handed me a photo-copied, handwritten checklist of suggested items to bring. "You can do more once you're in shape, but if you do, you won't have time for much else. Why kill yourself? It's supposed to be fun, right?"

Now that I was confident about the sixty- to seventy-mile average, I started dragging and dropping pins on Google Maps from one town to the next, starting in North Carolina and making my way farther south and then west. Staying off interstates, I'd calculate and record the distance from A to B, then drag A ahead of B to another town that looked to be sixty or seventy miles away and calculate B to A. I'd look for campgrounds, motels, and restaurants in each town, recording anything noteworthy.

As real towns and real highways we'd never heard of started to redefine the fabric of the country for us, that far off, fuzzy dream started to come into focus—and the three of us started getting psyched. Every few days, I scheduled a rest day, trying to have at least one rest day per week. Then there would be extended breaks in places of interest or places where we knew people and had a place to stay. I'd map out a few towns per night, playing with different routes and using Google Maps' "Street View" as much as possible to try to find roads that looked safe.

The plan was to graduate in May 2011, get a temporary job in a restaurant (or something like that) to save up some money, leave in February or March 2012, and return to New York in September or October. When I was finally done with the mapping, the route totaled just under 10,000 miles. It would take 216 days (157 biking days and 59 rest days). The trip would start on Monday, February 27, 2012, and end on Saturday, September 29, 2012.

At the time, these dates seemed far into the future. February 2012 was still more than two years away! But we had a real date circled on the calendar now—and that made the whole thing much more tangible. We were speaking it into reality.

***

When I told my parents that we'd be back home on September 29, which was, coincidentally, their wedding anniversary, and that we'd be ending the trip in Manhattan's Little Italy at La Mela, my favorite Italian restaurant in the city, they were skeptical to say the least. My dad would believe in me and support me in just about anything, but he was actually *laughing* at me.

Then his voice became more serious. "I mean, how could you possibly know the exact date you'll be back from something like this? It's ridiculous. You've never gone more than a few miles on a bike. You've never camped before, except in our backyard when you were a kid. There's no way you can be that precise about when you'll be back . . . if you make it at all."

Up to the challenge and a little ticked off now, I asked, "You wanna bet on it?"

Dad laughed again. In his trademark, kind-of-joking, "alright, tough guy" voice, he said, "I'll tell you what, if you're back in Manhattan on September 29, after biking to California and back, La Mela's on me. I don't care how many people are there." He seemed to really get a kick out of just the *thought* of something that absurd.

"Okay, sounds good," I said. "I'm holding you to that."

I have tremendous respect for my dad. He's smart and level-headed, and a man of pure integrity. He's the first person you want to speak to when something goes wrong, because he always has a solution. And he's the most moral and most loyal person I'd ever met in my life. I have tremendous respect for my dad, but I don't always agree with him.

***

Once we had dates and a route, the excitement started to grow back at school over the course of junior year. Alex, Mango, and I started talking about it more, among ourselves and with our teammates and other friends. Soon, word spread about the big "bike trip," and other friends started asking if they could join. Between myself, Alex, Mango, and Ranley, we were already at three bikers and four total people. Ideally, the group wouldn't get *too* big, but when friends starting asking, our attitude was, "Hey, the more, the merrier."

The first new joiner was Ty Siam, the other quarterback in our class (besides myself) and one of my closest friends on the team. Ty was from Kansas, so we planned to stay with his family for an extended rest about halfway across the country, just when I figured we'd need one. Alex, Mango, and I invited Andy Wade, another teammate, by silently handing him a written invitation in an envelope in a dark, crowded bar one night; we held it out, obstructing his path as he came around a corner. He grabbed it and tore it open without asking any questions and immediately accepted. A couple of others were more loosely committed.

At one point, the group was up to eight total people. Mango set up a website, biketrip2012.com, with a professional-looking red, white, and blue trip logo and a countdown clock to February 27, 2012, on it. We had over 800 days to go when the clock first started. The main purpose of the site was to raise money for the foundation via PayPal, but we'd also put the itinerary on it and planned to post photos to it as we went, so family and friends could follow along.

Now that the group was growing, there was even more talk about it around campus. Some people thought we were crazy. Some people straight up laughed out loud when they heard about it. Some thought it was awesome. Most were really intrigued—even fascinated—by the concept, whether they thought it was a good idea or not.

To anyone who asked about it, I said the trip was a sure thing. "It's happening," I'd say. "Cross country and back. There and back." *There and back* even became a kind of mantra for the trip between me, Mango, and Alex.

***

When senior year came around, you could feel the pressure on our class to land interviews and get job offers. To put the money you or your parents invested to good use. To stay in the flow and keep following society's steppingstones: do your homework in high school, study for the SATs, get into college, graduate, get a job, get a mortgage, get married, have kids, save for retirement. To deviate from that path is to fall behind, and fall short of society's expectations. Or your parents' expectations. Or *your* expectations. Or so it seems.

I went on a couple of job interviews on campus as a senior, but was met with blank stares and looks of concern if I mentioned wanting to take a year off to bike all around the country before I started.

Despite the interview pressure, senior year was fun and fairly carefree for most of us (especially in the spring, after football was over and we had a lot more free time), but you started to hear this chatter going around the seniors, like rumors of impending doom, of the "real world," and how much everyone was dreading it. Not me! Not *us*. Not *yet*, anyway. *We* were biking across the country. Living for adventure. Seeing new places with every single sunrise. Real world? We thought that could wait a year.

But ... inevitably, our bike trip group of eight started to dwindle. There's a stark difference, I guess, between a college kid's outlook as a junior, when they know they'll be back on campus the following year, and as a senior, when they know they *won't*. Ty had decided he was going to grad school, so he was out. The other new joiners dropped out one by one, and soon we were back down to the Core Four—me, Alex, Mango, and Ranley.

The Core Four became the Core Three when Ranley dropped out. He needed to finish up a few credits and wouldn't be ready to leave on time. Now we didn't have a driver, which changed the whole complexion of the trip. With Ranley out, our sag wagon was out as well. Now we'd have to bike unsupported, carrying all our clothing and gear on us. This would make the cycling itself *much* more difficult—especially in the mountains—and we'd be much more exposed to the elements.

Although we'd miss Ranley, I think the three of us kind of embraced the challenge. Having to camp out and improvise more, and having to carry all of our possessions, seemed like things that would add to the experience. And again, Alex and Mango enjoyed camping and had become good at it. There was something mesmerizing, too, about packing up all your belongings onto a bicycle and riding it as far as you could, until you reached the ocean on the other end of the country, and then turning around and doing it again. It would be such a departure from any hint of normal life.

About midway through senior year, though, Alex received a good job offer from Barclays, where he'd interned the summer before. He felt that he had to take the job. He was *out*. I was crushed. At first the news was kind of shocking to me—I never thought we'd have eight, or even six, but I thought for sure that at least the three of us would follow through on the commitment. We'd been talking about it for almost two years! But I understood where he was coming from, too. Again, that pressure you feel as a senior is very real. It's stronger than you think it's going to be. And I knew he was feeling it, too, from his parents.

Plus, there were no athletic scholarships in the Ivy League, full or partial. Our parents were paying full price for us to go to Cornell. Naturally, there's an expectation there to use your degree and get that first job.

When Alex dropped out, I began to really worry. I wrote him a long, handwritten letter, trying to convince him to reconsider. That the job, or *a* job, would be there for him when we got back. That there would be plenty of time for the city life in New York. I drove home the notion of it being a once-in-a-lifetime opportunity. He told me he appreciated the letter, because "it really made him think about things." But it wasn't enough. The letter had failed. His decision remained unchanged.

I was determined to make it work with Mango. It would be just the two of us now, unsupported. It would be a major challenge going with just two—physically, but even more so, psychologically. I thought the social dynamics would be much better with three.

Despite dropping out, Alex still joined me for the New York City Five Boro Bike Tour in May 2011, a few weeks before we graduated. The forty-mile ride from Battery Park to Staten Island, through all five of the city's boroughs, would be the farthest I'd ever biked in one day by a large margin—it was a big steppingstone as I worked up to the sixty- to seventy-mile average day.

After the ride, as we rode the free Staten Island Ferry with our bikes back to Battery Park, where our car was parked, I noticed that the new World Trade Center's Freedom Tower (before it would be known as One World Trade Center) was *just* starting to rise above the rest of the Lower Manhattan skyline. It was good to see.

On the bus ride back to Ithaca that evening, we heard the news that Osama bin Laden had been killed by US forces—a major victory for the country and President Obama.

***

On the last day of the investment banking class I took senior year, Professor Mike Troy asked me where I'd be working starting that summer. I told him I wouldn't be starting a career yet and explained the plan. In real life, the teacher is not always the master, but Mike Troy was. He was big time on Wall Street.

"Really?" he said, in response to my unorthodox answer.

I was expecting criticism now, or at least a wisecrack. But he surprised me.

"Well, nobody was ever on their deathbed saying, 'Man, I wish I worked another day.'"

I'll never forget that statement.

Right after graduation, at which the filled football stadium was oddly dotted with a rainbow of rain umbrellas to shield spectators from the hot sun, I moved back home to live with my parents and started working as a pizza delivery guy at Spuntino, the nearby Italian restaurant and pizzeria that my family would dine at just about every Friday night. My plan was to work there for six months, from June to Christmas, to save up some money for the trip. I actually liked the job most of the time—and on a rainy night, especially a rainy Friday night—you could easily go home with $250 cash. Not bad for a few hours of driving around, following the GPS, and blasting music, smelling the pleasant aroma of steaming pizza. And people were always happy to see you when you got to their front door. Of course they were. You were the pizza guy.

There was a "Share the Road" street sign with a bicycle symbol near Spuntino that I passed often—it was a constant reminder of why I was doing what I was doing. To live the dream, you have to pay your dues.

I had plenty of gear and things for the trip to buy with my pizza and graduation money, but fortunately, I didn't have to purchase a bike. A bicycle *and* Harley cross-country veteran named Billy Iaia had generously given me a very expensive Roubaix Expert, a fast and super-light silver and black bike that he had taken on long rides himself. He became a great mentor to me, too—before the trip started and as it went on. Sadly, just a few years after we first met, Billy died from a heart attack on one of his cross-country motorcycle trips, making the conversations we had all the more fleeting and cherished. Billy had done a number of long bike rides, but only went from coast to coast once. He was planning on doing it again when he turned sixty, but he never made it to sixty. His son Will did the trip instead in 2017, following in his father's footsteps, screaming in the middle of the Nevada desert, cursing him out for inspiring him to do this crazy thing, and ending at the same Long Island bar Billy ended at, where everyone welcomed him home. There, I returned the Roubaix Expert back to the family.

***

When Christmas came and I graduated from my pizza delivery job, I took two weeks completely off from any physical activity. The plan was to start training right after New Year's. We had Christmas dinner that year, in 2011, at Nana Mac's. Christmas at Nana Mac's was always special. It had such a classic feel. The gift opening, in the living room, where the tinsel-draped Christmas tree was, was always joyfully chaotic. The room was so full of people, gifts, scurrying little kids, and wrapping paper that you couldn't even see the burgundy carpet underneath it all.

As he was sitting at Nana Mac's dining room table and I was standing nearby, Uncle Kevin got my attention.

"So this, ah, little adventure you're goin' on . . . What route you takin', 80?"

I explained that it was technically illegal to bike on interstates unless there was no alternative. "On the way back, though, there's a stretch of I-90 in Wyoming that we have to take. There's nothing else out there," I explained.

A look of confusion and pure disgust blanketed Uncle Kevin's face. "Hold on a second," he said. His eyes narrowed as they locked on me. "What do you mean *back*? You're coming *back*, too? What are you, *out of your mind*?" he shouted across Nana Mac's dining room table, in his trademark New York accent.

The room got a little quieter. I thought of all of his insane stories—all the crazy things *he'd* done. Asking to be transferred to Bushwick, the war zone and epicenter of the crack epidemic, where cops would be shot at from rooftops. Following the lye attacker back to his apartment. Chasing the gunman through the bodega. Posing as a Westie with a Chinese gangster. Getting thrown off a goddamn Brooklyn roof. How could *he* think I was out of my mind?

At this point, despite any further pushback from my family, or other "red lights," I was resolute; I was doing this.

I got some interesting gifts for Christmas that year. Convinced that I was in way over my head and had no idea what I was doing, my family bought me a number of books, with titles like *How to SURVIVE Anything, Anywhere*; *National Geographic's Complete Survival Manual*; and *The Complete Book of Long-Distance Cycling*. My parents bought me a small one-person tent (a requested gift), and my sister Cailyn bought me a can of bear spray (another requested gift, but I pretended to be surprised when I opened it).

"You get harder and harder to shop for," she responded, dryly.

My two blond-haired, blue-eyed sisters were in each other's phones as "Sister Golden Hair," and both had a flair for Hollywood. Before moving to LA, Annie was a model and went to NYU. Living in Manhattan, she did well in the industry, and played a leading part in Tiësto's music video for "Red Lights" in 2014 (she's the blonde girl in the black leather jacket, who picks up her diner waitress friend to hitch rides across the desert on motorcycles and in the back of a pickup truck, ending up at a huge Tiësto show in Vegas, where the Dutch DJ invites them up on stage for shots of Jäger). When Annie and I met Donald Trump at a Ranger game in 2015, two weeks before he announced he was running for president, he extended his hand for me to shake and said, "I like your taste." I responded, "That's my sister."

Cailyn, the younger sister, went to Penn State. The "cool one" of the family (and also self-proclaimed *Star Wars* and *Marvel* nerd), she later lived in Brooklyn, loved dive bars and traveling around the world to off-the-beaten-track places, savored the change of seasons, snorkeled with killer whales in Norway, and started a promising career in production—working long hours but quickly amassing an impressive list of major movies and TV shows on her résumé, while climbing the production ladder just as expeditiously. If Cailyn gave you a compliment, you knew you deserved it. She might very well be a producer one day—but if you ask her, she'd be just as happy shucking oysters or working on a fishing boat in London.

***

To start 2012, I did the unthinkable. With Ranley and a few others, I went into Times Square for New Year's Eve, the very last place you'd find a native

New Yorker—on any day of the year. It was a bucket list type of year, I guess, right from the start. Then, on Monday, January 2, the day the world went back to work, I started training.

Since it was the middle of winter in New York, I couldn't really ride outside. So I relied on stationary bike workouts that my college strength coach, Tom Howley, had given me. He used them for conditioning with the Cornell Men's Ice Hockey team. Coach Howley was one of the best strength coaches in the country, and someone I admired and respected a great deal throughout college. A tall man with a carrying voice and unrelenting energy and intensity, he always encouraged us to know one speed, saying, "The way you do anything is the way you do everything."

When Coach Howley heard about the bike trip, he called me into his office, which was adjacent to the team weight room. He was excited and wide-eyed as he peppered me with questions, then handed me a single sheet of paper with ten stationary bike workouts on it.

"The one time I tried these," he said, "the fat just fell right off me." Just the *idea* of this bike trip was right up Coach Howley's alley—and unlike most, he didn't think the whole thing was a joke.

I didn't own a stationary bike, so I trained in a tiny yellow room in a strip mall across the street from the Dix Hills Diner. It was a chiropractic office with a single stationary bike in the middle of the floor. My mom knew the owner, so she got the keys for me. The office was vacant in the early mornings, so I had it to myself. Staring at the four yellow walls under unappealing fluorescent light as I pedaled, I tried to picture what I'd see on the actual trip . . . the Rockies, the redwoods, the deserts, the cities, the forests, the rivers. They seemed unattainable. They seemed a different world.

Coach Howley's stationary workouts were short but intense, lasting thirty to forty-five minutes each. I was always completely drenched in sweat by the end of them. They depended on your heart rate, so I had to wear a heart rate monitor, and each workout had a colorful name, such as "Illegal in 9 States . . . and 3 Provinces!!"

My plan was to train indoors with these workouts, working up from doing them three days a week to four to, eventually, five, then go for a trial run outside

65

with some gear on the bike, then rest for a full nine days before the actual trip start on February 27. As the weeks progressed and I started getting into better shape, the stationary workouts didn't get easier—they actually got significantly *harder*. As my cardio improved, I had to work harder and harder to get my heart rate up to the required levels to complete the workouts. Luckily, biking didn't seem to bother a lingering hip flexor injury from senior year nearly as much as running did. I mixed it up, trying all the workouts on Howley's sheet, but I did my favorite two the most often: "Mount Everest," and the most difficult of them all, "Buffalo Street . . . in 3 feet of snow!":

"Mount Everest"		"Buffalo Street...in 3 feet of snow!"	
Warm Up	3:00	Warm Up	5:00
130-140 BPM	1:00	150 BPM	5:00
150-160 BPM	2:00	155 BPM	4:00
160-170 BPM	3:00	160 BPM	3:00
165-175 BPM	4:00	140 BPM	:30
Easy Ride	3:00	155 BPM	4:00
130-140 BPM	1:00	160 BPM	3:00
150-160 BPM	2:00	165 BPM	2:00
160-170 BPM	3:00	150 BPM	:30
165-175 BPM	4:00	160 BPM	3:00
Cool Down	3:00	165 BPM	2:00
		170 BPM	1:00
		150 BPM	:30
		165 BPM	2:00
		170 BPM	1:00
		175 BPM	:30
		160 BPM	:30
		170 BPM	1:00
		175 BPM	:30
		MAX	:15
		Cool Down	3:00

In early January, Nana Mac called me. She wanted to take me to Hemingway's in Wantagh for lunch and then to a bike shop nearby called Brands Cycle & Fitness. She thought I should talk to the people who worked there, pick their brains. I needed to start buying other equipment, too, such as panniers, tools, water bottles, cycling clothes, etc.—pretty much everything except the bike. At lunch, Nana Mac, the matriarch, begged me to be careful on the trip. I very clearly remember her saying, "This family doesn't need another tragedy." Those words had some serious weight to them.

After lunch, we drove over to Brands, just down the street, right next to the Wantagh train station. Established in 1954, Brands is, perhaps, Long Island's best bike shop. I wheeled my silver and black Roubaix Expert into the store and told the first employee I saw there, a young guy, about my plan. "I need to buy panniers and the other gear for the trip," I explained, trying to sound like I knew what I was talking about.

"We have panniers," he said. "But you can't put 'em on *that* thing. That's a racing bike. You need a *touring* bike."

I didn't know the difference. I thought a bike was a bike! Nana Mac and I looked at each other. She was frozen in place, in her big winter jacket. Her eyes were wide.

I spoke to a few other employees about touring bikes, and it seemed the best option was a Trek 520. I came back another day and bought a brand new one there for $1500. That was a lot of money to me, but what choice did I have? You can't do a bike trip without a bike!

I spent the better part of a few days at Brands that January, trying on clothes, comparing pannier shapes and sizes, talking to the employees, learning how to use some of the tools. They said a kickstand would be useless once the bike was loaded (I wanted one anyway) and recommended not adding an extra cushion to the seat. An employee who cycled in the 1988 Seoul Olympics sized the bike for me, adjusting the seat to make sure everything lined up perfectly. The most veteran and legendary employee there, though, was a man in his seventies named Jaime Castro. He'd cycled across the country several times. Of everyone at Brands, Jaime helped me the most. He was encouraging and excited for me, but I could tell he had some legitimate concerns about my experience level. He was grandfatherly in that way. He asked me to send him a postcard from somewhere random—in the middle of nowhere, preferably. Confidently, I promised him I would.

The cat was out of the bag, though, when I finally had to ask someone to show me how to change a flat tire. I was dreading this particular question, and didn't even *think* about asking Jaime, but eventually, I couldn't push it off any longer. They looked at me in disbelief, as if to say, "*How far* you think you're going again?"

For the first time, they realized I didn't know *shit* about cycling.

5

CURVEBALL

"Float On" – Modest Mouse

A few days before Eli Manning and the Giants defeated Tom Brady and the Patriots in the Super Bowl for the second time, I got a call from Mango. He'd hurt his knee snowboarding. It was a torn MCL. *He was out.*

I couldn't believe it. Torn MCLs normally don't require surgery and can heal themselves in a couple of months (unlike the ACL, the MCL receives enough of a blood supply to heal itself), but we were supposed to leave in just over three weeks. And even after it healed, it wouldn't be a good idea to bike all day on it—we both knew that. I scrambled for a solution, considering all options, but it was time to face reality—he was out. That was it. The trip, the dream, wasn't happening. The whole thing didn't really fully register in my head until he showed up to the Super Bowl party a few days later on crutches, his knee wrapped in a large brace.

Then I thought about our conversations over the last few months. As the trip got closer and closer, it occurred to me that he was clearly worried about leaving his job. He didn't end up getting a more temporary job after graduation like I did. He hadn't told his boss yet about the trip. He didn't seem to be preparing like I was, with the equipment purchasing and the training. I knew that knee injuries are more common on skis than on a snowboard, where your legs are more locked in. *Was he faking it?* Mango was a good friend. I didn't think he was, but I definitely couldn't rule it out. I wasn't that naïve. Whether he was or wasn't, it didn't make a difference. He was out. *Everyone* was out.

The day after the Super Bowl, I decided to continue training—I had just two weeks of training to go before the nine-day rest period. I wasn't sure what else to do. The thought of waking up on February 27, in my parents' house, on a dreary winter day—with no job and no bike trip ahead of me—was nothing short of depressing. I stared out my childhood bedroom window at the lifeless, leafless trees and midday gray sky behind them and thought about how it'd feel to do the same thing on the twenty-seventh. In the silence of the moment, I could hear the clock ticking on my wall. It seemed to get louder and louder. *Tick . . . tick . . . tick . . . tick . . . TICK . . . TICK . . .*

Maybe, I thought. *Just maybe*, I could give it a shot alone.

I thought about it for a few seconds. It sounded idiotic. Senseless. Silly. *Who would ever want to do something like that alone?* Certainly not me. I'm not *that* crazy. *Seven months alone?* I'd never even spent an entire *day* alone. *Ever*— in my whole life. How would I handle that kind of loneliness? I had absolutely no idea—there was no precedent in my life for it in any shape or form. Would I meet friendly people? Or would most people think I was strange for traveling on a bike by myself and avoid me? Would I be bored to tears after the first day? And then there were the frightening logistics of the matter. 10,000 miles is the distance from New York to Sydney, more than the diameter of Earth (8,000 miles), and nearly the circumference of Mars (13,000 miles). *How could I bike that alone?* It was impossible.

Cycling with at least one other person isn't just about safety or moral support—it's about *drafting*. When one cyclist follows directly behind another, they pedal in a lower-pressure environment, with much less wind resistance. Even if there's no wind at all, it's much easier to pedal as the follower. Different studies have come to different conclusions, but the general consensus is that it's 20% to 50% easier to bike when you're drafting behind someone. When you're alone, you never get a break.

My parents were appalled that I was even *considering* attempting the trip alone. They thought I'd be robbed and murdered on the side of the road as I slept in my tent. Or maybe hit by a car. They kept telling me that a transcontinental trip is something that only trained, experienced cyclists would embark on.

My mom certainly took Mango's injury as a sign. "A *lot* can go wrong on this trip. God opens doors and closes them, John Michael," she lectured me. "This door is officially *closed*."

As the final couple of weeks counted down, I could feel anxiety rising in me, to a level I'd never experienced. Sometimes I had trouble sleeping at night, a mostly new problem for me, but I kept going to the strip mall to train early in the morning, sometimes driving through heavy snowfall to get there. It was the heart of winter in New York. January is usually the coldest month, but February always seems to be the snowiest. The week after the Super Bowl, I was up to training five days a week, Monday through Friday. The following week, I went Monday through Thursday. For the last day of training, on Friday, February 17, I was hoping to get outside and crank out sixty miles for the first time—as a trial run, weather permitting. Luckily, it was an unseasonably warm day with clear skies.

The route I decided on went from my parents' house in Dix Hills to Port Jefferson and back—exactly sixty miles. I put the panniers on the bike for the first time and threw a few sweatshirts in them to weigh them down a little, trying to make the trial run somewhat realistic. As I turned out of the driveway, I tried to imagine getting back home 226 days later, on September 29, and thought, *Today, Port Jeff and back. In ten days, California and back. No big deal.*

From my parents' house, I headed up toward Huntington Village via Park Ave, then turned right on 25A, a hilly and unnerving road with potholes, broken glass, a skinny shoulder, and heavy traffic. It was a hell of a way to break into road cycling. On the Five Boro Bike Tour, all the roads were closed; it was just cyclists. This was my first day *ever* riding on a road with heavy car traffic, and it was *way* more dangerous than I'd imagined. The road's small hills were giving me trouble, too, and all I had were a few sweatshirts in my bags! *What the hell was I getting myself into?*

The only food I brought with me was a banana. I figured it would be my lunch. *Big* mistake. I felt okay in the morning, but about midway through the day, my legs began to seize up. They began cramping uncontrollably. Sore to the touch. My knees ached, and my butt hurt badly. I dragged my feet to push the pedals, slowly creaking along. My legs had gotten a little stronger, and I was beginning to get into good cardio shape from the stationary workouts, but I was clearly not in any kind of road-cycling shape, and the banana wasn't nearly enough fuel. I mean, not even close. Starting at only about twenty-five miles in, I needed to take frequent breaks for my heavily fatigued legs. On multiple occasions, I found a grassy spot and just collapsed on my back, arms and legs outstretched like I'd been shot by a sniper. I'd just lay there, exhausted enough to fall asleep.

When I only had about seven or eight miles to go, I started to *really* struggle. I literally couldn't move the pedals anymore, so I pulled over at a deli. I couldn't remember having ever been that hungry in my whole life. I was *extremely* weak, to the point that I had trouble just walking up to the deli door. The Gatorade and overstuffed footlong hero I bought were delicious and revitalizing, but also pretty expensive—they cost more than I thought I could spend for lunch each day of the trip. (Now that I was going to be alone, my budget would have to be tighter. *Way* tighter. There'd be no one to split motel and campground rates with.) As I scarfed the sandwich down and gulped the Gatorade, I could only think about one thing. *How will I be able to afford to eat this much?*

If you divided the $15,000 I had in the bank by 216 days, I only had about $70 to spend each day, on average. I'd been expecting to have over $200 a day to split between three of us, which would've been significantly more practical. And if it had been four of us with the RV, we'd have the big upfront cost of buying or renting the RV, but we'd need to spend much less on food and lodging every day (the two largest daily expenses) because we could both cook and sleep in the RV. On my own, $70 a day wouldn't be enough, especially if I had to eat like *this*. Camping out every single night and carrying cooking supplies would've helped the budget, but they weren't practical options.

The last few miles weren't easy, and it was getting cold late in the day, but the fuel from the footlong hero and Gatorade made all the difference in the world. I finally biked down my childhood street, past the little incline that felt like a mountain on a bike when we were kids, and turned into the driveway feeling exultant. I'd made it! Sixty miles!

I hopped off the bike and went through the front door, victorious. The first person I saw inside was my mom. I told her about the day. It felt like I'd been gone for a week. I told her I was tired but felt pretty good.

"I think I'm ready!" I proclaimed happily as I finished my story.

"You're not ready," she said without hesitation, clearly disgruntled.

***

In my final days at home, I learned that the Marty Lyons Foundation wouldn't back me. They thought it was too dangerous. Worried about liability, they wouldn't promote or acknowledge the trip. This would make fundraising a lot more difficult. As the last few days counted down, it seemed that all the chips were falling against me. My friends were out, my parents were as vehemently against it as ever, and now not even the foundation I wanted to raise money for would support me.

Before I left, the only person who truly believed that I could do it was my little brother, RJ, who's seven years younger than me. When I was the captain and quarterback of my high school football team, ten-year-old RJ was the water boy. He'd come into our huddle and pass out the water bottles, wearing an extra jersey one of the coaches tossed to him. A few years later, *he* became the captain and quarterback of the team and set just about every passing record for the school, throwing most of his touchdowns to his best friend, DJ ("R-J, D-J" became a chant). He then went on to be the starting quarterback for all four of his years at Bucknell University, where he broke the 133-year-old program's all-time single season passing yards record as a junior and was voted Quarterback of the Decade for the 2010s. The kid grew up . . . I mean, he *really* grew up—eventually to a strong 6 foot 6, 250 pounds. As I was getting ready to leave for the bike trip, though, RJ was only seventeen.

A few days before I left, RJ told me he was excited that the family was planning to fly out to see me over Memorial Day weekend, when I was scheduled to be in Big Sur.

"Yeah, if I make it," I answered, without much confidence.

"You'll make it," he said with conviction.

On Friday, February 24, the day before I left (somehow I had convinced my parents to drive me down to North Carolina the next morning to drop me off), I found a photo of a yellow "Share the Road" street sign, identical to the one I used to pass delivering pizzas, and made it my Facebook profile picture.

I also posted an "out of office" message to my Facebook profile: *Biking cross-country and back. Leaving tomorrow for NC, back home in NY in September. Very limited phone.* Sophie Dawson was the first to comment: *No big deal.* Chris Li wrote, *Dude, bike to Hawaii!* But Keith Brennan's comment got the most likes: *I ran this trip with my eyes closed, you'll be fine JM . . . seriously though, best of luck. I'll be waiting at the finish line with a Dos Equis for you, because you, my friend, are the most interesting man alive.* I laughed out loud.

We had a fun farewell dinner that night at Pancho Villa's, a Mexican restaurant with potent margaritas (you'll feel the first one, but once you have a second you can forget about driving). The dinner had been planned for some time—it was supposed to be a sendoff celebration for all four families (mine, Alex's, Mango's, and Ranley's). Instead, it was a smaller group—ten or so from my family, plus Alex, Ranley, and a few of our college friends. The festive atmosphere, pitchers and pitchers of dangerously delicious frozen margaritas, and the hard-to-believe realization that it was my last night home with my family and friends before going solo into the wild for seven months was a hell of a concoction for getting rip-roaring hammered. We must've been there for five or six hours. The night was a blur, but it was a good time and a hell of a kickoff.

As I went back and forth between the front door of my parents' house and the open trunk of the white Suburban in the driveway the next morning, packing the car with a blistering headache and bowling balls weighing on my eye sockets, Mom stopped and looked at me as I passed her.

"You look like shit."

"Thanks, Mom," I politely responded, and kept walking.

She continued to look at me disapprovingly. I knew she thought I was doing something wrong, taking an unnecessary risk. This worried me a little, to be honest, because, again—Mom always had such impeccable judgment. She was almost always right about things. But there was no turning back now, as horrible as I felt that morning as we loaded the bike and the rest of my equipment into the Suburban. This trip was happening. This trip was happening *now*.

As the ten-hour car ride got underway, wind gusts swayed the 7,700-pound Suburban on the upper level of the Verrazano Bridge, rocking it violently and making my dad grip the steering wheel tight, with both hands, to avoid hitting the median. Growling and howling, the angry New York Bay gusts seemed to manipulate the four-ton steel tank of a vehicle as if it were a cheap pool float. I'd never really noticed wind from inside a car.

We drove all day down I-95, through New Jersey, Delaware, and Maryland, past Philadelphia, Baltimore, and Washington, DC. The sun set as we drove through southern Virginia, and we finally stopped for dinner in rural Rocky Mount, North Carolina, just off 95, at a rundown BBQ joint I found on my phone. As we walked in, the neglected buffet and harsh fluorescent lighting weren't welcoming. Neither was the staff. As we ate, though, I could tell Mom was enjoying the place, despite its lack of atmosphere; she always loved trying new places and new things—and I was already missing her because of it.

I started to feel this pit in my stomach growing larger, demanding my attention. *What am I doing? Imagine eating at this place* alone? *That's you for the next seven months.*

As we laughed and talked as we ate, relishing this strange little mini-adventure the three of us had found ourselves on, I was glad they were there with me. But it also felt weird; it would be the last time I'd see my parents for a very long time. It felt like I was saying goodbye for years, or maybe even forever—at least on this Earth. What a strange, lonely thought. One day, perhaps, I'd have to. But how are you supposed to deal with losing your parents? Your heroes. Your biggest fans. Your first and most important teachers and role models. It's one of life's most daunting obstacles, no doubt. Perhaps the only way is to find purpose, and love, and another home—in a family of your own.

At around 11:00 p.m., we finally arrived at our destination. The Suburban pulled into the dirt driveway of a one-story house, in the darkness, parking beside a weeping willow tree laden with Spanish moss. I hopped out, happy to stretch my legs and finally get out of the car, and walked right up to the front door, knocking energetically. As my parents caught up behind me, the gregarious owner of the home swung open the door with a big smile.

"Fritz!" I exclaimed.

"Hey, it's the Nittis!" he shouted back, pretending to be surprised.

We all gave him a big hug. He was married at the time, and introduced us to his wife, Rochelle ("Ra-Ra" for short), whom we'd never met.

Fritz was only forty-six, but he looked far younger—at least ten years younger. His New York accent had picked up a slight hint of a Southern accent, the result of nearly two decades down there, which confused people. He was lean and fit, with a tan, resembling a thirty-something Matthew McConaughey. Fritz could connect with complete strangers like nobody I'd ever seen, striking up conversations with ease. This didn't happen too often, though, because it seemed like he couldn't walk a block in Wilmington without knowing someone or being recognized.

After my parents and I dropped our bags in our respective bedrooms, we walked over to the home's full-fledged bar, which had its own room. The bar was impressive—long and wooden, with a tap and a TV—and had plenty of character, adorned with thousands of photos on its walls. Looking like an authentic Irish pub, it was a far cry from your typical household bar.

The name of the bar?

McFritz's Pub.

Of course.

Uncle Brian never got to see the dream come to fruition, but Fritz made sure it still happened. As he and Ra-Ra poured our first beers from behind the bar, he told us about the epic St. Patrick's Day parties McFritz's Pub hosted every year—rowdy, all-day affairs that would've made Uncle Brian proud.

"Just about every single person in Wilmington makes their way through these doors at some point throughout the day," he said proudly, gesturing toward the large, double-door entrance to the room.

Sitting there, I imagined the annual scene. The Irish pride and revelry of St. Patrick's Day. In New York City, it was a good day to be a firefighter. My uncles would always march in the parade down Fifth Avenue. No matter how many bars they went to with their firefighter buddies afterward, they always made it home that night to join the rest of the family for Nana Mac's party, complete with Irish music, corned beef, cabbage, and potatoes.

We raised our glasses at McFritz's Pub to Uncle Brian, proposing a toast to him and the start of a good bike trip, as he would have done. There was no place in the world that I'd rather start off from.

The clock was about to strike midnight—the date would fittingly change to February 26—2/26. We skimmed through my itinerary and talked about some of the places I'd see.

Fritz asked, "So what are some of the most random, desolate places, you think?"

Kimberly, Oregon, came to mind first—the itinerary said I was supposed to be there on June 27 (Day 122). The directions I'd written out to myself read, "19 south to Kimberly. You're there when you see the post office. There's nothing else."

Fritz got a kick out of these instructions. "Hey, at least we can send a care package to the post office so you don't go hungry that night."

I learned that night that Fritz is one of the best guys in the world to grab a beer with. We sat at the bar telling stories about Uncle Brian for another four hours, laughing until 4:00 a.m. Then we watched the tribute video to him, made by his fellow Engine 226 firefighter, Chris O'Donnell. I didn't want him to know, but I could see a couple of tears trickling down Fritz's face as we watched. My eyes watered up too. It had been over ten years. But Fritz couldn't replace a friend like Brian. Time was meaningless.

When the same video had played at the reception of the memorial service in 2001, I looked across the room just as it ended. My eyes met five-year-old Brianne's, Uncle Brian's eldest child and only daughter. There were tears in her eyes; she was fighting as hard as she could to hold back an all-out sob. It broke my heart—it was the most painful thing I'd ever seen. I wanted to run across the room and hug her, but we were too far apart, with too many people between us. In that moment, cruelly seared into my memory now, I couldn't help but think, *Why did this happen?*

The five of us went out for breakfast the next morning to Sweet 'n' Savory (the place later made it onto Guy Fieri's "Diners, Drive-Ins, and Dives" and named a Bloody Mary on its menu "The Sexy Firefighter" after Fritz), and then I said goodbye to Mom and Dad from the restaurant's parking lot. It wasn't easy.

I later found out that my mom cried on the drive home. She didn't think she'd ever see me again.

After they left, Fritz drove me around Wilmington. We stopped at his firehouse, and I met some of the guys he worked with. We drove down to the beach, past the house of an old girlfriend. Past a Chick-fil-A, the renowned chicken chain I'd never tried (it hadn't made it up to New York yet).

"That stuff's like crack," Fritz acclaimed.

Then we went back to the house for a few hours and Fritz suggested that I try to take a nap, since we'd been up so late the night before and tomorrow was now the big day. I went into my bedroom and laid on the bed. Alone in the room, the nerves came roaring back. Trying to fall asleep just made them worse. I wondered if I was ready. I wondered if I'd quit. I wondered if the trip would change me at all. I wondered if I'd crash or get hit by a car. I wondered if I'd *survive* this trip. Was I making a terrible mistake?

Hanging out with Fritz felt like hanging out with Uncle Brian. It was weird and nostalgic. In the years to come, he'd come up to visit New York, and I'd come back down to visit Wilmington. He'd teach me how to surf and stand-up paddleboard, introduce me to his firefighter and lifeguard friends, as well as Wilmington's favorite local beer—a citrus IPA called Tropical Lightning—and bring me to the bars he took Brian to when he visited back in the '90s. We'd often have deep, philosophical conversations late into the night from his porch or the dock by his house. Uncle Brian was often a topic of conversation as well, of course. Fritz would still talk to him, sometimes.

By the time I visited in 2019, Fritz had been promoted to battalion chief. When I visited again in 2022, after a shark swam right by us as we surfed one morning (a first for me), we rode bikes to the bars by the beach late that night toward a mute but minacious lightning-filled sky. As we rode, Fritz broke the silence by loudly humming the unmistakable opening riff of George Thorogood's "Bad to the Bone," out of nowhere. He repeated it twice, and then I started singing, with my best Thorogood voice, on cue. We went back and forth, trading lyrics as we rode our bikes, like two kids in the '80s. "I just saw him over my left shoulder," Fritz said, referring to Brian. "He was laughing."

As I've gotten older, Fritz has become one of my best friends. He once told me that I was an old soul, and he was a young soul—and that's why we got along so well, as close friends would, despite our twenty-two-year age gap. In *soul* years, we were aligned. But he's more than just a great friend. He's an especially important person to me because he was Uncle Brian's best friend. I thought that starting the bike trip in Wilmington would be perfect for this reason.

So I was elated, of course, when Fritz told me he'd start out the trip *with* me, on *his* bike, for the first few miles. This way I wouldn't have to start alone.

The night before Day 1, he handed me $500 in cash. I told him I couldn't take it, but he insisted.

"No, I . . . I can't take that money. I appreciate it, Fritz, but I can't."

"Yes, you can. Take it. Come on—take yourself out for some nice meals. Or get a few extra motel rooms instead of camping out on the side of the road somewhere. And make sure you hide each bill in different parts of your bags. Don't put it all in one place," he advised.

Reluctantly accepting the generous gift, I did what he said, distributing the $100 bills throughout my bags.

Fritz, Ra-Ra, and I went to Tower 7, a modern, SoCal-style Mexican restaurant and bar in Wrightsville Beach for my last dinner before the trip. As we sat at the bar (when you eat out with Fritz, he always prefers to sit at the bar), which was adorned with white string lights and an impressive assortment of little bottles of hot sauces, we talked about the trip and whether I'd write a book about it one day.

"Man, I wish I could bike across the country," Fritz said as we ate, with a kind of wistful envy. "You'll have some tough days," he continued, his tone right-sizing, "but you'll get through them."

A vote of confidence like that, from someone I'd looked up to for so long, was yet another gift. *Fritz really thinks I can do this*, I thought.

"What are you gonna do about the Badlands, though?" he asked.

Fritz seemed most concerned about the Badlands, the most remote areas in the middle of the country. We talked about it a little bit, but I didn't really have a good answer. I didn't have a good answer for his next question, either.

"So . . . if you write a book one day, what's your title?"

"No idea. That would be one of the toughest parts, you know? Just coming up with a title."

The three of us sat for a few moments in silence, chewing on both that thought and the delicious fish tacos. Fritz seemed to think hard for a few seconds, looking down at the ground and tapping his hand on the polished wooden bar. All of a sudden, a light bulb went off.

"I got it! How about I quit my job and come with you. We can attach a trailer to the bike. You pedal, and the old man'll enjoy the ride, sitting in the back with a helmet and a blanket—just takin' in that beautiful country. You can name the book *Me and Fritz.*"

The three of us burst out laughing and couldn't stop.

Then we finished our margaritas and drove back to the house so I could try to get some sleep.

As I went to sleep that night, I knew I was about to get out of my comfort zone like never before. I knew it would be good for me . . . that I would *grow* from the experience, but the fear and doubt I felt in me was very real . . . and very hard to ignore.

***

There was nothing particularly novel about biking across the United States. Thomas Stevens, a twenty-nine-year-old English man, became the first person to do it back in 1884, when he cycled a penny-farthing from San Francisco to Boston. Now, hundreds of people have been doing it every year for decades. But biking across the country *and back*? I'd never heard of anyone doing that. I kept googling and googling and couldn't find anyone who had done it. I was sure it had been done, at some point. It *had* to have been. I became less sure, though, that someone had done it solo, completely unassisted. And that intrigued me. To do something, potentially, that no one had ever done before—or at least that very few people had ever done before—was exciting. In fact, 10,000 miles is enough to cross the country more than three times. Maybe it would be one of the longest bike rides in the history of the United States. The Guinness World Record for longest journey by bicycle in any single country would be set six years later, in 2018: a 15,744-mile ride in India.

In 2017, climber Alex Honnold accomplished one of the most impressive and daring athletic feats of all time when he free soloed the 3,000-foot El Capitan, the world's most renowned and intimidating rock face, in Yosemite National Park. To "free solo" something is to climb it without a rope—meaning you either execute the climb perfectly . . . or fall to your death. Some climbers look down on free soloists as reckless, suicidal. Others marvel at their bravery.

In the thrilling, Oscar-winning 2018 documentary *Free Solo*, Honnold rationalizes his choice to take on his very risky dream when he says, before the attempt, "The thing is, anybody can be happy and cozy. Nothing good happens in the world by being happy and cozy. Nobody achieves anything great because they're happy and cozy . . . you face your fear because your goal demands it. That is the goddamn warrior spirit."[4]

On the morning of February 27, 2012, the big Day 1 that we'd started counting down to over 800 days prior, I woke up excited. I'd slept better than expected, only waking up a couple of times. I felt good. Ready to go.

I got dressed and we threw the bike, the panniers, and the other gear into the back of Fritz's pickup truck, and the two of us left the house. On the drive to Wrightsville Beach, we stopped at a Panera for breakfast. And there, for some reason, the nerves returned with a vengeance—to the point that I couldn't eat the oatmeal I ordered.

As we sat by the window (Panera didn't have a bar, of course, so Fritz was okay with sitting at an actual table), Fritz was his usual bubbly self, full of energy and excitement for the big day. Laughing, telling stories. I, on the other hand, didn't feel like myself at all. I felt like I was about to *throw up*. I forced a couple of spoonfuls of oatmeal into my mouth, knowing I'd need the energy, washed them down with apple juice, and reluctantly threw out the rest.

We walked outside and got back into Fritz's pickup truck. There was no turning back now—I had to push the fear aside. The countdown clock had hit zero. It was time.

PART II
THERE

ME AND THE ROAD

NORTH CAROLINA
FEBRUARY 27

"Ramble On" – Led Zeppelin

A little after 8:30 a.m. on Monday, February 27, 2012, I dipped the rear wheel of my bike in the Atlantic Ocean at Wrightsville Beach, North Carolina, to officially begin the trip. There was this cross-country cyclist tradition I had read about, where the biker starts the ride by dipping the rear wheel of the bike in one ocean and ends it by dipping the front wheel in the other ocean, so that the journey completely takes them and the bike from coast to coast, in the fullest sense.

The sun broke through the gray, overcast sky over the pier, giving the water a pristine aqua color. As the waves rolled in with white foam and the chilly Atlantic tide gently ebbed and flowed over the rear tire, and my bare feet sinking into the cool and soothing sand, Fritz captured the formal start—the baptism—by taking my picture. I had explained to Fritz that I planned to dip the front wheel in the Pacific two and a half months later at the landmark Santa Monica Pier in Los Angeles, so he decided to get Wrightsville Beach's slightly lesser-known Johnnie Mercers Fishing Pier in the background of the photo for consistency.

"You know—pier to pier," he reasoned.

Coast to coast. Ocean to ocean. Pier to pier. There was symmetry and tradition and circumstance in it. I liked it.

After the tire dip, I carried the bike over the sand back to the pier parking lot, where I was tasked with fully loading it for the first time. Looking back on the trip, it's amazing to me that I hadn't tried doing this yet. Procrastination at its finest.

Fritz helped me place the rear pannier bags on the rack; these twin units would carry the bulk of my gear, including all the clothes I'd wear for the next seven months and tools to maintain the bike. The two pannier "bags" were actually sturdy, structured compartments, joined by a strap that stretched over the rear rack, which the bags rested on by way of metal hinges covered with rubber. When the filled panniers were draped over the rack, they created a nice, flat surface about three feet wide that I needed to make good use of.

Here's what was included in the pannier bags:

- Bike Clothes: Four pairs of bike shorts (I'd wear Under Armour compression shorts underneath them); five or so Nike Dri-FIT moisture-wicking t-shirts (I didn't wear those professional-looking jerseys with sponsor logos on them because I didn't like them—I wasn't a pro or even serious cyclist by any stretch, so I felt out of place wearing them); one reflective black rain-resistant windbreaker; five pairs of black mid-calf socks to ride in.
- Casual Clothes: One pair of sweatpants; one pair of comfortable, lightweight pajama pants to sleep in; one pair of jeans; three or four pairs of boxers; two pairs of casual shorts; three t-shirts; three pairs of casual socks; one pair of board shorts to swim in.
- One green pin bag for dirty clothes. I figured I would need to do laundry after every five days of biking or so. I ended up never wearing completely dirty clothes; if I was out of clean biking gear and couldn't do laundry, I at least washed a pair of bike shorts, compression shorts, and a t-shirt in a sink somewhere with hand soap. I knew that, most days, I'd be sweating a lot, and to keep from getting sick or getting a skin infection, hygiene needed to be a top priority.

- Shoes: One pair of cycling shoes that clipped into my pedals; one pair of sneakers; one pair of flip-flops.
- One bath towel and a bright orange, ultra-absorbent ShamWow towel that Fritz had given me that morning, insisting I'd need it at some point.
- My navy blue FDNY hat.
- A small three-ring binder with the route and itinerary printed out (with turn-by-turn directions for all 10,000 miles) as a physical back-up to my phone.
- One pen.
- One spiral notebook to serve as a journal, stored in a large Ziploc freezer bag in case rain seeped through.
- Bike Tools: Finish Line bike chain lubricant, a chain brush (which kind of looked like a giant toothbrush with black bristles), a few spare bike parts, and an Allen key multi-tool.
- Bright yellow rain covers for the panniers.
- Sunscreen.
- Iodine tablets, in case I couldn't find drinkable water.
- The bear spray from Cailyn to ward off threatening bears (or people, I figured).
- Some backup food (including oatmeal packets and cans of soup). I thought oatmeal would be my go-to breakfast because it was cheap, easy to carry, and loaded with energy for its weight. I was so sold on this oatmeal plan that I bought a huge box of it at Costco before I left and dispersed about fifty packets in assorted flavors into every crevice, nook, and cranny in my bags. I couldn't move a single piece of gear or clothing, it seemed, without displacing a packet of oatmeal. To serve it, I brought a replica New York Yankees batting helmet plastic cereal bowl with me—I'd ordered it from the back of a cereal box as a kid, and had used it for cereal all the way through college. Before I left, I thought I could get by with a packet or two of oatmeal every day for breakfast. I quickly learned, though, that this wasn't nearly enough.

Within a few weeks, my ideal go-to breakfast became a tall stack of banana-nut pancakes, coffee, water, and a large cinnamon roll with plenty of icing. I was able to find some version of this hearty breakfast in more places than you would think, usually at very reasonable prices (often under $10 total). It was a lot more expensive than a packet of oatmeal, of course, but well, well worth it. Fueling up on carbs every morning had a significant impact on how I felt the whole day, and for some reason, I felt best after pancakes and cinnamon rolls.

Right in the middle of the two panniers, directly on the rack itself, I was able to perfectly fit my toiletry bag with my toothbrush, toothpaste, razors, etc. (Because the toiletry bag sat directly over the rear wheel, the bottom of it was often sprayed with a perfectly straight line of mud on wet days.) Then, we layered my tent bag, sleeping bag, small pillow, and rolled-up sleeping pad on top of the panniers and toiletry bag, attempting to balance it all as best we could. We strapped everything down with three bungee cords that connected to the rack. Fritz seemed to really know what he was doing when it came to packing everything and securely strapping it all down, so it was a good thing he was there for this.

In the front handlebar bag, I kept items I needed to access throughout the day:

- My phone and charger.
- My wallet.
- A digital camera.
- A few spare tubes.
- Tire levers.
- A pocket knife.
- Clif Bars and bananas.
- The small bike headlight.
- My biking gloves (the type that left the fingertips exposed).
- Sunglasses (when I didn't have them on).
- A somewhat heavy bike lock (that I basically never used).

- A weather radio that provided a detailed report of your current location in a creepy, robotic voice.
- A pair of lightweight running shorts to throw over my bike shorts during the day (I decided I was *not* going to walk into any café, store, gas station, or public place wearing just bike shorts).
- A duct tape wallet that my little cousin, Sophia, had made in school and given to me. I kept in it a stack of Uncle Brian's mass cards, which Nana Mac wanted me to give to firefighters and other people I'd meet across the country. The cards had his photo on them, wearing the FDNY Yankee hat with the sunset behind him.
- A relic of St. Therese (a tiny square of fabric from a piece of her clothing, taped to a card) that Nana Mac had given me—an item that was very important to her, which she felt would protect me.
- Fritz had given me a large bumper sticker that he created to honor Uncle Brian. It was a red Celtic cross design with an image of a traditional fire department badge Maltese cross overlaying it. In the arms of the Maltese cross, it read "FDNY – Never Forget – 9/11/01." Over the center of the overlaying crosses was a green shamrock with "Mac" written in gold.

On the top of the handlebar bag, there was a small, clear, plastic zipper compartment that I could access as I was riding. Here, I kept my iPod and any notes I had for the day (directions I'd written out, addresses, names, or phone numbers I might need to call that day).

In the center of the handlebars, the guys at Brands Cycle & Fitness had set up a digital speedometer and odometer that I made heavy use of each day. I'd reset the odometer each morning so I could track how many miles I'd completed as the day progressed. The computer also logged total trip miles. I also had a tiny hand pump that conveniently attached to the top tube part of the bike frame, directly underneath it, so it wouldn't be in the way. I'd inflate the tires to 110 psi, so inflating a new tube took well over 100 full pumps. I had 28 mm Continental Gatorskin tires and used the corresponding 28/32 tube size.

I was able to carry five water bottles with me: two on the front exterior of the rear panniers (one on each side), two on the bike itself by the traditional spot (on the frame by the crankset), and one on the side of the handlebar bag. The bike was a mixed silver/gold pewter color, like the helmet of the Tampa Bay Buccaneers, with "Trek 520" displayed boldly across the frame, which had orange water bottle holders.

The bike itself weighed about thirty pounds. All the gear weighed at least eighty. I weighed over 200 lbs when I started, so everything together weighed a whopping 315+ pounds, which is the equivalent of a barbell with three 45-pound plates on each side and heavier than an offensive lineman in the NFL.

***

At about 9:00 a.m. on February 27, 2012, I got on the bike in the pier parking lot and started riding with Fritz and his friend, Jason. It was reassuring to begin the journey with two other people, as opposed to being on my own. It certainly remedied some of that "Day 1" apprehension, even if it was just for a few miles. Fritz led the way and Jason was behind me, so he could keep an eye on all the gear and make sure nothing fell off.

On Day 1, I was bound for Myrtle Beach, South Carolina. Once I got moving, the nerves started to settle—in part because I really had to focus; what I was doing felt *nothing* like riding a bicycle! With the full weight of the gear on it, the heavy two-wheeled monstrosity felt unbalanced, cumbersome, and extremely slow in responding to my movement. I was clumsily wobbling along the street much more than "riding." Crawling before I could walk. It took an unbelievable amount of effort and balance to turn the bike just slightly. On a few instances, I had to quickly clip out of my pedals and hop off the bike before I toppled right over. I'd just smile and wave back to Jason when this happened, signaling back to him that I was okay, but really, I was thinking, *How the hell am I going to bike 10,000 miles like this?*

We must've taken the scenic route through Wilmington, because I think it added almost 15 unexpected miles to my day. After we saw the better part of

Wilmington, we arrived at the aptly-named Cape Fear Memorial Bridge. And there, we had a problem. There was no other way to get across the river to continue south along Route 17, but there was absolutely no shoulder on the loud, narrow, busy bridge. Bikes were certainly not allowed.

Unsure of exactly what to do, the three of us lifted our bikes onto a narrow metal divide between the road and the guardrail and walked them across the precarious, industrial-looking, steel, vertical lift bridge. Cars and trucks were honking and whizzing by us a few feet away. We had to shout to hear one another.

"His mom's gonna kill us," Jason said to Fritz, out of my earshot.

My heart was practically in my throat by the time we made it across.

Fritz had a big smile on his face when we finally made it over. It was a bit of a chaotic setting for a goodbye, but he wished me luck with a hug and a slap on the back on the side of the highway, and we parted ways.

"Just you and the road now," he said. "Good luck, buddy." Fritz took a photo of me pedaling away down Route 17 and sent it back to my parents.

From that point on, I was on my own. A lonely feeling sank in immediately.

A little while later, it started to rain. The air had a slight burning aroma to it, a fragrance that was distinctly North Carolinian. I realized that I didn't need to turn too much, so I didn't have to worry about maneuvering the bike as much as it seemed those first couple of miles. But the highway wasn't friendly. It was straight, flat, cold, and monotonous.

With nearly every passing car and truck, my pulse quickened and my hands gripped the handlebars a little tighter. I'd never biked on any highway before, and I realized it was going to take some getting used to. I felt very exposed, very vulnerable. The velocity of the traffic passing so close to me was shell-shocking and constantly stressful. *What if someone was texting and driving—or tired or distracted somehow, and they swerved off the road a little? What if they didn't see me? What if they were drunk? Or under the influence of something?*

All of that, of course, was completely out of my control, so I tried not to focus on it. My dad always used to tell us growing up to "Control the controllables"—easier said than done, but that's what I tried to do.

The other thing about biking on the highway that I didn't really think about prior to the trip was the specific nature of the shoulder. On Day 1, I got to know "rumble strips" pretty well, because Route 17 had plenty of them. Rumble strips, also known as "sleeper lines," are the tiny divots in the side of the road that are used to alert or awaken inattentive drivers if they begin to drift out of their lane into the shoulder. "Tiny," of course, is a relative term.

In a car at 60–70 mph or so, running over them has a vibrating effect, giving the driver just enough of a "buzz" to politely wake them up. On a bike going 12 mph or so, running over them is much like operating a jackhammer, violently shaking your entire body and causing you to hold on for dear life.

The problem was, on some shoulders, it was difficult to avoid the strips because there was hardly any room. On some stretches of Route 17, for example, the white line and the rumble strip were only inches apart, as were the rumble strip and the end of the pavement on the other side. Navigating such narrow real estate on such a wobbly, unstable bicycle was no easy task, especially on Day 1.

I would come to learn that most shoulders had much more space between the rumble strip and the end of the pavement, especially on interstates. I wouldn't like interstates, though, because they'd have a lot more debris, which made me more prone to flat tires; plus, it's illegal to cycle on them unless there's no alternative route, and there'd generally be more trucks and even faster-moving traffic on them. Sometimes there really would be no alternative, and sometimes I'd just do it anyway, because it'd be a lot more direct.

Many shoulders didn't have rumble strips, and some roads didn't even have *shoulders*. In the case of the latter, I would need to bike just inside the white line, sharing the lane with cars and trucks. Those were the most dangerous situations, of course, especially on two-lane highways when drivers in my lane had to account for oncoming traffic as they passed me.

Right away on Day 1, I figured out that I needed to take a break every ten miles. When I took a break, I usually tried to find a grassy area to sit down on, and would eat a Clif Bar or a banana and drink plenty of water. Including time taken for breaks, I was averaging about ten miles per hour (so my average cruising speed in the beginning was about 12–14 mph on a flat road with no wind).

I took my lunch break on Day 1 at a McDonald's in Shallotte, North Carolina. As I ate my first meal alone on the trip, I was feeling down. I sat in a booth, eating a Quarter Pounder with Cheese, looking out the window at the bike, with its yellow pannier rain covers on. I had hoped I wouldn't need those covers much, but here it was—only halfway through Day 1 of 216—and they were already on.

The lonely feeling intensified as I ate. My family was gone, Fritz was gone. It really was just me and the road now. And the bike. I didn't want to go back out there, in the cold rain, exposed to the road and the elements with nobody with me. But where else could I go? I couldn't go home—buying a bus ticket back to Long Island after half a day would be beyond embarrassing. It would be demoralizing. It would be a failure of epic proportions to me to give up on Day 1. I had been thinking about this trip and planning for it for a long time. There was no turning back now.

Reluctantly, I cleared my McDonald's tray and went back outside. It was still raining and still cold, but I climbed back on the bike and started pedaling.

HEADWINDS AND STRANGERS

SOUTH CAROLINA
FEBRUARY 27 – MARCH 4

"Against the Wind" – Bob Seger

Soon after my sad lunch at McDonalds, I came to the South Carolina border, which was the first state border I crossed and the first fragment of positive momentum I felt. Contrasting with the gray skies and soggy atmosphere, the bright baby blue South Carolina welcome sign was a sight for sore eyes. It was a sign of measurable progress—and on Day 1, I needed it badly. It was a crucial morale booster. I took a photo of it and decided at that moment that I would take a photo of every state welcome sign I came across. I would immediately send the photo to my parents, which always made them happy.

A little farther down the road, in a more remote area, a man shouted at me to flag me down.

"Where ya headed?" Steve, the owner of Island Hoppers Bike Shop, would be the first of many to ask this question.

I was too ashamed to admit that I was attempting to bike to California and back, and that it was only my first day, so I told him I was biking to Florida (it wasn't a lie—I really *was* biking to Florida—I was just planning on going a little farther after that, that's all). He was happy to hear it and offered a few words of encouragement and a free tube. He gave me a scouting report of the road ahead and how much farther I had to go, which also became common practice for locals I spoke to.

A few miles after I had waved goodbye to that supportive bike shop owner, an enormous bird (a crane, I think) sprang up out of nowhere from the side of the road a few feet away, startling me so much I nearly leapt off the bike, wheeling away from it toward the middle of the highway (luckily, there wasn't any passing traffic at the moment). I must have really looked like a New Yorker; from my reaction, you would've thought it was a gigantic pterodactyl that had escaped from Jurassic Park. Even more frightening was the fact that I started *singing* about the bird after that—evidence, perhaps, of the delirious, punch-drunk state of exhaustion I was in.

That was a very big bird . . .
Oh yes, a very big bird, that I sawww,
Oh, oh-oh, on the side of the road

A little later, as I was slopping along the wet pavement in North Myrtle Beach, on a busy stretch of road with a very narrow shoulder, a car slowed down and rolled down the window so a man could scream at me, at the top of his lungs, "*Use the sidewalk!*"

I jumped, surprised by the encounter, and promptly rode right up onto the sidewalk, obediently following orders. I pictured the guy laughing and high-fiving his buddy as they sped off. People feel big with two tons of steel around them—my dad would always say that. I would become tougher with more time on the road, but on Day 1, I was a little timid and a little naïve. The highway wasn't friendly. Not even a minute later, I felt stupid for adhering to the guy's unnecessary command, and I quickly realized that it was much easier and much faster to be on the road, despite the congestion and shrinking shoulder. So, after a block, I left the sidewalk and dipped back into the road. From that point on, I never biked on the sidewalk again.

Surf shops, mini-golf courses, high-rise condos, bars, seafood restaurants, and bargain beachwear/swimwear stores adorned with large, concrete sharks to greet vacationing customers were springing up along the roadside late in the afternoon, under the gray, darkening sky, and soon I was officially in Myrtle Beach. Day 1 was in the books, and I was much more psyched than I thought I'd be. In fact, I was ecstatic. I felt like I had completed the whole trip. I ended up going about ninety miles on Day 1, more than I had originally planned for and almost 50% more than an average day, so it was a hell of a way to break myself in. I sent the image of the Myrtle Beach welcome sign back to my parents, and they were elated; my mom, especially, said how proud she was of me. *I guess they thought I'd give up on Day 1,* I thought.

That night, I was lucky enough to have a condo to myself—that I didn't have to pay for. A friend from Ithaca, Debbie, and her husband, Drew, had reserved their condo for me for two nights. It was on one of the higher floors of the building, with a great view of the Myrtle Beach strip, which was illuminated by the time I walked in, around sunset.

I was cold and wet when I arrived, but I still took an ice bath before I did anything else, because my legs and butt were killing me from riding all day. I was in a great deal of pain *all over* my body, really. Everything hurt, and it only got worse when I got off the bike and started to cool down and tighten up. Setting up the bath required multiple trips to the ice machine on another floor to fill up the tub in the condo, but it was worth it. Immersing yourself in icy water in February, after you've been out in the cold rain all day, might not sound like a particularly great idea, but an ice bath is the best way to get your legs to recover fast—I knew that from college. The next day was a rest day to help with recovery too.

After the numbing, but invigorating, bath, I took a hot shower and went out to grab literally the closest food I could find, a personal pizza, for dinner. As I sat in a booth, waiting for the pizza to be ready, feeble from fatigue and hunger, my sister Annie called me. It was only the end of Day 1 and I was already very lonely, so it was good to hear her voice. She had handwritten me a long, encouraging letter before I left, and echoed some of the same sentiments—that this trip would be a *great* thing, and that I'd look back on it fondly—over the phone that night, when I needed it most. I also spoke to my parents and Fritz when I got back to the condo, thanked everyone who had sent me a supportive text that day to wish me well, including Alex, and went right into a deep sleep.

Breakfast the next morning was *extremely* lonely. It was the first time in my life eating at a real sit-down restaurant alone, and the fact that I was the only single patron in the whole, eerily quiet pancake house only added to it. Myrtle Beach is a ghost town in February. When you eat in a restaurant alone, you kind of get the feeling that the server feels bad for you; I could detect it in the waitress's tone of voice that morning as I ate my pancakes and made small talk with her. It's not a good feeling. An empathetic "How we doing over here, hun?" was a phrase I would get used to hearing.

It's hard to eat a meal alone when you're not used to it. In college, we ate in groups and I always seemed to know people in the dining halls. In high school and before, we always ate dinner as a family. But as I walked back to the condo, I remember being happy. Happy that I'd had the guts to leave home and take on this journey on my own. Happy that this big trip I had planned for and thought about so much the previous few years was actually underway. It was exciting— the beginning of a long adventure with no certain script. It was so completely different from anything I'd ever done. I felt incredibly *free*.

* * *

Apparently, one day off wasn't enough, because I was still very sore from Day 1 when I got back on the bike the morning of Day 3, which worried me. What troubled me much more, however, was the *wind*. I only needed to go thirty-seven miles, but the wind slowed me down considerably, making each of those thirty-seven miles a real chore. What was supposed to be an easy half-day became a full day of work, and then some.

On one bridge into Georgetown, South Carolina, the wind was so strong that I actually thought it was going to lift me right off the bridge, so I ducked down as low as I could on the bike, just trying with all my might to keep the pedals moving. I remember having a new appreciation that day for the old Irish blessing, *"May the road rise to meet you, may the wind be always at your back."* I picture a beautiful, emerald, Irish prairie when I hear that, with a charismatic cobblestone road unfolding over a soft hill. Maybe some sheep. But, so far, my road had met me with unforgiving rain and bellowing trucks, and the wind was always obnoxiously *in my face.*

When I got into Georgetown, I asked a man on the street for directions; I was trying to find my way to Johnson's Marina & Campground for the night. I'm not sure if he had teeth, but it sounded like he didn't, and he had a very different way of talking; I thought to myself, *That guy's a character right out of a movie.* About five minutes later, I looked up at the town water tower to read, "Georgetown, SC: A Character City."

I met another Georgetown character when I got to the campground, this one even more colorful. His name was Billy Johnson, the owner of the marina and riverside campground. He was in his early sixties and had a deep tan, short blond hair under a baseball cap, and a strong Southern accent. He had a Southern tough-guy way about him, for sure, too.

Everyone else staying at the campground had their own RV, but since I was just on a bike, I rented my own personal "trailer." It was more of a metal box, actually. It looked like a miniature version of one of those shipping containers you'd see stacked at a seaside port, one on top of the other. When I called in advance, it was supposed to be $45 for the night. When I got there and they saw me, they knocked it down to $30 (I don't know, maybe they felt bad for me).

After talking with Billy and his wife, Ella, for a little while, he offered me a Coke, and when he heard about the trip cause, he said, "Well, we'll have to just give you your money right back then." They let me stay for free. And the kindness from these perfect strangers didn't stop there—he picked up a hamburger in town for me that night, on him, and invited me for coffee at their home by the river the next morning.

Ella called the *Georgetown Times*, and a reporter came to take my photo with Billy and to write up a story about the trip and the Marty Lyons Foundation. In the photo, Billy had his arms crossed, with a badass, serious look on his face—no smiling—next to me and the bike. Noticing this and trying to match him, I put on kind of a half-tough face and narrowed my eyes a little, but in the photo you could tell I was trying, unsuccessfully, to hold back a smile. He said he'd send a copy of the paper to my parents back home.

Conversation topics with Billy that afternoon ranged from cars to guns to bedbugs, but the one thing he seemed most excited about was *apple cider vinegar*, of all things. I had absolutely no idea what it was at the time. He said a trusted doctor once told him it was the best single thing you could possibly ingest, but no other doctor would ever admit it, since "they'd lose business."

"It clears your arteries and prevents ya from gettin' sick," he continued. "I been takin' a tablespoon a day for twenty-seven years now, and I've never gotten sick. *Never!* I saw an interview on TV with a fella who just turned a hundred 'n' six, and when they asked him how he did it, he said, 'Well, the first thing is the Good Lord above, and the second . . . is apple cider vinegar.'

"Since you're still young," he told me, "you'll prolly live to a hundred 'n' fifty if ya start takin' it now. Make sure, though, you get it with the mother."

"With the *what*?"

"With the *mother*. It'll say it, just like that, on the label there. With. The. *Mother*," he said, spacing out the text with hand gestures.

He even let me try some. It was as intense and nasty as you'd expect vinegar to taste, and set my throat on fire as it went down. He seemed pleased that I took a shot of it, though, without watering it down. Sure enough, the yellow bottle said, right on the label, "WITH THE MOTHER."

* * *

It was raining the next morning when I woke up in the shipping container, so I decided to delay my start a little, hoping it would let up. I had a longer-than-expected coffee with Billy on his riverside porch, talking politics and guns (at his preference).

After the coffee, he drove me to Food Lion so I could pick up some peanut butter, bread, and bananas. Then, he walked me into his house to show me his gun collection, which comprised about fifty rifles. He said he'd never give up his guns, no matter what—you'd have to kill him—and that it was his constitutional right to have them. One was made in 1907; another, a bayonet, had been used in the Mexican-American War.

I was grateful for Billy and Ella's hospitality. They even said I could stay another night if I wanted to. I wasn't expecting kindness like that from perfect strangers, and the Johnsons were the first on the trip to offer it.

Billy had one request before I left: "You make sure you give us a call, now, when you make it back to New York, alright?"

I promised I would, thanked them for their generosity, and went back outside to get the day started.

The third day of biking, from Billy's campground to Charleston, South Carolina, was absolutely *brutal*—just a painful, long, windy, rainy day from hell. From the campground, I walked the bike down a long, dirt path, through a wooded area, back to the road, and grudgingly climbed back on for more torture. My muscles ached as I sluggishly labored forward through the humid morning air, my legs lashing out at me for making them move. Even the bike seemed tired. And pissed at me. It creaked and squeaked along, seemingly already fed up with this tedious chore of an exploit.

I had some serious doubts about making it to Charleston that day, and much more severe doubts about the trip in general, worse than ever before. *What the hell did I get myself into?* The months ahead of me were beginning to feel like a prison sentence, certainly not a "vacation."

I said those exact words to Dad on the phone one night, and he replied, "Well, it's not a vacation. It's an adventure."

He was right, and it made me feel a little better. For the first time, I felt that my parents were behind the endeavor.

Back on the highway, I crawled through the wind, holding on when gusts picked up and wondering what a tailwind would feel like. A short while later, the rain returned, pelting me at times, so that it felt more like hail, and the pain in my butt was excruciating from too much time in the seat (it was immensely sore, to the touch), which made me need to break every five miles as I biked along

Route 17 through Francis Marion National Forest. I had anticipated a hard couple of weeks to start the trip, but I hadn't expected *this*. This was misery.

The lone highlight of the day was stopping for lunch at a place on the highway called Seewee Restaurant. Cold and soaked to the bone from the rain, I sat in the back room alone, watching my bike get drenched outside through the window, but warming up a little with some delicious she-crab soup and a shrimp po boy.

A little later, as I approached Charleston, the road got very congested and exceedingly dangerous because of construction zones and non-existent shoulders. Eventually, I came upon Arthur Ravenel Jr. Bridge, the largest and most treacherous bridge I would cross the entire trip—it made crossing Cape Fear Memorial Bridge on Day 1 look like a stroll through Central Park. It was one last, enormous hurdle I needed to scale before finally arriving in Charleston to finish the day.

As I got onto the bridge, I remember just understatedly thinking, *This is not good.* The bridge was much larger and busier than I had anticipated when I mapped out the route, and I knew it was no place to be riding a bicycle, but there was basically no other way into Charleston—so I decided to put my head down and just get over the damn thing as quickly as possible so I could finally end the damn day. The sun had come out just before I crossed, but I literally feared for my life as I climbed up and over the monstrous, modern-looking, suspension bridge, which had a slim shoulder, gusting wind, and fast, heavy traffic, high above the Cooper River.

When I was a little more than halfway over the bridge, I heard a siren and saw an ambulance speed by. I thought to myself—*Shit, I might need one too.*

Then, I heard another siren. I turned my head slightly and thought I saw a cop from the corner of my eye—it almost looked like he was pulling up behind me to pull me over! I'd never heard of a bicycle getting pulled over by a cop, so I wasn't sure, at first, if I was the one being targeted.

I didn't know what to do, so I quickly looked straight ahead again and kept pedaling, pretending I didn't notice the siren. I also wanted to get the hell off that bridge as soon as I could. The siren continued to blare, though, as I obliviously scrabbled slowly along.

Then, I realized the cop was directly behind me, a few yards away. I continued to look straight ahead. Suddenly, I heard a loud, booming, Gestapo-like voice over the police car intercom. It bellowed three words I'll never forget, emphasizing each distinctly:

"STOP THE BICYCLE!"

Then I was sure it was meant for me, and I couldn't pretend I didn't notice anymore. I stopped and waited, feeling defeated and guilty, ready to get a ticket or arrested. He pulled up to my left and rolled down the passenger side window to give me a hard, perplexed stare, as if I perfectly fit the description of the local insane asylum escapee who actually thought he was going to make it to freedom over Arthur Ravenel Jr. Bridge.

"Bikes aren't allowed on this side," he said, eyes locked on me with the same baffled expression on his face, which implied, "Are you fucking *kidding* me?"

I told him I saw the protected walkway on the other side of the bridge, but couldn't figure out how to get over there. He understood, to my relief, and could easily tell I was an out-of-towner.

"I see you're going a long way," he said, nodding to my bags and all my gear. "Just get off at the first exit, okay? I'll give you an escort so you get there safely."

I was certainly planning on getting off at the first exit anyway, but I didn't mind having a *police escort* the rest of the way, to say the least. *What an incredibly kind, unexpected gesture.*

As I rode through Charleston, past its signature pastel-colored houses and stout palmettos, it was getting dark. Away from the wind and the highway and the noise and the bridge and the mayhem, I breathed an exhausted sigh of relief as I slowly pedaled down an old, quiet street that was peacefully meandering its way into dusk. Finally, I could relax. I had cut it close that day, in an array of ways.

I got to the Comfort Inn and immediately collapsed on the king-sized bed. It felt like the most comfortable bed in the world. I didn't even leave my room to explore Charleston, a place I wanted to see. I had planned on walking around the charismatic colonial town, eating at a nice restaurant, maybe checking out a rooftop bar or two, then going on the "Ghosts of Charleston" walking tour, which I had heard was a great way to see the history-rich, supposedly haunted town after dark. Instead, I iced my ass, had a can of Campbell's Chunky soup from my bags for dinner in the hotel room, and passed out.

***

The next day was more of the same. There were long construction zones, I almost ran out of daylight and water for the first time, which I was learning were both precious commodities in this new life, and the sun was hot and strong. I felt like I was riding for weeks, but, somehow, it was just one day.

As it got more remote, places like boiled peanut stands ($4 for a pound) made for good roadside snack stops. On a desolate stretch, late in the afternoon, though, with just trees and marshland around me, I was out of water and realized how much of a predicament I could get myself into by running out. Dehydration set in incredibly quickly, and I started feeling awful. Any energy I had was gone, my body somehow ached even more, my mouth and throat had dried up, and—worst of all—I had a splitting, excruciating headache. I cursed myself for not conserving better earlier in the day. Miles slowly, agonizingly, went by. I started to feel that I literally couldn't go any farther without drinking some water.

Finally, I saw a sign for the Carolina Cider Company a mile up the road. What a stroke of luck! I don't think I'd ever seen a cider store in my whole life up to that point. The store's slogan was "A taste of the lowcountry" and the sign out front read, "Black Bing Cider, Peach Cider, Jams, Jellies. Free Samples."

Literally about as content as I could be, I gulped down a Peach Cider and a Black Bing Cherry Cider in a rocking chair on the front porch of the old store, and of course, guzzled some ice-cold water and filled all five of my water bottles with it. I could actually feel the fluids reviving me, cooling my esophagus down to my stomach, and then circulating through the rest of my body. After a few minutes, my thirst was quenched and the headache quickly dissipated.

That day, I learned about the need to conserve water; drinkable water wasn't going to always be easy to find, and it was imperative to go out of my way to fill up all five of my water bottles whenever possible.

If I prayed for water that day, the prayer was answered the following day, because water *came*. It came in the form of biblical-like, flooding rain. Luckily, it was a scheduled rest day in Beaufort, South Carolina. The rain came down in sheets, and I could see that the Howard Johnson parking lot had turned into a respectable swimming pool as I timidly peered out from my motel room window, very happy to be inside.

I spent most of the day on my bed, watching *Indiana Jones* and other movies on TV, without much desire to move. I joked to my parents on the phone that I knew it was going to pour that day, two years prior when I made the schedule, so I decided to make it a rest day. I could hear the relief in their voices—they always sounded more at ease on rest days. I was actually pretty worried, though, about being able to keep to the itinerary. This was only Day 6, and biking in that kind of rain definitely would not have been feasible.

After a lot of fast food the first few days, which I wasn't used to, I was craving a healthy meal, so I walked over to an out-of-place Swiss restaurant next door, in the downpour, and picked up some sautéed mushrooms and chicken cordon bleu for dinner. I noticed that someone had written on the website (there was a place on the biketrip2012.com homepage for visitors to post comments) that she had seen me riding in the rain, the day I rode to Charleston. She commented that the whole thing was "awesome and meaningful," which gave me a little lift of motivation. I had no idea who she was or how she found the website, but I decided that I needed to have some kind of sign made that read "biketrip2012.com" so that when drivers saw me they could find the website and cause, if they were interested.

I also got some great advice and some much-needed words of encouragement from Billy Iaia. We had been messaging back and forth on Facebook:

Billy: I know the bike will hold up and I know u will hold up. Just remember if your mind says stop, keep going – your body will tell you when it's time to call it a day. Remember, eat good and drink all through the day, every 15 minutes. If u need it or not. And keep your eyes on the road at all times. Make sure u know what's behind u at all times. Let me know how u feel along the way, and remember, we live in Denver so u have a place to stay.

Me: Ok thanks a lot Billy I really appreciate it. In Beaufort, SC, now . . . some tough headwinds the last couple of days.

Billy: Get on the bike at 5 a.m. and do your hard riding early, no wind. Winds start up around 10 or 11. Remember the longer you're on the bike, the more the body takes a beating. Good luck and take it all in.

Getting an earlier start definitely helped, but the remorseless wind continued, day after day. Bob Seger's "Against the Wind" played over and over in my head (at that point, it was the theme song of the trip). It was worse near water, and especially awful on or near bridges, which were plentiful while I was still tracking along the East Coast.

As I approached one bridge, a gust was so stifling that the bike slowed to a barely moving crawl, then stopped completely! I tried to kick my heels out, just before I hit 0 mph on the speedometer, remembering the bike shop guy's advice to "be like Dorothy from *The Wizard of Oz* and kick your heels" when clipping out as a beginner, but I couldn't. My cycling shoes were stuck in the pedals, and I couldn't kick them out. The wheels came to a standstill, so I slowly—very slowly—toppled over onto the muddy grass on the side of the highway, landing hard with a thud.

Almost immediately, a pickup truck pulled onto the shoulder behind me, and a little girl, maybe six or seven years old, hopped out of the front passenger seat and shouted out to me, "Are you okay?!" in a sweet little voice.

Simultaneously demoralized and heartened, I answered, "Yes, I'm okay," turning my head to wave to her father in the truck from the ground, still clipped into my pedals.

8

QUIT, MAN

GEORGIA
MARCH 4–9

"Georgia on My Mind" – Ray Charles

After I passed the Georgia welcome sign, which, of course, had a peach on it and said, "We're glad Georgia's on your mind," I hit Savannah, where I stayed at a Days Inn. A couple of good guys from a nearby air force base bought me a couple of beers as I ate a burger and a basket of fried shrimp for dinner, sitting at the lively bar on the hotel premises.

The next day, I turned inward away from the coast to start a westward track through the southern tier of the Peach State. Here, the towns got smaller and more spread out, I passed signs that said things like "Brush your mind with the word of God. It prevents truth decay," and everything got noticeably less expensive. I stayed in a motel one night in Jesup, Georgia, for just $35, which shocked me. It was great news, though—I had to be pretty miserly if my savings account was going to last me seven months.

I could feel myself getting further and farther from what I was used to. The idea of a $35 motel room certainly gave me a more positive outlook on my budget and how often I could afford to sleep in a real bed; some *campgrounds* were almost that price. I figured the less I had to camp, the better I'd feel. Food was relatively cheap and easy to find in these towns, too, especially since they almost always had the usual chains like McDonald's, Subway, Pizza Hut, Taco Bell, KFC, Domino's, Chipotle, etc. That same night in Jesup, I went to a Taco Bell across the road, and the guy at the counter slid out a tray of soft beef tacos about ten seconds after I ordered them. Like a bad actor from a low-budget '70's commercial, I actually said, "Wow, that was *fast*." He just replied, "Fast food, sir," with a slight nod and tip of his Taco Bell visor.

I almost never ate fast food before the trip—maybe a few times a year on the road or on the way to a game or something—but it had become the most viable option for me as I went, so I began eating it regularly. It was cheap, quick, and convenient. I needed to eat a lot, and I couldn't imagine trying to go grocery shopping or carrying a camping stove with propane canisters and bowls, plates, etc.; it just wouldn't work.

As I left Jesup the next day, the wind died down a little (at least, in part, I think, because I was getting farther away from the coast) and I started to feel significantly better on the bike. My average cruising speed got up to 17 mph, a delightfully brisk pace compared to the 12 mph or so I had been averaging, especially compared to the windier days when I'd dip down to 10 mph or even into the single digits.

I was pumped, and actually started to enjoy riding a little bit for the first time—it's a lot more fun, I learned, when you can go faster. A *lot* more fun. I thought about Billy Iaia's words of wisdom, and how the more time you spend on the bike, the more your body takes a beating. Since I was sticking to a schedule with predetermined miles each day, the faster I went, of course, the less time I'd have to spend on the bike, the fewer pedal strokes I'd have to take, and the more recovery time I'd have at the next destination.

In Waycross, Georgia, I "Couchsurfed" for the first time. A couple of months before I left, my sister Cailyn told me about this relatively new social media site called Couchsurfing.com. The two parties that the website joined were "surfers"—travelers on a budget looking for a couch to crash on for free— and "hosts"—a group that I hoped was comprised of well-intentioned Good Samaritans with strong morals, a solid upbringing, and plenty of food.

When my profile was verified, I tried to find as many hosts along my route to send a "Couchsurfing request" to. I found a decent amount, which helped the budget and was a great way to meet some very interesting people as I went. The hosts I'd stay with were always happy to help me out, and seemed to genuinely enjoy the experience as much as I did. Even for those who hosted all the time, my trip was unique and piqued their interest; conversation never ran dry over a meal, and they were glad to become part of the adventure.

The first time, however, was a little awkward, I have to admit, especially because it was the first time for the host, as well. When I arrived at Michael's house, the twenty-eight-year-old Florida State grad who had accepted my request, the two of us—two Couchsurfing virgins—kind of just looked at each other in his Waycross driveway, slightly suspicious of one another and not really sure what to do next. After that initial encounter, there was nothing at all strange to me about crashing on a perfect stranger's couch for the night, in a place I'd never been, and most of the hosts hosted routinely.

I Couchsurfed again the next night in Valdosta, Georgia, with a guy in the army around my age named Cody Hoover. Cody and I had a chance to talk over breakfast the next morning before I set out. Because he was in the military, I thanked him for his service and gave him one of Uncle Brian's mass cards, which clearly meant a lot to him.

I felt sore and irritable leaving Valdosta, thinking negative thoughts. *I really miss home, and this is only Georgia. Living out of my panniers is already getting old. I don't have enough time to recover between rides. I'm in pain every morning.*

Adding to my frustration, I started to hit the first real hills and the first real heat and humidity of the trip on the same damn day—in between Valdosta and Thomasville—and I worked up a full, dripping sweat that soaked my shirt under the hot Georgia sun. Despite wearing "sweat-proof" 30 SPF, my exposed skin was getting visibly redder, and I had an agonizingly unquenchable thirst, probably in part because the water in my water bottles was hot enough to make tea with. It was only early in the day, and I already felt beat.

I remember seeing the city limit sign of the small town of Quitman, Georgia, that morning and reading it as "*Quit*, man," as I took a break to have a

Cool Mint Chocolate Clif Bar, sitting against a brick wall on the outskirts of town by the sign, head hung low, continuing to bake in the sun. When we were kids, my dad never let us win and always used to tell us that the words "Quit" and "I can't" shouldn't be in our vocabulary. Quitting should be the furthest thing from our minds in any endeavor, to the point that we barely know what it means.

I imagined him saying that as I thought about the name of the town, dehydrated and disoriented from the heat, sweat dripping and skin burning. On this day, however, in that scorching Georgia sun and suffocating Southern humidity, "Quit" was an appropriate word and a tempting concept.

The distance ahead of me was becoming a bulky burden on my mind; taking it a day at a time was easier said than done. I *knew* how far I really had to go—I couldn't lie to myself. I had a whole continent ahead of me, and then another one after that. My thoughts started down a slippery slope of rationalization: it'd be a quick bus ride to Tallahassee or Atlanta, and a quick flight home from there. Nobody expected me to complete the trip on my own—not even me; the truth is, I never would've even *considered* it if I'd known I'd be alone. *I had made it pretty far on my own, right? No disgrace in cutting it short.* In many ways, going home felt like the logical—and right—thing to do.

I continued sitting there against the brick wall, facing east, my back recalcitrantly turned toward my westward destination. The melting Clif Bar and sizzling water from my water bottles didn't satisfy. Sweat dripped. Skin burned. The thick hot air was making me feel nauseous. Home called to me, urging me to come to my senses, save my money, cease the physical misery and senseless danger I was putting myself through on a daily basis, and end this hellish escapade of naiveté and delusion. But I couldn't bring myself to quit. No matter how much my legs ached or how hot and exasperated I was as I sat there, I just couldn't do it, for whatever reason. Something prevented me.

I got up, faced west again, got on the bike, and kept going past Quitman. I didn't feel like I had much of a break, especially since I didn't sit in the shade, but I decided to focus my thoughts on the fact that I was staying in a "real" hotel that night in Thomasville, where there would be wonderful *air-conditioning* (I was definitely beginning to develop a new appreciation for the simple comforts in life). Since the trip, anytime I think about quitting something, I think about the day I passed through Quitman, Georgia. I think about the day I *didn't* quit.

As I approached the Florida border the next day, the hills got more intense. The day started with a middle-aged Black woman pulling over next to me as I took a break on the side of the highway, rolling down her window, asking me where I was going, and handing me a rolled-up piece of paper, saying "Have a blessed day."

Before I realized it was a $20 bill and tried to give it back, she had closed her window and begun to drive off. I was beginning to feel guilty from all this random kindness from perfect strangers—it was *really* incredible.

Buffett and Other Buffets

FLORIDA
MARCH 9–13

"Who's the Blonde Stranger?" – Jimmy Buffett

I took a less-traveled back road into Florida, so there was no welcome sign (of course, I was disappointed about that; I was kind of looking forward to a bright orange "Sunshine State" welcome). Instead, on the Florida border itself, in a wooded, secluded area, I spoke to an eighty-three-year-old woman named Lucille as I rested at her mailbox. She owned a ton of land, she told me, because her grandfather or great-grandfather was a plantation owner. Now, all her children and grandchildren were her neighbors, since she had all this extra land to spare.

The trees in the Florida border vicinity were distinct; they were large, very old, overarching oak trees, draped with ghostly, cobweb-like Spanish moss, a natural Halloween decoration of sorts, that drooped down low. The trees blocked out most of the sunlight. They appeared wise in a way, yet kind. Sad in their posture, yet beautiful in their elegance. They seemed a little guarded, too, as if they surreptitiously used their serpentine branches and thick Spanish moss to conceal entrances to disguised, fabled worlds that roadway travelers weren't supposed to enter.

Later, I had lunch at a sandwich shop in Havana, Florida, (a guy washing his car in his driveway recommended it) and the elderly White couple that owned the shop treated me to some oatmeal cookies, a piece of cake, and a map of Florida, in addition to the sandwich and sweet tea I ordered. They were genuinely concerned about me, because there was a front approaching nearby Tallahassee.

After that, the day took a turn for the worse—but not because of the weather. It started getting very hilly, which I didn't expect in Florida. To get over some of the steeper climbs, I started standing up on the bike for the first time, which didn't initially seem to cause any issues. I was almost to Greensboro, Florida, on Route 12, on a steep climb off the seat, when suddenly I heard a crash and felt intense drag coming from the rear wheel. I had no idea what it was. My immediate reaction was that it was a flat (I'd never had a flat tire before on a bicycle, so I didn't know exactly what it felt like).

I hopped off and realized the rack had detached from the bike and sent the panniers and all the gear crashing to the pavement! I backtracked and searched for the loose parts and screws, squatting and crouching down to find them on the side of the highway as traffic zoomed by, then moved the bike and all the gear up the road a little to a safer location under a tree. Luckily, I found all the little pieces scattered along the pavement. Nothing was broken, to my relief, and I thought I knew how to get the rack back on, but for some reason, I couldn't fit it back on properly to tighten it again. I was getting flustered and frustrated because I was wasting time and valuable daylight.

Finally, I left my gear under the tree, hiding it from view from the highway, and biked a little farther up the road into town, to a general store, for help. A Black man there named Charlie helped me get it back on. It turned out that all I needed to do was loosen the screws a little *more* so the attachment bars would fit through the holes on the rack, before tightening the screws all the way again with the Allen wrench on my multi-tool.

I offered Charlie $10 for his help, but he wouldn't take it. All he said was, "No, you travelin', man. You travelin.'"

There's something about a traveler, I suppose, that everyone can relate to and sympathize with; journeys, in all forms, are respected—especially long ones.

I put all the gear back on and got back on the road, but the mishap had cost me a lot of valuable daylight. Standing up on the bike and swaying all that weight back and forth is what had loosened the screws on the rack and caused the detachment. From that point on, standing up on the bike to climb a hill was no longer an option. I wouldn't do it again for the remainder of the trip, no matter how steep the ascent.

It was getting very dark along Florida Route 12, an unlit, two-lane highway, and I was worried about cars seeing me, so I forced myself to ride as hard as I could for the last twenty miles or so into Bristol, Florida. I was tired, but anxiety from riding on a remote highway in the dark kept my legs pumping hard through intense, fiery muscle pain. It felt like the last sprint of a spin class in a way, but lasted twenty whole miles.

I was uneasy about taking my sunglasses off too. A high school friend of my mom's had been struck by a rock kicked up by a car as it passed him on his bike, blinding him in one eye—she warned me to always keep my sunglasses on for this reason. Of course, I knew the odds of a rock striking me directly in the eye were minuscule at best, but I figured thousands of hours on a bike would bring those diminutive odds up just slightly, and, well, you can't get a new eye—so I decided I wasn't going to take any chances. For basically the entirety of the trip, I kept my sunglasses on when I was on the road.

For the last few miles, it was completely dark. I couldn't see a thing. Headlights from passing cars helped me see the upcoming road and whether there were turns. I was extremely worried, and just hoped that the small reflectors on my bag and windbreaker jacket were large enough and bright enough for cars passing at 65+ mph to see me.

I was exceedingly relieved when I saw the lights of Bristol, a tiny Panhandle town at the intersection of Florida-12 and Florida-20, and even more reassured to find a motel. There was never a person in the history of the world that was as happy to arrive at the Snowbird Motel in Bristol, Florida—I guarantee it. The dull blue sign with white letters glistened in the darkness, beckoning to weary travelers. A choir sang in harmony. The penguin mascot I imagined jumped out of the sign and waddled over to greet me with open flippers. To me, it was an oasis in the desert, proof that I had survived the dark highway and lactic acid in my legs and made it to shelter.

I walked to the only restaurant in town still in my bike clothes and reflective windbreaker, and hit the buffet hard, loading up my tray in the run down, basically empty establishment. I didn't know what half the stuff in the buffet was, but I didn't care. It was fuel and I was on empty. Pretty much everything was fried.

As I walked over to a table with my food, a middle-aged White man said to me, very slowly, in a deep Southern, and probably drunken, drawl, "My son says you look like a *space*man," and chuckled with his kid at their table in a strange, condescending way. He was referring to my black windbreaker, which had small, reflective, silver sections on the front and back, which, I guess, in some way, made me resemble a NASA astronaut to the duo.

As I ate in my corner table alone, somewhere in the Panhandle backcountry of Florida, I felt very far from home.

It may sound like a miserable night—alone, eating in that run-down, crappy restaurant (the fried shrimp wasn't bad, at least), sleeping in a fleabag motel room that reeked of cigarettes, being made fun of by a little kid. But I was actually fairly happy. After the day I'd had, I was grateful to have a full stomach, a roof over my head, and a bed, and thrilled to have made it off that dark highway without incident.

I slept soundly that night and woke up sore and groggy the next morning, but excited to make it to Panama City Beach, where it happened to be spring break!

My hotel, the Days Inn Panama City Beach, was absolute pandemonium. Technically, I was out of college—but I was only twenty-four, more than young enough to fit into the chaos, drinking games, and reckless college crowd on the beach. I met some new friends for the weekend, including an Australian crew driving across the US that I would meet up with again in New Orleans (oddly, our schedules overlapped, even though they were driving, and I was biking), a firefighter from Alabama that I gave one of Uncle Brian's mass cards to, and another group from Ohio—including a pretty blonde stranger I'd meet up with again a few months later in Cleveland (she didn't believe me at first, of course, when I told her I'd biked to Florida). We had a blast that night at Spinnakers, a big beach club with live country music. For the first time on the trip, I felt like I really *was* on vacation, after all.

The ride from Panama City to Pensacola, Florida, was awesome. The beautiful, bike-friendly road went right along the beach, in very close proximity to the shore, and boasted an unhindered view of the Gulf (no dunes, no people, and there were no buildings, because it was a protected nature preserve). It was overcast, foggy, and desolate, but it was certainly a very enjoyable afternoon. Such pristine stretches of beach are rare in the world now, especially in Florida, where the shoreline is such prime real estate.

In Pensacola Beach, I had dinner at Flounder's Chowder House, a preferred hangout of Jimmy Buffett, a favorite musician of my parents', whose music I grew up on. A more obscure track, Buffett's 1984 song "Who's the Blonde Stranger?" played in the background as I had a fried fish platter, flounder soup, and a $2 margarita at the bar, talking to the bartender about Jimmy, who he knew personally.

The next day out of Pensacola was another very long one, starting with a long, flat bridge with trucks and heavy traffic that connected Pensacola Beach to Pensacola. I got a late start that day and was beginning to notice a pattern: late starts led to bad days and early starts led to good days. Coincidence? I was beginning to realize it wasn't. Billy Iaia's advice was consistent with this correlation as well. Soon after the bridge, I crossed into Alabama.

FREE BEER

ALABAMA
MARCH 13–15

"Sweet Home Alabama" – Lynyrd Skynyrd

After I crossed into Alabama, whose welcome sign unexpectedly read "Alabama the Beautiful" instead of "Sweet Home Alabama," I had lunch at Hickory House BBQ in Robertsdale, which offered free beer. Yes, free beer. Usually when you see a sign that reads "Free Beer," the word "Tomorrow" is under it in smaller text; this one, however, was actually legit. It even said right there at the bottom of the menu: "FREE BEER: Seriously, It's Free!"

Normally, I wouldn't have a beer when I still had biking to do, but I had to get one; I mean, how often do you see that? I'd never seen it before in my entire life, and I don't expect to ever see it again. I asked the waitress why it was free, and she just shrugged "I don't know." Since then, Hickory House BBQ has gone out of business (I wonder why).

Later, after passing a large battleship, I approached the Mobile skyline. I took one look at the narrow, crowded Bankhead Tunnel into downtown Mobile and decided there was no way I was biking through it in my right mind, which meant I had to go way out of my way, up and around on Route 90, to cross a bridge. As I crossed, the sun was about to set. Then, just after that, I came to a railroad crossing where a freight train was crawling by and finally came to a complete stop. I saw smoke ahead—the train was stuck, causing me to take a second detour. The train blockade and bridge roundabout cost me time and daylight, and meant that I would have to ride through Prichard, Alabama, after sunset.

The town of Prichard was notable, but not for anything good. The area was definitely sketchy at best. Prichard was one of those places where it was hard to tell if a person on the street was running for exercise or running *from someone*. It was a little unnerving to be riding through the town, where the violent crime rate was about six times the national average in 2012, in the dark. I had my pocketknife and bear spray ready to go if needed. I didn't end up having any problems, and a person or two even helped me with directions.

After coasting through Prichard as quietly and inconspicuously as possible, it was a relief to see some familiar faces in Drew and Michele Alston, who picked me up on the side of the road at Spring Hill College, ending a very long, rough day for me. Drew was the punter on my college football team, and was probably one of the better punters in the country my senior year. After graduating, he got married and became an officer in the National Guard, and also worked as a car salesman at the Mobile Honda dealership. I took a rest day at the Alstons' and ate a lot. I was beginning to realize that I was losing weight fast and literally couldn't eat enough calories to replace what I was burning each day.

After a tough time getting into Mobile, I'd also have a tough time leaving. As I put my bike back into Drew's car to drive back to Spring Hill College (he understood that I couldn't cheat and even said, "Not on *my* watch"), I noticed that the front tire was flat—it was the first flat of the trip, and I wasn't sure exactly how to fix it (I'd never done it before on my own). Of all the objects that my tires had gone through so far (glass, potholes, pieces of metal), it looked like it was a standard staple that did me in.

Drew helped me replace the tube, and I set off, stopping at a pizza place called Mellow Mushroom for an early lunch. With large concrete mushrooms to shield outdoor diners from the sun, it had this hippie atmosphere to it, and the people who worked there were really interested in my trip. As Drew said,

"They're real chill when you walk in, like, 'Hey, you want some pizza, man?'" His review was spot on.

I was almost out of Mobile on a busy commercial road when a pickup truck coming from the opposite direction made a left turn into a McDonald's, failing to give me the right of way. I was going fast. Unfortunately, he didn't see me until it was much too late.

I tried to brake as hard as I could, but couldn't stop, and went into his passenger door hard, bouncing off it and hitting the pavement. Just before impact, I got a comically close-up view of the look of horror on his face when he finally saw me, just a few feet away. I must have had a similar expression on my face too.

He felt terrible, immediately recognizing that he was at fault. He was really apologetic and legitimately worried, but I knew right away that I was fine, so I didn't make a big deal about it. I had a couple of small cuts on my elbow, and the base of my palm throbbed with pain, but I was actually much more concerned about the bike—which seemed fine, too, to my relief. The seat had been turned all the way to the side, which takes a lot of force without loosening it first, but it was a quick fix. No damage had been done.

Wild Hogs, Gators, and Snakes?

MISSISSIPPI
MARCH 15–17

"The Pascagoula Run" – Jimmy Buffett

Shortly after the pickup truck collision, my spirits were lifted near the Mississippi state line (the welcome sign read, "Welcome to Mississippi: Birthplace of America's Music"), when I stopped at a fruit stand and Jesse, the elderly man who worked there, tossed me an orange and handed me some strawberries and cold water, free of charge.

At the end of the day, I stopped for an ice cream bar, and the man there gave me a free hot dog, asking how it compared to Nathan's in Coney Island. I didn't lie, saying it was "different," and then the woman who worked at the store gave me $10 "for lunch tomorrow." As it turned out, another very nice woman named Maria Pollock bought my lunch the next day anyway, at a good seafood restaurant on the Mississippi coast called White Cap; she said she would donate to my cause, too, explaining she had tragically lost her young daughter to a brain tumor.

Soon after arriving in Pascagoula, Jimmy Buffett's "The Pascagoula Run" playing in my head, I crossed paths with another cross-country cyclist for the first time, which was a bit like running into another American in Turkmenistan. We were immediate friends, and had thousands of questions for each other.

Kurt had almost completed his north-to-south journey from Minneapolis to Tampa and was also by himself, except for his little Chihuahua named Alexander that rode in the small trailer he towed behind the bike. I imagined that it would've been very nice to have a companion like Alexander to travel with; it can get lonely on the road. But it would also be another thing to worry about and more stuff to carry, so I wasn't envious. I couldn't imagine fitting dog *food* into my limited carrying space, much less the dog itself!

I was only a few blocks from where I was planning to stay that night. A big family I found on Couchsurfing.com had a large tent ready for me in their backyard. Because I'd be camping out in the yard and not actually sleeping in their house, I figured they probably wouldn't mind if Kurt came, too, so I invited him along.

Our hosts, Troy and Susan Butts, had a family of eight, and made their living in Pascagoula, Mississippi, as farmers and beekeepers. They grew their crops and kept their bees in their relatively small backyard and didn't have much. But they were more than content with their lifestyle and more than happy to host both of us that night. They even cooked a big, hearty chicken dinner, with more than enough food to fill us.

Before we went to sleep, we all talked out on the back porch under the stars for a long time. It was predominantly the adults who were talking; the kids would listen all around us, shoeless and wide-eyed. Conversation topics ranged from astronomy and constellations (Troy knew a lot about the stars and gave us all a lesson, pointing out that Venus, Jupiter, and Mars were all clearly visible that night), to astrophysics and the expansion of the universe, to dumpster diving, and what a queen bee went for on the market in those days (I don't remember the exact figure, but it was much more than I would've thought). And of course, Kurt and I had biking stories to share.

Every once in a while, the family would all go inside to pray together and then come back out to the porch. They were Muslim, but White. Each time they went inside to pray, I thought about all the Americans across the country who had begun to fear or hate Muslims and the general concept of Islam since 9/11. Then I looked at this incredible, gracious, kindhearted family, a family so full of love for America, for each other, and for perfect strangers. There was nothing to fear, hate, dislike, or question. Watching them, I was reminded of the need to explore our world as much as we can and embrace the diversity of our interesting, multicultural planet. Of the need for acceptance and compassion. Of the beauty of unlikeness. My thoughts shifting from the past, to the present, to the far future as I looked on, I was also reminded that, if humanity is able to spread into space and colonize other worlds in the centuries to come, that they're likely to be less ethnically and religiously diverse than Earth today. As thrilling as it may be to imagine "New Earths" in the future, with their infinitely unfathomable unearthly landscapes, none of them may ever be as demographically fascinating as the one we're on right now.

Luckily, the tent we slept in that night in the backyard was really big. There was more than enough room for myself and the two unexpected guests (the second, of course, being Alexander the dog). The sound of birds chirping woke me up the next morning; they were birds I'd never heard before—exotic-sounding and soothing. There's something very tranquil about waking up in a tent too. On the bike trip, it always took me a second or two to remember where I was; after all, my location was different every morning, and the fact that I woke up in places like the backyard of a Muslim, beekeeping, farming family in Pascagoula, Mississippi, in a tent next to a stranger from Minnesota and his Chihuahua dog, was a lot to remember first thing in the morning. I was beginning to get used to bizarre situations like this, though, and was beginning to thrive on them. *Where would I wake up the next day?* That was always an interesting question.

Kurt and I exchanged intel on each other's upcoming routes (we were going in opposite directions) and he had some invaluable bike maintenance pointers for me, most importantly how to clean the chain properly. He took one look at my chain and made a face of complete disgust, saying in a chopped, nauseated tone as he began adroitly cleaning it, "Yours is ... lookin' ... pretty *gritty*, dude." Mine was filthy next to his.

Kurt's method of cleaning the chain turned out to be an excellent one— one that I'd abide by the rest of the trip. Cleaning the chain, I learned, is probably the most critical maintenance you can do for your bike. It's like changing the oil in a car. He would hold a towel and run the chain through it, attempting to "dry" the chain as much as possible. Previously, I had thought that a greasy, lubed-up chain was best, but Kurt assured me that an oily chain would only pick up more dirt, sand, and grit, which would wear on your gears and crankset and diminish the life of your chain. So from that point on, I was diligent about it, cleaning the chain at least every week or two. First, I'd get any big pieces of grit out of the chain with the chain brush. Then, I'd apply one drop of Finish Line Dry chain lube to each link and run the chain through the towel a few times, one hand holding the towel and the other hand turning the pedal of the inverted bike.

At this point, I felt myself beginning to transform into a traveler, not the type that stays in chic hotels and sees the landmarks with a tour guide—a *real* traveler. A backpacker, a nomad, a drifter. I was learning that you don't miss much when you travel by bicycle; you're immersed in every sight, sound, and smell. You're part of it, really. And you experience every little town on the map in one way or another, often staying in communities overnight that don't get many out-of-towners.

Being alone added another dimension too—it forced me to be more outgoing than I would've been otherwise; it forced me to be more outgoing than I'd ever been in my *life*. Human beings have this innate social need. Being on my own put this to the test; it forced me to approach people, to go out of my way to talk to them. Of course, much of the time it was easy because people would see the bike and be naturally curious. When you're alone, you become more approachable too. Conversations almost always started with them asking, "Where ya headed?" Even if I had just one other person with me, I would be much less inclined to go out of my way to engage in conversation with perfect strangers.

In the very beginning of the trip, I was more worried about being alone than anything else; but after I had a couple of weeks under my belt, I began to appreciate it. It was *adding* to the overall experience. It enhanced the feeling of freedom. It forced me to *grow*. I learned, too, that to really travel, it's essential to spend some time with the people of a place. Sure, it's nice to accumulate some check marks on your things-to-see bucket list, but the experiences that stay with you the most won't be found in any travel guide or tourist map. It's the faces, the conversations, the laughs that'll stay with you the most.

* * *

I biked along the Gulf Coast much of the next day out of Pascagoula, and stopped that night at the West Hancock Fire Department in Pearlington, Mississippi—the last night before I'd reach New Orleans. I knocked on the firehouse door and explained my situation, and they let me camp in the fenced-in yard. Pearlington was bayou backcountry, I learned, and I *still* decided to camp, even after the firefighters offered a bed inside and told me there were 200-pound wild hogs, gators, and snakes in the area. The fence would keep out the gators and hogs, but "probably not the snakes," they said. I guess I was just in the mood to camp—and test out my tent for the first time.

Before going to sleep, I hung out with the crew, who were hosting another group of firefighters from Pennsylvania there to help with construction. Incredibly, the area was still recovering seven years after 2005's devastating Hurricane Katrina, the most destructive and economically impactful storm in US history. I gave the chief one of Uncle Brian's mass cards as a small token of my appreciation for hosting me, and he said they'd hang it proudly in the firehouse. They were amazed by his story. He was a comrade to them, a fellow firefighter, who made the ultimate sacrifice on the country's darkest day. A fallen brother. It didn't matter that New York was over a thousand miles away. He was one of them.

I could hear coyotes howling in the distance as I tried to fall asleep that night in my tent. There wasn't much room to maneuver in that sarcophagus of a shelter (not even enough to sit up straight), and the sleeping pad I breathed into to inflate didn't give me as much cushion as I'd hoped for. Sleeping on an inch of air is a lot better than the hard ground, but it still isn't much, and even as tired as I was, it was somewhat difficult to finally drift off to sleep.

When I awoke the next day, the tent was soaked in morning dew and covered with mosquitoes. Luckily, the rest of my gear was dry in the firehouse garage, and no mosquitoes got into the tent; I could see them perched, though, drawn in by the CO_2 I exhaled all night, I imagine, and ready to invade as soon as I reached for the zipper.

I almost forgot it was St. Patrick's Day. It was fitting that I woke up at a firehouse that morning. Since FDNY firefighters had the privilege of marching in the annual NYC parade, St. Patrick's Day was always Uncle Brian's favorite day of the year.

I wore my neon yellow/lime green Nike Dri-FIT shirt for the occasion, the closest thing I had to true green, and was excited to ride into New Orleans for The Big Easy's version of the celebration. The city's signature event, Mardi Gras, was just a few weeks before, and I lost count of all the purple and green beads I saw on the side of the highway on the ride there.

As I biked through the bayou, I discovered that I couldn't really take a break. If I stopped moving for more than just a few seconds, six to eight large mosquitoes would immediately land on me, all at the same time. I imagined a lot more would come if I stayed put. Not wanting to find out, I kept the pedals pumping fast enough so that they couldn't land and didn't take any breaks, to the ire of my quads and calves.

Storms and Cotton Candy Swamps

LOUISIANA
MARCH 17–24

"Thunderstruck" – AC/DC

Every time a tractor trailer passed me on the highway, it came so close and went by with so much velocity that it actually jolted me forward a little with the wind current it carried. On the first few days of the trip, I hated this, of course, as any normal human being would—it was terrifying. But by the time I'd reached Louisiana, approaching New Orleans on US-90, I was pretty much desensitized to it. Extra tired from camping the two previous nights, and possibly a little delirious, I even started *appreciating* the "truck boosts," as I began to think of them. Even though I was a few feet from certain death for *hours* on this highway, the truck boosts were a welcome distraction from the fact that, if I took a break, or even slowed down for just a few seconds, I'd be attacked by a swarm of big-ass swamp mosquitoes.

When I arrived in New Orleans—the first major checkpoint I'd reached on the trip—on schedule, I was ready to celebrate. I checked into my hotel (an old little place in the heart of the French Quarter called the Ursuline Guest House); had a delicious, real-deal shrimp po boy from a little, very un-touristy deli called Verti Marte that the person at the hotel front desk recommended; and picked up a six-pack of Dos Equis before walking over to the sea of green that was Bourbon Street dressed up for St. Patty's. There, I was supposed to meet the Australians, who I'd met back in Panama City Beach—but never did because some of them were still "pretty sick" from the night before. I ended up very randomly running into my friend, Ryan Ostrower, from back home, at Bourbon Street Blues Company, and joining his brother-in-law's bachelor party for the rest of the night. I always seemed to run into Ryan randomly back home, but *this* encounter was on a whole different level.

The next day was a needed rest day. After another Verti Marte shrimp po boy for lunch, I ate at Acme Oyster House (Fritz's recommendation) for dinner. As Fritz would do, I ate at the bar, enjoying the company and humor of "Hollywood," the engrossing and somewhat eccentric professional oyster shucker. I had a great time in New Orleans.

I had some good tailwinds as I headed north out of New Orleans, which made for great cycling despite an ugly industrial backdrop highlighted by the Shell Norco Refinery, one of the largest petrochemical plants in the United States. The scene was reminiscent of the New Jersey Turnpike. It reminded me of my favorite family Christmas card growing up (and the only one we ever took that was my idea).

I was in high school at the time, my two sisters were also teenagers, and my brother was a little kid. Instead of taking a normal family photo, with an alluring sunset or some foreign, picturesque landmark in the background, such as the Great Pyramids of Egypt, the Taj Mahal, or the Eiffel Tower, I thought it would be unique to take it in front of the Linden Cogeneration Plant in the heart of the industrially ugly New Jersey Turnpike, just past Staten Island. So Dad pulled the car over to the shoulder and the four of us kids hopped out in the rain. Mom snapped the photo—three of us smiling brightly, my teenaged sister visibly unhappy because we woke her up and made her get out of the car on the Jersey Turnpike in the rain—with an appalling, awful scene behind us, complete with unsightly smokestacks, repugnant metal distillation towers, and dystopian flames, topped off with a rainy, dark gray sky. The card was superb. It read, "Season's Greetings. With love from no place exotic. – The Nitti Family."

***

Somewhere just south of Gonzales, Louisiana, I got a flat tire and spoke to a local named Bryan as I changed it on his front lawn. Bryan was a big, friendly guy with a long ponytail. Since I was an out-of-towner, he offered to give me a tour of the local swamp if I helped him move something down the river that he called a "two-person job."

"We can do some gator-spotting too," he said, which would be my compensation for the labor. I'd never seen an alligator in person, and my schedule called for a very short day of biking into Baton Rouge the next day, so I agreed to help him the following morning.

It turned out that the objective was to move a colossal, full, tool cabinet, that was literally the size of his little speedboat, down the river; it was *definitely* a two-person job. When we finally loaded it, it looked ridiculous—the boat looked ready to throw in the towel and start sinking right then and there.

Bryan steered the boat from the back, and I sat in the front. My job was to hold the drawers of the cabinet in as best I could as we bounced along the water, the tools clamoring and bouncing along with us, trying with all their might to break out and swim to freedom. The drawers took turns as accomplices to the stir-crazy, wannabe-fugitive tools, sliding open one at a time and making my job much more onerous than I ever could've anticipated. They did this randomly, like they were trying to keep me guessing. One by one, I'd close the drawers with one arm while trying to hold the cabinet and stay in the boat with the other. We were *flying* down the river. I thought, at one point, that the tool cabinet and I would fly right out of the boat into the gator-laden swamp water, but we made it and accomplished the mission—no tool, nor drawer, nor passenger left behind.

We spotted gators basking in the sun along the way, slowing down at times to avoid scaring them, and later took small canoes deeper into the bayou swamp forest, where it was quiet and a little unnerving knowing that the prehistoric predators could be lurking underneath us. I felt like I was on the TV show *Swamp People* on the History Channel. Bryan actually mentioned the show, because the river we were on was one of its filming locations. The swamp had a very odd smell to it—one I certainly didn't expect. To me, it smelled like *cotton candy*, of all things.

When I said this to Bryan, he laughed. "I bet you're gettin' a whiff of the sugar refinery just down the river. 'Cause it sure as hell ain't the swamp!" he said with a hearty laugh.

That afternoon, I got back on the bike for an easy half-day of riding into Baton Rouge.

***

For the most part, Baton Rouge was a rough and dangerous city, so the place I stayed at on its outskirts—the decrepit Vel Rose Motel—represented it fairly well. The motel office was an isolated structure in the middle of the central parking lot, and was fortified with barred windows that had a small opening, like a ticket window, for me and the manager to exchange cash for keys. Of course, I was pretty damn hungry from biking and moving a tool cabinet down the river, so I ordered a large pizza and cheesy bread from Domino's as soon as I got to the room. It took two extremely long hours for the food to arrive, so it was free, but I would've paid double for it to come in fifteen minutes, without a doubt.

After dinner, on the walk over to do laundry at the motel's outdoor machines, a local group of construction workers staying there warned me of a really ugly forecast the next day—a big storm with widespread tornado watches throughout Louisiana and Arkansas. I went to sleep worried, and set my alarm extra early.

Before sunrise the next morning, I wheeled the bike through the dark, beat-up parking lot of the broken down Vel Rose Motel, ready to take advantage of a little extra adrenaline. I was determined to beat the storm. It was supposed to be at its worst at midday, so beating it was a reasonable endeavor, or so I thought.

I got off to a blistering pace, making great time with a slight tailwind under very dark, extremely ominous skies. The sun never really rose that day. Night had simply endured into morning. I had made it almost twenty miles on US-61, which ran parallel to the nearby Mississippi River, when it finally showed up and caught me. Swirling wind picked up, ruffling the leaves on the trees around the highway, turning them upside down and exposing their lighter green underbellies. The sky grew even darker, its menacing clouds and rumbling thunder building to a crescendo with the other elements, and pompously raised the curtain for one of nature's favorite old-time acts. It was the commencement of a thunderstorm.

Flashes of lightning lit up the sky, increasing in frequency and ferocity. Thunder clapped vehemently, growing louder and quickly gaining on its more fleet-footed counterpart. The hair on my arms stood straight up; I almost couldn't tell if it was from fear, or from the curious feeling that the air all around me had somehow become saturated with electricity.

At that point, the storm turned up its favorite AC/DC track, daring me to keep going. I knew the skies would open up any minute, and the rain would be pouring. As exposed as I was on the bike, I couldn't help but imagine being struck by lightning. I remembered hearing reports of lightning-strike survivors saying they felt like they were hit with sledgehammers over the head, or "had the taste of battery acid in their mouths" just after. I wasn't sure how they knew what battery acid tasted like, but I certainly didn't want to be able to make my own assessment.

Then I felt a couple of drops of rain, and knew it would be a minute or two at most before an all-out downpour began. I sped up and pulled into the first building I saw a little farther down the road, the "Highway 61" gas station on the right, in an otherwise wooded area. I propped the bike up outside, protected under the larger-than-usual gas station canopy, and went into the mini mart for shelter and to take a look at the radar. The news was already on inside, and the radar looked awful—it showed a big green, yellow, and red blob that enveloped the entire Gulf Coast. It wasn't clearing anytime soon, without question. Then I looked out at my bike and saw that I had another damn flat. Second one in just three days. Then the skies opened up, on cue, and the rain came down in torrential, cascading sheets. Lightning struck closer than ever now. Thunder roared, angrily shaking the ground. Between the rain, lightning, radar, and flat,

I decided to raise the white flag. I wouldn't make it to Woodville, Mississippi, as I had planned.

The next guy who pulled into the gas station had a pickup truck. His name was Eddie Morse. Eddie amicably offered a ride, so I threw the bike in the flatbed, and he drove me ten miles north in the pouring rain to the closest hotel, the Best Western, which didn't have vacancy. So then he drove me to the next one, the Magnuson Hotel, which did have a room. (He even offered to drive me back to the same gas station the next morning, after I explained that I didn't want to cheat.)

When I got to the Magnuson Hotel, it was still before 10:00 a.m., so I took advantage of the hotel's complimentary breakfast for my second breakfast of the day. Uncle John called to check in on me; he had seen the weather report from New York. The storm was certainly big enough to warrant the decision to stop riding for the day, but I was off schedule for the first time, and wasn't happy about it—I felt defeated and down.

I checked into my room and quickly became bored; it was still morning, it was going to rain all day, and I had nothing to do. But since I had some downtime, I decided to take the bike apart, clean it and the chain, and rotate the tires (with the weight of the pannier bags, the back tire was wearing a *lot* faster than the front). I fixed the flat too.

When I was just about done putting it all back together, there was a knock on the door. I wasn't expecting anyone, so I went over to the door a little suspiciously and cautiously answered. It was one of the hotel employees, holding a large cardboard box with lunch and dinner in it that the hotel staff had prepared for me, free of charge. They also gave me a discounted rate and wished me luck. I was speechless.

Early the next morning, Eddie picked me up again and drove me back to the Highway 61 gas station. Not even two miles into the day, I got *another* flat and my pessimism reached its absolute peak. That was three flats in four days. My stomach was in knots. I could feel my blood pressure building, like a volcano about to blow, and my thoughts, once again, turned very negative. I wanted to scream as loud as I could as I changed that flat. *Was I going to get one every two miles now? I'd never make it home.* I started to imagine the thousands of flats I would have across the country at that rate, and all the tubes I would be going through—another 4,500 tubes would be pretty expensive. At $8 a tube, that would be $36,000.

Each flat I had on the trip (I'd have about twenty-five total) was a little bit of an ordeal. I had to take all the gear off, flip the bike upside down, take the wheel off, use my tire levers to pry off the tire, take the tube out, try to find the hole (and the culprit), decide whether to replace the tube or try to patch it (usually I just replaced the tube), put the tire and wheel back on, pump it up with my little hand pump, then find something to prop the bike up against so I could put all the gear back on (once all the weight was on the bike, the kickstand was useless, as advertised). In the beginning, the entire process took over half an hour. Eventually, I could do it in fifteen minutes.

Most of the time, flats were caused by tiny pieces of wire in the road that looked like twisted staples. I later found out that this wire usually came from blown-apart truck tires. My bike tires of choice were Continental Gatorskins, known to be some of the most impenetrable, widely-available models on the market. Broken glass was almost never an issue, but even the Gatorskins were no match for the stingy bits of wire—which, of course, were almost impossible to see in the road. Every time I came across a mangled, obliterated truck tire, though, I knew to steer clear of it as much as I could. I always held my breath as I passed one. I carried only one spare tire with me, and usually four or five spare tubes.

Besides the inconvenience and the time they wasted, I didn't like flats because they sometimes put you in an especially precarious position. If there was no way to get off the highway (this would happen on busier roads, like interstates), you were forced to change the flat on the shoulder. This kind of situation always brought to mind a tragic incident that occurred only a couple of years before my trip.

I went to high school with an avid cyclist named Matt Scarpati, who was struck by a drunk motorcyclist as he was changing a flat tire on the Wantagh Parkway bike path (just off the highway) on Long Island, killing him at just nineteen years old. I remember attending his wake, seeing the unfathomable pain in his parents' eyes as they greeted us beside the casket. Every time I had to change a flat in an exposed position, that memory was with me. Matt Scarpati should have lived another seventy years. It was a grim reminder that being on the highway is truly hazardous, especially when you're not in a car. Because of Matt, there's now a guardrail protecting joggers and cyclists on that path.

***

I finally passed the Magnuson Hotel again. I felt like I was playing catch-up the rest of the day. I wanted so badly to get back on schedule; I was about half a day behind. I crossed back into Mississippi, going through Natchez late in the day and crossed the milestone Mississippi River back into Louisiana as the sun was getting ready to set, which was the highlight of the day. As I crossed it, I looked down at the river, which was wider than I expected and a surprising chocolate milk color. I stayed in Vidalia, Louisiana, that night, a little town on the edge of the river.

The next day out of Vidalia was an opportunity to get back on schedule. It was my first day biking on flat, really open roads, and I decided I was going to try to make it all the way to Bastrop, Louisiana, which was where the itinerary said I should be that night. I started at dawn in very thick fog and ended after dusk, twelve hours and 104 miles later. It was my first century (100-mile) ride ever, a milestone for any cyclist. Many consider a century to be cycling's equivalent to running a marathon.

At some points that day, the shoulder was rough and bumpy, so I rode along the actual road, along the white line, to the chagrin of a few cranky drivers, who honked resentfully. At this point, though, I was a little tougher than I was on the first few days of the trip, so the honking didn't bother me much.

Literally on mile 100, just outside Bastrop, as I once again became light-headed and slightly delirious with fatigue, I hit the remarkably steep Red Hill after 99 miles of completely flat terrain. A very long time ago, Red Hill had supposedly saved the town of Bastrop from one of the Mississippi's worst floods.

Apparently, this act of heroism, and all the glory associated with it, had gotten to its head, because Red Hill taunted me. In a deep voice, it shouted out arrogantly, "You want this century, *bitch*?" as I started to climb. I didn't say anything back. It continued, "Come on. Come get it, little bitch." It was almost completely dark, I had a slow leak in my rear tire, which slowed me down, and my legs were unconditionally surrendering and screaming for mercy as I climbed the hill. It felt good, though, to get to the top without having to get off and walk the bike. A victory for sure. Humbly, I didn't say anything back to Red Hill—I decided to take the high road.

I was completely drained as I approached Bastrop at the end of the day, but happy to be back on schedule. See, the schedule was becoming everything to me. It was my guide, my rock, my map to actually pulling this crazy thing off. As long as I made it to the town I was supposed to be in, I was doing my job and was on track to make it back home by the end of September.

Four miles later, I was in Bastrop, and I couldn't wait for my head to hit the pillow in a real bed, but the first motel I came to didn't have vacancy—and the woman at the desk said there weren't *any* places in town that did that night. There was nowhere to camp, really, and I so painfully needed a bed to sleep in and a real roof over my head. So I wandered around a dark, empty Bastrop on my bike trying to figure out what to do. I felt homeless. I *was* homeless. I even tried to get into a church, thinking it would be a place of refuge for the tired, the poor, the huddled masses—but the door was locked.

Utterly dejected, I walked back down the church steps to the street and continued farther into town. A few minutes later, I came across a vintage-looking corner café and breathed a slight sigh of relief—at least I'd be able to get something to eat.

As I walked in, a large, middle-aged, mostly bald, White man was walking out. As we nearly bumped into each other at the door, he said, in a friendly Southern accent, "Sorry, it's eight o'clock. They just closed. You *just* missed it."

I wasn't surprised. Missing it by less than a minute was perfectly in line with my luck that night. I started talking to the man, and he offered a ride to go get some food, so I threw my bike in the back of his pickup, and we drove to a nearby Taco Bell, where the conversation continued as I ate a sleeve of tacos. His name was Mark, and he was known by his friends and the local townspeople as the "mayor" of Bastrop because he was so outgoing and seemed to know everyone in town. He was funny, too, teasing and joking around with people everywhere we went.

He told me the local Walmart was a mistake. "It was meant for Bastrop, Texas—not Bastrop, Louisiana—but they didn't realize the mistake until after it was built! Ain't that a hoot?" he said.

I wasn't sure how a mistake like that could possibly be made, but it was definitely funny, and the Walmart *did* seem extraneously immense for such a small town.

As we spoke in the Taco Bell booth, I could tell he was mulling something over in his mind. I just kept talking, trying to prove I was relatively normal. I guess I didn't convince him, because he called the sheriff to come by to check me out. Yep, he literally called his sheriff friend, who drove the sheriff car directly to the Taco Bell parking lot.

When he pulled up, I gave a slight, awkward wave and couldn't help but smile. This was yet another ridiculous situation I'd gotten myself into, and I felt the humor in it immediately. He rolled down his window and told Mark there wasn't much he could do.

"I can't really run a background check on him," he explained, the expression on his face saying, "Come on, Mark, we're not the goddamn *FBI*." Then the sheriff told me about a park nearby. "Now, I'm not saying you can camp there. I'm just saying I ain't gonna bother ya if ya do." I had the sheriff's approval—a small town's key to the city.

At that point, Mark finally decided to trust me and help me out, but more so than I ever could've imagined. He set me up with an entire house to myself across the street from his—it was the house he grew up in and hadn't been able to sell yet after his parents passed away. When we got to the house, I wheeled the bike into the room I'd be sleeping in and started to unload it so I could fix the slow leak, as Mark set up the pullout couch for me to sleep on.

As I unpacked, Mark said something that caught me off guard, to say the least. "You must be sore from all that ridin' . . . I could give ya a massage if ya want. I've been told I have *magic hands*." After a brief silence, he exclaimed, "Nothin' weird," putting his hands up.

Something was certainly weird, but I was so tired, and in complete disbelief of what he'd just said, that I wasn't sure how to respond, so he kept going on and on about his magic hands, until, finally, I cut him off. I politely but firmly declined the massage offer, telling him he had done enough for me already. I thanked him for the generous accommodations and told him I'd see him for breakfast the next morning.

I couldn't believe how things had turned around that night; I'd been despondently walking through the streets just an hour or two before, and now I had an entire house to myself! Feeling grateful, I fixed the slow leak on my rear tire, took a hot shower, and slept solidly that night, happy to have my first century in the books.

The next morning, I bought Mark breakfast, which he appreciated very much, at PT's Eat-A-Bite, the same corner café we'd met at the night before. Shortly after hitting the road, I came to the Arkansas border, where I stopped to take the usual photo, with the bike leaning up against the welcome sign. I also sat down to take a water/Clif Bar break. The welcome sign was adjacent to a small church, surrounded by nothing but woodland, with a crowd outside; there was a funeral going on.

As I sat there eating my Clif Bar, reading "Welcome to Arkansas, The Natural State. Buckle Up for Safety," on the sign, the pastor of the church came over to me and offered some fried chicken, dinner rolls, and Sprite from the funeral, which I was happy to accept as extra, free fuel. The pastor was surprisingly young—my age or younger.

"I'll pray for you in your travels," he said.

LOOKING FOR RED LOBSTERS

ARKANSAS
MARCH 24–30

"Running Up That Hill" – Kate Bush

Headwinds, heat, and hills with slow, gradual, constant inclines made my first afternoon in Arkansas an arduous one, and late in the day I had run completely out of energy. I was extra beat up from the century the previous day; I felt dehydrated, my legs were slow and heavy, and I had a headache.

Unbelievably exhausted, I took a break on the side of the highway and actually laid down on the pavement, resting the back of my head on the hard concrete. It was oddly comfortable. I stared up at the sunny blue sky with its white, puffy clouds moving over it, bone-weary and beaten, content to stay resting in that position with arms and legs stretched out, sprawled on the shoulder. I thought about what my friends and family back home would think if they could see me at that moment. To drivers, I probably looked dead. Once again, I seriously doubted I could finish the trip. *I gave it a shot*, I told myself, *but California and back is just not going to happen.* 10,000 miles was impossible. Hell, I doubted I could finish the *day*.

I stopped in Pine Bluff, Arkansas, and stayed at a "real" hotel, a Comfort Inn, because it was right across the street from a Red Lobster, which I decided I wanted to try (I'd never been to a Red Lobster, and at that point, I figured I might as well try every single restaurant chain in the United States on the trip). Excited for a big meal and a comfortable bed, I ordered a beer, made quick work of the Cheddar Bay Biscuit basket, and chatted with the waiter for a while, since I didn't have anyone else to talk to. Somehow the conversation turned to some ridiculous idea I had for the chain—a seafood brunch or something, so the intrigued waiter brought out the manager to discuss it with me.

The manager, William Furlow, was a large, middle-aged Black man with a big smile and an affable personality. He sat down in my booth and was easy to talk to. I was grateful for the company, and we spoke for a long time as I ate my appetizers and overly large seafood platter. I told him about the trip so far and the cause I was riding for, explaining that the Marty Lyons Foundation raises money to grant wishes for chronically and terminally ill children aged three to seventeen.

His eyes lit up. "Well, that means something to me," he said, in a different, even more engaged tone of voice. "My five-year-old son had leukemia," he explained. "And when the Make-A-Wish Foundation sent my family to Disney World, it was literally a turning point in his recovery from the chemo and everything he was going through."

The trip was such a morale booster for the boy, he explained, that his physical condition started to measurably improve after it.

"He's now in remission," he said, graciously. "The trip saved his life, as far as I'm concerned. What you're doing is important. Keep going," he told me, with stone-cold sincerity. "And I'll tell you what I'm gonna do. Your meal tonight is on me. And I'm going to call other Red Lobster restaurants in the state to make sure they do the same. Just let me know what your route is going to be."

I was floored. William's story gave the whole trip a new sense of purpose. It expanded the mission of the Marty Lyons Foundation to me. It would make those steep climbs, heavy headwinds, and lonely days a little more manageable. I thought of the kids who would directly benefit from the money we were raising; maybe one of *those* wishes would be a turning point too. William's generosity was motivating; he believed in what I was doing so much that he was going to go out of his way to help me continue on, to contribute to finishing the mission.

I thanked him a few times, shook his hand with everything I had, and wished his son well.

Over the next few days, I found myself in a situation I certainly never thought I'd be in: biking through Arkansas looking for Red Lobsters. The very next night, I ate at another one in Little Rock. The manager was actually expecting me, and as promised, it was free. After dinner, I continued on toward the house I was going to Couchsurf at that night in Little Rock. Riding on Markham St. on the way there was like riding a roller coaster. Your momentum from each downhill portion was just about enough to get you over the next hump, which made it pretty fun.

My hosts that night—Alex, Tracie, and Luke—had also just graduated college. When I got to their house, we went out to the backyard for a bonfire. We sat around the fire, the aroma of its crackling, smoky scorch reminiscent of summer and adventure, drinking beer and telling stories.

My favorite was one of Tracie's. When she was little, she recounted, she was playing in her yard when a cute little animal scampered over to her. She thought it was a puppy, so she started hugging, petting, and playing with it. She even picked the adorable thing up, carrying it proudly to go show her parents. When her mother saw it from a distance, however, she was struck with horror, because it wasn't a puppy her young child was holding in her arms—it was a baby *wild hog*. And the mother hog wasn't far behind. The wild hog in Arkansas is colloquially known as the "razorback," which is the beloved mascot of the University of Arkansas—and you know what, it might be the fiercest mascot in all of college sports. Razorbacks are big, ugly, snorting, drooling, big-fanged, brutish beasts, more than ever when one of their young is threatened.

Tracie's parents screamed out to her to drop the baby hog, but the mother hog was already on her way. As the squealing monster of a mother stampeded toward Tracie and the baby hog, Tracie's father began shooting his rifle from a distance to try to scare it off. Little Tracie finally dropped the hog and escaped unhurt, but her parents took her to get glasses the very next day, and she'd had them ever since.

A little while after Tracie told her story around the bonfire, I started sneezing uncontrollably, to the point that it was downright embarrassing. I stood up and started to walk toward the house, sneezing like I had never sneezed before. I didn't know what was going on—all of a sudden my eyes burned like I was in a sandstorm, and my nose was gushing. The sneezing didn't stop. It was a wicked allergy attack, something I'd never experienced before. Whether it was a different type of tree pollen down in Arkansas or a plant or something in that backyard that I'd never been exposed to, my body reacted viciously to it—it was almost a little scary. I was worried, though, for other reasons—I thought they'd think I had some kind of contagious disease and would kick me out to the streets of Little Rock that night. I was a perfect stranger to them, trying to make an impression that I was a normal, non-threatening person so they wouldn't take back their commitment to host me for two nights.

The next day was a rest day in Little Rock, and the allergies continued as we played old-school records and watched an old movie called *Airheads* (1994), about a failed band that holds a radio station hostage until they play their demo tape. We prepared and enjoyed a fresh, healthy, home-cooked fish dinner in their kitchen. It was *so* good to have a home-cooked meal, and cooking with strangers was fun and kind of bonding.

The following morning, Tracie drove me to a CVS to get some Claritin before I set out. The allergies were still intense, so even though the package said to only take one, I figured it wouldn't hurt to take two—to catch up a little. I hit the road and didn't think anything of it.

As the sun rose higher in the sky, the day became very hot and muggy, and the terrain started getting hilly as I approached the Ozarks north of Little Rock.

About halfway through the day, I had become extremely lightheaded, to the point that I felt like I was drunk or drugged. I pulled over to the left side of the road to take a break at a donut shop. I sat in the cool, dark, air-conditioned donut shop and had some ice-cold water and a couple of sweet, frosted donuts, happy to be out of the sun and humidity. I felt better afterward, and got back on the road with a lot more juice in my legs.

A while down the road, though, now deep into the afternoon, I saw oddly familiar train tracks, hugging the road just feet away and running parallel to it. Still fairly dizzy and empty-headed, I thought it must have been the most potent déjà vu I'd ever had, and kept riding. About thirty seconds went by. *No, I've definitely seen this before*, I thought to myself, countering the perceived déjà vu. *But the tracks weren't on this side . . . No, they definitely weren't . . . Shit, they were on the* other *side.*

Then a terrible, sinking feeling came over me as I realized I was biking the wrong way, retracing the route I had covered that morning! After the donut break, I'd gotten back on the bike and started going in the wrong direction, disoriented from the combination of the extra Claritin and the heat, for ten to fifteen miles!

It was a costly mistake—it turned a seventy-mile day into well over a ninety-mile day, which was brutal with the hills and heat, and cost me between two and three hours. If it weren't for those railroad tracks, though, I might've not realized the gaffe until I was all the way back to Little Rock!

I was extraordinarily angry at myself. I wanted to punch myself in the face. I cursed myself when I finally approached the donut shop again, shaking my head, and then finally smiling a little when I passed it, pointing forward, as if to confirm with myself the right way to go, like the bumbling scarecrow in *The Wizard of Oz*. Sometimes you just have to laugh at yourself.

Late in the day, I was officially in the Ozarks, the first real mountains I'd ever tackled on a bicycle in my life. In a zone, I pedaled hard to make up time. With weary legs from an already long, sweltering day, it was a real test.

I was elated to arrive at a hillside Best Western, albeit belatedly, in Clinton, Arkansas, that evening a little before sunset, again thankful that I had planned for a "real" hotel that night and badly needing a shower and something to eat. I walked the bike up the steep driveway to the elevated parking lot of the hotel, seeing a large snake slither across the pavement at the top, and checked in. Then I showered and walked over to a Pizza Hut a few doors down for dinner.

Eating at Pizza Hut always evoked a certain nostalgia—it reminded me of being a kid in the '90s. I remembered its red, pilgrim hat-shaped roof, homey interior with red booths and stained-glass lamps, carpeted floor, trademark salad bar, and large sign by the entrance that read "Please Wait to be Seated" in old-fashioned font. Then there were the breadsticks, the pan pizzas, and the translucent red plastic soda cups. Mom often took me and my three siblings there on school nights when Dad was away on business trips. This Arkansas Pizza Hut was a little different, but it still reminded me of being a kid. I thought about those days back in the '90s as I sat at my table, this time alone. Hungry from the long ride that day, I easily finished a whole large pizza, which was a lot more than the other patrons ate. When I asked for the check, with the scrap-free, oily, pizza pan beside me, a few minutes after it was brought over to me, the waitress looked like she was going to faint.

GREAT PLAINS GHOSTS

MISSOURI
MARCH 30 – APRIL 1

"Turn the Page" – Bob Seger

After some grueling climbs in the heart of the Ozarks and a night at a campground in Harrison, Arkansas, where the owner kindly offered me some homemade split pea soup for dinner, I crossed the Missouri border on Friday, March 30, and was greeted with a flat tire in Branson, my destination that evening.

I got the flat because Route 76, the main road in Branson, was strewn with debris from a tornado that had struck the small city just a month prior. It was jaw-dropping to see such destruction; it literally looked like a war zone. A motel was ripped wide open, right in half, part of it completely intact and the other part reduced to twisted steel and crumbled ruins. I was out of tubes, so I just walked the bike the rest of the way to the house I was Couchsurfing at that night, instead of changing the flat. This turned out to be a mistake, though, because the extra pressure on the wheel resulted in a broken spoke, which was one of the few things I couldn't fix with the tools that I carried. Luckily, the bike shop in town was still open and fixed it for me.

My host that night, Michael, helped me get a good feel for what Branson was about in the few hours I had to explore it. Branson is a unique little town and attracts a good number of tourists for its variety of somewhat old-fashioned live entertainment. Michael was the editor of the *Branson Update*, which promoted the live shows, so we went to see a show called *The Haygoods* for free. The show was basically a concert of all different kinds of music performed by a single family. Picture the Von Trapp Family Singers from *The Sound of Music* singing modern songs you'd hear on the radio today. It was a little strange, but interesting and kind of funny to me. The youngest kid, about seventeen years old, wasn't there. Michael said, "After being in music and show business his whole life, and after being home-schooled since birth, he was having second thoughts about what he wanted to do with his life, so his family sent him to Africa to do some volunteer missionary work to think it over and realize how good his life really was."

From Branson, I rode to Mt. Vernon, Missouri, and the road began to *really* flatten out and you could see for miles. With the Ozarks behind me, I had reached a new phase of the journey: The Great Plains. In Mt. Vernon, I stayed at a motel called the USA Inn and ate a surprisingly delicious dinner at a truck stop buffet called Country Pride across the highway. It was just me and a bunch of truckers loading up our plates at the buffet; the scene was reminiscent to me of Bob Seger's classic song "Turn the Page." Every once in a while, a voice came over the intercom at the truck stop, saying something like, "Shower 6 is now available," which made me laugh to myself.

Sometime when I was in Missouri, it had occurred to me that, up to that point in the trip, dogs had chased me just about every single day. Something about bikers fascinated them, I guess—or maybe, unlike a car, a bike was something they figured they had a chance of actually chasing down. If the dog was big, it definitely worried me, but they usually gave up the chase after I started sprinting on the bike. Most of the time, I was more concerned about the dog getting hit by a car (they often ran across the road to begin the chase). Some, however, were a little more determined to catch me, and it took a lot of work to outrun them—especially because it was difficult to accelerate the bike at first, as heavy as it was.

They all barked loudly, except for one. My favorite dog, in Arkansas, didn't want to catch me at all and didn't make a sound. He was more than content just running on the grass along the roadside with me for a little while, in a completely non-threatening way, ears flapping with his gallop. He was a welcome traveling companion, even if just for a few moments before he peeled off.

Cows also found me interesting, for whatever reason. Herds of cows would stare at me like I was some kind of alien, wide eyes fixated on me, trying to figure out what the hell I was. Frozen in place, they would slowly turn their heads in unison to watch me as I passed. Once, I stopped to try to snap a photo of them. As soon as I took out my camera, they suddenly broke into a frantic run away from me, moving in unison like a school of fish.

The next day, out of Mt. Vernon, made it very clear how much of a difference the wind could make. In the United States, as you get into flatter, more desolate country, the highways become very straight and spread out, and intersect one another at perfect right angles, creating a grid effect on the map, almost like a very stretched out city. I thought it was ironic that a grid is the most efficient means of roadway planning in only the most populated and least populated areas of the country. Navigating had become much simpler out there, but with nothing to break it, the direction and strength of the wind had become exponentially more crucial.

The controlled nature of the grid also created the perfect opportunity for a little wind experiment, to see just how much of an effect it really had. There was a south wind that day, so, as I went directly north on Route 97 toward Lockwood, Missouri, I was able to cruise with the tailwind at a swift 22–24 mph. In Lockwood, however, I had to turn left and began riding precisely west. Even though it was just a crosswind and not a direct headwind, the stiff south breeze slowed me down to just 10–12 mph. That's less than half as fast as I was going when I was biking north! It was a tremendous difference—and the wind was only moderately strong that day.

I had never cared so much about the weather until 2012, but I'd *especially* never cared so much about the wind. With the gear and panniers catching so much of it, like sails, the wind made all the difference in the world. When I checked Weather.com every morning and night on my phone, I went straight to the wind speed and direction—this indisputably told me if I was going to have a good day or a bad day. I'd even get a little nervous sometimes as it loaded, awaiting the verdict. Imagine caring *that* much about the damn wind?

I didn't know it at the time, but my tribulations with it were just beginning. The Great Plains' gales would prove to be the country's most challenging obstacle for me, both on the way to the West Coast and on the way back, perhaps more so, even, than the great Rocky Mountains.

The two main obstacles for long-distance cyclists, of course, are mountains and headwinds. The general rule I came to accept was, where there were mountains, there was no wind, and where there was wind, there were no mountains. I quickly learned that I'd rather bike over a mountain than deal with a headwind any day. Mountains are more intense obstructions for cyclists, I think, but they have known identities, fixed dimensions, and both qualitative and quantitative benefits that headwinds lack. Mapped, discovered objects, they have names, elevations, grade percentages, and histories. You see them coming. You get mentally prepared for them—even psyched, in a way. You focus your energy, grab a sip of water, and your adrenaline gets pumping, preparing your body for a workout.

Defeating a mountain is an invigorating, uplifting feeling for any traveler—whether you're on a bike or on foot. Hell, it's even a victory for someone driving a *car*. Mountains have galvanized romantics, poets, monks, philosophers, songwriters, and adventurers for centuries. Iconic titans of nature, they've been benevolently assimilated into religion, art, history, and lore by myriad cultures, from all different points in time. When you take them on riding a bicycle, they'll make you work and sweat for sure, but the tried-and-true custom stands that, when a cyclist adequately tackles a mountain's climbs, they're rewarded with a view and then an exhilarating, rapid descent that makes up for lost time spent on the slow, grinding ascent. Most of the time, it's fair, predictable, even contractual; you put your work in, and then you get compensated.

Headwinds, however, don't play by those rules. They have no names, no dimensions, no histories, and no benefits. They can't be discovered, can come out of nowhere, and are seldom predictable. You can't even *see* the bastards. There's no reward for beating them, and there's no way to make up the time they take from you. No, headwinds don't give refunds, and they don't inspire. They slowly suck the morale out of you like leeches, draining your energy and confidence and putting your patience to the absolute test. They literally extract the breath from your lungs and make oxygen seem like a rare commodity.

Like invisible ghosts, they haunted me all the way across the country—but especially on the Great Plains. I kept thinking they'd go away, but they always came back.

In the next town, whose water tower I could see for miles as I approached it on the open plain, I took a welcome lunch break from the wind and sun. Supposedly, Cooky's Café in Golden City, Missouri, was "world famous," especially for its pie. It was also a popular spot for cross-country cyclists, since it happened to be along the TransAm route—one of the most-taken cross-country routes. I scarfed down two beef brisket sandwiches and a slice of peach pie for lunch, and the staff had me sign a journal that all cross-country cyclists signed when they stopped there; they said I was the first that season. Golden City looked like a movie set for a tornado scene—it just had that vintage, heartland feel to it. It was obvious that the café itself, a prototypical old, Midwestern diner, situated right on Main Street in the middle of town, had been there for decades without any attempts at renovating it—which I was grateful for.

Later that day, I crossed the Kansas border and, soon after, was in Pittsburg, Kansas, where I would finally get a much-needed, long break. As I took the picture of my bike next to the Kansas welcome sign, I felt like it was the last day of school before a vacation. I was giddy and excited to see the Siams, the family of my college buddy Ty, who I'd be staying with for the entire upcoming week. I was in desperate need of sleep and extended physical rest. More than anything, though, I was looking forward to seeing some familiar faces. It'd been a long time.

15

KANSAS HOSPITALITY

KANSAS
APRIL 1-13

"Wish You Were Here" - Incubus

"I thought the whole *thing* was an April Fool's joke," Khamis angrily exclaimed into his cell phone, in his Middle Eastern accent. "Until this *man* shows up at my door!" His tone transitioned from anger to authentic surprise.

We were out for ice cream. He was speaking to his son, Ty, and, of course, he was kidding. A witty Pitt State University chemistry professor, with large round glasses and a kind face, Dr. Khamis Siam was a charismatic, generous man with an incredible sense of humor. The date was, in fact, April 1, and the Siams were going to host me for a very long time—an entire week (six rest days), which would be my longest stop of the trip. Ty was in grad school back at Cornell, but his family was happy to host me anyway. I was desperate for a break, and in very good spirits when I pulled up to the Siam home—a brown and beige house with Tudor architectural elements on the exterior—in Pittsburg, Kansas, a small town in the heart of Heartland USA along The Sunflower State's eastern border.

Khamis, his amiable, thoughtful wife, Dua, and Ty's sister, Nisreen, were my hosts. The hospitality they showed me throughout the rest week was nothing short of extraordinary. I had my own room, a very comfortable bed, and unlimited access to Ty's red pickup truck, a Dodge Ram. When I drove the truck around town, locals must have thought Ty was home—people would honk their horn, shout out at me, wave their hands. Obscured by the windshield, I waved or honked back, just so they didn't think he was being rude.

Ty was a legend in Pittsburg. An all-state quarterback for the Pittsburg Purple Dragons, with a big red pickup truck, living the American dream. His nickname on his high school team was "The Beast from the Middle East," and he had an interesting fact on his Facebook profile: "Coconuts kill more people every year than sharks do." Perhaps destined for a career in football and data analytics, he eventually went on to work for the New York Giants as Director of Football Data and Innovation.

We went out to a nice dinner every night, to the family's favorite restaurants around town—except for one night, when Dua cooked a traditional Middle Eastern dish called *kufta*, which was delicious. For the second time in just a few weeks, a Muslim family had opened their home and shown me astonishing kindness, at a time in the United States when fear and "Islamophobia" were bringing out the worst in many Americans and making Muslims throughout the country feel increasingly anxious and discriminated against.

I slept in late every day and had a big breakfast every morning, alone in their dining room, scarfing down French toast, Pop Tarts, cereal, eggs, and more. I noticed my appetite was catching up with me. I was even *hungrier* on the rest days, even after a *few* rest days. By Kansas, I had lost a decent amount of weight already—somewhere around ten or fifteen pounds.

I was noticing some strange food cravings too. Extreme long-distance cyclists often describe weird food cravings they have on their journeys, sometimes for food they didn't even know they liked. I was beginning to learn that mine was for Twizzlers Pull 'n' Peels, for whatever reason. I had a bag of them right by my bed that week with a bunch of water bottles.

Even though I slept in late every day and was very inactive, I was still somewhat productive in Pittsburg. I got a much-needed haircut at Ray's Barber Shop on Main Street; had a red sign made out of tarp-like material that read "BIKETRIP2012.COM" to tie to the back of my bags; bought a couple of t-shirts, including a blue Kansas University shirt that read "Rock Chalk Jay-hawk," with the beloved red and blue bird mascot, with its oversized yellow beak; and took the bike for a full tune-up and new tires at Tailwind Cyclists—the best bike shop in town.

The seasoned bike shop owner was surprised that I wasn't taking the Trans-Am route that continued through Pittsburg. "It's much safer," he said, explaining that there were a few designated routes like it that went across the country.

I didn't even know routes like that existed. Unlike most bike shops, his was accustomed to cross-country riders. It seemed, though, that he'd never encountered someone mapping out their own route.

I also did an interview for the Pittsburg newspaper over lunch one day, with a respected reporter in town named Nikki Patrick, a forty-seven-year veteran journalist, known to be an absorbing storyteller. Her column, "Patrick's People," was a staple of the town, and now I was lucky enough to be a part of it. She wrote a great article about the trip to that point, the upcoming terrain I'd face, the Siams, my parents, the Marty Lyons Foundation, the flat tires I'd had, Uncle Brian, and Fritz. She described it as "a trip of a lifetime." Nikki passed away just two years later, in 2014, at the age of sixty-eight. I was fortunate to meet her in 2012 and be a brief part of her long-celebrated column.

At night after dinner, we'd go over the Siams' Iraqi next-door neighbor Nazar's backyard patio to chat about life and a multitude of random things, from earthquakes and fault lines to travel websites and the origins of Pizza Hut, which started in Kansas. I enjoyed exploring Pittsburg, the classic middle American town that it was.

Kansas has the distinction of being in the *extreme* center of the United States, and in the center of an area with a high propensity for severe weather—an area known as Tornado Alley. The exact geographic domain of Tornado Alley is up for debate, but it's generally accepted as the central corridor of the United States, where warm, moist air from the Gulf of Mexico; warm, dry air from the Southwest; and cold, dry air from Canada all meet—often violently. By some definitions, Tornado Alley stretches from North Dakota all the way to Alabama—but its core is known to be northern Texas, Oklahoma, Kansas, and Nebraska. The backbone of the United States. The chosen battleground for rival, domineering air masses.

There are more tornadoes in the US than any other country, by far.[5] One day, there was footage on the local news of a tornado hurling tractor trailers through the air, tossing them like they were toy trucks. I couldn't help but picture myself in the news clip, flying alongside the airborne trucks on my bike. A chill went down my spine. I prayed I wouldn't see one when I got back on the road.

I was scheduled to get back on the road on April 8, Easter Sunday. I took the red pickup to the town's large, traditional church on my own and met the family for a big farewell brunch afterward on Main Street, where they told me I was welcome back any time to stay in their home again. They actually asked me to please make sure I came back one day. I was reluctant to leave—I felt like I had become a part of their great family. They took care of me like I was their own son.

As I left, Dua gave me a miniature doll of the Tin Man from *The Wizard of Oz* with a surprising (and creepy) gray baby-doll face with opening eyelids, a quirky souvenir to remember Kansas.

***

On my first full day riding in Kansas, the landscape was wide open, and very green. Much of it was flat, but there were some significantly hilly areas, too, which I definitely wasn't expecting. I thought it would be "flatter than a pancake," as some actual research has suggested (most of the state *would* turn out to be extremely flat, after that first day). But I was surprised at first. One of the great things about travel is that a new place is never exactly how you expect it to be. It's always at least a little bit different.

After being with the wonderful Siam family and their friends all week, I was reminded of how lonely the highway can be. I wasn't exactly happy to be "back to reality." I realized, too, that my "reality" had become so strange—so unique—outside and exposed on the highway all day, riding for miles and miles.

Physically, I felt really, really weird too. I was well-rested, but completely out of rhythm. After a week of inactivity, my legs had to kind of relearn how to ride my cyclopean, two-wheeled contraption that was my bike, and it felt incredibly awkward. It almost felt like Day 1 all over again that morning.

After a few hours, though, my legs woke up, I got back into the swing of things, and I was happy to continue the trek. It felt good to get the blood pumping again, and to feel that high that a workout can give you. It was a beautiful day, and I even had a little bit of a tailwind, which would continue through most of Kansas, to my pleasant surprise. For the first time in a while, the bike was absolutely silent as I rode—not the slightest hint of any creaking, grinding, or squeaking. Just smooth, easy cruising. The guys at Tailwind Cyclists did a commendable job on the tune-up—it literally felt like a brand-new bike. Such exemplary work is never guaranteed, I would learn.

Up until Kansas, I was afraid to listen to my iPod. I was an inexperienced cyclist, who had never biked on a highway. I wanted to hear every car, truck, horn, person, dog, bird, insect, and slightest sound without any distractions. But by Kansas, I was used to being on the highway all day and had built up a solid desensitization to its dangers. Kansas introduced me to long stretches of flat, usually treeless, desolate road, with great big skies, open green fields, and faraway horizons, where the infinite road would lead to a single, seemingly impossible-to-reach vanishing point. Highway traffic had thinned out significantly too. So I figured *what the hell*. I put my ear buds in (AirPods weren't released until 2016, so the wires dangled down to the handlebar bag), put my iPod on random play, and my world literally and instantaneously changed. The first song that came on was "Wish You Were Here" by Incubus. The wonderful sound immediately gave me chills, pumped some adrenaline into my legs, and provided a welcome soundtrack for the sunny countryside I was taking in.

From that moment, I listened to music every single day as I rode. Most of my iPod comprised classic rock—Led Zeppelin, the Stones, the Eagles, Van Morrison, Bruce, U2, Neil Young, Steely Dan, Fleetwood Mac, Tom Petty, Billy Joel, ZZ Top, CCR, Queen, Bob Seger and the like. That was mixed with a good amount of alternative rock from the '90s and later, like the Chili Peppers, Green Day, Stone Temple Pilots, Alanis Morissette, Nirvana, Pearl Jam and Blink-182, and even some '80s music, like Madonna, and new music such as MGMT, Passion Pit, Empire of the Sun, The Knife, Matt and Kim, Modest Mouse, The Black Keys, and new Eddie Vedder (my sister Cailyn added the latter group for me, in an effort to bring me into the current century). There was also Wayanay (a South American group from the Andes Mountains that played soothing Peruvian pan flute music that I always loved), Johnny Cash (a favorite of Papa Mac's), Simon & Garfunkel (a favorite of my dad's), Jimmy Buffett, and much more.

I *loved* it, and I realized, for the first time, that the world would be a lot duller without it. Music was a barrier, a blanket, a new weapon for me against the highway. Acoustic familiarity in visually uncharted territory. It gave me such an advantage compared to the dry drone of the highway. I almost felt like I was cheating.

When you listen to your iPod *all day*, "random play" isn't quite random enough, I learned. I eventually figured out that the best way to maximize the variety of my iPod was to just play the entire song list, A to Z, or, in my case, "Acadian Driftwood" by The Band to "1979" by The Smashing Pumpkins. Every once in a while, I'd sing along. *Why not?* Sometimes I knew every word, sometimes I pretended I knew the words, and sometimes I tried hopelessly to keep *up* with the words, especially with R.E.M.'s "It's the End of the World as We Know It (And I Feel Fine)"—like Chris Farley and David Spade in *Tommy Boy*.

At this point in the trip, I was becoming a more seasoned rider, and I had developed a routine that I came to love and rely on. I'd wake up, pack up all my stuff, eat breakfast, and hit the road as soon as possible. The hardest part of the day was the first few slow, painful miles, when every muscle in my body was tight and irritable, and the last thing in the world I felt like doing was riding a bike. I treated the first five miles as a warmup, to get the blood flowing.

When the odometer hit five miles, I'd try to find a grassy spot on the side of the road for a water break and a full stretch. Warm muscles stretch better. I'd also do as many pushups as I could do in one set and a two-minute plank, in an attempt to maintain some kind of base upper body and core strength. I called this daily morning stop the "Five-Mile Water/Stretch." Of course, it didn't really need a name because I was the only one it applied to. But it had a name anyway.

After the break, which was usually about twenty minutes, I felt like I was sufficiently warmed up and stretched and could get the real riding started. I also could start listening to music. I only allowed myself to listen to my iPod *after* the Five-Mile Water/Stretch. It was a reward for getting the day underway. A mind trick of sorts. I think that, with any big project or task, you have to find little ways to reward yourself. If you sprinkle in little incentives along the way, it's easier to keep going. Music was helping me—there was no doubt about it. Studies have suggested that plants might grow faster and cows give more milk when music is playing[6]; maybe it's a stimulant for *all* life.

Another strange ritual that became a trusted part of my routine was the "1:00 Checkpoint." The goal was to hit a certain number of miles, typically at least thirty or forty, by 1:00 p.m. Usually the goal was getting to the halfway point by that time. Hitting this daily goal was actually cut close fairly often, which would send me sprinting like a cyclist in a Tour de France time trial, for really no good reason, just before 1:00 p.m. Sometimes I made it only within a minute or two. Busting it to make the checkpoint didn't really make sense—I know. Nobody was watching and there was no tangible reward for making it, of course. But the little victories were important. Small bursts of momentum are morale boosters, and anything is easier when broken down into parts. If I was on track to make the checkpoint, I was on track to finish the day. If I was on track to finish the day, I was on track to finish the trip. My dad was charting my progress on a big map back home. He'd penciled in the entire planned route, then went over the completed portion with a Sharpie as I went. I often thought of him updating the map, going over the road I was on with a giant Sharpie coming down from the sky.

I ended up making it across nearly the entire state of Kansas without even having to *look* for a place to stay. The Siams knew a family in Independence, my next stop, who knew another family in Winfield, the stop after that. I stayed with Gina and Andy McLenon in Independence on Easter night. They knew Bobby and Donna Smith in Winfield, so they gave them a call to let them know I'd be on my way there the following day. The Smiths had no problem putting me up for the night, either; Bobby was an avid cyclist, so he had a lot of questions about the trip. They didn't know anyone in Medicine Lodge, which was the much smaller next town—but the Kansas hospitality would continue anyway.

As I approached Medicine Lodge in light rain under a dark gray sky, I knew I'd have to improvise; the motel I saw didn't have vacancy, and the weather didn't look conducive to camping. I saw some teenagers in their front yard and casually asked if I could camp there—they said they'd have to ask their parents. I never thought I'd ever be able to ask such a bizarre question so casually.

When I met the parents, Lee and Carla Capansky, I was once again trying to make the impression that I was a normal person, which isn't easy to do when you're riding your bike across the country alone in the middle of Kansas. I told them that I had set up a website for the trip.

"You should check it out," I said, hoping it would help legitimize my odd request. I was about to give the URL when Carla cut me off.

"Hold on," she said. "Let me guess . . . ImNotASerialKiller.com?"

I acted surprised. "How'd you know?"

She laughed, and they let me sleep on the couch inside, which was a very good thing, because a strong thunderstorm rolled through that night. I woke up to the sound of thunder in the middle of the night, extremely grateful to have a roof over my head. It's not easy to take in a perfect stranger. It's weird. But people still do it. And that's a testament to the good of humanity, to me, as much as anything could ever be.

We all had a quick breakfast together the next morning, including their nephew, who was my age and on his way to his first day on the job, operating a forklift at the wallboard plant in town, where Lee worked for a long time. I could tell Lee was proud of him.

The day leaving Medicine Lodge was chilly and damp. Early in the day, a woman stopped her white truck on the side of the highway and handed me $15—just because she knew the Capansky family and had heard about my trip.

When I stopped for lunch in Coldwater (a curiously appropriate name for the chilly, damp day that it was) at The Lazy T, I had an oversized, beef-heavy taco salad, a cheeseburger, a steak sandwich, a plate of french fries, and some hot chocolate. When the owner Wayne Thompson, a real nice guy with one of those long, old-fashioned mustaches, heard about what I was doing, he said "It's on me," even though I'd eaten enough to easily feed a family of four.

There were kids at the restaurant, too. They asked me all kinds of questions and wanted to take photos with me, as if I'd just won the Tour de France. One thing I loved about the trip was that little kids could appreciate what I was doing just as much as adults—I could tell by their reactions when their parents explained it to them. Kids can relate to riding a bike as well as anyone, and they seemed to fully understand why I was embarking on such a journey, maybe even *more* so than their parents.

Being that it was April, the heart of tornado season in Kansas, I biked through a few tornado warnings, which always worried me a great deal. One day, I had to take cover from heavy rain at a secluded, empty church in the middle of a field for about half an hour. I sat outside, but was covered by a roof supported by an arched colonnade that overlooked a central courtyard. Every once in a while, I got up to look over the open field, which I couldn't see from where I was sitting, to see if I could spot any tornadoes on the horizon. The conditions were prime for one, but I didn't see any.

There was one day, though, that I was *sure* I would see one. I'd heard about the warnings the afternoon before, on the day I started out from Medicine Lodge. Kansans know when a threat is legitimate, so I was taking anything I heard extremely seriously. I ended that afternoon in the tiny town of Ashland, where I had to call the owner of the town's uninhabited motel at his home to come drive over to drop off the key. When I opened the motel room door, the room was extremely tiny—so minuscule, in fact, that the bed occupied just about its entire square footage. The bike barely fit! I had to squeeze it between the foot of the bed and the room's window, which looked out at the empty parking lot. I immediately turned on The Weather Channel to prepare for the next day.

The Weather Channel's TOR:CON Index, which estimates the risk of a tornado in a given area, was very high for the following day in the area I would be biking through; it was an 8 out of 10, meaning "a very high probability of a tornado," or about an 80% chance of a tornado occurring within a fifty-mile radius. The map on the TV was an eerie dark red. The creepy, robotic voice of my yellow handheld weather radio, a second opinion, wasn't making me feel any better. I was worried.

Of all the things I thought I might encounter on the trip (bears, snakes, highway traffic, sketchy people), tornadoes were what I feared most. In fact, tornadoes had always been my greatest fear, *period*. The thought of seeing one live for the first time in the exposed position of riding a bike was almost paralyzing. It's quite irrational for a Long Island, New York, kid to have a fear of tornadoes—I know. I'm not sure of its origin, but I think it's very likely that it could be the 1996 movie *Twister*, starring Helen Hunt and Bill Paxton. The first time I watched *Twister* was at Uncle Brian's house when I was a kid—it had just come out on VHS, and he was psyched to put it on for me and my younger sister, Annie. Annie and I, seven and nine years old, respectively, watched *Twister* and then *Independence Day*, a double feature of 1996 thrillers that we might have been a little young for, but were ecstatic to finally see. Mom wouldn't have let us watch them at home. But Uncle Brian was cool like that. And smart. If you want to occupy two kids under ten years old for a few hours, a couple of PG-13 blockbusters about cow-tossing tornadoes and highly intelligent, strategically invading aliens with weapons of mass destruction should do the trick.

I sat on that motel bed because there was nowhere else to sit and had a can of Campbell's Chunky soup for dinner because there was nothing else to eat. As ridiculous as the room was, it was kind of cozy. I felt safe in the moment, in part because I knew the next day I would be very exposed and more likely than ever before to come face-to-face with my greatest fear.

I'd never seen a tornado with my own two eyes, but part of me *wanted* to, to be honest. What scares us very often thrills us. But I certainly didn't want to see one from my bike. No sir. My plan, however, in the event that I *did* come across one without any shelter around was to lie flat in the ditch alongside the road. Most of the roads in Kansas had some type of ditch that ran parallel to the road, for water drainage purposes. A lot of people in Kansas recommended this act of desperation if I was in an open area and couldn't find shelter. The logic was that any debris that was flying around would more likely fly *over* me if I was lying flat in the ditch. The solution wouldn't protect me from the tornado itself, of course, but the odds of the tornado itself going directly over me were minuscule compared to the odds of life-threatening debris crossing my path. And again, it was a last-ditch effort (literally).

I slept surprisingly well in the tiny motel room, despite my nerves, but got up extra early. After some deliberation, I decided *not* to sit the day out, despite the 80% TOR:CON Index, my terrifying robot weather radio, and the recurring tornado nightmares I'd had since I was a kid. The best way to get over a fear is to just face it, right?

The day was significant for other reasons, too—it was supposed to be the longest of the entire 216-day trip. Yes, facing my greatest fear had perfectly lined up with the longest day in miles on my schedule. 116 miles from Ashland, Kansas, to Guymon, Oklahoma. April 12, 2012. On its own, a day to prove something to myself. And now, a day to face my fear, and prove something more.

NO FEAR, I thought, picturing Uncle Brian's locker.

As I left the Ashland motel under charcoal skies that early morning, I heard the foreboding, chilling sound of wind chimes, the tornado siren's gentler cousin, and that eerie, menacing, opening music—with the hurried orchestra crescendo to mimic a sudden gust—from *Twister* in my head.

As I got some miles behind me and got a sweat going, my jitters subsided. I saw plenty of ominous skies and cloud formations that day on remote, open highways, and there was some light rain. But, luckily, no tornadoes.

I had lunch at a little burger place called Bob's Drive-In in Meade, Kansas, and saw on the news that motorists had been stranded on a nearby highway the night before, because they were suddenly buried by hail. Yes, *buried by hail*. Even the locals were perplexed, looking up at the TV perched above the lunch counter with seemingly unfamiliar uneasiness. After lunch, the sun came out, dissolving my fear once and for all.

But that's precisely when the wind started. It was picking up fast, directly in my face, and stronger than ever before.

Toward the end of the day, as I was battling extreme headwinds that were keeping me crawling at a painstaking 8 mph, a cop pulled me over. I was about ten miles outside Liberal, Kansas. He wanted to inform me of another tornado warning and tennis ball-sized hail they were expecting at 5:00 p.m. Yes, *tennis ball-sized* hail.

I looked at my watch—it was 4:50. I had ten damn minutes.

"Well, I don't see any supercells around—and you have a helmet, so you'd be alright for a little while," the cop said. "If you get caught, though, call 911 right away, and we'll have a pickup come get you and your bike."

I had a question before he left. "This wind," I said. "Uh, is this *normal?*" I thought to myself that *there was no possible way it could be normal*. I still had plenty of Great Plains country to cover, and this kind of wind was going to make my coming days and weeks pretty miserable if it continued much longer. I was looking for some peace of mind, but the cop wasn't going to give me any.

"Welcome to Kansas."

That's all he said, with a very slight hint of a smile. Then he peeled off toward Liberal..

Kansas, after all, is named after the Kansa tribe. Kansa, a Siouan word, is known to have some reference to the wind, possibly meaning "people of the wind." The Kansas wind that day was more brutal than any I'd encountered (it was probably at least 20–25 mph, directly against me, its constancy relentless), and it took everything I had to finish the day.

For the last nine miles of the day, I tried to imagine I was somewhere else. I let my physical surroundings evaporate around me as best I could and kind of closed my eyes, trying to separate myself from my situation. Trying not to grimace, I imagined that I was back in my hometown of Dix Hills, New York, riding the old nine-mile loop I'd done a few times as a workout when I was home from college. My forgiving, familiar, friendly, windless neighborhood was an oasis in my mind. I imagined passing the landmarks one by one. *There's my high school on the left, I'm about a quarter of the way home . . . now I'm halfway—turning around at the Expressway, now I'm passing Signal Hill, the elementary school . . . here's the home stretch on Caledonia Road, here's the left turn onto my block.*

Needless to say, I couldn't go any farther when I finally got to Liberal (or pulled into my driveway, in my mind), even though I was supposed to keep going on the schedule. The day was over, anyway. The sun was about to go down, so I didn't have much of a choice. The day—again, scheduled to be the longest of the trip at 116 miles from Ashland, Kansas, to Guymon, Oklahoma—had slyly gotten away from me, and I wasn't happy about it.

I had dinner at Pizza Hut and slept well in the motel next door that night, but I was pissed. I felt defeated. I had fallen short of the goal that day by a long shot—a good forty miles.

THE WALKER

OKLAHOMA
APRIL 13–14

"Drivin' My Life Away" – Eddie Rabbitt

The next day was supposed to be a rest day, but I biked the forty miles to Guymon, Oklahoma, instead, to get back on schedule. The Oklahoma panhandle wasn't green like Kansas. It was dead and brown, with even less to look at.

As I approached Guymon early in the afternoon, after miles of barren badlands, I saw a man from a distance, wearing a sombrero and an orange reflector vest, pushing a cart. There were no people or buildings at all on this stretch of highway, and hardly any cars. The rising heat from the pavement obscured his distant figure in the sultry sun, making him appear wavy and spirit-like. *Was he a mirage?*

I thought he was selling tacos or something on the side of the road, so I figured I'd stop for a bite when I finally got to him. I imagined I'd be a welcome customer in such a desolate, lonely wasteland of a marketplace. I thought he'd greet me warmly.

As I got closer, I could tell he definitely wasn't a mirage *or* a taco vendor; he did, however, seem eager to talk, so I pulled over to say hello. Embarrassingly, I couldn't clip out of my pedals as I slowed down (a missing screw from the clip in my shoe had been giving me problems for weeks) and I went crashing to the pavement, yet again.

He rushed over to see if I was alright. I assured him I was fine and tried to downplay the humiliating fall. It must have seemed like I had just been introduced to the common contrivance known as the bicycle, and decided to try riding it for the first time in the middle of Oklahoma.

"I'm fine, I'm fine," I said. "This, uh...this happens."

His name was Ebram Megally. He was born in Egypt, and he was walking across the United States. Yes, *walking*. And people thought *I* was crazy. Like me, he had just graduated from college (Boston College). Like me, he was going from coast to coast (his route was LA to his home in Boston).

We were almost exactly halfway across the country when we crossed paths in the panhandle of Oklahoma, traveling in opposite directions. Our modes of transport were different, of course, but we were immediate compatriots with similar daily challenges. I respected the hell out of him. There's no way I could've ever had that kind of patience. To *walk*? You've gotta be kidding me. I'd go out of my mind.

We kind of acknowledged and appreciated the humor in our ridiculous situations, on that dusty, remote, unsightly highway—and seemed to fully recognize the irony of our crossing paths, almost precisely in the center of the country. One lifeform finding another, in the most unsuspecting of places. It was good to talk to someone out there, in the middle of nowhere. I didn't think I'd find someone on the highway traveling more slowly than I was, either.

I took a photo of him with his cart and he took a photo of me with my bike.

***

Exactly ten years later, to the day, on April 13, 2022, I would meet Ebram again, for drinks in Manhattan's Bryant Park on a warm spring evening. We picked up where we left off in Oklahoma. As we caught up, I learned that his parents had also been staunchly against his trip. He began to look at food purely as fuel and carried peanut butter and bread, as I did, and endured his share of physical discomfort, including brutal blisters on his feet. As I went through tires every couple of thousand miles, he went through sneakers every 500. And like me, he'd experienced the kindness of strangers, who did more than just take him in for a night—they welcomed him as part of their family, and sometimes even unloaded their problems on him in one-on-one conversations, as if he were a therapist. Perhaps the combination of his very approachable personality and the fact that he was passing through town, likely never to return, made him a perfect candidate for that job. Sometimes people just need to be *heard*.

Unlike me, though, Ebram had a full appreciation for the dangers of the highway before setting out. He'd even written his eulogy before he left. He didn't want people to say, "He died doing what he loved." Because he knew he wouldn't love it. And he *didn't* love it. He was doing it to challenge himself. To see what he was made of. Somewhat small in stature and "never known as an athlete," as he put it, nobody back home thought he could do it—until he proved them wrong and proved something to himself. Something lasting.

"Anytime something's hard and I feel like I can't do it," he said, ten years later, "I think of that trip, and I *know* I can do it."

***

Several days prior to our crossing paths in Oklahoma, Ebram had spent a few rest days with a very kind family in Dalhart, Texas.

"Selene and her husband are really great people," he told me on the side of the highway. "I'm sure they'd have no problem letting you stay."

So he gave me Selene's phone number and texted her to let her know I'd be coming through Dalhart and needed a place to stay. I was planning on getting to Dalhart the following night, after a night in Guymon. Dalhart was only seventy miles from Guymon, a typical day's distance, but I had *no idea* how difficult it would be to make it there. I was literally about to be tested like I'd never been tested in my entire life, both physically and mentally.

After arriving in Guymon, Oklahoma's remote panhandle town, and checking into the Pioneer Motel, I ate at a legit Mexican restaurant next door that was attached to a gas station. I knew I was getting closer to the Southwest; the Mexican food was getting better and better. The name of the place was "Mexican Restaurant," and it served the most authentic Mexican food I'd ever had.

Earlier in the day, I'd finally fixed my broken shoe, which needed a new screw. It had been a nuisance for weeks but was starting to become unbearable and a legitimate hazard since I kept falling, unable to clip out of the pedal. I called the bike shop in town ahead of time, and even though the owner, Rick, wouldn't be around, he left a box of screws in the law office next door for me to search through. The only screw in the box that was old and lackluster was the only one that was a perfect fit. That's pretty good luck for Friday the thirteenth.

When I got back to the motel room after dinner, though, I checked the weather on my phone and my heart sank fast. It seemed my luck had changed: 35 mph sustained winds the next day, with 54 mph gusts? *Fifty-four* miles per hour? *Directly* in my face? *Are you kidding me, Weather.com?*

On April 14, 2012, I got up real early, before 5:00, and wheeled the bike across the street to have breakfast at a small donut shop that had its lights on. It looked like one of those old-fashioned ice cream stands, a free-standing structure surrounded by a parking lot, with bright lights and large glass windows that made it easy to see inside. It was dark everywhere else, so the place stood out.

It was Saturday morning, and it seemed that nobody else in Oklahoma had woken up yet, besides me and the Asian woman behind the counter at the donut shop. I had an egg sandwich and a couple of vanilla frosted donuts, taking my time because I didn't want to start until it was light enough to see the road—and, more importantly, for the highway traffic to see me. The day was going to be a very long and hard one, there was no way around it. I had come to learn that 15 mph headwinds made for a tough day. But as high as *54 mph*? That sounded completely insane. I couldn't imagine what it would be like out there. I was about to be up against a force of nature that was traveling just a hair shy of the standard US highway speed limit, directly against me.

From Guymon, Oklahoma, to Dalhart, Texas, US-54 goes directly south-west, in a perfectly straight line. The wind that day was coming directly from the southwest. In other words, I'd need to battle a monster 100% direct head-wind for a full seventy miles to make it to Dalhart and finish the day. There was only one very small town between Guymon and Dalhart, but since I had a family to stay with in Dalhart, I was hellbent on making it.

54 mph isn't too far from the strength of hurricane-force winds (74 mph), and it's well above the tropical storm and gale-force threshold of 39 mph. A 55 mph wind is considered a "whole gale." A 10 on the Beaufort Scale, it's "seldom experienced on land," and can result in broken trees and structural damage.[7] Sure, I could've chosen to take the day off, but the thought of sitting around all day and the fact that I had just gotten back on schedule pushed me out the door. Plus, the cunning, unpredictable wind could do the exact same thing the following day, and maybe the day after—I could never count on it dying down. Whenever possible, I had to ride. Otherwise, I'd never finish. Part of me also wanted to take on such an outrageous challenge.

I hit the road stressed, feeling rushed and anxious, like I was already run-ning out of time. It was very cold. The sun, obscured in a burnt-orange, cloudy, dusty haze, was very low in the sky when I first set out, and didn't provide any warmth or much light. In the haze, it didn't even look like the sun—it looked like another planet, or a menacing, dark orange moon in some exotic far-off star system.

The constant stream of tractor trailers blowing by me with their headlights on made it even colder; it was one after another after another, a constant bar-rage of bursts of frosty air pushing me along. It was a different world. A harsher world. And a solemn reminder that the highway is a realm in which a motor vehicle is the assumed method of transport. Just like you're not supposed to swim amidst ocean tankers or hang glide in the company of 747 jumbo jets, you're not really supposed to *bike* on an isolated major highway in Oklahoma with gargantuan tractor trailers in the near dark. It's just something you don't do. But there was no alternative to 54 out there, in the middle of Oklahoma. And I had to try to get ahead of this crazy wind.

I wouldn't be surprised if I was the first person *ever* to bike on this particular part of 54, actually. My ears and jaw hurt in the cold air. 54 was an old, rough, narrow road with reddish pavement and a very small, beat-up shoulder, surrounded by Oklahoma dust. It rumbled constantly with the weight and force of the trucks, as if it struggled to support them. I was nervous. Even after being on the road for over a month and a half, the situation on this stretch of 54 felt especially precarious. The speed limit was high—it had to be between 70 and 80 mph, and the tractor trailers buzzed by me just a few feet away. Clearly, I hadn't picked the right route when I was mapping this absurd trip out in my college dorm room.

This is what I get for charting my own course, I thought. *Why didn't I just take the TransAm route like everyone else?*

I had to steel myself to look forward, hands tightly gripping the handlebars. Because there was so little room to work with, it was a bit of a balancing act, too, to stay between either the rumble strips and the white line or the rumble strips and the end of the pavement. The humming behemoths were relentless. I hoped that every one of those truckers had had their coffee that morning. Their margin for error—and mine—was frighteningly minuscule.

Perhaps embracing the insanity, I kind of felt a bond with the truckers that morning too. It was just me and them, the only living things for miles. We had the same mission—to keep heading southwest. To find daylight and morning, to get to our destination. To have a warm meal. To sleep in a bed. They were humans like me, not robots or self-driving trucks. I imagined them looking out for me, paying a little extra attention in the seconds that they passed me. I imagined them surprised to see me biking in such an inhospitable environment at such an hour, but rooting for me as a result. I even imagined us listening to the same song. There was an old country, kind of folksy song by Eddie Rabbitt that came on my iPod from time to time called "Drivin' My Life Away." It's a great road tune—one of the best, I think. If there was a song the truckers and I were simultaneously listening to that early morning, I decided it had to be that one.

***

Highways are the most dangerous places we'll commonly encounter in our lives, but we don't really think of them that way. Many of our most obvious fears as human beings, like spiders and snakes, are a result of evolution. These fears don't make much sense in most parts of today's world. Our cavemen ancestors passed these fears down to us, simply because those who were naturally afraid of things like spiders and snakes survived more often; it's a classic example of Darwin's theory of natural selection. Those traits live in us today, ancient gifts of fear that have grown somewhat dispensable with time.

I remember learning about this in my college psychology class taught by Professor Tom Gilovich. None of today's top killers (things like heart disease, stroke, cancer, and car accidents) strike fear in us in quite the same way—they aren't quite like those "evolutionary fears." Most of us would rather ride in the passenger seat of a car than have a harmless spider crawl up our arms, right? But this is perhaps only because evolution hasn't caught up yet. We *should* be at least slightly afraid of highways, because around 40,000 people die on them in the US each year.[8]

In the future, with the proliferation of cars that drive themselves, the highway will no longer be so deadly. I imagine future generations will look back on the archaic days when every individual vehicle on the road was susceptible to human error, similarly to the way that we look back on the mayhem of the Middle Ages.

"Everyone actually used to control cars, going seventy-five miles an hour, or as fast as they wanted, by *themselves*, with their hands and *feet*?" they might wonder. "And some would even try to do this when they were *drunk*, or looking down at their phones?"

But that day hadn't arrived by 2012. The roads were still a place of pandemonium and human error, even more so with smartphones, which were a relatively new thing. And of course, the odds of dying on a highway were certainly higher for a cyclist, the uninvited guest. The vulnerable alien trespasser. I knew the facts before I left, but I had never really grasped how incredibly dangerous biking across the country is, especially on highways like US-54 in Oklahoma.

My generation—the millennial generation—could easily be the last to teach their kids how to drive. It's sad in a way. I enjoy driving, and soon it will be kind of a lost art. One less skill passed down from parent to child. One less rite of passage. I always felt that driving gave me the ability to think deeply, more than I ever could as a passenger, especially on long trips. A kind of meditation. The long-celebrated tradition of car ownership may very well become obsolete too—likely to become a convenience for the wealthy and another victim of the share economy. Truckers, too, are a dying breed, making a living off a soon-to-be extinct occupation as self-driving trucks become a much more economical option. The benefits will more than make up for all of this, though, I suppose. No more innocent people killed by drunk or distracted drivers. That alone would be enough justification. But artificial intelligence will bring new moral dilemmas too; not all accidents can be avoided.

Consider, for example, the Trolley Problem. Imagine an unstoppable trolley going down a track toward five people tied to the rails with rope, and an alternative track (that the trolley could be redirected to) with one person tied to it. Imagine that you have control of the lever that could redirect the trolley, but can't stop it. Do you allow five people to die by doing nothing, or actively kill one by redirecting the trolley? In the event of an unavoidable accident, will autonomous vehicles sacrifice the lives of their passengers to maximize the total number of lives that could be saved? Instinctively, human beings wouldn't necessarily react in such a manner. But self-driving cars *might*. According to Isaac Asimov's three laws of robotics, when a computer program encounters an unsolvable problem like the above, it stops and asks for human intervention.[9,10] But, of course, there isn't time for that in the pivotal seconds of a car accident. How will self-driving cars weigh the risk for those inside the vehicle against those outside? How will pedestrians, joggers, and cyclists be factored in? How will artificial intelligence determine who lives and who dies?

As car accidents decrease in frequency, car insurance companies, which thrived in 2012 (it seemed that every other TV commercial was for GEICO, Progressive, or Allstate) will likely need to shift their focus to other types of insurance.

Ironically enough, shortly before I left, there was a campaign in which the English-accented GEICO "gecko" (who everyone felt like they knew personally because of the company's ridiculously aggressive advertising strategy) was getting ready to embark on a cross-country journey to make sure Americans everywhere knew they could be saving 15% or more on their car insurance by switching to GEICO.

As he begins the journey in the first commercial, he remarks, "Well, I've made it out of the parking lot. That's a good start," poking fun at himself for being so small, as he often did.

I thought the similarities between his 2012 journey and mine were funny—and I'd be lying if I said that first commercial didn't cross my mind when I wobbled out of that pier parking lot in Wrightsville Beach, North Carolina, on Day 1. *Well, I've made it out of the parking lot. That's a good start.*

***

As the sun crept higher in the sky on 54, I had mixed emotions. I wanted it to rise so that the trucks could see me better, and so that I could warm up. But I thought of Billy Iaia's words of wisdom—and I knew the wind would start later in the morning. In the early hours after dawn, the wind wasn't too bad, and I was pedaling hard, trying to get as many miles under my belt as I could.

A little later, I took a quick break for a snack at a gas station in Texhoma (on the border of Texas and Oklahoma, not surprisingly) with billowing storm clouds in the distance. Sitting in a booth in the gas station mini mart, I spoke to my mom on the phone; she sounded nervous and worried, as she always did when I called from the road. I didn't stay on long. I knew I had to get moving.

THE BEAST

TEXAS
APRIL 14–16

"Full Force Gale" – Van Morrison

Back outside in Texhoma, I took the obligatory photo of the bike leaning up against the "Welcome to Texas" sign and crossed the border. The wind was picking up astonishingly quickly, making my first pedal strokes in Texas a real grind. As the day wore on, the truck traffic slowed down, and the shoulder widened, but the wind was getting so intense that it was actually difficult to *breathe*.

When I stopped at a Dairy Queen for lunch in Stratford, the only other town I'd go through that day, it was an incredible relief just to be inside. I felt like I could finally catch my breath. My pace was slowing to the point that I was pretty sure I wouldn't make it to Dalhart. I texted Selene to tell her I was going to give it my best shot, but that it wasn't looking good because of the unbelievable strength of the wind.

In her reply, she wished me luck and wrote: *I know . . . it is A BEAST.*

I'd never heard anyone describe the wind like that.

Going back outside after lunch was disheartening. The Beast was reaching its peak, gusting to an angry roar and causing me to dip down to just 3 or 4 mph, which is just barely enough to stay upright on a bike. The fastest I was able to go was a crawling 6 mph. All the cattle on the roadside ranches were lying down on the ground—something I'd never seen before. *Did it take too much energy for them just to stand upright in this wind?* It had to be the reason.

Dirt kicked up often, whipping my skin and caking and accumulating on my face and arms. Tumbleweeds were *flying* by me at ridiculous speeds, bouncing with fury along the pavement; it was like a video game trying to dodge them at times, dipping to the left or right. I didn't even think tumbleweeds were real things—I mean, I knew they were *real*, but I didn't think they were common. I thought they were almost fictional figments of old-time Wild West movies, added for effect. Texas proved their existence to me with humorous abundance, and their size and velocity made them formidable agents and accomplices of The Beast, which was now firing on all cylinders.

At one point, I actually turned around and started biking northeast back toward Guymon, just to see what it would feel like to have that kind of tailwind. I barely had to pedal! It was like cruising on a catamaran; my wide panniers were my sails, filled and stretched to capacity. It was amazing. When I turned back around again, I wanted to scream in frustration. I imagined screaming at the top of my lungs in complete silence, as if I were underwater, The Beast rendering me mute, drowning me in its vehemence.

The Beast seemed content with the cattle bowing down to it, but insulted by my perpetuation. So it raged with even more intensity, to the point that I literally could not breathe. I had to gasp and gulp the air and dust with my mouth in order to get enough oxygen. Like a satanic sultan, The Beast seemed to stand straight up, tilt its head back, and slowly lift its arms, with outstretched palms, over its head, as if summoning the full force of its fury, as a swirling, dusty vortex enveloped it—answering its calamitous call. The Beast howled, crowning itself the monster of all headwinds.

I was at my limit. Actually, I was beyond my limit. But I kept going, mustering up as much tenacity as I could find in the nooks and crannies of my bones. Steeling myself forward. Begging myself not to quit. Separating mind from body, but imploring my brain to keep sending one ironclad, repeating signal to my legs: Just. Keep. Moving.

Sisu (pronounced "seesu") is a unique word in Finnish culture. It's one of those wonderful words in other languages that doesn't have a direct translation to English. But it roughly translates to "guts" or "strength of will." When you're depleted, exasperated, and have given absolutely everything you have but are still coming up short, you reach deep down and use your *sisu* and do it anyway. It's like a special kind of gutsy Finnish magic, a secret weapon we can summon as a last resort. I'd never used my *sisu* quite like this. Every single minute was a remarkable challenge. It was easily the hardest day of the entire 216-day trip, and the most mentally challenging, physically strenuous day of my entire life, without exaggeration. Yes, taking on The Beast was nothing short of a religious experience. It took every ounce of mental fortitude and *sisu* I had to continue battling its suffocating, relentless torrents.

So often we think "If I could just get through this day" . . . or week, or month, or even year. We wish we could jump through time to something better. To something more comfortable or more fun. To something less busy, less stressful. It's human nature. My dad never liked that mindset, though. He always used to say "Never wish any part of your life away" to us as kids and teenagers growing up. It's often hard to do, but his point was that the hard times in your life are still *your life*. They still count.

As we get older, life seems to go faster and faster—maybe because each passing year is a smaller and smaller percentage of our lives to date. Maybe because we get into a comfortable routine and can kind of go on autopilot, at times, as the everyday world becomes less mysterious and fascinating to us as adults than it was when we were kids. Whatever the reason, our relationships and our *time* are the most valuable assets any of us will ever have. So don't wish away the days until your next vacation. Or until the weekend. Or until summer. That was my dad's message. We owe it to ourselves to soak it all up as best we can, and try to "enjoy," or at least *be present*, at all times, even the hard times. I pictured him saying "Never wish any part of your life away" on that Texas highway, and even on my toughest day, it resonated.

But my legs were in a lot of physical pain too—and that can be difficult to ignore. The Beast seemed to be thoroughly enjoying my terrible day. But I was offending it, belittling its power, by continuing straight into its full force with just a bicycle, and it was becoming increasingly irate. I stopped to take a break in the middle of nowhere, and took my gloves and sunglasses off, as I usually did, and placed them on my handlebar bag. I reached for a water bottle and took a few satisfying sips.

Just a second later, The Beast swiftly picked up one of my gloves in a sudden rage and chucked it far off the road, somewhere into the endless, sunny field of dirt and shrubs, just to add a little insult to injury. I ran after it, but it had traveled so far that I couldn't find it!

As I searched, venturing far into the field, and crouching down to look between dried-out shrubs, The Beast let out a hearty, bellowing laugh. "HA-HAHAHA . . . *GO FETCH, FUCKER!!!*" it shouted like a madman. I was in disbelief. *The bastard's playing games with me now too.*

Thinking the glove was gone for good after several minutes of searching, I finally found it and made the long, demoralizing walk back to the road, shaking my head and gritting my teeth—but even more determined to finish the day.

Late in the day, I was out of water. This time, unfortunately, there was no cider store. Actually, there was no *anything*. The highway was extremely remote, with nowhere to find food or water. At one point, I saw a building on the horizon, but as I got closer I realized it was just an abandoned gas station. With no water. The usual symptoms of dehydration set in: my mouth dried up and a bad headache ensued. My muscles shook with fatigue. I pulled up to the abandoned gas station, anyway, to seek shelter from The Beast for a few moments and noticed a pay phone hanging off the hook, dangling eerily in the wind. There was no sign of civilization as far as the eye could see. It had a post-nuclear, apocalyptic feel.

When we were thirsty as kids at the Bronx Zoo or somewhere on a hot day, my mom used to tell us to "swallow our spit." She really did. "You're not thirsty, just swallow your spit." I remember doing it too. Maybe she was preparing me for this exact moment.

Raising four kids isn't easy. But she raised us to be tough. If we said a bad word, she'd wash our mouths out with soap. We probably deserved it. When I was a very little kid, after all, I once turned to her as I brushed my teeth and said, "I hate this fucking toothpaste." She also used to tell us, when we were fighting or acting up in the back seat of the car, that the "EJECT" button on the car stereo, which would spit out CDs, would actually eject *us* from the car—like fighter pilots abandoning a crashing jet.

"You see this button? Look—it says 'EJECT.' If you guys don't stop it *right now*, I'm pressing it."

We totally believed her.

A little while later, I could start to see the light at the end of the tunnel as the Texas sun turned in and called it a day, beckoning to The Beast to follow. Just after sunset, I finally got to Dalhart. *Fourteen hours* after I left Guymon. Yes, it took me fourteen long, excruciating hours to cover seventy miles—that's an average of just five miles an hour.

I made it. I was relieved. Very relieved. But I was too tired to feel proud. I was barely able to pedal. I stopped at the first gas station I came to and was barely able to *stand*. I slowly limped inside and bought a large Gatorade, gulping it down in a few seconds; the feeling of it trickling down my dry throat and filling and cooling my stomach was unbelievable. It was like I could actually feel my veins dispersing the liquid throughout my badly dehydrated body. Then I bought another, and gulped it down just as quickly. I felt dizzy, and my vision was blurred.

Partially resuscitated from the Gatorade, I took out my phone and called my little seven-year-old cousin, Gianna. My Uncle Tony had told me she wanted to talk to me for some reason when I made it to Texas. She had some fascination with Texas—maybe from a TV show or a school project. I wasn't exactly in a jovial mood, but I had planned to call her that day, and I wasn't going to back out now.

So I called, and as soon as I heard her cute little voice on the line, I put on my best Texas twang and said, in a deep voice, like a cowboy from a hundred years ago, "Hi, Gianna, I'm in *Texas*."

I could hear her giggling on the other end of the line, which definitely made my day. I laughed, too, right there in that gas station mini mart, and felt happy to have finished the day. Psyched to have conquered The Beast. And blessed to have my little cousin, thousands of miles away, put a smile on my face for the first time that day. I almost forgot how sore and depleted I was. Maybe we always have the ability to smile. Maybe we always have the energy to laugh.

My morale was lifted even more when I met the Schumachers, another incredibly kind family. We immediately clicked. I had just finished a fourteen-hour bike ride through hell. My face and arms were covered in dirt, and I was ready to collapse when I arrived. They had people over when I got there, though, so I had to meet everybody with dirt caked all over my face.

When the company left, we talked as I ate a delicious dinner that Selene had prepared; it was refreshing and wholesome to have a home-cooked meal. The Schumachers were really fun, down-to-earth people. We were instant friends, randomly joined by Ebram, the Egyptian-American walking across the country.

Even though I was back on schedule, my body was wrecked. The Beast had certainly taken its toll. I was aching worse than ever before, all over my body. Since the wind was supposed to shift and come out of the northwest the next day (to be another direct headwind, of course), and since I liked the Schumachers so much, I decided to stay an extra night in Dalhart and realize the rest day I was supposed to get in Guymon. I didn't even have to ask them to stay an extra day—they offered it before I even considered it.

Dalhart is a small, relatively unknown town, but it makes for the subject of a great trivia question. Almost unbelievably, the northern Texas panhandle town is geographically closer to the capitals of six other states (Oklahoma, Kansas, Nebraska, Wyoming, Colorado, and New Mexico) than it is to Austin, the capital of its own state. There's no better testament to just how big Texas is.

After a coma-like sleep in an upstairs bedroom I had to myself, I woke up on Sunday morning and went to church with Selene, her husband Steve, and their daughter, Sam. After church, we watched *Indiana Jones and the Temple of Doom* on TV, drank beers in the backyard, and had another delicious dinner. Selene had her own catering company and was an excellent chef, and Steve knew how to grill a steak like a true Texan. For dinner, we had a fresh salad, homemade bread rolls, sweet potato fries, and home-grilled ribeye, aged and cooked to perfection. No steak sauce was required; Steve said it ruined it. And to ask for some, it seemed, would be a terrible insult.

At around dusk, Steve, who made his living as a crop consultant, took me for a drive back out into the open plains to see one of the largest feedlots in the world, which held about 150,000 cattle. As we approached in the car, I could see an endless landscape of cattle in the early darkness, fenced in and crowded tightly. I couldn't help but feel a little bad for them. It didn't look like the cattle ranches I'd seen from the road. It looked like a kind of prison camp, where they'd wait on an assembly line to be slaughtered and turned into burgers and steaks.

Steve slowed the car down and rolled down the window. "You know what that smell is?" he asked.

It smelled like shit. I mean, it was overwhelming. I didn't really want to blurt that out, thinking I might insult his home state. Remember, I was their complete stranger guest. But without question, the correct answer was shit.

Luckily, he answered for me. "We call that the *smell of money*."

The next day, I left Dalhart and headed northwest toward the New Mexico border.

AIN'T NO MOLEHILLS

NEW MEXICO
APRIL 16–25

"Ain't No Mountain High Enough" – Marvin Gaye and Tammi Terrell

The New Mexico welcome sign was all beat up; it even had bullet holes in it. It looked like something from Looney Tunes or a prop from a Wild West movie set. It read "Welcome to New Mexico. The Land of Enchantment" with green and red chili peppers, which seemed to dance festively, despite the bullet holes.

I was excited. I felt *really* far from home now. The open cattle ranches of Texas evolved into open desert country in New Mexico. Somehow, it was even drier and more desolate. But it wasn't the classic sandy kind of desert with cacti and scorpions and the like. Not yet, anyway. It was more like dried out, yellow and brown grassland—but with mesas and other southwestern features you don't see as much in the Heartland.

A day behind again, I was worried about keeping to the schedule. But unlike before, stopping early because of the wind could have very palpable consequences. I was getting into a part of the country that didn't necessarily have towns every sixty or seventy miles. I wondered where I'd sleep, where I'd eat, and most importantly . . . where I'd get water.

On the first full day of riding in New Mexico, I found myself in the predicament that I feared. The headwinds were so strong that I had to stop early, before I could make it to the next town. Well, there was a "town" on Google Maps that I was coming up on, called Gladstone, but when I got there, I realized it was just a gas station and mercantile store. Luckily, the owner of the Gladstone Mercantile, Thelma Price, said I could camp there.

The inside of the store was warm and cluttered, stocked with basic groceries and sundries and cowboy boots and hats, and adorned with old-fashioned lamps and souvenirs like Coca-Cola clocks. I bought the old store's Cowboy Burger and a chocolate bar for dinner and a quirky New Mexico postcard with aliens and other things on it to send to Jaime at the Brands Cycle bike shop back on Long Island. He asked me to send a postcard from somewhere random. The Gladstone Mercantile in the middle of barren New Mexico seemed to fit the bill.

I pitched the tent next to the store, using a pile of firewood and a picnic table I propped up on its side as a very necessary wind break. The bike leaned against the pile of firewood, in the small space between the wood and the tent. I watched the sunset as I brushed my teeth in the open field away from the tent, rinsing with my water bottle, and spitting into the yellow grassy dirt, then sat cross-legged on the ground for a few minutes, appreciating the unique moment, and gazing at the orange, pink, and purple sky, waiting for the sun to completely slip under the horizon.

Once it did, I walked back over to the wood pile and got in the tent. The temperature was plunging fast, and the wind was actually picking *up*—I was used to the sunrise turning *on* the wind and the sunset turning it *off*. It ended up being very windy and cold all night, getting down into the thirties.

I put the rain cover on my tent to trap more heat and slept in my windbreaker, the warmest piece of clothing I had. I was *just* barely warm enough to fall asleep, and there wasn't any traffic noise coming from the nearby road. Just the constant, white noise of the tent flapping in the wind, companionably. The noise gave me the exciting feeling of being on an expedition, like I was on my way to the top of Mt. Everest.

The next day, after two pronghorn antelope leapt in a single bound across the road in the distance ahead of me, I could see the snow-capped Rockies on the horizon. It was the first time I'd ever seen them in my life. Like a mirage or some type of cruel illusion, the far-off mountains seemed to never get closer, no matter how many miles I put behind me. They were a new and welcome backdrop, though, no matter how unattainable they appeared. The Rockies were a major milestone for my long westward trek, as they'd been for pioneers on the Oregon Trail nearly two hundred years prior. I was getting to California, slowly but surely.

That day, I passed an abandoned, supposedly rattlesnake-infested pink house that I was warned to stay away from, and a fairly large, brown dust devil, which was eerie because it looked a lot like a tornado—a strange one, though, with a bright blue, sunny sky behind it.

Finally, very late in the day, the deceiving mountains seemed to be getting closer. And bigger. I passed beautiful wild horses of all different shades and colors, grazing with endless open horizon to their east and formidable Rocky Mountains just to their west. Soon after, I got to Cimarron. The town's welcome sign read "Welcome to Cimarron: Where the Rockies Meet the Plains." I loved that sign. It made it official. I was in the Rockies.

A couple of years before the trip began, my high school friend, Ranley (who was going to drive the RV), and I called a random motel along the route to get a sample room rate so we'd have an idea of how much to budget for in that part of the country, and really just for fun. It was somehow kind of fun, as a college kid, to speak to a motel owner in New Mexico from my parents' basement on Long Island. The old landline phone, with its coiled cord, was our connection to some faraway place we'd only heard and read about. All we had to do was dial ten digits.

And as it turned out, we picked a winner. We called the Cimarron Inn and spoke to the owner, the colorful Mrs. Deb Sanders. After we talked rates and about the different rooms they had, I asked her about Taos, the next town on the map after Cimarron. I asked her about the "Taos Hum" since I saw it ranked somewhere online as the "#1 unexplained phenomenon in the world," ranked above the likes of Stonehenge, Bigfoot, the Bermuda Triangle, and the Loch Ness Monster. It seemed worth asking about.

"The Taos *what*?" she replied, in an energetic and tough, don't-mess-with-me Southern accent that took me a little by surprise.

"The Taos Hum," I passively asserted, then went on to explain how some residents and visitors of the town had been perplexed and annoyed for years by a low-frequency "hum" in the air that nobody could explain, according to what I'd read.

There was a pause, dead air on the other end. Then, speaking slowly for emphasis, she said, "That's a hippy dippy crock of *shit*."

Surprised, on the other end, Ranley and I looked at each other, ready to burst out laughing.

She continued, "Son, the only thing they'll sell ya in Taos is bullshit. And sometimes . . . *cow* shit."

When I checked in and met her in person at the Cimarron Inn, she actually remembered the conversation, which seemed like ancient history to me, when I brought it up. I didn't think she'd remember.

"That cow shit thing . . . my husband always says that," she said, laughing amicably. She was a really nice woman—much less intimidating in person.

We talked for a while and took a photo together out front, and then she showed me to my room, "The Fishing Room." The fishing-themed room was decorated with nets, hooks, and different types of fish all over the walls, with a turquoise quilt on the bed.

On the walk over, I met a middle-aged construction worker named Dayne, who had been staying at the motel for weeks, a few rooms down.

He asked me about the trip, handed me a $20 bill, and said, "You gotta come raid my fridge, man. I have all this food, but I'm outta here tomorrow. Going back to Denver."

I thanked him and said I was alright, but he insisted.

"Come on, man. I *know* you're hungry!"

Well, he was obviously right about *that*, so I took him up on his offer. I followed him back to his kitchen, fired up the stove, and made six large bacon and egg breakfast burritos for dinner (yes, six), eating and eating until I was finally full—like a great white shark that had luckily stumbled upon a whale carcass—as he told me about how he and his friend used to play around with their skateboards in the snow as kids, attaching planks to the wheels.

"The difference between the two of us is that he stuck with it," he said, a little despondently. "He started Burton Snowboards."

After I ate and cleaned up the mess I made in my generous neighbor's kitchen, I went back to my room and started feeling lousy, the way you do when a really bad cold is coming on. I felt like I had razor blades in my throat, and although I was even more tired than usual, I couldn't sleep well.

The next morning, I started climbing the Rockies. No more open, windswept plains. Now my days were full of pine trees and mountains and crisp air and beautiful scenery. But *steep*, brutal climbs. Way tougher than ever before. These monsters made the Ozarks look like little molehills.

Deb Sanders said the first twenty-four miles that day would be my "toughest climbs yet," and she was spot on. It was also my first day battling a full-fledged cold, which was extra-burdensome in the thinner mountain air.

The first pass I went over was an entirely different kind of climb from what I was used to, and again, I couldn't stand up. As I'd learned in Florida, standing up and swaying back and forth would loosen the screws that connected the rack to the bike and, eventually, detach it. When you approach any kind of climb on a bike, you instinctively stand up. It's just what you *do*. In the hardest part of a spin class, when you crank up the resistance, you *stand*. It was the way I'd trained and the way I knew how to ride a bike since I was a kid. But I *couldn't* on this bike, on this trip. And that made the Rockies much, much more difficult.

That afternoon, I approached the extremely steep, 9,101-foot Palo Flechado Pass. It was a grueling ascent, much more so than even the first pass that day. The most intense portion was up two miles of heavily wooded switchbacks. I was sweating and breathing hard in the cold, damp air, my breath clearly visible as misty smoke rising from my head. The term *palo flechado* means "tree pierced with arrows" in Spanish. According to the sign at the top, its name may be attributed to a Taos Pueblo Native American custom of shooting one's remaining arrows into a particular tree near the pass following a successful buffalo hunt.

The way down the pass into Taos was an exhilarating eighteen-mile roller coaster. I was going fast, having fun, and relieved that my work for the day was done, until the sky darkened again, and I started getting pelted, *hard*, by little pellets of freezing rain! It felt like a sudden barrage of wasp stings all over my face, arms, and legs—wherever skin was exposed.

In an abrupt panic, I pulled into a driveway dug into the slope of the road and sought quick shelter under an overhang, the static noise of ice falling from the sky growing stronger and louder, beginning to roar like a waterfall.

I had only been there a minute or two when an elderly, white-haired woman came to the door, and to my pleasant surprise, invited me inside. Her name was Connie. Intelligent and good-humored, she had a warm personality and was easy to talk to. It wasn't her house; she was house-sitting. The owners made pottery and used their home as a gallery, so there was ornate, mostly burnt orange, pottery everywhere, delicately placed on an abundance of fragile glass shelving. The upscale home was exquisite, with substantial floor-to-ceiling windows and a commendable panoramic view of the alpine landscape, albeit now partially shrouded in icy mist.

I sat on the couch by the fireplace to warm up, and we talked for a good while. We both seemed to have a mutual appreciation for the unexpected company. We eventually saw small patches of blue sky through the windows, so I got back out there and cruised the last fifteen miles down into Taos to end the day, feeling fortunate to have come across shelter, warmth, and good conversation when I needed it most.

I was frozen when I got to the Taos Inn, an historic place that greeted visitors with its burnt orange adobe exterior and blue and yellow condor sign with bright red and pink neon letters. The room was cozy and warm, with authentic New Mexican decor and a fireplace. I ordered the famous Chile Relleno Platter for dinner at Doc Martin's, the homey hotel restaurant, and finally slept well, despite my now-horrible cold.

Before retiring for the night, I responded to another message I got from Billy Iaia:

Billy: R U STILL RIDING ACROSS AND R U LOVING IT?

Me: Yes, loving it! I'm in Taos, NM right now. Crossed a 9000 ft pass today in the Rockies!

Billy: Great job. I hate u because you're out there riding and I'm on the couch. Enjoy the ride of your life. You will talk about it the rest of your life, so take it all in. Have a great ride tomorrow.

It was ironic that he said, "Have a great ride tomorrow," because the very next day I had my close call with the herd of elk crossing the road on that dark, steep, never-ending mountain pass, and stayed with the elderly Native American couple, the Ulibarris, I randomly encountered in the tiny town of Tierra Amarilla. From there, as the scenery transformed from mountains into southwestern desert country, I rode to Dulce, where I spent a rest day at the Best Western on the Apache reservation to try to get over my cold.

The next day, I went eighty-two miles to Aztec, New Mexico. I felt good because of the rest day, despite some heat. Late in the day, I stopped at Trujillo's Country Store & Lounge for a Powerade, and the woman at the counter told me that actor Steve Carell had stopped there a few years back while riding his bicycle. The woman said he looked exhausted. While she didn't recognize him, she offered him some complimentary tea. He later sent an autographed card to thank her.

In Aztec, I Couchsurfed with Ginny and Steven Jones. I had a guest room to myself with a full bed in their basement. They cooked dinner for the three of us and took me out for ice cream, like an aunt and uncle I hadn't seen in a while.

Before I went to sleep, Steven warned me, "If you hear something late at night, don't be scared."

He explained that he usually rises at 3:17 a.m. to hang from his inversion table in the basement and then takes a long soak and reads the paper before going to work.

If it had been my first time Couchsurfing, I might've thought this routine was strange, but at this point, I was unfazed.

The next morning, Ginny took me to see the Aztec ruins (they were actually Anasazi ruins, but the settlers' mistake survived in the town name).

I passed through Farmington and Shiprock later that day. Shiprock is named after a rock formation that looks like a tall-mast pirate ship marooned on the desert horizon, easily visible from the highway. I ended the day in the Navajo village of Beclabito on the reservation by the New Mexico/Arizona border. I didn't have anywhere to stay, but the Navajo let me stay in their community center, and I was offered free hot food from the gas station across the street.

In the community center, I slept in my sleeping bag in the middle of the floor, on top of couch cushions. I also had access to a bathroom with a shower and cold water from a water fountain. A kind man named George Kelly, who worked at the nearby Navajo coal mine, arranged the setup for me.

When George and his wife stopped by the next morning to say goodbye, I told them that, although I didn't know for sure, I thought I might've been one sixty-fourth Navajo. I explained that my grandmother had come across evidence at one point in her life that suggested she had a great-great-grandparent that was Navajo, which would make her one sixteenth Navajo, my dad one thirty-second Navajo, and me and my siblings one sixty-fourth Navajo. The Kellys got a good laugh out of that.

19

Cruising through Colorado

COLORADO
APRIL 25–26

"Achilles Last Stand" – Led Zeppelin

From Beclabito, I went through the Four Corners, the only place in the US where four states meet, and I stopped at the monument there in the middle of the desert. There's a small gold-plated plaque with the precise meeting point. I put my index finger on the dot at the intersection of its perpendicular lines so that my single finger was in Utah, Colorado, New Mexico, and Arizona at the same time.

I bought some Navajo Frybread at the stand outside the monument (topping choices were powdered sugar, cinnamon, and honey) and cruised down a hill into Colorado, going so fast that I went right by the large, wooden "Welcome to Colorful Colorado" sign and had to turn around to go back for the photo with the bike.

Approaching Cortez, Colorado, I biked through a sandy desert with miles of towering, eroding mesas that looked like giant, neglected sandcastles.

When I woke up in Cortez early the next morning, I thought Moab, Utah, was two days away at best. I was a day behind schedule from the rest day I took for my cold, but it wasn't too big of a deal since I had two rest days scheduled in Moab. I left the motel just after sunrise; it was a nice day, with congenial blue skies. My iPod played Led Zeppelin's "Achilles Last Stand," my favorite Zeppelin track, as I cruised at a brisk speed through green rolling hills, my legs feeling unusually strong in the early morning hours. In a groove, I listened to the song over and over again, the pedal strokes syncing with the fast-paced beat, cruising down the downhills and grinding up the climbs, fast and easily.

With bright green fields in the foreground and snow-capped peaks in the background, the rolling, hilly road was agreeing with me. The whole *morning* was agreeing with me. There was no wind, my energy was up, and I was making excellent time. The sun felt great in the crisp morning air, and the miles were piling up behind me pretty quickly.

MARTIAN DRIP CASTLES

UTAH
APRIL 26 – MAY 1

"Up on Cripple Creek" – The Band

After an early French Dip lunch in Dove Creek, Colorado (about thirty-five miles in), at a little hole-in-the-wall place named the Dove Creek Dinner Bell (pretty much the only place to eat in town, as far as I could tell), I was all of a sudden at the Utah border. The burnt orange and sky blue welcome sign had a cool-looking artist's rendering of Moab's iconic Arches National Park on it. It was my favorite welcome sign so far. As I took the picture of the bike leaning up against it, the prospect of making it all the way to Moab creeped into the back of my mind.

I had planned on making it as far as Monticello, Utah, that day. When I got to the town around 3:00 p.m., with plenty of daylight left and some gas left in the tank, I was feeling ambitious and decided I'd shoot for Moab. With no towns between Monticello and Moab, still over fifty miles to go, and storms in the forecast that afternoon, it'd be a fairly risky move. But I was feeling good. At this point in the trip, I was finally starting to feel that I was in good cycling shape. That I was hitting my stride. It took until Utah.

I had a second lunch at Wagon Wheel Pizza in Monticello. At this point in the trip, I'd figured out that I couldn't go more than about forty miles without stopping for a full meal. So, on most days, one full lunch would suffice. But on long days, I needed two.

As I ate the pizza in the warm pizzeria and started to relax and get out of cycling mode, I decided to give myself a little extra motivation to make it. I called The Gonzo Inn, a more upscale hotel in Moab that was well beyond my usual budget, and reserved a room for that night, which, at that point, was non-refundable if I didn't make it. I ended the call and took a deep breath. There was no turning back now—it was Moab or bust; I couldn't afford to lose that money.

Minutes after that phone call, I heard the rumble of thunder from inside the pizzeria. Just as I left, the thunderstorm showed up, so I sat in a Texaco mini mart on the outskirts of Monticello for over an hour to wait it out, reluctantly burning precious daylight.

I finally got back on the road at nearly 5:00 p.m., with fifty-four miles still to go! The math didn't add up—fifty-four miles was way too far to go after 5:00 p.m.—but something told me I'd make it if I gave it a shot. I thought about the day so far—how I'd felt and the pace I was able to sustain. And the opening lyrics of that Zeppelin song I'd played over and over on that April morning. Something told me I should go.

I started pedaling hard right out of the Texaco parking lot, on wet pavement from the recently departed storm. Luckily, I had a bit of a tailwind, and it was mostly a slight, steady downhill, all the way to Moab, so I was making incredible time. I was hit with some light rain, but there was little traffic on the barren road, and the scenery around me was completely otherworldly. It got stranger and stranger as I went, in the late afternoon light, with enigmatic red rock formations that made me feel like I was biking on Mars. Mars base prototypes have actually been built in Utah because the conditions there do, in fact, come closest to simulating those of Mars—beyond just the optics.

I ended the 117-mile day, the longest of the trip, by pulling into Moab just as the sun was setting. I'd made it. It was a monumental day for me—a 117-mile, sunrise-to-sunset ride, from Colorado to Utah. A major moral victory. I was back on schedule, my cold was finally gone, my legs were beginning to feel like they were in serious shape, and I'd just finished an invigorating day, in which I'd combined two full scheduled days of biking into one. My reward was two rest days in Moab and a relatively luxurious hotel room with a heavenly bed to sleep in. I'd cycled ten out of the previous eleven days and covered nearly 700 miles, many of them in the Rockies, so I desperately needed the two-day break.

I was so happy, and on such a high, that I did the unthinkable—after I ate dinner at a '50s-style diner, I walked into a bar, *alone,* for the first time in my life. I had this kind of sad picture in my mind of walking into a bar alone, like it was something that only real loners did, or maybe struggling alcoholics. I had thought it was far, far, worse than eating at a restaurant alone. But that night, I didn't care. I was psyched, and ready for a victory beer. I was proud of myself. I felt I deserved it.

Woody's Tavern was big, loud, and rowdy. It was a Thursday night. I sat down at the only open barstool and ordered a beer, feeling slightly awkward and unsure how I'd start a conversation with anyone, or *if* I'd start a conversation with anyone. I didn't have the bike with me to spark anyone's interest, so I was just a normal loner with no friends, sipping a beer at the bar, feeling a bit like an uninvited guest. I didn't know a single soul in all of Utah, let alone at this crowded bar. I missed the bike, wishing it were sitting next to me. *It deserved a victory beer, too, didn't it?* I didn't make it 117 miles on my own that day, after all.

Instead, it was locked up in a dark storage room. The Gonzo Inn was the first hotel that didn't let me take the bike into my room. The hotel was used to having bikers—mountain bikers, that is—and didn't want to deal with the inevitable mud and mess. That actually made sense, but I was pissed and objected hard when they told me when I checked in earlier in the night, in a tone that suggested there was no way in hell I was following their stupid rule.

As I sat at the bar, I reflected on that exchange and was kind of surprised at myself for reacting so vehemently (and immaturely), especially to such a reasonable request. My reaction, I realized, was a testament to the peculiar bond that I'd formed over time with the bike; it was beginning to be a stronger connection between a person and an inanimate object than I'd ever thought possible.

We'd become buddies in a way. We relied on each other, simultaneously experiencing the ups and downs that a crazy, long adventure is guaranteed to provide. And I didn't have anyone else. Finally, I understood Tom Hanks's connection with "Wilson" the volleyball in the movie *Cast Away*.

As my beer disappeared at the bar, leaving a few foamy traces in its tracks on the glass, I still hadn't spoken to anyone. I contemplated going back to my comfortable bed across the road and going to sleep. I was paying good money for that bed. But nothing memorable comes from going back to your bed and going to sleep. So I took another gulp of beer and jumped head-first into the large group's conversation next to me, just like that. That may not sound like such a big deal, but it was a big deal for me, especially at the time. They seemed like cool people—around my age, maybe a year or two younger. A mix of girls and guys, maybe twelve of them. They welcomed me into their group. I ended up hanging out with them for the rest of the night, and the next two days.

I definitely couldn't afford to stay at The Gonzo Inn for another two nights, so I checked into the nearby Ramada the next morning, after sleeping in late. I went out to lunch and explored the town a little, bought new cycling shoes at the bike shop, then hung out by the hotel pool in the afternoon, where a dad playing with his kids in the pool overheard me speaking to someone about the trip. He started asking me questions, and eventually offered a place to stay in Idaho. Incredibly, their house in Sun Valley, Idaho, was precisely on my route back to the East Coast. Just off the very road I planned to bike on. I was scheduled to get there in July. I got his contact information and promised to take him up on his offer.

That night, I met up with the group again at Woody's, and we met a group of Brits our age traveling the world. One of them, Faye, said she quit her job at a bank in London and now was just traveling from country to country, without too much of a plan. We laughed, realizing we'd both be completely broke when we got back home. I tried not to think too much about it, but the reality was, I'd be very lucky to finish the trip before my bank account hit zero. No more Gonzo Inns, perhaps.

The next day, I met up with my newfound friends, and we drove through the alien, Martian landscape of Arches National Park, just outside town, marveling at the natural stone arches and outlandish rock shapes, meticulously sculpted by thousands of years of wind and erosion. Here, the terrain was even *more* bizarre than Mars, with giant drip castle-like red rock formations that resembled a surreal Dalí version of The Red Planet. We hiked off a trail over some rough rock to a cliff, to get an off-the-grid view of the iconic Delicate Arch (the one on the Utah license plates). I took a picture of a guy we spotted far below us; he had a camera in one hand and a beer in the other, his feet dangling very precariously off the edge of the cliff. *If he slipped, would he drop the beer or the camera to catch himself?* The drop below him was seemingly never-ending—I couldn't even see the bottom. He was just taking in the view of the Arch, sipping his beer, about as carefree as could be. He wasn't taking photos. Sometimes after a long day at work, or if I'm running for a Manhattan subway and *just* miss it, I think about that guy on the edge of the cliff, not a care in the world, absorbing it all, smelling the roses of the Delicate Arch and sipping a beer in a kind of meditative state, apparently not thinking too much about the past or future. Maybe we should all remember to take moments like that and focus on what's in front of our very *eyes*, not what's on our phones or TVs, or on images in our heads of the past or perceived future. Maybe we all need to remember, sometimes, to be more like the guy on the edge of the cliff.

When we got back into town at the end of the day, people had lined the streets with lawn chairs and blankets to watch the annual outdoor car show's vintage cars roll out of town. I had spent that morning walking around the show, as The Band's "Up on Cripple Creek" played over the speakers, taking photos and sending them back to Uncle John, a classic car aficionado. Watching the cars roll out seemed to be a tradition to mark the end of the late-April event each year.

As I stood among the onlookers, a sense of wonderful simplicity, of timeless magic, came over me. There was something special about watching this parade of classic cars, of all different models and colors, rolling out of Moab, spectators savoring it as much as the drivers, the red rocks around us glowing a warm orange in the late, late afternoon light. Rainbows of mint and sea foam greens, rangoon and vermillion reds, sky and dolphin blues. The cars just kept coming, proudly strutting their stuff and apparently relieved to be out of the garage, out from under the cloth that concealed their winters. They seemed to revel in the fresh air; it was like they had spring fever, revving their motors and reverberating their 1950s sound waves through the arid, increasingly crisp evening air.

For my last night in Moab, I hitched a ride with a couple of people from the group to a house party a little farther outside town than I'd bargained for. Everyone was drinking and planned to crash at the house, which was big . . . but I had to ride the next day and needed to get back to the Ramada in town. Uber didn't exist yet (except in a few of the world's largest cities), it was way too far to walk, and it was too late for the Moab taxi service, so I began to worry about getting back. I asked one of the new faces for suggestions. She said, "That's *your* quest," in a cold, aloof tone that suggested she was under the influence of something other than alcohol. Clearly, she didn't care, and I was beginning to realize how incoherent everyone was around me. Suddenly, I felt very alone. And too far from where I was supposed to be.

After another hour or so at the party, trying to come up with a plan, I saw a face I recognized. It was one of the guys that worked at Rim Cyclery back in town, where I'd just bought the new pair of bike shoes. Luckily, he and his girlfriend offered to give me a ride back to the hotel. They seemed at least as drunk or high (probably both) as everyone else, but I didn't have a choice—it was my only way back.

I don't remember exactly how the conversation in the car went, but it ended with him warning me about the Native American reservations I'd be riding through, and the ghosts I was almost guaranteed to encounter on them. As we pulled up to the hotel, the guy kept talking about the ghosts. His parting remark was, "Remember man, they can't hurt you. They can only make you hurt *yourself*."

"Okay, thanks a lot," I answered, and promptly got out of the car.

I didn't get back to my room at the Ramada until 4:00 a.m., but three cups of coffee, a whole plate of fruit, and a stack of banana walnut pancakes a few hours later, at the crowded Pancake Haus next door, gave me the boost I needed for the uphill climb out of Moab.

The two days off had me feeling refreshed, even after some partying and late nights. I retraced my route through Mars back to Monticello (the only significant retracing I did the whole trip), then continued southwest through Blanding toward Mexican Hat, which was barely a town.

I really enjoyed the ride that day, especially at the end of the day; the golden-hour sunlight danced across the rock formations, reflecting thousands of shades of orange, red, and brown. The Dalí Martian landscape had transitioned to sensational, jagged old western scenery with an unbelievably diverse autumnal color palette. The home stretch to Mexican Hat was one of the most breathtaking portions of road in the entire country. It was dreamlike to bike through. At the very end of the day, I passed a rock formation that looked like a balanced upside-down sombrero, some sixty feet wide, resting atop a mesa, which explained the origin of the town's name.

I had dinner outside as the sun went down at The Swingin' Steak restaurant, just off the road. A couple of tables away from me, the cook had a cowboy hat on. The grill he stood over was swinging back and forth, rhythmically, over a fire, with the sunset behind it and country music playing in the background. The place was authentic and old-fashioned. Quaint and coarsened. I sat back and soaked it all in—breathing in that cool, charred, southwestern air—as I waited for my dinner, extremely grateful, perhaps for the first time, that I'd had the courage to leave home and embark on such an uncertain journey, alone, two months prior. I was grateful that I didn't quit in Quitman, Georgia, or at any other time in those first few brutal weeks. I realized that I didn't mind being alone so much anymore. I could do what I wanted, stay where I wanted, ride when I wanted. I was alone but very free.

A very nice retired couple sitting near me, who were making their annual road trip to their summer home in Colorado, generously bought my dinner without my knowing. After I ate and spoke to the couple for a while, amazed at their random generosity, I sat back down at my table and called my parents. I sat there and spoke to them, telling them that I was doing just fine, watching the guy flipping steaks and burgers as the fire leapt at the swinging grill with the sunset behind it. I got a room upstairs at the inn there, so once it was completely dark, I walked upstairs and went to sleep.

The next morning, I approached "Forrest Gump Hill." In the classic 1994 film, Forrest ends his cross-country, years-long run, which partially inspired my trip, at this very hill, with the rock spires of the iconic Monument Valley in the background. With a long beard and a red Bubba Gump Shrimp Co. hat on, he stops running, turns around to face his followers, and says, "I'm pretty tired . . . I think I'll go home now," and begins walking home. His multi-year, multi-thousand-mile run was over, just like that. I recognized the spot right away when I got to it. There was even a sign there on the side of the road, as if the run had really happened, that read, "Forrest Gump ended his cross-country run at this spot, 1980."

Battling a headwind, I descended Forrest Gump Hill and slowly approached the stone spires of Monument Valley. I made a left turn off the highway toward the visitor center, which had an absolutely astounding view of Monument Valley's "mittens," which are decidedly the most iconic scene of the American West. The mittens and surrounding mesas and buttes are in movies, dating back to old western films, and make countless other appearances in pop culture. There's even an emoji for one of the mittens (it comes up when you type "desert" into a message, along with the cactus emoji and the camel emoji). Seeing the mittens up close was truly awe-inspiring; it was so much more impressive in person than I thought it'd be. In Navajo, Monument Valley is called *Tsé Bii' Nidzisgaii*, which means "Valley of the Rocks."

As I looked out over the incredibly scenic valley, a group of about ten middle-aged Asian male tourists surrounded me and the bike, rapidly snapping photos with their large cameras and talking among themselves inquisitively in a language I couldn't identify. I felt like a UFO that had just crashed in the desert.

Without speaking, one of them offered an orange, which I happily accepted. The curious chatter and photos continued as I just stood there, beginning to peel the orange.

Finally, one of them asked, "How long . . . have you been . . . on the road?"

I felt most of their eyes shift from the bike to me. "About two months," I said casually, simply answering the question.

Then there was complete silence. The chatter and picture-taking had come to an abrupt stop. You could hear the wind whistling as the men stood around me, suddenly frozen in place.

After a few long seconds, the group suddenly—in perfect unison—burst into a harmonized fit of loud, *hysterical laughter*, startling me at first. They were laughing so hard, and for so long, that I started laughing too. I don't know, maybe they thought I was kidding. Or maybe they just thought I was crazy.

CHLORIDE POPCORN

ARIZONA
MAY 1–8

"Don't Bring Me Down" – ELO

Right after I left Monument Valley and got back on the main road, I crossed back into Arizona and Couchsurfed in Kayenta. My host, Colin, was in his mid-thirties and worked at the hospital clinic around the corner. We had a good talk over a simple pasta dinner with "three-buck chuck" (as he called it) red wine. He explained that he loved Couchsurfing, but had only hosted. He'd never even once "surfed," which was the way I was exclusively using the service. The all-time host had met the all-time surfer.

I'd always thought for sure that the surfer was getting the better end of the deal, getting a free place to stay. But Colin didn't see it that way.

"Couchsurfing gives me the opportunity to travel without leaving my apartment. People from all over the world come through here. It's actually pretty cool," he said.

I told him I was getting a lot out of it, too, beyond just helping the budget. "I can't camp all the time, and it's more fun than just staying in hotels or motels, you know?"

"Yeah, staying in hotels every night just seems kind of *soulless*."

He apologized for not changing the sheets on my bed after a German Couchsurfer had slept there the night before, a detail I probably didn't need. "She was hot, though," he said, "and I think that counts for something."

The next morning, we sipped delicious French press coffee—which Colin was proud of and particular about—over breakfast, and he packed up some pasta and sliced avocado in a Ziploc bag for me to have later as a roadside snack. He was off to work; I was off to the highway.

After biking through a long stretch of Arizona desert that day, I stayed in Tuba City, Arizona, at a modern hotel on the Hopi Reservation, where the time was one hour behind what it was across the street (the time zones were pretty confusing in this part of Arizona). Thinking the outdoor hot tub at the hotel would be good for tired legs, I bought an orange cream slush from Sonic and hopped in with it.

After about a minute and thirty seconds of peace and quiet by myself, I was joined by an entire Navajo family in town for a funeral. The hot tub was suddenly full, with ten to fifteen people in and around it. They were really friendly, though, and good-humored—*in oddly good spirits for being in town for a funeral,* I remember thinking. Most of them were women—of all ages, from little kids up to the elderly grandmother, the matriarch of the family. I told them I might be one sixty-fourth Navajo. They seemed to like me, so they decided to give me a Navajo nickname. I was intrigued by what they might come up with. After some deliberation, they decided they would call me *bilagona*, which they later told me means "White guy."

It was a long, tough day out of Tuba City, but the end of it was extremely rewarding. On 64, I looked to my right and saw an almost unimaginable sight. A void in the Earth so vast it didn't look real, like an artist's rendering of some cataclysmic event in which the Earth was splitting in two.

Of course, it was *the Grand Canyon.* One of the Seven Wonders of the Natural World. I'd never seen it in person. You hear so often that major world attractions don't live up to the hype—take the *Mona Lisa,* for example. After finally seeing it in person, I definitely did *not* think the Grand Canyon was one of those things. Teddy Roosevelt might have praised it best: "Leave it as is," he said. "You cannot improve on it. The ages have been at work on it, and man can only mar it. What you can do is keep it for your children, your children's children, and for all who come after you, as the one great sight which every American should see."[11]

After about eighty tough miles that day, I found a motel somewhere in Grand Canyon Village and easily downed two colossal chicken pot pies in the cafeteria for a satisfying dinner.

The next day, I headed south toward Williams, had my first flat since Missouri, and capped off the day with dinner at lively Pancho McGillicuddy's to celebrate Cinco de Mayo. From Williams, I hopped on I-40 (my first interstate of the trip) even though it was technically illegal, and then continued on the longest intact stretch of the old Route 66, the famed American highway that once stretched all the way from Chicago to the Santa Monica Pier in Los Angeles. On the way to Peach Springs, Arizona, I stopped for lunch in Seligman, the inspiration for Radiator Springs in the animated Disney movie *Cars*. Like the fictional town in the movie, Seligman (on 66) received fewer visitors after nearby I-40 was built, which bypassed it—so it became a kind of forgotten town.

The place I ate at in Seligman was a prototypically kitschy, quirky Route 66 burger stand called Delgadillo's Snow Cap Drive-In, founded in 1953, and known for pulling pranks on patrons. At the outdoor counter, I ordered a burger and a shake. When I asked for the shake, the girl behind the counter extended her hand. When I asked for a straw, she held out a handful of barnyard hay.

After a night in Peach Springs and a stop at the Route 66 Hackberry General Store, I biked through Kingman, Arizona, then started heading north toward Las Vegas, approaching a couple of Arizona blips on the map along the remote US-93. Blips with colorful names. First, there was Santa Claus. Then, Grasshopper Junction. I had planned to make it to Grasshopper Junction, where I figured I'd free camp. The name of the town likely comes from disgruntled pioneers who were struggling to make their way west (other towns in Arizona such as Tombstone, Contention, Booze Crossing, and Hookers Hot Springs share a similar sentiment[12]), and I'd imagine refers to the swarms of grasshoppers that can blanket the Las Vegas area in years when rainfall is above average.

I had plenty of time as I biked, so I often came up with mantras for the day, slogans of sorts that would repeat over and over again in my head. They usually contained the destination for the day in some capacity, and were often corny or alliterative or rhymed. Sometimes I imagined printing the mantra on a t-shirt and wearing it for the day.

On this day, my imaginary t-shirt said "GET TO THE JUNCTION" with a big grasshopper on it. This was the slogan—the mantra—that I kept repeating in my head, over and over, pushing myself to keep pedaling through the desert in the general direction of Las Vegas.

When I finally "got to the Junction," though, there was nothing there but a closed, beat-up little convenience store with a rusty tin roof and a person-sized painting on its exterior brick of a green grasshopper dressed like a cowboy drawing a gun. The tree next to the store was the only tree you could see for miles in any direction you looked.

With the store being closed, I couldn't even get anything to eat. The sun had just set, it was beginning to get cold, and my stomach growled impatiently. I noticed a large sign pointing east that read "Chloride: 1860 Historic Mining Town—4 Miles," so I climbed back on the bike and rode the four long miles in the dark. I later learned that the odd ghost town was a onetime silver mining camp and known for its collection of junk art—including a flamingo made out of a motorcycle gas tank, a tin man with a blue hat, and a caterpillar made out of bowling balls. There are old telephones on the graves of its cemetery.

Approaching Chloride, the first and really *only* sign of life I saw was a mostly dark VFW building, with a muffled sound coming from inside. I walked up the steps to the building and opened the door, realizing that the sound was ELO's "Don't Bring Me Down," playing loud and clear on the old-fashioned jukebox inside, to a large and otherwise empty, dingy, dimly lit room, with a few vacant, cheap catering hall-style tables and chairs.

I walked up to the bar on the far end of the room, and the bartender, an elderly woman with an anomalous face, offered me some popcorn. After a couple of minutes awkwardly eating popcorn a few stools down from the only person sitting at the bar—a narrow-eyed, blank-faced older man that didn't seem eager to talk—I decided not to stay, and the woman kindly directed me to a motel around the corner. The motel didn't have any available rooms, but the owner let me sleep in a used room with one clean bed for just $20. To this day, any time I hear ELO's "Don't Bring Me Down," I can't help but think of eating popcorn in Chloride, Arizona.

OUT OF LUCK?

NEVADA
MAY 8–12

"Walkin' on the Sun" – Smash Mouth

The next afternoon, after lunch at the Last Stop rest stop in Arizona, where I spoke with a biker gang that said they'd seen me at the Grand Canyon a few days before, I crossed into Nevada as I passed right by the Hoover Dam, crossing a bridge named after Pat Tillman, who was killed serving in the army in Afghanistan after giving up his NFL career just after 9/11.

Soon after, as the landscape became more populated and built up, I mistakenly biked through some freshly-put-down wet pavement, which got badly caked onto my tires. I couldn't get all of it off, and the mess resulted in a flat soon after.

All of that delayed me significantly, so I soon found myself on a major, unlit freeway approaching Las Vegas, completely in the dark. I could see the neon lights of the strip glowing in the far distance, easily discernible from the dark desert around it, but I had a ways to go. The traffic was fast and heavy, with monstrous trucks and a small shoulder. The most dangerous part was crossing where exits were, where the shoulder disappeared.

An overwhelming fear came over me—that feeling you get when you're sure you're not supposed to be in a situation, and you just want to get out of it. I was pretty sure I was going to be struck by a semi. I could see the headline the next morning: *OUT OF LUCK: FOOLISH CYCLIST STRUCK AND KILLED ON NEVADA FREEWAY APPROACHING LAS VEGAS IN THE DARK.*

But then, the 1997 song "Walkin' on the Sun" by Smash Mouth came on my iPod, and it was curiously comforting. For some reason, it calmed me down. It reminded me of being a kid in the '90s, listening to the song on the radio. The ridiculous danger started to almost, somehow, become *fun*, as twisted as it sounds. I turned up the volume, partially drowning out the roar of cars and tractor trailers blowing by me. The song just seemed to fit the scene. Maybe it was the retro kitsch vibe of it, which seemed to align with the southwestern Route 66 theme of bright neon lights popping up in the middle of the desert. I kept playing the song over and over, surviving the dark, treacherous highway three minutes at a time.

As the neon lights got bigger and brighter, I started to believe that I'd make it to Las Vegas unscathed. But then—flashing lights and a blaring siren behind me! I was being pulled over. Again.

This time I decided to be proactive, since there wasn't much room on the shoulder. So I left the bike and walked over to the cop's driver-side window, hoping that wouldn't be perceived as threatening.

When the window came down, I was shocked. She was young and pretty, probably even younger than I was.

"Is cycling legal on freeways?" she asked with a puzzled look on her face, which surprised me even more.

I replied, "Yeah . . . I think so," the only answer that seemed even remotely appropriate.

She gave me directions for an alternate route from the exit I had just passed, so I climbed over boulders from the highway up to the exit ramp above, struggling mightily to carry the bike.

Once I was off the highway, an incredible feeling of relief came over me. I could feel my heart rate plummeting. I could finally take a deep breath. I grabbed a Slurpee at a 7-Eleven just off the exit ramp and was at the famous "Welcome to Fabulous Las Vegas" sign just a few minutes later.

Over the next couple of days, I would be hosted by Paul and Dawn Shultz and their children, Eric and Ali, who were in middle school and high school, respectively. I'd never met him, but Paul Schultz was one of Uncle Brian's best friends from high school. Ali is Uncle Brian's goddaughter, as is my sister Cailyn. As I waited to be picked up, a very large Eastern European fellow, who legitimately looked like he could win World's Strongest Man, was admiring my bike.

"Can I pick up?" he asked, in his Eastern European accent. The crowd of people around us began to look on.

"Sure!" I said, knowing it wouldn't be so easy, even for Mr. Olympia over here.

He picked it up directly over his head and screamed loudly as his face turned beet red, struggling a bit to hold it. It brought a slight smile to my face, to see him struggling with it. Chuckling to myself, I took his picture with the bright neon sign in the background, as did many others around us, the bike suspended over him. After a few seconds, he set it back down.

Paul and Eric arrived a few minutes later. After a good night's sleep, I got the bike tuned up the next day, and they took me out to the Nine Fine Irishmen pub (where Dawn waited tables) for dinner, in the New York-New York Hotel & Casino. Uncle Brian's name was on a plaque on the wall there, which was dubbed "The Wall of Fine"—they wanted to make sure I saw it.

Then, Paul and I went to play some blackjack, and I actually won a little money. Beginner's luck, perhaps.

Paul was psyched. He said, "You're one of the few. They don't build these things by losing money!"

The next day was Take Your Son to Work Day, so Eric joined Paul and I on the family boat (which Paul didn't work on, of course), and we had a great day out on Lake Mead. It was a hot, sunny day, so when we jumped off the boat into the crystal-clear water, just above the Hoover Dam, it somehow felt thirst-quenching. It felt great to dry off, too, in the hot, arid air as the boat sped off.

After spending the morning on the boat, I took Eric to try the brand new, much-hyped Doritos® Locos taco at Taco Bell that afternoon (which we both approved of), so we had some time to talk one-on-one. He was a great baseball player, but seemed especially inspired by Uncle Brian's story. Before I left, he gave me a large coin with the FDNY logo (which included the Twin Towers), with "New York City's Bravest" on one side and an FDNY Maltese Cross on the other, with "343" in the middle, and the names of all five NYC boroughs. The item was clearly important to him, but he wanted me to have it for the rest of the trip.

When Eric got older, he became a wildland firefighter in Montana—where he fought massive wildfires—then later joined Las Vegas Fire & Rescue, always wearing an Engine 226 patch under his helmet.

I later found out that just after I left, Paul was upset because I reminded him so much of Uncle Brian. He wanted to drive out into the desert to check on me, but Dawn convinced him not to. He called Nana Mac, telling her that Brian's spirit was strong in my soul.

***

I-15 was the only road that cut across the inhospitable Mojave Desert to connect Las Vegas to Los Angeles—so I-15 it was, for four straight days. Death Valley, which is just north of the Mojave, is well-documented as the hottest place on Earth; it has bright red, stop sign-shaped warning signs for hikers that say *STOP: Extreme Heat Danger. Walking after 10AM not recommended.*

Again, it was actually legal to bike on interstates in situations like this, when there is no alternative. That doesn't mean it was safe, by any means. From Vegas, the final five days to finish my cross-country ride would end in Primm, Nevada; Baker, California; Barstow, California; San Bernardino, California;

and Santa Monica, California. I was 295 miles from the ocean, a sight I absolutely couldn't wait for. Five days from that front tire dip.

On the first night in the desert, I stayed at a cheap hotel and casino in Primm, Nevada, which was right on the California state line. Primm was a mini oasis of casinos, surrounded by desert—your last chance to gamble, I guess, before crossing into California.

The next morning, I wheeled the bike across the carpeted casino floor, right through all the slot machines and flashing lights and gaming sounds, past a couple of cigarette-smoking stragglers still playing the slots from the night before, and took the picture of the bike leaning against the blue and yellow "Welcome to California" sign a little down the road. I almost couldn't believe that I'd made it that far, from the Atlantic Ocean to California. It didn't look anything like the California I knew, though, in the middle of the desert like that. *Am I really here?*

I sent the photo back to my family and my sister Annie posted it on Facebook. It was nice to know that my family was proud of me, that I'd already accomplished something real at that moment.

A HORSE WITH NO NAME

CALIFORNIA PART 1
MAY 12–20

"A Horse with No Name" – America

Baker, California, was aptly named, because it felt like I was descending into an oven as I approached it. The air was stifling—so hot that it was hard to breathe it in. These desert towns were perfectly spaced for me, though, because they occurred about every sixty miles, with basic rest stops about halfway in between them. I stayed in the towns at night and had lunch at the rest stops, where I could refill my five water bottles. I had to conserve water, for sure (I only had one chance to refill them per day), but the rest stops, at least, made it possible to cross the desert without trying to carry an additional water supply—which wouldn't have really been feasible with the way the bike was packed.

Unfortunately, however, the rest stops didn't have food—all they had were vending machines with candy and chips, which didn't do me much good. So I had to settle for peanut butter sandwiches and Clif Bars for lunch each day, sitting at picnic tables under outdoor canopies that only partially blocked the sun. The stops were crowded, with busloads of interstate travelers taking bathroom breaks and stretching their legs in the sultry desert air. The only indoor areas were the bathrooms, so there was no air-conditioned respite. The desert heat

217

made me drowsy and lethargic. This was only exacerbated by inadequate lunches and a short supply of water. My exposed skin was burning, even with 30 SPF.

***

Whenever my iPod wasn't playing in the desert, I had the same song stuck in my head—America's "A Horse with No Name" from 1971. It was a classic desert song with a catchy tune—the type that easily gets stuck in your head.

Thinking about that song, I realized I'd never given the bike a name. Many people had asked me, "What's the bike's name? Aren't you going to name the bike?" I guess long-distance or serious cyclists often did that. I *had* started to feel a bond with the bike, since Utah. I considered naming it Talulah, the proposed, but rejected, name of the Jamaican bobsled in the 1993 Disney movie *Cool Runnings*, loosely based on the real Jamaican bobsled team at the 1988 Calgary Winter Olympics. The scene has some interesting dialogue for a Disney movie:

SANKA: So what are we going to name the sled?
JUNIOR: How about . . . Talulah.
REST OF TEAM: *[Laughing]* Hahahaha. Talulah!!
SANKA: Ta-LU-lah. Sounds like a two-dollar hooker! How'd you come up with that?
JUNIOR: That's my mother's name. *[Embarrassed silence, then team converses in agreement that Talulah is actually a good name]*
SANKA: *[to Derice]* What's it gonna be, star? What are the people gonna be screaming when Jamaica takes the hill?
DERICE: I say we call it, "Cool Runnings."
JUNIOR: Beautiful, I like it.
YUL: Very strong.
COACH IRV: Nice, very nice, but...what exactly does it mean?
DERICE: Cool Runnings means, "Peace be the journey."
Team: *[Toasting]* Cool Runnings![13]

Ultimately, I didn't name it Talulah or Cool Runnings or *anything*, for that matter. I decided it would remain without a name, save for "the bike." I hoped it wouldn't take offense.

Since it was the only road that connected Vegas to LA, I-15 had heavy traffic with large trucks. The shoulder was wide (thankfully), but also dirty, littered with debris. I got a flat one day. Luckily, it happened right before a rest stop. As I changed it at the rest stop, I spoke to a grandma in her fifties named Sharon, who worked there. She offered a place to stay in Barstow, so I happily accepted.

After a good dinner a few hours later, at Peggy Sue's 50's Diner on the outskirts of town, where a father sitting in the booth next to mine posted to biketrip2012.com to thank me for showing the bike to his young son, the night took a turn.

Sharon lived with an even younger grandmother, who had a fourteen-year-old and a sixteen-year-old, who had just had a baby. There were lots of other people in and around the house, too, and nobody was particularly friendly.

When I arrived, they were all getting ready to watch the pitbulls fight in the dirt lot yard. I saw a roach scurry across the floor. The fourteen-year-old and I watched a bootleg movie after everyone else suddenly disappeared. I couldn't wait to go to sleep on the couch (so I could wake up and leave), until I found a random guy named Carmine sleeping in the chair *right* next to it. He snored horribly all night—I mean, the worst snoring you can imagine. He sounded like he was slowly dying. I hardly got any sleep, which added to an already-tough next day through headwinds and over a dangerous, heavily trafficked mountain pass on I-15 into San Bernardino.

As soon as I descended into the LA basin over the pass, the temperature was significantly cooler. You could feel it right away. Finally, I was no longer in the desert. I stayed in San Bernardino that night at the Wigwam Motel, a Route 66 staple. Each room was a free-standing concrete "teepee" with a fairly standard motel room on the inside. I went to sleep excited—ready to finally complete the Atlantic to Pacific journey the next day and see my good friend Bruce Lagnese.

The next day, while approaching Rancho Cucamonga on Foothill Boulevard/Historic Route 66, I fell and hit the pavement hard as I turned into a gas station for the Five-Mile Water/Stretch and a 5-Hour Energy. I tried to turn in a rain puddle, and the rear wheel lost traction. I landed on my right side *hard*, right on my hip bone, resulting in a big, nasty, multi-colored bruise that hurt to the touch.

A new rule was born: *Never* turn in a puddle.

Despite the bad start, it ended up being a fun day of biking through the LA metro. I went through busy, crowded streets with lots of energy and things to see. My mind was always occupied and busy, which was a change of pace that I liked. It was exciting.

Cutting across the heart of LA, I took Route 66 to Sunset Boulevard to Santa Monica Boulevard all the way to the end (the Santa Monica Pier is the end of Route 66). It was nearly eighty miles from the Wigwam Motel to the pier—a full day of biking just to get across the massive LA basin. Seeing the ocean for the first time from Santa Monica Boulevard on that gorgeous, sunny day was absolutely incredible. I'd made it!

As I made my way over to the touristy Santa Monica Pier through large crowds, I got off the bike and started walking, looking around, and literally bumped right into Bruce. He handed me a margarita in a plastic cup and gave me a big bear hug. I couldn't have imagined a better greeting after a bike ride across the country.

"You made it, buddy." Bruce was shocked that I'd arrived on time, to the day and hour, to the Santa Monica Pier. And I knew that it took a lot to shock Bruce. He kept saying, "This is unbelievable."

Bruce is one of my dad's best friends from Westbury High School on Long Island, but has been living in Studio City in LA for a while. He's the funniest person I've ever known, without question. He had a very lucrative career as a financial advisor/manager for some of Hollywood's biggest stars, including Jennifer Aniston and James Earl Jones. He spoke his mind freely, which sometimes led to conflict—but he was always honest. He didn't bullshit you—*ever*. In his mid-fifties, he wasn't married and didn't have kids, but he usually had a beautiful, younger girlfriend. He spoke slowly, profoundly, with extremely self-deprecating humor. When I told him I was writing a book about the bike trip and that he'd be in it, he asked what chapter. I said in the twenties, and that the title was "A Horse with No Name."

"Seems pretty late for such an important character," he quipped. "Am I the horse?"

When Bruce made up his mind, that was *it*—there was no going back. One day, for example, he decided to give up skiing. He just quit, cold turkey. The problem was, he was only about halfway down a mountain when he quit—so he took off his skis and hiked the rest of the way down. I can picture him saying, "*That's* it. Fuck this," and huffing down the mountain. I wasn't there, but I can almost guarantee you that's exactly how it happened. He gave every piece of ski equipment he owned to my dad and never skied again.

Driving in LA, he once accidentally cut off another car. So, at the next red light, the heated guy pulled up to him and flipped him the bird.

Keeping his cool, Bruce rolled down his window and said, "Hey, I'm sorry."

"Fuck you."

To Bruce's credit, he once again said, "Alright, I'm sorry. I was wrong, I cut you off. I know."

Then the guy did something that Bruce wasn't going to just sit there and take. He extended his index finger and thumb to create the shape of a gun and extended his arm, pointing it at him. Yes, sir, that crossed the line.

So Bruce reached down and took out his handgun and pointed back, saying, "Oh yeah? This is what the *real* fuckin' thing looks like, bud!"

The shell-shocked guy hit the gas and sped off.

I was so thirsty at the Santa Monica Pier that I gulped the margarita Bruce handed me like it was a lemonade. Perhaps hoping I'd savor it a bit more, he told me (in great detail) about how difficult it was to bring that margarita outside, as it was against the rules to take drinks to-go. At first, the waitress at The Lobster restaurant wouldn't let him take it. But Bruce had already made up his mind that he was going to welcome me with a margarita in hand. Bruce told her the whole story of the bike trip, how I told him I'd be there on that specific day (May 15) at 5:00 p.m., years beforehand, how I'd be arriving, on time, in about fifteen minutes, on and on.

"So can you just put a margarita in a plastic cup so I can take it outside to him?"

"No."

"But that's why I told you the *story* . . . "

"Alright, alright," she finally agreed, albeit reluctantly.

Bruce 1, The Lobster 0.

We walked down to the end of the pier and then down to the beach. He took the photo of me dipping the front wheel of the bike into white, crashing waves, with the pier in the background. The bike and I had made it from coast to coast, ocean to ocean, pier to pier, officially. It was a familiar celebration—a tire, a pier, a photo, a margarita, and a great friend.

I stayed with Bruce, his girlfriend, Shelly, and Shelly's eight-year-old daughter, Makayla, for four rest days at Bruce's house, which had been Drew Barrymore's childhood home, in Studio City. I was totally spoiled; I'd come a *long* way from sleeping on that couch in Barstow a couple of nights before. I had a brand new, state-of-the-art guest room with a connecting bathroom and a really comfortable bed. At the house, Makayla was always running and jumping around, laughing, singing, and playing with Sparky the dog. She beat me in a game of handball (played with a kickball) in the driveway, against the garage door, and I was actually *trying*. She kept adding new rules, though.

Doing his best to help me maximize my rest days, Bruce arranged two professional massages for me with his attractive British masseuse and threatened to kill me one night if I accepted Shelly's invite to go help feed her horses early the next morning, because he knew I'd planned to sleep in (he even took his handgun out of a futuristic compartment on the wall, saying, "In case you were wondering how I'd do it. . ."). We hung out by the pool and hot tub in the backyard; went to high-end restaurants, like nearby Casa Vega, for dinner each night; and spent some time at Bruce's golf club, where he was a well-respected member and leader. Members included the likes of Jack Nicholson and Sylvester Stallone.

One night, Bruce and I were smoking cigars with a bunch of members at the club, and Bruce had the floor, telling everyone about the trip and how I was about to bike up the coast and "hang a right" near Portland to head back to New York. He had the place rolling.

"And another thing," he said. "This whole thing really tells you something about the *job* market right now, doesn't it?"

More hearty laughter and puffs of thick cigar smoke.

As we climbed into Bruce's sleek convertible to drive home, he said, "You know what? I really had fun tonight. I really did."

I got the feeling he didn't say that very often.

Bruce was practical, seasoned, and street smart. Very successful, but unpretentious. He had a clear sense of right from wrong. And under the layers of crude self-deprecation and profanity, sometimes brutal and off-putting honesty, and an occasionally twisted sense of humor—a very big heart.

As we talked in his backyard one afternoon, just the two of us, smoking cigars, Bruce suggested that my goal should be to raise more money for the Marty Lyons Foundation than I spend on the trip. Otherwise, he said, the foundation would have been better off if I had skipped the trip and had just given them the money I would've spent.

"Look, it's great that you're having this experience," he said. "But you have to think about it purely from the foundation's perspective."

If I couldn't raise more than I spent for my own expenses, the trip would be a failure. I have to admit, I hadn't thought of it like that. But he was definitely right.

I was on pace to spend about $15k over the seven months, which was literally every penny I had in the bank, so the fundraising goal became $20k from that point forward. It was fitting that Bruce was the one who helped me determine this goal. In some ways, he was like an uncle or a father figure to me—a father figure who could say things in a way my dad couldn't, such as when Bruce told me as a teenager, "Hey, there's only two ways you can fuck up. I mean, there's plenty of ways you can fuck up, but there's only two ways you can *really* fuck up: Number one is drive drunk. Number two is get someone pregnant. Don't do either of those things, and you'll be alright."

I looked to my dad when he said that, sitting next to us. He didn't say anything, but he nodded, his face confirming the validity of the advice while acknowledging he could never say it to me quite that way.

But more than anything, Bruce is just a really good buddy. Like Fritz, I kind of forget we're so many years apart sometimes. He once told me, "If I could buy stock in you, I would." There's no better music to a twenty-something's ears. Since that day on the beach on September 9, 2001, I'd always felt that if you have something positive to say about someone, you should just tell them. They might remember it more than you'd think.

* * *

On Sunday, May 20, I said goodbye to Bruce and Shelly, and their neighbors gathered at the end of the driveway to watch Makayla ride her miniature bike, with its pink and white streamers, with me to the end of the street. I said goodbye and watched her pedal back to the small crowd of waving neighbors. It was the beginning of a new stage of the journey.

The day started with a tough climb over a canyon on Beverly Glen Boulevard, which broke an early sweat and made me feel rusty. After that, I stopped at the Santa Monica Pier again. I walked the bike to the very end of the pier, paused for a few moments as I looked out at the ocean, turned around, and walked all the way back.

Then I started pedaling north on the Pacific Coast Highway.

THE PACIFIC COAST HIGHWAY

CALIFORNIA PART 2
MAY 20 – JUNE 11

"Electric Feel" – MGMT

It was tough getting back on the road, as it always was after an extended rest, but I had a short day of biking to Malibu—only thirty-five miles—to break back into it that first day. Plus, I was on the PCH! Not much to complain about. I'd been looking forward to this stretch for a long time. I liked having the Pacific Ocean dependably on my left. I liked the thick, salty air and the beachy scent of fish and seaweed. The aroma of clam chowder brewing and fresh bread baking in upscale seafood restaurants along the road. It was all so new and refreshing. The desert on the other side of the mountains seemed a world away.

I met my good friend from college, Jack Campbell, and his wife, Nicole, at their beautiful Malibu condo that first night, and we went to one of those fancy seaside restaurants, Geoffrey's, for dinner. Jack played linebacker at Texas Tech before transferring to Cornell, where he was one of the best players on the team at defensive lineman. He worked on his family's vineyard in Bakersfield a couple of hours away, where they lived with their infant son, Jack, but made sure to drive out to the coast to meet me when I was coming through.

I fell asleep to the sound of the waves crashing against the rocks of Malibu in the condo that night, then finally swam in the Pacific Ocean the next day, a scheduled rest day. Jack jumped in too.

The day after that was a full day of biking up to Santa Barbara, where a man at Bruce's golf club named Rob Robertson let me sleep on his boat, docked in Santa Barbara Harbor. He'd given me the keys a few nights before—the night we all smoked cigars at the club. The boat was a welcome addition to the list-of-interesting-places-I'd-slept-recently that I was quickly compiling.

The following day was brutal, with intense headwinds that forced an early stop in Lompoc. The whole way out to California, I kept telling myself, *The wind mostly goes from west to east, so once you're in California, it won't be as bad for the rest of the trip. Just make it to California and you'll be in the clear.* Well, I was wrong. That long day out of Santa Barbara told me that headwinds would still be a very big part of a typical day.

On the PCH, I saw *way* more cyclists than I'd seen in any part of the country, and they all had one thing in common: they were all going south. Every single damn one of them. I was the only idiot going north. This was because of the *wind,* of course. It was almost always coming from the northwest. It was a cruel joke. As I shifted my general direction on the journey from westward to northward, the wind was happy to shift as well, to remain directly in my face.

Some of the cyclists kind of looked at me in surprise, as if they were thinking, *Why would this guy choose to go* against *the wind?*

One guy even shouted out, "You're going the wrong way, dude!"

I waved and shouted back, "I know."

From Lompoc, I biked through Vandenberg Air Force Base and got back on schedule the evening of May 24 by making it to Morro Bay just as the sun was going down over Morro Rock, a large volcanic plug at the harbor entrance that added immensely to the particularly beautiful sunset.

I asked a local on Main Street where to eat. Without a hint of hesitation, he replied, "Tognazzini's Dockside—that's where the locals go." When you ask for a recommendation, that's exactly what you want to hear: *That's where the locals go.*

So I biked down to the restaurant, which sat right on the water next to Crills Salt Water Taffy, and ordered the Seafood Quesadilla. It was so big and dense—and filled with delicious crab, shrimp, and other seafood—that it filled me right up, which was no easy feat after a long day of biking. I stayed at the charming mom-and-pop-style Bayfront Inn, a little down the street, after spotting it on the way to the restaurant.

I faced more intense wind the next day, passing Hearst Castle and a beach full of loud, barking sea lions, before starting a steady climb into the winding, soaring cliffs of greater Big Sur, the climax of the entire Pacific Coast Highway, and perhaps the most beautiful stretch of coastline on the planet. It was this section of the PCH I most loved and remembered from driving it as a kid with my family. It's a place of natural drama, a land of extremes. I was loving it even more as an adult, from the unique perspective of a bicycle.

This part of Route 1 or Highway 1 (the other names for the PCH) was especially twisting and winding, with thick and methodical fog that predictably loitered into the late morning, lofty cliffs jutting out above the clouds, oddly colorful mountains with pink and yellow flowers and maroon shrubbery that descended into surprisingly bright turquoise water, unparalleled bird's-eye views of waves exploding dramatically into unforgiving boulders, Pacific horizon sunsets, and the beginnings of towering trees. Despite the steep cliff drop-offs that were often just feet from the road, the small or non-existent shoulders, the often-heavy traffic, and the never-ending blind curves, it was a joy to ride. The salty ocean breezes made it consistently cool, and looking out at the brilliant blue water and white waves crashing into the shoreline boulders never got old. I was beginning to feel very lucky, actually, that I would get to look at the Pacific Ocean every day for an entire month, as I made my way from Los Angeles to Portland.

That night, I stayed at a little inn right next to a place called the Whale Watchers Café—it was all part of Gorda, an isolated mini-town on a very remote stretch of the coast—where the traffic thinned out and there was no phone service. Gorda is known to have literally the most expensive gas in America at times, because it's so remote. The inn there was a good deal, though, because the carpeted room had a fireplace, a lot of space, a large painting of rough waves crashing over sharp Pacific rocks, and large windows looking out over the PCH and the Pacific—where it was apparently very commonplace to spot passing whales as they migrated.

It was getting stormy in the late afternoon and looked like it was going to rain, so I was really happy to find a place to stay in lieu of camping (especially since it was the Friday of Memorial Day weekend, typically a very hard night to find a hotel). My family was on a flight out to San Francisco to come meet me. I was incredibly giddy and excited that they were actually on their way as I played a game of Bananagrams with a couple of strangers at the café.

My family spotted me on the road at the very end of my ride the next day, from their rental car, which was lucky, because we were both running late. I didn't even realize it was them right away. A red car going in the opposite direction honked at me, but cars honked at me pretty frequently. I didn't realize it was them until the red car turned around and started following me as I coasted down a hill to the Big Sur Lodge. There, I saw and finally hugged them all— Mom, Dad, Annie, Cailyn, and RJ—right on the side of the highway next to the Big Sur Lodge sign, for the first time in three months. It felt *so* much longer than that.

It was a memorable Memorial Day weekend. Dad treated us to excellent dinners at the upscale Ventana Inn and Rocky Point Restaurant in Big Sur, where we celebrated Mom's fifty-first birthday. We hiked to Pfeiffer Falls one day, and then they drove (I biked, of course) the thirty-five miles up to Monterey the next day, over Bixby Bridge, Big Sur's iconic open-spandrel arch bridge that appears in countless car commercials. My family stopped on the north side of the bridge and watched me slowly bike over it.

At the hotel in Monterey, where the rooms opened to an open-air hallway, with vistas of the Pacific that made the ocean appear close enough to jump into, we smoked cigars on the beach and drank lots of Jameson at dinner at the urging of my sisters. Annie was twenty-two and Cailyn was nineteen; but apparently, they both smoked cigars and drank whiskey now, like two old men.

The next morning, we went whale watching, which was incredible. We really lucked out—it was one of Monterey Bay Whale Watching's best days. We saw tons of humpbacks; one even jumped high into the air, with a graceful splash landing like it was auditioning for a Pacific Life commercial. Then, at the end, just before the four-hour tour was due to wrap up, we were lucky enough to run into a pod of orcas! Coming across orcas occurred much less frequently, so the tour operator decided to follow the pod.

The ocean's top predator, orcas, or "killer whales," have been known to hunt other whales, including humpbacks—and even great white sharks. Studies have shown that great white sharks regularly flee from orcas, and even avoid areas where they've encountered them for up to an entire year.

I could sense the tour operator's genuine excitement when his voice came over the intercom: "Ladies and gentlemen, I'm pleased to announce we'll be extending our cruise today! Well, we've really got a treat for ya. Looks like there's a pod of orcas hunting down a harbor seal just to our west, so we're gonna take a little detour to go investigate."

The boat cheered in excitement, delighted to go find the hungry killer whales—all except RJ and Mom, who had been throwing up off the back of the boat for the entire four hours.

At one point, the killer whales were right in front of us, tearing apart the poor harbor seal and rendering the water a bright red—it was hard to believe it wasn't *Planet Earth* footage we were watching. The wild orcas were a sight to see up close, with their intimidating, tall, black dorsal fins and signature large white spots above their eyes, which likely evolved to protect their actual eyes by providing a false target for predators. Sick as he'd ever been, RJ looked straight down at the water, hands gripping the side of the boat.

"RJ, look up! Please look up, just for a second—you might not see anything like this again in your entire life!" Dad pleaded. RJ acknowledged him by slowly raising his index finger, but continued to look straight down without saying a word.

Later that day, Lonnie at Sudz Laundromat in Pacific Grove let me do my laundry free of charge and made a donation to the Marty Lyons Foundation.

We had dinner that night at Isabella's on Monterey's Fisherman's Wharf, home to probably the best New England clam chowder I've ever had, and enjoyed our last night together as a family.

It was hard to say goodbye again the next morning. Mom begged me not to bike on major highways anymore, so when they watched me bike away from the hotel, I stayed on a bike path until I was out of sight. Then I got back on the freeway. Ironically, a little while later a California Highway Patrol car pulled me over.

As the cop flicked his lights on and I came to a stop, he said over the inter-com, booming loud and clear, "*Not the best place to be ridin' a bicycle*," in a very sarcastic tone, which actually made me laugh. It was true. It wasn't the best place to be riding a bicycle. I was desensitized to being pulled over at this point, and this officer seemed to have a better sense of humor than the others—I wasn't too worried, and he didn't end up writing me a ticket. But after that, I had to get off the freeway (all California freeway entrances clearly said, "No Bicycles," so I couldn't play dumb).

Inching closer to the Bay Area, I stopped that night at the beautiful Costa-noa Resort in Pescadero, looking to camp. The place had a range of accommo-dations, from upscale hotel rooms to cabins to yurts to a campground. I ended up getting a yurt for the night, which was basically a framed white tent with wood flooring and a real bed. With the lack of insulation, it got cold in there in the middle of the night, but the bed was heated with an electric blanket, which was *really* nice.

Long before I went to sleep, though, I went to the resort restaurant and had a pot roast dinner at the bar. A guy named Mark Schaaf overheard me talking to the bartender about the trip as I ate, and said, "Your dinner's on Google's tab tonight." Mark was a high-level guy at Google, there for a team-building retreat for the company's mobile ads division. He would later go on to be the CTO at Instacart, another major Silicon Valley company.

Mark invited me to join the large, overwhelmingly very-young group for drinks upstairs, so of course, I went—and ended up hanging out with the group late into the night. At first, my story was that I was a new summer intern that had just joined, and that I'd come over from the Yahoo mobile ads division, where I'd interned the previous summer. They believed me, at first, but by the end of the night everyone knew I was the biker who crashed the party (they were pretty smart, obviously).

It was a really fun night, partly because of the spontaneity of it, and after we sat around a fire under the stars into the early morning hours, the team invited me to a large breakfast. At breakfast, I spoke to another high-level guy, who was having trouble fathoming how or why I'd biked so far, for so long, and how I still had so far *to go*. And he, especially, couldn't comprehend how I was so *upbeat* about it. "Well, you definitely have the right attitude," he said, shaking his head.

I biked into San Francisco that day, stopping for lunch on the way at The Main Street Grill in Half Moon Bay. As I approached The City by the Bay in the late afternoon, MGMT's "Electric Feel" playing on my iPod, the hills became extreme. I passed golf courses, Golden Gate Park, and the Presidio before finding myself in the heart of the city.

The iconic crimson-and-gold cable cars shook the ground as they rumbled by, bells ringing. A high-pitched, flute-like sound in the streets was somehow reminiscent of the 5:00 whistle that announced quitting time for Industrial Revolution factory workers, or the whistle of a steam engine rolling into town, full of excited, weary travelers in their top hats and dresses. The sound took you back more than 100 years if you closed your eyes. The downhills were so steep, though, that you'd be out of control in about a second and a half if you weren't careful. So my eyes remained open. I'd always loved San Francisco.

Despite the city's traditional charm and lovable landmarks, 2012 was the beginning of a homelessness epidemic in San Francisco and other temperate West Coast cities, fueled by housing affordability issues and drug addiction. People living in tent cities and on sidewalks was beginning to become commonplace. The problem has put the city on the brink of a public health crisis, with the potential for disease outbreaks not seen since the Middle Ages.

The West Coast issue brings to light an even larger-scale problem facing the US in the 2010s and 2020s, especially in rural areas—the Opioid Epidemic.

Since I graduated high school in 2006, six people from my high school class have died from drug overdoses. *Six*. Most of these deaths occurred a few years after high school, but the most recent was in 2018. Clinical studies have shown that medications, like methadone, can be highly effective in treating opioid addiction, yet most drug treatment centers don't use them, saying they "replace one drug with another." With drug overdose deaths involving opioids increasing exponentially between 2012 and the end of the decade[14], maybe it's time to change this approach.

I had to walk my bike up one side of the extremely steep Lombard Street; I then biked down the other side, the top of which was a major landmark of the city because it's known as "the most crooked street" in the world (in 1922, the homeowners of the street decided it was too steep for comfort, so they decided to give it eight sharp turns to make it more manageable). Biking down it was tricky. I had to squeeze the brakes as much as I could, and slowly navigate the eight sharp turns without losing my balance and crashing to the red brick below. There were also slow-moving cars to contend with.

From the crooked street, it was only a few minutes to the hotel at Fisherman's Wharf, where I was meeting my oldest friend, Brendan Murphy. Our parents were friends, so we'd known each other literally since birth; I was born about three months before him. Decades before our parents met, my great-grandfather, "Pop," lived right beside Brendan's great-grandmother in Brooklyn—their back-to-back backyards shared a fence. It was an extraordinary coincidence.

Pop had fought for Italy and the Allies in World War I, alongside the United States. He survived a German mustard gas attack by following a cat that had climbed up a tree, literally peeled his army uniform off in strips after weeks of nonstop rain on the front lines trapped in a trench, and barely survived a German prison camp by using a napkin to collect the breadcrumbs from the single piece of bread he was served each day, so that nothing was lost.

"The crumbs made the difference," he told my dad, decades later. He swore by it.

Pop lived to ninety-six years old. I was a baby when he died, so, technically, I met him. There's even a picture of me, my dad, my grandfather, and Pop together—four generations in one photo, made possible by breadcrumbs.

Brendan's great-grandmother didn't know Pop as the hardy, gritty, tough-as-nails, trench warfare and prison camp survivor that he was, though; she just knew him in Brooklyn as "the gentle neighbor who loved to feed the birds," and sometimes climb his tree.

Brendan and I had gone on family vacations to the Outer Banks, visited each other in college, backpacked through Europe, run with the bulls in Pamplona, and gone on countless other adventures. So I wasn't really surprised when he told me he was flying all the way out to San Francisco just for the weekend (I had two rest days scheduled).

He called me a couple of months before when he was booking his flight. "Alright, so . . . I'm booking my flight . . . so . . . you're gonna *be* there, right?"

I promised him I would. He'd never been to San Francisco, so we explored and did some sightseeing, then saw the Giants play the Cubs at my favorite baseball stadium (other than Yankee Stadium, of course) after pregaming at the 21st Amendment Brewery down the block—whose signature Hell or High Watermelon beer is bizarrely (and wonderfully) served with a slice of watermelon. The Giants won the game, and went on to win the World Series that year.

After the game, we walked to Kells Irish Pub near the TransAm Pyramid. Apparently, there was another McAleese family, this one straight from Ireland, that owned a string of West Coast pubs named Kells. Paul McAleese owned the one in San Francisco, Patrick McAleese owned the one in Seattle, and the family had two other establishments in Portland. The West Coast McAleese brothers were as charming and friendly as they were swashbuckling and colorful, much like their East Coast counterparts—my uncles. There was no relation as far we could tell, but McAleese is a very rare Irish name, so it isn't such a stretch to imagine a connection going back a few generations. (While rare, the name McAleese is known in Ireland; Mary McAleese was the eighth president of the country from 1997-2011. On a visit to New York in 2002, she asked about Uncle Brian when she saw his name on a memorial and then sought out and met our family.) Paul certainly treated us like family, welcoming us to his handsome, very lively pub and buying all our beer. I tried to pay for our drinks, but he wouldn't have it. In fact, I've been back to his bar in years since, and I still can't pay for a drink there. "Get the fuck outta here" is all he'll say, in his thick Irish brogue.

There are things about the US that Paul doesn't like, and he'll be vocal about them. But he'll also say, "America is the greatest *idea*. Ever. In the history of the world."

I gave him one of Uncle Brian's mass cards that first night we met. It was obvious that he was genuinely thrilled to have it, carefully handling it as if I'd just given him a fragile piece of pottery worth millions of dollars. It was clear that he felt a connection to our family and our loss, whether we were related in some crazy way or not.

Brendan and I did more sightseeing the next day and had dinner on Fisherman's Wharf, where we had a long conversation. I could tell he was happy for me for the experience I was having, for making it to California and not giving up—as a true friend would be. Somehow, the conversation turned to relationships and marriage—a topic we'd almost certainly never covered before. Why would we? We were twenty-four. He was at a point in his life where he'd been out of college and in the "real world" for a couple of years, and his relationship with his college girlfriend was kind of at a crossroads. I certainly wasn't a relationship expert by any stretch, and I hadn't even experienced the "real world" yet, but I told him what I'd always felt about relationships and marriage.

I said, "I think deciding who to marry is the most important decision you make in your life," echoing advice from Nana Mac. "And if you're with the right person, it's the easiest."

He broke up with his girlfriend soon after.

Our parents were having dinner together at the very same time that night, back on the East Coast, and we spoke to them on the phone. Brendan's dad, Kevin, kept saying how lucky we were to have the travel experiences we'd had, at just twenty-four years old. When we travel and go on vacation, we're very *present*—it's hard not to be. It's one of the best things about traveling.

Kevin was writing a spiritual book at the time, titled *The Three Rooms*. The core message of the book suggests that the best way to achieve happiness and fulfillment is to live in the present, or keep our thoughts in "The Present Room," and that depression and anxiety can only exist if our thoughts are in the Past or Future Rooms, respectively. Here's one of my favorite passages:

> Let's go back to some of the feelings you experience in the Past Room, like anger, jealousy, bitterness, and regret. What do they all have in common? They are all rooted in fear. When your thoughts are stuck in the Past Room, they are dominated by fear. Now let's look at some of the feelings you experience in the Future Room, like stress, anxiety, pessimism, and lack. What do they all have in common? They, too, are all rooted in fear. Finally, let's look at the feelings you experience in the Present Room, like peace, joy, appreciation, and compassion. What do they all have in common? They are all aspects of love. You can't find fear in the Present Room because it cannot coexist with love. There is only love, and only love is real. Therefore, only the Present Room, where you experience love, is real.
>
> – Kevin Murphy, *The Three Rooms*

I can't help but think of Uncle Brian's locker when I read this. *NO FEAR*.

In 2021, toward the end of the Covid pandemic, Kevin received shocking news. He was diagnosed with an aggressive form of prostate cancer at age sixty. He beat it, though. There isn't a doubt in my mind that his unrelenting optimism and spirituality had a lot to do with it. Or *everything* to do with it. He's always been one of the most positive-minded people I've ever known.

Later that night, we met up with one of Brendan's college buddies and had a night out on the town, staying out way later than we should have. Abandoning the maturity of our dinner conversation like a sinking ship, we partied like we were in college again and got kicked out of a '50s-style diner late at night after someone in our crew threw up everywhere.

When I first woke up the next morning, I rolled over and lazily looked at the clock radio between our beds, thinking, *Hmm, that can't be right.* Then my heart leapt right out of my chest as I jumped up, jolted by sudden shock wave of adrenaline.

I shouted at Brendan, *"Wake up! We overslept!"* which prompted a *Home Alone*-like mad frenzy at fast-forward speed to pack up his things and get him to the airport. It was a valiant effort, but Brendan missed his flight back to New York. He ended up having to take the red-eye later that night and went straight into his office in Manhattan the following morning.

***

While Brendan was at SFO, trying to get on another flight, I was making my way over the Golden Gate Bridge. I considered the Golden Gate to be the journey's symbolic halfway point. The bridge was about halfway up the PCH, which was the middle stretch of the trip. The bridge, constructed during the Great Depression and considered to be a symbol of American perseverance, with its burnt orange towers and cables, often shrouded by "Karl," the name locals have affectionately given to their frequent fog, is *so* impressive in person.

Back on the PCH the next day, another cyclist caught up to me. Finally, someone else heading north. The tall White man's name was Peter Dewaard, and he was a bit of an odd sight. Riding a bike with three wheels, he had a British accent, small round glasses, and a long, streaming, silver ponytail. The third wheel was directly behind the back wheel, and carried small panniers of its own.

Peter and I started talking as we rode, but it was more like screaming because of the wind. Between the wind and his thick British accent, there were times that I couldn't understand a single word he was saying. There was barely any shoulder and a decent amount of traffic, so definitely *not* enough room, in my opinion, to be riding side by side, carrying on a casual conversation. I hugged the white line, and Peter was right in the middle of the two-lane high-way, flirting with the double yellow line on the curvy, coast-hugging PCH. He didn't seem to mind the cars repeatedly honking at him, and later told me that he usually rides right in the middle of the road *anyway*, so cars are forced to slow down and pass him as they would a slow-moving vehicle.

Traveling a little lighter than I was, he went ahead of me as it got more mountainous. I crawled over a steep, but scenic, oceanside bluff at the very end of the day (I swear I've seen it in a car commercial), eating Skittles Mom had sent me in the mail between switchbacks for a little extra energy. I didn't think I'd ever catch him, but when I hopped off the bike to check out a motel in Fort Ross, I saw him waving and calling from a distance.

"John, Johhnnnnn! Over here!" He offered to split his two-bed motel room.

Since it was cold and rainy and would be half the cost, I happily took him up on it.

For dinner, we traded food in the room. He gave me a peanut butter sandwich and a can of peaches in exchange for a Clif Bar and a 5-Hour Energy, two food items he'd never tried or heard of. We shared the large bag of Skittles (he called them Ski'les) for dessert. He said "porridge" instead of oatmeal, and, of course, "holiday" instead of vacation. Instead of showering, he took a long bubble bath in the motel room bathroom before we went to sleep early.

I only had $10 cash on me, so I bought him breakfast the next morning with my credit card to pay him back for my share of the room (Venmo wasn't really a thing yet). We rode a mile down the road and stopped at the plush Timber Cove Inn for an expensive, but delicious, strawberry pancake breakfast. It was a fancy, quiet place with a few other tables of people and considerable ocean views.

For at least ten minutes after we sat down at our formal, white cloth-covered table, Peter kept his old-fashioned bicycle helmet on, balanced high atop his head. For some reason, this was *hilarious* to me. I could barely contain myself; inside, I was laughing hysterically. The older couple sitting next to us seemed to be entertained by the sight of us, and by our conversation.

After breakfast, Peter went ahead of me. After I stopped for the Five-Mile Water/Stretch, I knew I wouldn't catch him.

That day was a long one up the coast to Fort Bragg, where my grandfather on my dad's side, Papa Nitti (Pop's son), was stationed during World War II, waiting to be sent to Japan. If the US hadn't dropped the bombs on Hiroshima and Nagasaki to end the war, he would've been sent, and I almost certainly wouldn't have been born, whether he survived or not.

I had a rest day in Fort Bragg, then camped out in the redwoods the next night, just south of Garberville, as the road turned away from the coast and into thick redwood forest. After Fort Bragg, Route 1 ended for good and merged with 101. For the rest of the way, the PCH would be 101.

The forest campground I found was full of motorcyclists there for the Redwood Run, a big annual biker rally that weekend. The bikers welcomed me as a fellow biker, Harley or not. One group picked up a burger for me and handed me a $20 bill with it, "for the road." I found a nice spot under a tremendous redwood tree to pitch my tent and hung out with another group at the campsite next to mine around their campfire, drinking beer and eating tri-tip and peanuts. We sat there, telling stories and talking about life, late into the night. The whole thing was a big party, with campfires and music everywhere, the orange fires glowing amongst dark, gigantic redwood trees, under a very nearly full moon. It looked like the cover of Greta Van Fleet's *From the Fires* album—and was reminiscent of the final, celebratory scene of 1983's *Star Wars: Return of the Jedi* on the forest moon of Endor, but with burly bikers with tattoos and black leather jackets instead of little teddy bear-like Ewoks with walking sticks and spears.

Waking up in a tent in the redwoods the next morning was astonishingly peaceful. The day would end up being one of the most enjoyable days of biking of the entire trip. Maybe *the* most. It would take me through the heart of the redwoods, one of the world's most inconceivable and awe-inspiring places.

The Pacific Coast Highway meanders its way in and out of pockets of redwood forest, sometimes transitioning abruptly from windswept ocean cliffs to deep, dark, quiet, fairy tale-like woodland. There are, perhaps, no other places in the world where the forest so dramatically meets the sea.

There was one particular stretch of redwood forest that was most memorable. It's a small stretch between Phillipsville and Pepperwood, in Humboldt Redwoods State Park. I turned the music off for this stretch, so it was just me and the forest. Incredible quietude. Maybe it was because the road in this particular pocket ran parallel to the bustling 101, which is a major freeway at this point, and so it had barely any traffic at all. It might as well have been a thousand miles away from the freeway, a thousand years ago. Maybe it was because the road was so narrow and the trees were so enormous that it barely felt like a road at *all*. Whatever the reason, its name certainly helped make it my favorite. It was an epic name, of sorts, that seemed to adequately suit the road's majesty. This stretch, a legendary road out west, is known as the Avenue of the Giants.

The world's tallest trees, redwoods can live to be over two thousand years old and have been on Earth for 240 million years, surviving the asteroid impact that killed off the dinosaurs.[15] The largest have trunks twenty feet wide and grow to heights of nearly 400 feet—much taller than the length of a football field. They once inhabited a much-larger portion of the planet, but are now only found in Northern California and Southern Oregon, near the coast.

To properly give a sense of just how old these trees are, imagine the oldest fence in New York City—the wrought iron fence that surrounds the FiDi's Bowling Green in Lower Manhattan, built in 1771. The fence that was across the street from George Washington's Revolutionary War headquarters. The fence that has seen the entirety of American history—from watching a revved-up mob tear down the park's lead statue of King George III after hearing the Declaration of Independence read aloud for the first time in 1776 (before melting the statue down for ammunition to use against the British); to surviving New York's Great Fire of 1835, in which virtually all of Lower Manhattan was reduced to rubble on a night so frigid that firefighters' water supply was frozen (before consuming all of New York City, the fire was eventually stopped by the Marines by blowing up buildings along Wall Street in an act of desperation to create a literal firewall[16]); to witnessing the construction of the nearby Brooklyn Bridge in the late nineteenth century; to accompanying generations of twentieth century Wall Street workers taking their lunch breaks beside it; to reveling in joyous ticker-tape parades for Amelia Earhart, international dignitaries, Nelson Mandela, JFK, the Apollo XI astronauts when they returned from the moon, and the New York Yankees after World Series victories passing it; to feeling the horrific rumble of the Twin Towers collapsing a few blocks away at the start of the twenty-first century; to celebrating the US Women's World Cup soccer team, to discreetly photo-bombing tourists' photos of the petite *Fearless Girl* statue defiantly standing up to Wall Street's colossal *Charging Bull* in 2017. If you visit the fence today, there's a sign on the south end of it, by the National Museum of the American Indian. It reads:

BOWLING GREEN FENCE
ERECTED BY THE COMMON COUNCIL IN 1771, THIS FENCE
SURROUNDS NEW YORK'S EARLIEST PARK. THE PARK WAS LEASED
IN 1733 FOR USE AS A BOWLING GREEN AT A RENTAL OF ONE
PEPPERCORN A YEAR. PATRIOTS, WHO IN 1776 DESTROYED AN
EQUESTRIAN STATUE OF GEORGE III WHICH STOOD HERE, ARE
SAID TO HAVE REMOVED THE CROWNS WHICH CAPPED THE
FENCE POSTS BUT THE FENCE ITSELF REMAINS

For years after the bike trip, when I was living by Battery Park, all "Bowling Green" meant to me was that I was home. It was my subway stop—a particularly quiet one at night by Manhattan standards—on the north end of Battery Park, just a couple of minutes on foot from my apartment. I walked by it all the time, but it took years for me to finally realize the Green and its fence had seen so much.

Now again, imagine that inanimate fence, and its 250-year history, and multiply it by eight. That's two thousand years. That's how long many of these individual redwood trees in California had *lived*. Now, multiply it by a *million*. That's how long this hardy tree species has survived on this planet. A million times longer than the United States of America.

The towering ancients rendered a pleasant shade, allowing just enough light to trickle through to create an air of mystique, constructing this otherworldly sanctuary one couldn't help but feel blessed to enter. The shade from the trees made the middle of the day feel like late afternoon, and late afternoon feel like something else altogether. It had to be the most magical place on Earth. Stopping for a breather was like pausing for a moment of silence in a great Gothic cathedral, sunlight transcending through stained glass windows. This, no doubt, was a holy place. This was God's work. And it felt more sacred than any manmade structure could be. Like gargoyles on the cathedral roof, the treetops seemed to whisper secrets amongst themselves. It was as if I could almost hear them, faintly, with the ruffle of the occasional, delicate zephyr—secrets hundreds, and even thousands, of years old, no one person could ever know. They were proud of these secrets, and proud of their grandeur, but still welcoming, allowing you to become a part of their abundant history, even for just a minuscule moment in their time.

It was definitely a positive, welcoming kind of vibe, supporting the ancient belief that good spirits lived in trees. And maybe, just maybe, it felt this way because there was more of a connection between people and the redwood trees than I'd realized. Years after I had my experience biking through the redwoods, National Geographic interviewed Sammy Gensaw, the young Native American leader of an environmental activist group named the Ancestral Guard. He revealed an interesting Native American custom that goes back hundreds of generations:

> For the Yurok tribe there is a tradition that when a baby is born the father takes the after-birth (the placenta) and places it at the root system of a baby Redwood tree. They take care of that tree the same as the child with the belief that the health and spirit of both are now linked.
>
> Science now tells us that mycelium connects all Redwood trees in the forest. If a tree is sick, the forest knows and sends energy its way. By putting our genetic material at the root systems of these trees for thousands of years we have also become part of this interconnectedness. It's something spiritual for my people but I also believe it's probably true on a molecular level.[17]

The redwoods accepted me into their beautiful world as a quiet, harmless passerby. Yes, as some of the oldest living organisms on Earth, they demanded your respect. But there was this indescribable feeling of embrace. Infused with, but resistant to, the passage of time, these great-grandfather trees had an alluring wistfulness about them, evoking a perplexing nostalgia indifferent of one's past. The soaring trees were a snapshot of another epoch, a window to another world. They were a powerful reminder of the brevity of our stay on this unique planet. *These trees that shield me from the sun were here long before me, and they'll be here long after I'm gone.*

And, too, the cyclist could appreciate the redwoods so much more than the motorist, on multiple sensory levels. You could look up and see their utter immensity. Inhale their heavy, pristine oxygen. Smell their fern. Taste their bark. Touch their cool shade. Hear their silence.

On a few occasions, there were long, grueling climbs in the Redwoods—easily the steepest since the Rockies—followed by exhilarating forest roller coaster rides. Those downhills were some of the most memorable of the entire trip.

I stayed at a motel in Fortuna that night, then stopped at the Lost Coast Brewery in Eureka for lunch the next day. I first heard about the remote "Lost Coast" by nearby Capetown when my high school calculus teacher, Mr. Ciolfi, told the class about when he and his brother flew out to "find" it by surfing its renowned, secret-spot-feel waves. As they were about to hop in the water, though, they came across an orca that had just washed up, rolling in the surf. It had a tremendous chunk of flesh bitten out of it—a bite that could have only come from a great white shark. Despite traveling all that way, the brothers decided not to stick around. The coast remained Lost. At the brewery, I asked a couple sitting next to me to watch my bike through the window while I went to the bathroom.

When I thanked the guy when I got back, he said, "I've always admired the 520."

He was referring to my bike, of course—a Trek 520. His face was sincere and approving, with a long, distinguishable goatee. He said he used to work at a bike shop, which sparked a lengthy conversation about the trip as we ate lunch. James and Sarah Smith lived in nearby Arcata, and offered to put me up that night.

James and Sarah competed every year on Memorial Day weekend in the Kinetic Grand Championship—a three-day, forty- to fifty-mile race in Humboldt

County, in which participants navigate giant bicycle-powered sculptures through sand dunes, water, mud, and roadways. It was the "Triathlon of the Art World," and the couple just happened to captain the perennial powerhouse team, a team they called "The Tempus Fugitives." I was immediately intrigued. I mean, how could you not be? The rules of the competition state:

> Bodies are our only Batteries. All energy used to move your sculpture forward on the course must be Kinetic, not potential, which means no batteries or other form of stored energy can be used for propulsion except for the calories stored in your Pilots. Acceptable energy sources include: Pilots, wind, sun, gravity, and friendly aliens (from another planet, not another country) as long as they are presented to officials before the start of the race.[18]

The 2012 vehicle of The Tempus Fugitives was a giant cockroach, dubbed "The Apocalyptic Cockroach," because December 21, 2012, was supposed to be the end of the world, according to some doomsday sayers, since it was the end of the Mayan long count calendar. (I remember Ty Siam saying in college, "Either the end of the world is coming . . . or the calligrapher got tired.")

James and Sarah couldn't wait to show me their humungous bug, which weighed in at about 2,000 pounds and could seat four pedalers. We drove all the way over to their garage workshop just to see it. They said it was pretty expensive and a ton of work to build the thing (and it showed—the functionality, art, and engineering were all really, really impressive), so they were planning on beating it up with baseball bats, etc. and reusing it for 2013's race, where they'd call it "The Post-Apocalyptic Cockroach."

We grabbed beers at the Redwood Curtain brewery nearby and later had a fun steak, salad, and corn-on-the-cob dinner with their friends back at their house.

"Welcome to Marijuana Country," they said, as we clinked glasses.

Arcata is known for its weed, for whatever reason. As soon as I got back on the freeway the next morning, I was greeted with an overwhelming whiff of weed wafting through the air. Marijuana Country indeed.

It was another beautiful ride through the redwoods on the way to Crescent City, my last stop in California before crossing into Oregon. A senior Canadian couple, appreciating the forest by their car, stopped me as I passed them. They were eager to talk, and insisted that I take a large glass bottle of fresh maple syrup with me; it was from their farm in Quebec. I didn't have any room in my bags and didn't want to carry any more weight, so I politely declined the offer. But they insisted, so I crammed the heavy bottle of syrup into my rear panniers, making a mental note to use the stuff as soon as possible so I could get rid of it. I then passed a giant statue of Paul Bunyan and his blue ox Babe in the forest in Klamath and asked a tourist to take my picture in front of it, mimicking Bunyan's waving gesture like a little kid on a field trip.

The redwood forest in the late afternoon was so thick that sunlight barely transcended it, adding to the aura and enchantment. It was no wonder that other cultures have special words for this magic—words such as *komorebi* in Japanese and *waldeinsamkeit* in German, which have no direct translation to English. *Komorebi* roughly translates to "the interplay of light and leaves when sunlight shines through trees" and *waldeinsamkeit* to "the feeling of being alone in the woods, connecting with nature." The redwoods were certainly deserving of special words like these. They'd earned them. Being in the forest has also proven to have physical benefits for people, as well as psychological. Studies have shown that being around trees reduces stress and strengthens your immune system.[19]

There were a couple of winding climbs at the very end of the day in the darkening forest, then a descent into Crescent City on the coast, where I stayed at the Curly Redwood Lodge, a motel built with the wood from a single redwood tree (yes, just one tree) that was struck by lightning decades ago. The motel was clean and old-fashioned; it seemed nothing at all had been changed since the 1960s or 1970s.

I had a big breakfast the next morning at the restaurant across the road, called Fisherman's. When the waitress asked if I wanted syrup for my pancakes, I told her I had some—then took the large glass bottle of maple syrup from the Canadian couple out of my windbreaker pocket, feeling a bit like Will Ferrell in *Elf* as I opened it and poured it generously over my pancakes.

A Last Look

OREGON PART 1
JUNE 11–24

"Only the Ocean" – Jack Johnson

I crossed into Oregon on Monday, June 11, and stayed at Motel 101 in Gold Beach for $50, which was a good deal—especially because it included a free continental breakfast (albeit a very limited one). The ride from Gold Beach to Bandon was notable because I was pleasantly surprised when I stopped for lunch at The Crazy Norwegian's Fish & Chips in Port Orford. It was easily the best fish and chips I'd ever had in my life.

As I ate dinner in Bandon that evening, at a Chinese restaurant, an elderly couple out to dinner with their neighbors in the booth across from mine overheard me asking the waitress about motels and campgrounds in the area. A little later, the woman, Alexis Proctor, went out of her way to come over to my table to offer a place to stay. I was slightly ahead of schedule (because I had originally planned a detour to go whitewater rafting on the Umpqua River with my college roommates when they were still part of the trip—and you can't really sign up for a whitewater rafting trip alone), so I decided to stay with her and her husband George for two nights at their lovely, modern home in Bandon, near the beach.

I had the upstairs loft to myself—it had a very comfortable bed with warm flannel sheets. Knowing that I was on the raw, misty, rainy, rocky Oregon coast made the flannel sheets seem even warmer. Alexis and George made me feel very much at home; I felt like I was staying at my grandparents' house. We watched TV and played board games before going to sleep.

George Proctor was an eighty-seven-year-old World War II veteran. I listened to his stories over breakfast the next morning. George and I sat and talked for a couple of hours in their kitchen; I always considered it a real treat to speak to someone from the Greatest Generation. There weren't many WWII vets left. Both my grandfathers had served in the military (Papa Nitti in WWII, Papa Mac in the Korean War) and had since passed. If they could come back for a day, I'd ask them to tell more stories. War stories. Love stories. *Any* stories.

Of course, my grandfathers can't come back; for a couple of hours, though, I felt like I had a piece of them back, in the form of George Proctor. So I asked for stories, and he was willing to tell them. He told me about how he was drafted and stationed in Borneo, about his world travels and how he once rode a train from San Francisco to North Carolina, and a bunch of other anecdotes. My favorite story, though, and certainly the funniest, was about him and his friend John Henry. George and John were transporting beer rations between their ship and the port in Borneo during WWII when a case of beer went overboard, toppling off the small boat they were on. John Henry quickly jumped in after it, wrapping his arms around it and claiming it was his because of the "Salvage Rule." He shouted out, "Salvage Rule! It's mine!" The military police fired a few gunshots in his general direction, ordering him to give it back. John audaciously fired back and was court-martialed, but won in court because he was, in fact, *correct* that anyone who salvaged something that had gone overboard had the right to keep that object. The military police ended up getting in trouble! We both got a good laugh out of that one, sitting in their quiet, sun-drenched kitchen that morning on the Oregon coast, some seventy years later.

Later that day, we took their golden retrievers for a walk on the beautiful boulder-strewn beach near their home, taking in the picturesque rocky coastline and playing fetch with the dogs as they ran around and barked loudly. Alexis and

George pointed out the different rock formations in the water and what they were named, notably "Face Rock," and farther away, to its northwest, "Cat and Kittens Rock." A large volcanic plug out in the water, Face Rock looked like a gigantic rock mermaid from an ancient tall tale surfacing—her eyes, nose, and mouth looking nearly straight upward, her ear just above the water line, and her hair flowing behind it. There was, in fact, a legend about her. But she wasn't a mermaid. It was a Native American story, and she was Chief Siskiyou's beautiful daughter Ewauna.

To greet Chief Siskiyou and Ewauna, who were coming to the coast from far away in the mountains, the four chiefs of the coast planned a grand potlatch, complete with large quantities of clams, mussels, salmon, elk meat, huckleberries, and wild honey. Armed warriors were watching so that Seatka, the evil spirit of the ocean, could not cause trouble.

After the feast, Ewauna went down to the beach with her dog, Komax, and her cat and kittens, which she carried in a basket. She had never seen the ocean before, thinking it was most beautiful, for she thought that, at last, she had found the place where the beautiful white clouds that she saw each day from her home in the mountains were made. Singing her dance song to the full Chinook moon, she dropped her basket, telling Komax to watch, and waded into the cool water. She began swimming, soon far from shore, paying no heed to the dog's cry of danger from the beach. The friendly moon became obscured, and suddenly she was grasped by a fearsome creature! It was the dreaded Seatka.

Komax, who had failed to make her hear his danger call, swam out with the basket and, as the monster seized his beloved mistress, he stuck his sharp teeth into his hand. Howling with rage he kicked the dog off, causing him to drop the basket. Grabbing the cat and kittens he threw them far out into the sea. Seatka held the girl tightly, trying to make her look at him, as his treacherous power lay in his eyes. This she refused to do, telling him she never would, keeping her face toward the friendly moon.

At sunrise her father awoke and finding his daughter gone gave the alarm. They all rushed to the sea. Fearfully they gazed out, seeing the dawn break through the white mist, and then they saw the beautiful face of Ewauna lying on the sea smiling up at the white clouds coming from the north. To the west they saw her cat and kittens and near the beach poor Komax baying for his mistress. Behind the large rocks near the shore sits Seatka, gazing at Ewauna still trying to catch her eye. But never, never does she falter. Many, many moons she has been there. Now they have all turned to stone.

-Written by Ottilie Parker Kronenberg (1865-1943).
As a young child, she often listened to "Mary," one of the last of the
Nasomah (Coquille) tribe, and delighted in the many
Native American stories Mary told her.

After the hearty omelet and toast breakfast Alexis made for me the next morning, I took photos with Alexis and George in their driveway, with their house behind us, to remember them. George passed away in 2016, at the age of ninety-two.

I got an early start, riding past Face Rock (or Ewauna) and through the nice Old Town section of Bandon, which looked like a weathered fishing village in Alaska, or Greenland—where buildings are painted certain colors to reveal what they are (red for store, for example[20]), which is useful when everything is buried in snow. Then I got back on 101 and made it as far as Reedsport that day, where I had terrible pizza that tasted like cardboard for dinner. *Not too surprising*, I thought, for Oregon pizza.

I slept in a little later than planned the next morning, and the Fir Grove Motel owner apologized, proudly, for the bed being "too comfortable," as I wheeled my bike across his parking lot. I made it to Waldport that day, a nice little oceanside town that was celebrating their "Beachcomber Days" weekend with live music and a big crowd, relishing the sunshine and unseasonably hot weather. My motel neighbors—a grandfather, father, and son—were celebrating Father's Day weekend with some crabbing, and offered me a beer and "the best crab we got" from the large pot that was the centerpiece of their parking lot setup. I spoke to my dad on the phone to wish him a Happy Father's Day, and it made me miss home.

The ride on Father's Day the next day was short (just forty miles), calm, gray, and misty, with more great fish and chips for an early lunch at the South Beach Fish Market just south of Newport. In Newport, I hid the bike behind a shed and walked along the beach to check out a seventy-foot, concrete dock that had washed up all the way from a fishing port in Japan—it was wreckage from the catastrophic March 2011 tsunami, which caused the Fukushima nuclear disaster. (In one of the greatest displays of heroism in modern times, over 200 Japanese retirees selflessly volunteered to clean up the radioactive contamination so that members of the younger generation wouldn't have to expose themselves.) The Japanese markings on the side of the dock proved its authenticity. It took a little over a year to float across the Pacific, and a crowd had gathered to quietly investigate, perplexed by the magnitude of its passive journey.

Later, I found a quirky, kitschy motel called the Historic Anchor Inn in Lincoln City to spend the night and a rainy rest day the next day. The place was reminiscent of Route 66, with historical trinkets and creepy mannequins adorning it. My room was old, wooden, and cozy, with more flannel sheets and a separate living room with a couch and TV. The wood-paneled bedroom had paintings of a weathered, gray-bearded fisherman, the rugged coastline, and a lighthouse, and an old-fashioned lamp in the corner, giving me the feeling of being in the sleeping quarters of an old tall ship creaking in the waves.

I rented out DVDs, including *Slumdog Millionaire* and *21*, and got theater-style, buttered popcorn from the front desk, happy to be inside and protected from the elements. And grateful for a hunkered-down, rainy rest day watching movies. The place was also a great deal—just $130 for two nights, with an included made-to-order hot breakfast.

As I tried the Inn's "Experimental Breakfast," the waitress told me her name was "Misty, like the weather." The local news announced the US Open winner that year was a devout Christian. The elderly White news anchor remarked, "It's nice to see some young fella athletes not afraid to confess their faith in Jesus." You'd *never* see that on the news in New York.

Early the next day, I stopped in Lincoln City for a long pause to look at the ocean from the road, high above the shore. It was the last time I'd see it before turning inland. It was a peculiarly long stop. I just kept staring out at it. It was an overcast, gray day. I've always considered the ocean to have these kind of magic healing powers, both physical and psychological. And much like the redwoods, it has such an abundant history and mystique, intertwined with countless legends and lore. The most mystifying thing about the ocean, I think, is its sheer size; more than 80% of it remains unmapped and unexplored by humans.[21]

I continued to stare out at the ocean like it was the last time I'd ever see it. The last time you ever see the ocean—for real—will you *know* it's the last time? Probably not, for the vast majority of us. Uncle Brian definitely didn't know on September 9, 2001. I remember the last time Papa Nitti came to the beach with us. Born a thirteen-pound baby on an ironing board in a fish market in Brooklyn in 1920, he was then in his eighties, struggling with Parkinson's; it had become difficult for him to make it down to the beach. When we arrived, he said, "Wow. Look at that *ocean*." Maybe he was one of the few that knew. Even though I was almost certain it *wouldn't* be the last time I'd ever see it, I looked at it that day in Lincoln City as if it were. And now I can say I've looked at the ocean like that, whenever the real last time may be.

Back on the road, I passed a sign that read "45th Parallel – Halfway Between the Equator and North Pole" and then made the big right turn—the one that Bruce joked about in LA—onto 18 and immediately picked up a nice tailwind into McMinnville. It was the first time on the trip I was headed east. I'd biked long stretches in every other direction, but not yet east. I felt like a veteran now, and it was reassuring that every mile I biked brought me a mile closer to home. For the first time on the trip, I was sure I was going to make it—the whole way, there and back.

In McMinnville, I took the gear off the bike (leaving it at the motel) and biked around town without it for the first time, looking for a place to eat. The bike felt feather-light and naked, and accelerated like a Corvette. It was a freeing, weird feeling to ride like that. From McMinnville, I continued through wine country the next day into Portland, one of the most bike-friendly cities in the world. There were wide, green, bike lanes and bike shops everywhere you looked.

I stayed with my mom's college roommate, Monique Topelmann, her husband, Lars—who was a professional photographer—and their two sons, Karsten and Finn. Karsten, eighteen, had just graduated high school and was on his way to the University of Oregon in the fall, and Finn was thirteen, still in middle school. They were both tall with thin builds and fairly long, wavy hair. Lars was bald, with a long goatee, which was his trademark. In their travels, a toddler in Ireland once called him "The Goat Man" and the name kind of stuck. I still think of him as "The Goat Man," actually. Monique had long dark hair and a pretty, natural-looking face that fit her free spirit and suggested she loved the outdoors.

The Topelmann family hosted me for three enjoyable rest days in Portland. On the first day, we dropped the bike off for its third tune-up, checked out Lars's photography studio, and went to their friends' barbecue. The occasion was a send-off for a German exchange student that none of the host families particularly liked very much (so it really *was* a celebration). We also went out for pizza at Apizza Scholls, a little, unassuming place on SE Hawthorne Boulevard, with partially wood-paneled walls, Portland-brewed IPAs on tap, including the best-selling Breakside Wanderlust, a super laid-back and friendly staff with beards and tattoos, and seriously outstanding pizza. It's been ranked as one of the top pizzerias in America, for good reason, and the locals know it as *the* place for pizza in Portland.

As we enjoyed the pizza at our table by the window, Karsten and Finn got us into a lengthy discussion about Led Zeppelin and *Lord of the Rings*, two franchises they were apparently huge fans of (especially the younger one, Finn).

"So you must love 'Ramble On,' then," I said enthusiastically, happy to know something about their passions.

They looked confused. "No . . . why?" Finn replied.

I couldn't believe they weren't aware of the connection. "Well, the lyrics of 'Ramble On' reference *Lord of the Rings*," I said, feeling a bit like an old, wise, nerdy man, who was about to drop some life-changing knowledge upon their young minds. "Yeah, there's a link there. They talk about Mordor and Gollum in the song."

It was pretty much an epiphany moment for them. Finn's jaw literally dropped. I was loving it.

While I was in Portland, Uncle Kevin called me. "You made it to *Portland*? Portland, *Oregon*? Are you kidding me? That's unbelievable. Keep goin', kid."

It took a lot to surprise Uncle Kevin, who very seriously asked me if I was out of my mind before I left, at Christmas dinner. I appreciated his call.

Lars was working on preparing for an upcoming photo shoot in LA for a new brand of rum called Naked Turtle. His task was to shoot all different animals lounging around wearing sunglasses. His personality seemed to fit this particular assignment well. Nothing at all seemed to ever bother him—other than the fact that he couldn't seem to find a small enough hammock to put a sloth in.

Frustrated, he kept talking about it around the house. "I've looked everywhere. I guess I'm going to have to make one. I'm going to have to somehow *make* a mini hammock . . . for a *sloth*. That's what it's come to."

Lars was like a kid in a lot of ways, too. When he wasn't working on the Naked Turtle project, he was flying a remote-controlled helicopter in the living room or making giant bubbles outside on the front lawn with Finn. Karsten engaged in such activities, but with reserve. Finn was still just a kid, so he jumped right in with no hesitation (as did I). Monique just laughed at us most of the time.

Monique and I drove around Portland one day, stopping at the International Rose Test Garden, Killer Burger (a local favorite), and Portland State's football stadium to say hello to my colorful offensive coordinator from college, Bruce Barnum, who had since joined the Vikings staff and would become head coach there in 2014.

Coach Barnum was known for being unapologetically himself—and for saying some head-scratching things from time to time, such as when his Portland State team traveled to play Southern Utah in Cedar City, Utah, and he had them stay up in nearby Brian Head the night before the game instead of down in Cedar City.

"I didn't want to stay in Whoville," he explained to the press. "We're going to stay up in the Grinch's castle. We are going to go down, play them Saturday, whoop up on them."

The angered Cedar City community, many dressed up as Whos from "How the Grinch Stole Christmas," showed up in full force, setting a new attendance record as Southern Utah won the game. Coach Barnum wished me luck and offered his cabin in Yellowstone if it was on my way.

Before I left Monique and Lars's home, we took a group photo in front of the fireplace. Karsten was out with friends, so Lars seamlessly photoshopped him in. There are perks to having a professional photographer in the family.

On the last night, Monique, Lars, and I went to the Portland Kells for dinner, where we met two more of the McAleese brothers—the owner Gerard, and Patrick, who owned the Seattle Kells at Pike Place Market. Patrick was a sturdy six-foot-six, with a young-looking face, a strong Irish brogue, a slightly devious, but amicable, grin, and thick white hair that looked far too white for his youthful face.

Patrick joined Monique, Lars, and me in our booth (a unique kind of booth, with wooden swinging doors that closed it off, a little like a prototypical Wild West bar—Patrick called them "snugs"), and we talked and laughed hysterically for a long time, over pints of Guinness, telling stories about Uncle Brian (Monique knew him, too, almost like a brother since she'd spent so much time at Nana Mac's years back), the West Coast McAleeses and all their shenanigans, and of course, the bike trip. Monique, Lars, and I had only met once or twice before, when I was a kid, and we'd *all* just met Patrick, of course, but the four of us talked and laughed and told stories like old friends.

Toward the end of the night, Patrick promised he'd be at the finish line in New York City in September. I laughed.

"No, I'll be there, brother," he reasserted, raising his glass. He wasn't laughing.

Lars rode his bike with me for a few miles the next morning, through downtown Portland, to see me off. I followed him through town, almost for too long. He pointed out the turn I was supposed to make. I guess I hadn't seen him waving.

"You're going *across the country*, dude! I'm just going home," he said with a smile.

We hugged and parted ways.

All of a sudden, I was on my own again for a long, hard, and hilly eighty-five-mile ride into White Salmon, Washington.

PART III
BACK

BEFRIENDING THE UNKNOWN

WASHINGTON
JUNE 24–25

"Rise" – Eddie Vedder

After crossing into Washington State, I was on WA Route 14 (its signs were labeled with a profile of George Washington with a "14" in the middle) for most of the day, high above the Columbia River and running parallel to it. At the very end of the day, there was a short but steep, grueling climb into the little town of White Salmon, where I found an inn—the aptly-named Inn of the White Salmon—a "cozy brick hotel with a lounge and garden," according to Google Maps. I had already paid to stay in the hostel part of the inn, which was very cheap, but a recent West Point grad reading in the garden offered the second bed in his room as an alternative, which would be a lot more comfortable. So I took him up on it.

The brevity of our conversation leading to the offer would have been a red flag to just about anyone, including me in my prior life. Well, the whole thing wouldn't have even *happened* in my prior life, obviously. But he seemed to be a legitimate West Point grad. Right or wrong, I trusted him because of it.

The Asian American man's name was Anderson Kim. He was on a month-long vacation before moving to Oklahoma, enjoying some kitesurfing on the

Columbia River. I'm glad I took him up on his offer, because I slept like a rock that night—it was probably the most solid sleep of the entire trip to that point. With a perfect stranger in the room, in the bed right next to mine. Perhaps I was, in fact, changing. The unknown had become far, far less uncomfortable. The strange had become the familiar.

27

Strange Terrain

OREGON PART 2
JUNE 25 – JULY 2

"Swimming in the Flood" – Passion Pit

Built in 1889, the Just-Us Inn is a simple Victorian farmhouse in the tiny town of Wasco, in the middle of one of Oregon's poorest and least populous counties. North central Oregon is a strange, barren, untold part of the state—and of the country, for that matter. Wasco's seasoned, discolored, cantankerous houses suggest they could've been built by hardy Oregon Trail pioneers, perhaps as final settlements. Rumored to be quite haunted, the Just-Us Inn was originally a courthouse—where trials and public hangings took place. Later, the courthouse became the Old Oskaloosa Hotel and a brothel of sorts; then it transitioned to offering nightly, weekly, and monthly stays. Paranormal activity "experts" have sworn by the presence of spirits at the inn and have even recorded interesting sounds—such as the clanging of glassware in the house's supposedly empty kitchen.

I stumbled upon the inn after leaving White Salmon, Washington, that morning and crossing over the Columbia River and back into Oregon at Biggs Junction. When I got there, there was nobody home. Dark, empty rooms. Perhaps "Just-Us" referred to the *spirits*. The inn's business card even read: *Come stay a day or month, there are always rooms. Where the spirits gather and the wind blows.*

I called the phone number on the front door. The man who picked up was far away—in Portland at the time—but he gave me the combination to open a compartment on the door to get the key to the house. He said he wouldn't be there until sometime the next day, but trusted me to leave the $40 fee in the top dresser drawer of the ground floor bedroom after staying the night.

After I unpacked my things, I put on my sweatpants (my family had brought them back to me on their California visit after I'd imprudently mailed them home) and watched TV on the couch in the quiet, very old-fashioned living room. I was very happy to have my sweatpants back in that old, drafty, empty house. Later, I found out there were a few other people boarding there—I think all of them were temporary workers servicing the multitude of wind turbines in the vicinity of the town. A few of them got back to the house for the day as I watched TV. After I explained who I was and what I was doing there, one of them offered a fresh piece of salmon.

"Some good protein for ya," he said.

I cooked and ate the salmon in the haunted kitchen the next morning for a hearty breakfast, left two twenties in the top dresser drawer of the bedroom, and hit the road.

Wasco has been called the "City of Windmills," and I found out why that day. The ride that morning took me through rolling green fields under gray skies, and seemingly thousands and thousands of white, spinning, wind turbines. They were in all directions, as far as the eye could see. Turbines like these were becoming more and more common across the country, but I'd never seen so many of them in one place. (The renewable energy sector in the United States was beginning to proliferate in 2012, but wouldn't pass coal in terms of monthly electricity generation until years later, in April 2019.[22]) There was basically no traffic, so it was just me and the sea of turbines, and the rolling green hills. And absolutely nothing else. It was an empty, alien landscape—dreamlike and unsettling at the same time. My iPod played Passion Pit's "Swimming in the Flood," added by my sister Cailyn—the music fit the scene *perfectly*, somehow. If you listen to that song, especially the beautiful, but slightly strange-sounding, string instrumental in the beginning, I can almost guarantee it'll take you to those desolate green fields and churning ocean of turbines—silently spinning, almost in slow motion. If you close your eyes and let it.

Later in the day, I started getting into the high desert country of central Oregon, making it as far as an aptly-named town called Fossil. From Fossil, I went through some really interesting country—not at all what I was expecting. The John Day River allowed the passerby to take a look back in time by exposing layers and layers of rocks and fossils—millions of years' worth. In the long process, the river had created a beautiful valley, its clean, flowing water surrounded by sun-drenched brown rock hills dotted with green shrubs and pine trees. The paved road was the only evidence that human beings had ever set foot here. I spoke to another cyclist that day in the small town of Spray (population 160); he was driving the sag wagon that day for a group of Boy Scouts on a week-long bike tour of the John Day River area.

I ended the day in Kimberly, Oregon, which made Google Maps, but wasn't a town—*at all*. In fact, there were no people there. Not a single person. Just two abandoned houses. This was the place that Fritz joked he'd send a "care package" to back at McFritz's Pub—he asked about some of the most random, desolate places I'd be going through; Kimberly came to mind, because the only thing in it, as far as I could tell from my research, was a post office.

I chose one of the two neglected houses, which looked like it used to be the post office (and a mercantile store), to camp behind. Its backyard was ghostly and bizarre, because it was fully outfitted with a deck and patio furniture—tables, chairs, and even cushions—but it was clear that nobody had used them in years. The setup disconcertingly suggested that whoever lived here picked up and left in a hurry. It'd been so long, though, that birds and bees had begun to take over the place, creating nests and hives in the nooks and crannies of the deck and veranda that attached to the house, which hung over the table and chairs. The bees didn't bother me, and I didn't bother them. We were both harmless invaders, making good use of space whose original inhabitants had long moved on, for whatever reason.

I swam in the adjacent John Day River and walked across some farmland on the other side of the road, bar of soap and towel in hand, to a field of high-powered sprinklers for an improvised shower. As I approached one of the sprinklers, I realized just how powerful this "showerhead" was going to be; it was the type that could spray water *hundreds* of feet. I looked around to make sure nobody was watching. No signs of anyone in any direction. Then I stripped down to just compression shorts, took a deep breath, and jumped in, dancing around the sprinkler in a circle as it rotated, just a few feet away, staying in the stream, naked except for my skin-tight black compression shorts. Then I soaped up and did it again. The water stung a good amount, but it certainly served its purpose; I felt very clean and refreshed afterward. Actually, it was a *great* shower. You couldn't ask for better water pressure!

When I got back to my campsite, I bought a root beer from the vending machine out front (it was mysterious to me that it was still on—the plugged-in, functioning machine was starkly incongruous with the rest of the deserted setting) and spoke to a group of teenagers passing by. They were on their way to fire a bunch of bowling balls into the river (or maybe into a mountainside) out of the makeshift cannon they had in the back of their pickup. Yes, they had a *cannon*. After we spoke, I reached down to grab the can of root beer and kind of just shrugged to myself as they peeled off, feeling a little bit old. *I guess that's what kids do for fun out here.*

I had the root beer, a can of cold Campbell's Chunky soup, a peanut butter sandwich, and a Clif Bar for dinner, sitting at the backyard table, listening to the buzz of the bees and the flutter of the birds, and wondering where the hell Fritz's care package was. I figured if I combined all of my backup food and snacks into a meal, I could kind of call it dinner. *Kind of.* Not exactly a Michelin-star worthy menu—but the *view* was absolutely first class. The golden mountain landscape beyond the river I looked out on as I ate glowed a brilliant brown and orange as the sun was setting behind me. This spectacular panorama was mine and mine alone. Not even the best restaurants in the world can offer *that*.

It was a sublimely beautiful early summer, late-June night—warm, but comfortable, with brittle, soothing air. The silence around me, other than the buzz of the bees and flutter of the birds, created an astonishing peace. A pacifying, organic respite after a long day. I placed chair cushions under my tent for an extra buffer before climbing inside as it got dark. I could hear coyotes in the distance as I looked up at a magnificent star-studded sky through the tent that night, and slept reasonably well—until roosters started crowing at 3:30 a.m.! It seemed pretty early, even for roosters. Agitated by nature's rude and unwelcome alarm clock, I felt like stumbling out of my tent, grumpily walking over and screaming at them, *You couldn't wait 'til FIVE?* I didn't do that, though. I stayed in my tent. Secretly, I'd always wanted my alarm clock to be a rooster—at least once in my life.

I stayed at the historic Hotel Prairie the following night in Prairie City, Oregon, before an early morning climb over Dixie Pass. My last couple of days riding in Oregon ended in the towns of Unity and Ontario, after desolate stretches of road. Then I crossed the river into Idaho the morning of Monday, July 2.

28

AD ASTRA

IDAHO
JULY 2–10

"Starman" – David Bowie

I loved Idaho from the moment I crossed the state line. Of the thirty-five states I rode through on the trip, it would end up being my favorite (California was a close second, but I *knew* California was beautiful. Idaho had the element of surprise). It was a good-looking morning, and I was making great time, passing potato farms right from the get-go.

I'd almost forgotten that it was nearly the Fourth of July. It was hard to keep track of time on the trip; days didn't have "feels" to them like they do in normal life. There were no Monday feels or Friday feels or Sunday feels. Dates, months, and holidays didn't have their usual feels, either. It was as if I'd become totally desensitized to the passage of time. So it didn't *feel* like the Fourth of July. Not even a little bit.

On July 2, I stayed north of the Boise metro area by riding through Emmett to Horseshoe Bend, where I rode down to a restaurant by the river named Kit's Riverside Restaurant (it was later renamed Locking Horns Riverside Restaurant under new ownership). The owner, Kit, let me stay in the house next to the restaurant for a price I named (it was an inn that hadn't opened yet). I suggested $40, and he agreed right away. Later in the day, I met Kit's little son, who asked me a lot of questions about the ride and then asked his dad why I was staying in the house if I had a tent with me.

"Well, sometimes he wants to sleep in a real bed, to feel like a *person* again," he explained to his son.

"Did you charge him?" the kid asked, right in front of me, surprising both of us.

Now his dad looked a little uncomfortable. "Well . . . yes."

"You're mean."

I almost laughed out loud when the kid said that. His father had charged me, but it was for a price *I named*—which was more than generous on the man's part. Especially since the accommodation was first-rate—an apartment with a kitchen and a living room, with an upstairs loft, new interiors, modern wood furniture, and floor-to-ceiling windows overlooking the Payette River. Kit could've easily charged a couple hundred a night for it, even in Horseshoe Bend, Idaho.

The stunningly beautiful, mountainous ride the next day to Lowman, Idaho, was one of the most scenic of the entire trip, and the main reason Idaho was my favorite state. The stretch from Banks to Lowman along Banks Lowman Road went through completely pristine, unspoiled, forested mountain country. The road ran parallel to the Payette River—at first meandering right beside it and then climbing high above it through mountains and towering ponderosa pines, Douglas firs, and Engelmann spruces. As the road climbed higher, the river on its right roared with churning whitewater rapids below, the commandeering water cascading and billowing past jagged rock formations beside it and atop smoothed-over boulders below it. The clean white and dark blue water sparkled in the sunshine, the mountains cast long and swaddling cool shadows, and the spotless air tasted astonishingly sweet. Surely this is what Earth looked like before there were people. Or at least before there was industry. I felt fortunate that day to see the country and experience untouched nature the way Lewis and Clark must have. It was a surreal morning and afternoon biking through the Idaho mountains.

When I got to Lowman, there wasn't much there at all. Nowhere to eat, nowhere to stay as far as I could tell. I found an abandoned hotel along the river. Figuring I'd camp behind it, I tiptoed my way around back, looking all around to see if anyone was watching. Nobody. Behind the forgotten wooden hotel, there was a patio with a hammock on it. It was a hot day with plenty of daylight left, so I cooled off in the river, despite the fairly strong current (it was my shower for the day), peeled off my wet compression shorts and left them to dry on the patio in the sun, and changed into some clean clothes. I had a can of cold Chef Boyardee for dinner, caked layers of Off! mosquito repellant onto my face and neck, and got into my sleeping bag in the hammock—figuring it would be a comfortable place to sleep that night. At first I was really comfortable, suspended above the ground, listening to the flowing river, but I couldn't fall asleep because it was still so light out; it didn't get dark this far north until nearly 10:00 p.m. at this time of year.

After sunset, I still couldn't sleep, and the temperature began to really plummet. I could actually *feel* it dropping—minute by minute, degree by degree. Because it would've been difficult to pitch the tent in such complete darkness, despite the full Thunder Moon, I stayed in the hammock, hopefully telling myself I'd eventually fall asleep.

But the air was quickly turning frigid. A couple of hours into the darkness, it had become far too cold to sleep, so I put my towel over my head to help warm the air I was breathing in, and tried not to shiver. More hours went by. Still not a wink. The air temperature had taken a nose dive from about ninety degrees when the sun was still out to about thirty degrees in the early morning hours—it'd dropped sixty degrees since I'd gotten in the hammock!

As the pre-dawn traces of light started to very faintly brighten the Idaho wilderness around me, I finally drifted off.

In what seemed just minutes later, I heard a trickle of water—but it wasn't the river. No, it was more of a *spray* than a trickle. Frozen solid, to the point that I almost couldn't move, I quietly, and very slowly, removed the towel wrapped around my face and turned my head.

I saw a very elderly man, about 100 years old, watering the plants near me with a hose. He was looking straight down, so I didn't think he saw me. I stayed frozen in place in the hammock, not wanting to be discovered as a trespasser and not wanting to startle him, thinking that doing so could possibly end his long life.

He gently walked along the edge of the patio, continuing to water the plants, then lifted his head slightly and pointed the stream directly at . . . my compression shorts! *I was caught!* Or so I thought.

But wait, *Why the hell is he watering my shorts?*

After he doused the shorts inquisitively for a few seconds, he moved on. Back to the flowers and other plants. At that point, I decided to get out of the hammock and get his attention, doing my best not to frighten and potentially kill him. After I'd explained myself, he didn't seem to care that I'd trespassed for the night, and even recommended a place down the road for breakfast.

"Look for a hot springs hotel and gas station a few miles down 21, on the left—they have a good breakfast," he advised.

The Fourth of July ride got off to a difficult start—my frozen muscles were almost impossible to warm up, and I got a flat from a thorn (the only thorn flat of the trip) just a couple of miles in, before I even got to the Five-Mile Water/ Stretch. I was also trying to wake up after what was the worst night of "sleep" of the trip by far.

I finally found the breakfast place. When I walked inside, thankful to finally feel some warmth, our centenarian gardener friend was sitting up at the counter drinking coffee. He nodded to me, and I nodded back. I sat at the stool right next to him, warming and waking up with six cups of hot coffee and a stack of filling sourdough pancakes. Feeling revitalized and amped up on caffeine, I hit the road again and enjoyed more mountain scenery as the temperature soared.

I hit a fairly large pass late in the day when I was tired and out of water. *Welcome (back) to the Rockies.* The headache from the lack of water was especially bad, compounded by serious sleep deprivation and too much coffee. I slugged over the pass, drained and dragging my bones. Another cyclist in racing gear and no baggage cruised by me near the top, shouting out, "See you in Stanley, man—for happy hour!"

Feeling dizzy from the increasingly severe dehydration, I cruised down the pass into Stanley, taking a beautiful photograph of a green field of brown and white cattle with beguiling snow-capped bluish-purple peaks behind them.

When I arrived in Stanley, a peach smoothie and purple huckleberry ice cream (huckleberry is a local favorite flavor) hit the spot and helped cure my dehydration headache, in the midst of very old-school-feeling Fourth of July festivities that were already in full swing. When I checked into the frontier-style motel in town, complete with farmhouse-like front porches that extended from its rooms, the person at the front desk told me that the entire town didn't have air-conditioning because it just wasn't needed, even in the heart of summer. This part of Idaho, it seemed, enigmatically turned into a refrigerator at night. I didn't need an explanation, though—my Antarctic night in the hammock was a first-hand account.

Just after it got dark, the fireworks show commenced. I had a great view from my front porch. I sat back and watched, enjoying one of the country's oldest traditions immensely, and feeling proud to be American. The familiar booms and crackles and whistles were comforting and nostalgic; I could've been back home watching the show at Jones Beach or Point Lookout, like we used to as kids. Fourth of July fireworks were the same in the middle of the Idaho wilderness as they were anywhere else, it seemed—except for one very distinct thing.

In between booms and crackles, as the next shells silently ascended into the dark night sky, leaving traces of swirling white light in their decelerating paths, you could easily hear the loud drone of what seemed to be thousands of mooing cows echoing off the mountains in the distance. MOOOOOOOOOOOOOOOOO. It was a thundering, constant, murmuring echo that reverberated through the still air that would have otherwise been silent, brimming with anticipation for the next detonation.

At first the noise puzzled me. But once I figured out that it had to be coming from the cattle in the surrounding fields, it made sense—they must have been terrified of the unnatural barrage of crackles and booms.

As soon as it was over, I passed out and slept like a rock for a solid ten hours. The next day, I went over the biggest mountain pass since New Mexico; it was called Galena Summit, part of the Boulder Mountains in Sawtooth National Forest. It was a slow grind up hairpin switchbacks, followed by a thrilling ride down into Sun Valley and Ketchum—which compose one of the most prominent ski resort areas in North America—as dormant and sleepy in the midsummer heat and greenery as a booming beach town is on gray winter days.

I stayed with a great family in Sun Valley—another reason Idaho was my favorite state. The Rutherfords lived halfway between Ketchum and Hailey. They were the family I met at the pool in Moab, Utah, about two and a half months before, who just happened to live right along my route back to the East Coast. Dean, a former professional tennis player, was in his forties—he was fit with slightly gray hair. His wife, Dominique, was thirty-six, also fit, with a pretty, kind face. They had two kids—Gavin had just turned nine on July third, and Lydia was six. Dean's mother, Leslie, was also staying with them at the time, visiting from Chicago. The family lived in an actual log cabin (a very nice one) with beautiful mountain scenery surrounding them—it was an idyllic setting, like something from *The Sound of Music*.

Dominique cooked delicious, eminently healthy meals, Gavin made a YouTube video titled "Me and John Biking," we all (including Grandma Leslie) played a genuinely fun and competitive game of wiffle ball in the backyard, we had a Nerf war (me, Gavin, and Dean) with Gavin's arsenal of Nerf guns, we lit small fireworks in the driveway as the family dog tried to eat them, and we went to see an outdoor ice show at the nearby ski resort. On the way back from the ice show, Gavin and Lydia yelled "*Skunk!*" in unison as we passed through a foul-smelling part of the woods in the car, exactly how *we* used to as kids, a generation earlier, all the way back in New York. Gavin had his ninth birthday party at the community pool on Saturday, July 7, and he really wanted me to be there, so I stayed an extra night, sleeping on couch cushions in the log cabin home office one more time.

On the morning I was leaving, as I got the bike ready in their garage and was about to say goodbye, six-year-old Lydia asked her mom a question I'll never forget.

"Mom . . . um, can John stay . . . *forever?*"

Dominique smiled and turned her head slightly as she looked down at Lydia, then gently explained why I couldn't stay forever—telling her that I had to ride back home to New York, back to my own family.

I have to admit, it was difficult to say goodbye to the Rutherfords—I liked them very much, and Gavin had become my buddy for a few days. There was a procession line of hugs as I said goodbye to each of them: Dean, Dominique, Grandma Leslie, Lydia, and finally, Gavin, who looked down at the ground. I felt like I was letting him down by leaving. I felt physically good after two rest days, but my soul ached a bit as I turned away from the house. I reluctantly waved one last goodbye as I biked down their street, with a little pit in my stomach. I wondered if I'd ever see them again. Suddenly, this place felt like another home, somehow. The difficult farewell made it an even lonelier day out in the desert.

But it also felt good to be back on the road, especially after I turned the music back on. As Route 75 goes south out of Sun Valley, it comes out of the mountains and back into barren desert. Heading east on US-26, I biked through Craters of the Moon National Monument & Preserve, a massive lava field on Idaho's Snake River Plain, in the south central part of the state (at over 600 square miles, the lava field is so large that it's easily found in a satellite image of the entire country). The road was the only pavement that cut through it, along its north edge. The black, volcanic landscape baked in the blistering July sun. It felt otherworldly and remote. While it didn't look like the moon to me, it still made me think of meeting legendary astronaut Buzz Aldrin when I was a kid.

* * *

Shortly after successfully landing the lunar module with only about sixteen seconds of fuel left, Neil Armstrong and Buzz Aldrin became the first two human beings in history to set foot on ground beyond Earth when they walked on the moon's surface. The mission was an incredible feat, especially for the time; as space historian Rod Pyle has said, "Basically, we flew to the moon using the processors you find in microwaves now." And they almost didn't make it back— improvising, Aldrin replaced a broken circuit breaker switch with a felt-tipped pen. Without such quick thinking, there would've been no way to power the lunar module's ascent engine to lift them off the moon, and President Nixon would've had to read his prepared backup speech, which included the macabre revelation, "Fate has ordained that the men who went to the moon to explore in peace will stay on the moon to rest in peace."

Fortunately, astronauts Aldrin, Armstrong, and Michael Collins returned to Earth safely—as international heroes. After hundreds of thousands of years of looking up at the moon—first wondering what it was and what it was made of, then later singing about it, painting it, writing about it, and photographing it—we'd finally made it there.

Renowned British cosmologist Stephen Hawking wrote in his final book, *Brief Answers to the Big Questions*, "We thought space was worth a big effort in the 1960s. In 1962, President Kennedy committed the US to landing a man on the moon by the end of the decade. On July 20, 1969, Buzz Aldrin and Neil Armstrong landed on the surface of the moon. It changed the future of the human race."

***

When I met Buzz Aldrin (in his late sixties at the time), I was a little kid in elementary school. We were at an airport in the Bahamas. My family was on our way back from vacation, and we were waiting to board the same plane.

Recognizing Buzz immediately, my dad (in his late thirties at the time) urged me and my sisters to go over and ask him how the moon was. You know, just casually. I was shy as a kid, though, so I really didn't want to go. After some deliberation and further encouragement from both my parents, I finally walked over, with my two little sisters behind me.

Without even introducing myself or saying anything else, I straight up asked him, "How was the moon?"

Buzz paused for a moment, looked up slightly, and then, fully respecting the question and speaking in a serious tone as if we were adults, looked at us and answered, "Dark . . . dusty . . . lonely . . .," putting careful thought into each word. "Though bright—in the sunlight."

His wife Lois looked on as we spoke a little more, seemingly charmed by the encounter, and proudly told us about how Buzz Lightyear from *Toy Story* was named after her husband. My sister Annie, true to form, later scribbled a handwritten letter for Buzz to read on the plane, and my mom was relieved, thinking he'd be an overqualified backup for the pilot.

Before we walked back, I asked him to sign my notebook. He did, but wrote more than just his autograph. Below his signature, he added "Apollo XI." Above his signature, he wrote a Latin phrase I'd never seen before. I had no idea what it meant, of course. He had written "AD ASTRA" in all caps.

Before he handed me back my pen and notebook, he pointed to the phrase and asked, "Do you know what that means?"

I shook my head, "No."

He said, "It means '*To the stars.*'"

* * *

In all the years since that memorable encounter, I've thought a lot about *AD ASTRA* and wondered why he wrote it. As a kid, I wondered why he didn't write "To the moon." *Ad lunam.* But as I grew older, I began to understand why. I think it's because he knew that his historic journey to the moon in 1969 was just the very beginning. And that it wasn't about the *moon*—the moon was just a steppingstone. It was about progress. Progress not just for the United States. Progress for *humanity.* Progress that would eventually lead human beings much farther into the final frontier. Armstrong even said, "That's one small step for man, one giant leap for mankind" as he took that iconic first step off the lunar module ladder. Buzz Aldrin, having executed that first landing and taken those first few steps beyond Earth, would be forever connected to that endeavor—in essence, *one small step . . . to the stars.*

NASA, Boeing, and Elon Musk's SpaceX are currently leading the effort to get to Mars. We may get to the Red Planet in the next decade or so and take the "next step" for humanity when astronauts land on another planet for the first time. Mining asteroids for rare metals (some asteroids are worth well more than the global economy) and terraforming Mars and the moons of Jupiter and Saturn to make them habitable for permanent human settlements may come after that, followed by landing on more distant comets (first in the outer fringes of the solar system, on comets in the Kuiper Belt, and then beyond the solar system, on comets in the Oort Cloud—a distant, spherical cloud of mostly stationary comets that surrounds the entire solar system).[23]

According to American physicist and futurist Dr. Michio Kaku, one way to the stars would be using comets as far outpost "gas stations" and steppingstones, much like how ancient Polynesian explorers hopped from island to island as they journeyed across the ocean thousands of years ago.

Comets in the Oort Cloud could be as far as around three light-years away, more than halfway to the Centauri triple-star system (the nearest star system to our solar system). Robots could be sent ahead of time to build refueling stations by mining the comets' minerals and metals and melting their ice to create drinking water, rocket fuel, and oxygen—in effect, creating "rest stops" in deep space to break up the first interstellar trips and provide respite for weary astronauts, nomads of the future. Kaku writes, "Instead of leaping to the next star in one jump, we might cultivate the more modest goal of 'comet hopping' to the Centauri system. This thoroughfare could become a cosmic Route 66."[24]

While interstellar travel seems more like science fiction to us today because of the sheer distances involved and the engineering challenges of creating spacecraft that can go fast enough, it's reasonable to believe that one day it will be possible—*if* we survive long enough. And if we can eventually create spacecraft that can go close to the speed of light, people on board would experience the effects of Einstein's theory of special relativity, which posits that the faster you move through space, the slower you move through time. With such effects, specifically time dilation and length contraction, reaching seemingly unattainable distances would become much more feasible. For example, if you could travel at 99.9% of the speed of light to the nearby, very bright star Vega, 25 light-years away, it would take just over 25 years to get there and just over 25 years to get back, from the perspective of people on Earth. But from *your* perspective, because you're moving so fast, the round trip would only take about 2 years. If you left at age 50 in the year 2050, you'd return to Earth at age 52, in the year 2100.[25] If you had any kids over age 2 when you left, they'd be older than you when you got back.

If we scale this up to greater distances, the effect becomes even more unimaginable. A round trip to the Andromeda Galaxy (the Milky Way's closest neighbor, 2.5 million light-years away) at a speed within 50 parts in 1 trillion of the speed of light would take only about 50 years from your point of view on the spaceship. *The Cosmic Perspective* states, "You could leave Earth at age 30 and return at age 80—but you would return to an Earth on which your friends, your family, and everything you knew had been gone for 5 million years."[26] In this way, special relativity could not only allow us to travel to the stars—it could allow us to travel to the future. Even millions of years into the future. Time travel is possible after all.

If you do the math, it should be possible to colonize dozens of planets within a few centuries and a good portion of the Milky Way galaxy within a few million years, even with relatively slow-moving starships (that can travel a few percent of the speed of light). If we take this idea that it should eventually be possible to colonize the galaxy and combine it with the reasonable (though unproven) notion that civilizations throughout the 100 billion or so stars in the galaxy (many of which have Earth-sized planets in habitable zones) are common, then run some conservative numbers, we come to the perplexing conclusion that the galaxy should have already been colonized by someone else—*a long time ago.*[27] The fact that we've found no evidence of other life in the galaxy, much less a galactic civilization, despite this logic, is known as the Fermi Paradox. So either civilizations like ours are extremely rare and we are truly alone, perhaps being the first intelligent life in the galaxy (it took two and a half billion years, a large chunk of the sun's total life span, for life on Earth to go from single cells to multi-cellular[28], so this is certainly possible); interstellar travel is even more difficult or expensive than we imagine and other civilizations are unable to travel too far from their homes; or, more darkly, civilizations destroy themselves before they attain the technology required for such travel, either by conflict or environmental degradation. Or, maybe there *is* a galactic civilization that hasn't revealed itself yet.[29] Fascinatingly, one of these four scenarios *needs* to be correct. We can only hope that it's not the third one.

Even the first scenario (that we're alone), which seems to be the least interesting at first glance, is quite extraordinary:

> If this is true, then our civilization is a remarkable achievement. It implies that through all of cosmic evolution, among countless star systems, we are the first piece of our galaxy or the universe ever to know that the rest of the universe exists. Through us, the universe has attained self-awareness. Some philosophers and many religions argue that the ultimate purpose of life is to become truly self-aware. If so, and if we are alone, then the destruction of our civilization and the loss of our scientific knowledge would represent an inglorious end to something that took the universe some 14 billion years to achieve. From this point of view, humanity becomes all the more precious, and the collapse of our civilization would be all the more tragic.
>
> - *The Cosmic Perspective, Fifth Edition.* Jeffrey Bennett, Megan Dona-
> hue, Nicholas Schneider, Mark Voit.

We, along with the next few generations of our children, are living at *the* most critical time in the history of humanity. Before his death in 2018, Stephen Hawking said that if we can survive nuclear and environmental catastrophe over the next two centuries, "our species should be safe, as we spread into space. Once we establish independent colonies, our entire future should be safe."

There is much about the universe, of course, that we don't understand—the vast majority of it, for example, is made of Dark Matter and Dark Energy, things we can't see and know very little, if anything, about—other than that they exist and have something to do with the structure and accelerating expansion of the universe, respectively. As American astrophysicist Neil deGrasse Tyson states,

> What we do know, and we can assert without further hesitation, is that the universe had a beginning. The universe continues to evolve. And yes, every one of our body's atoms is traceable to the big bang and to the thermonuclear furnaces within high-mass stars that exploded more than five billion years ago. We are stardust brought to life, then empowered by the universe to figure itself out—and we have only just begun.[30]

Today, the visible universe comprises somewhere around a hundred billion galaxies, each with hundreds of billions of stars. There are thought to be at least as many planets as stars. As incomprehensibly vast as the universe is (if our Milky Way galaxy were the size of the United States, our solar system would be the size of a quarter), a solar system like ours is rare. A life-supporting planet like Earth is also rare (exactly *how* rare is up for debate right now). Not so much because of its size or distance from its star, which are two important prerequisites to support and develop life (liquid water can only exist in a small sliver of the solar system, known colloquially as the "Goldilocks Zone"[31]), but because of some of its quirkier characteristics, such as the size of its moon. In fact, to attain such characteristics and support and develop intelligent life the way it has to the present day, Earth has undergone a series of improbable "lucky breaks" since its inception.

Sometimes I wish everyone could have the perspective of an astronaut, and could see the Earth from space, and see how fragile it is—a beautiful blue marble, an oasis in a dark vacuum desert. A "pale blue dot," to use the words of Carl Sagan. The Apollo missions were the first times that humans traveled far enough from Earth to see the whole of it. To see how finite it was. The photos were revolutionary. As British natural historian David Attenborough recalled, "It completely changed the mindset of the human population of the world."

Most of us living today will never have the privilege of going to space, but we can go in our minds. Imagine taking a solo trip across the galaxy, or the solar system, or even just to Mars. You would pass through an unfathomable volume of nothingness—nothing but empty space, desolation, loneliness, cold darkness, utter silence, and hostile conditions—for *years*. If you could actually take that trip, and see where we live on a larger scale, you'd appreciate every square inch of Earth *so* much more. And not just the beautiful parts, I think.

Such a trip would make even, say, New York City's Penn Station at night seem friendly—even inviting, upon your return. As you walk through the crowded train station, some people are dancing, singing. There's a guy playing Bob Marley on the steel drums by the Eighth Avenue subway. People are enjoying a meal. Talking to family members or friends on the phone. Randomly running into old acquaintances they haven't seen in years. Sure, they rush by you, in a hurry, sometimes bumping into you rudely or cutting you off, exuding self-interest. But who could blame them? They're just trying to make it in the world, to feed their children—maybe pay for their college. And they're just trying to make it home—just like you. In fact, the first person you saw in the train station upon returning from your cross-galaxy trip would probably be your new best friend. Their religion, or the color of their skin—those things wouldn't even cross your mind, let alone influence your judgment in any way. And from a cosmic perspective, the crowded and bustling train station would feel very warm and cozy, I think. Maybe not compared to your living room, with a crackling fireplace and a lit, decorated Christmas tree—but on a cosmic level, it would feel like a good childhood memory. It would all seem very human. And comforting. And nostalgic.

Maybe I'm strange, but I think about this often, witnessing the world—hearing the birds chirp in the trees, the chorus of crickets and katydids in the summer trees at night, and the waves crash and rumble on the beach (all sounds that would be enormously comforting to an astronaut in the silent vacuum of space)—but also driving through cities, sitting in traffic, and rushing through airports and train stations. Appreciating a blue sky—over a mountain, a beach, or a city skyline—as a thin boundary between a beautiful day and a dark, inhospitable place. It often crosses my mind—how good we have it. Even in the places that aren't really all that great, relatively speaking.

This perspective, this *cosmic perspective*, can be powerful. We all can have it and benefit from it, regardless of whether we ever go to space. In a way, it can be a gift. Neil deGrasse Tyson encourages us to "imagine a world in which everyone, but especially people with power and influence, holds an expanded view of our place in the cosmos. With that perspective, our problems would shrink—or never arise at all—and we could celebrate our earthly differences while shunning the behavior of our predecessors that slaughtered one another because of them." In his popular book *Astrophysics for People in a Hurry*, he expands on this viewpoint, writing, "The cosmic perspective not only embraces our genetic kinship with all life on Earth but also values our chemical kinship with any yet-to-be-discovered life in the universe, as well as our atomic kinship with the universe itself."[32]

We are living in an exciting time in history where a plethora of "exoplanets," a term for planets beyond our solar system, are being discovered, among other astonishing developments in the world of space exploration. The first exoplanet was found back in the early 1990s, but the numbers have picked up significantly in the last decade; now, thousands have been discovered. Most are found by calculating dips in a star's brightness as an orbiting planet passes in front of it (the Transit Method) or by measuring the wobble of a star as a planet orbits it (the Doppler Method). A good portion of the exoplanets found so far are "Hot Jupiters" (a nickname for a gas giant that orbits very close to a star—unlike our Jupiter, which is very cold); because they're so big and so close to their stars, they're easier to spot. The profiles of many of these worlds contrast sharply to the green and blue garden paradise that is Earth, though. On one of the closest, a large blue planet discovered in 2005, just sixty-three light-years away, it likely rains super-hot molten glass, *sideways*, with howling 5,000 mph winds and day-time highs around 2,000 degrees Fahrenheit, according to NASA.[33]

As we continue to hunt, though, we'll likely find a habitable world one day—in fact, we might have found several already. Kepler 22b is about 600 light-years away; it's only twice the size of Earth and has an estimated surface temperature of 72 degrees Fahrenheit. Proxima Centauri b, another Earth-sized planet, orbits our closest stellar neighbor only around four light-years away—though its red dwarf star's propensity for deadly solar flares is likely an issue, and it's not known if the planet's magnetic field is strong enough to deflect them. More are being discovered each year, and the James Webb Space Telescope, launched in 2021, will help us learn more about them. Whether any of these candidates contain atmospheres with water vapor or other conditions to support life remains to be seen, but we may one day come to the startling conclusion that the conditions necessary for life in the universe are actually somewhat *common*.[34] That would be a very good thing, of course. Humanity was born on Earth, but isn't meant to stay here.

If we achieve interstellar travel via antimatter engines or some other means, and finally make the long journey to the stars, "Mother Earth" could have a very new meaning in the future—our planet could be known as the beginning, the origin and cradle of humanity. *Our first planet*. This would make it an extremely historically important piece of the galaxy. Earth's stories would become old legends, cloudy tales of the galactic pioneers' ancient ancestors. Perhaps the search for habitable planets and the effort to go interstellar to reach them will unite nations over the next couple of centuries. Perhaps it will motivate children to become the next great innovators. Perhaps it will encourage all of humanity to think beyond borders and racial and religious differences. Perhaps it will inspire humanity to ponder our progress as a whole, the way Neil Armstrong and Buzz Aldrin's 1969 moon landing put an exclamation point on the hard work of thousands of people from around the world—and made humanity across the globe pause in wonder, even just briefly, and look back at how far it'd come. And look forward to how far it could go.

The next giant leaps will depend on choices we make today: how we invest in science and space exploration, how we mitigate the threat of nuclear weapons, how we teach and inspire our children, and how we choose to protect our children's home—the only home any of us have ever had.

What will the next hundred years bring? Will we perfect fusion technology, the "Holy Grail" of energy? Will we colonize Mars? Will we solve the "theory of everything" once and for all? Will we discover another intelligent civilization in the galaxy? Will we find the next Earth, another home for humanity? Whatever scientific milestones we achieve, avoiding nuclear conflict and conserving our rare, delicate planet are the most important things we can do as a species, if only to buy ourselves enough time to leave our home—and go *to the stars*.

AD ASTRA.

As Stephen Hawking said, "We are, by nature, explorers. Motivated by curiosity. This is a uniquely human trait. So remember to look up at the stars and not down at your feet. Be curious."

***

Just after finally biking out of the volcanic, black, scorching, desolate, unearthly Idaho desert that is Craters of the Moon National Monument & Preserve, I ended the day in Arco, Idaho, the birthplace of nuclear energy, and ordered the flagship Atomic Burger for dinner at Pickle's Place, a little hole-in-the-wall greasy spoon with a green-painted exterior and an image of a dancing pickle on its sign proudly unveiling the establishment's name and the friendly words "Home of the Atomic Burger" like Vanna White on *Wheel of Fortune*. The roof displayed "EAT" with unlit neon lights and the interior had old-fashioned, wood-paneled walls with foreign paper currency and coins taped to it.

After the ride from Arco to Idaho Falls the next day, I strayed from my budget and went for a big steak dinner at Outback Steakhouse because I knew the following day would be a rough one—probably the toughest day on paper of the whole trip (because of the combination of the terrain and distance), and I knew I had to fuel up.

Any way you cut it, the ride from Idaho Falls, Idaho, to Jackson, Wyoming, is a difficult one. The 109-mile southern route through Alpine, Wyoming, is easier, with flatter terrain, but it's also twenty miles longer than the 89-mile northern route through Victor, Idaho, which features the nearly insurmountable Teton Pass over Mount Glory and down into Jackson Hole.

When I stopped for lunch in Swan Valley, Idaho, where the two paths diverge, I had a last-minute decision to make. I ate and pondered, looking over Google Maps on my phone and asking the waitress for a scouting report. I finally decided to take the shorter, more difficult path over the problematic pass, knowing it would be brutal but hoping it would save some time. I'd learned at this point that any time the yellow line on Google Maps gets all squiggly, you're in for either a merciless ascent or a precipitous descent, and usually both. The map topography was often misleading because it's possible to have a fairly level road that cuts through mountains or runs parallel to a river. The topography couldn't capture that too well; the line of the road, however, didn't lie. If it was all jagged or haphazardly meandering, it was not by accident. It meant switchbacks, tolled with sweat and time.

The road started climbing fairly abruptly right out of the gate as I left Swan Valley—but that was nothing. It wasn't even a hint of a warmup for what would come later that afternoon. Already exhausted after the road descended again into Victor, a small Idaho valley town, I gulped a couple of Gatorades and bought a couple of sleeves of Gatorade Energy Chews at a gas station grocery mart, hoping they would help. I left the gas station, turned up the music, and braced myself. The climb started fairly steadily, with a straight road, then picked up as I approached the state line.

There are three signs in the vicinity of the Idaho/Wyoming state line on Idaho 33/Wyoming 22. The first has yellow lights on it and reads RETURN TO VICTOR WHEN FLASHING; the second is the "Welcome to Wyoming: Forever West" sign, where I stopped to take the photo; and the third, just beyond the welcome sign, reads STEEP MOUNTAIN PASS AHEAD - 10% GRADES. Collectively, they were like the sign for the witch's castle in the haunted forest in *The Wizard of Oz*—the one that reads, *I'D TURN BACK IF I WERE YOU!*

NEED FOR SPEED

WYOMING & MONTANA
JULY 10-24

"Get Over It" – Eagles

A sustained 10% gradient is about as intense as it gets on US highways (the interstate highway legal limit is only 6%). The steepest grades I'd seen up to that point, even in the New Mexico Rockies, were about 7%. I knew, because steep grades were almost always posted on yellow signs with a symbol of a truck going downhill on them, with the corresponding percentage. I usually loved seeing those signs at the top of a pass, because they meant there were some free miles ahead of me that didn't require any work—a reward for the work I'd just put in—and that I was effectively about to get on a heart-pounding roller coaster.

By comparison, the steepest sustained climbs in the Tour de France in the Pyrenees and Alps usually hover around 12%. The Col d'Izoard, at 10%, is known to be one of the most brutal climbs in the Alps and one of the tour's most signature stretches (it's often the final ascent of the race, making it particularly strategic). Of course, the Tour de France guys are elite cyclists with light bodies and super light bikes, and they don't have to carry eighty-plus pounds of gear.

Anything over 5% means you're really *grinding* up and really *flying* down. From what I've seen, the warning signs usually start at 3% to 5% in the US, so

that's basically where it starts to become precarious for truckers and RV drivers—where they have to start worrying about overheating on the way up and
losing control on the way down. I couldn't imagine what 10% would be like on
a bike—on the way up *or* on the way down.

After passing another sign that read WATCH FOR FALLEN ROCKS, I
got into the switchbacks of Teton Pass and the climb became just about impossible. The switchbacks were the big, looping, horseshoe-bend type, not quite
the tight hairpin type, but they were more difficult than I'd ever faced—without any doubt. In fact, I'm fairly certain that the climb was even more than 10%
at a few points—I think it was likely 11% or 12% at times—which, again, is as
intense as it gets on US highways. I've spoken to cyclists who have done the
TransAm (specifically Max Lippe and Anton Lindberg, who came in 9th and
16th place, respectively, in the 2017 edition of the grueling annual race from
Oregon to Virginia), and they said the same—11% or 12% is the steepest you'll
see on that route as well.

Interestingly, they told me some of their toughest climbing was in Ken-
tucky and Virginia (two states I didn't cycle through); even though the elevation of the Appalachians is much lower than the Rockies, many of the climbs
are just as difficult.

The bike just *barely* creaked forward as I climbed Teton Pass, foot by foot,
inch by inch. My legs were just *barely* strong enough to push myself, the thirty-pound bike, and the eighty-plus pounds of gear forward, even after being
conditioned by some 7,000 miles of cycling. The road was so steep that, with
every switchback turn, I had to stop and catch my breath and allow my erupt-
ing heart rate to recover. At each turn, I popped a Gatorade Energy Chew and
gulped some water. Sweat was pouring out of me and my chest felt heavy, like I
was having a heart attack. It was like doing consecutive sets of heavy squats for
hundreds of reps. And again, I had to remain seated. I couldn't stand up.

Sometimes, during intense climbs like this, my mind would wander off,
and I'd imagine what it was like to climb dozens and dozens of flights of stairs
in the World Trade Center with sixty pounds of bunker gear, as Uncle Brian,
Stan Smagala, Dave DeRubbio, Lt. Bob Wallace, and the other firefighters on

9/11 did, as the office workers were coming down. Then, in a fit of guilt, I'd quickly push the thought out of my head, acknowledging that it wasn't the same thing—and that I shouldn't compare what I was doing to *that*. But it still motivated me.

The pedals ground forward as slowly as they possibly could, almost at a standstill now. When I started the climb, the song "Get Over It" by the Eagles was playing on my iPod—I played it over and over again, until I reached the top and "got over" the pass. It's not one of the group's best songs, in my opinion, but it was starkly appropriate for the situation. I was breathing so hard at times that I was taking between one and two breaths per second, gulping the summer mountain air. Sweat dripped down my face and leapt off my chin, nose, and eyebrows.

For the final push, I ate the last Energy Chew and steeled forward, excited to be finally approaching the top, emptying any last bits of energy I had left in the tank and feeling the lactic acid wildfire in my legs like never before. As the road flattened at the summit, I began cooling down and slowly coasting. A deep exhale of relief.

For a peaceful, silent few moments, I took in an incredible view of Jackson Hole in the valley far below, as I coasted, with miles and miles of forest green Wyoming wilderness in view beyond it. The view was so much better than it would've been after driving up the mountain. I was exhausted and drenched in sweat, yet invigorated by the intense exercise and exhilarated to make it all the way up without having to get off and push. It was a big victory.

With my destination for the day in view, I decided *not* to take a break at the top. As I slowly accelerated into the 10%+ descent, feeling the quickening trickle of wind in my face as you would at the top of a roller coaster, I began to feel a need . . . for speed.

Feeling invincible and daredevilish, and likely not thinking clearly after the completely depleting and soul-taxing workout I'd just gone through, I took my hands off the brakes and just *let it go*. I just let it fly, challenging the bike to show me what it could do.

All of a sudden, the pavement dropped from under me and my speed picked up *exponentially*. After a few seconds, I cleared 30 mph—which is going pretty fast on a bicycle. Fast enough to warrant your full attention and focus, especially on a twisting mountain road. The mountain air felt amazing now, cooling me down and drying me off.

I checked the speedometer at the center of my handlebars again a few seconds after that: 36, 37. The fearless, but stupid, twenty-four-year-old in me didn't even *think* about reaching for the brake.

When I cleared 40, the adrenaline was pumping hard. 41, 42. *Okay, now I've never gone this fast.* I was blowing by cars at this point, banking to the left and then to the right, leaning into the curves of the sinking, serpentine mountain road. I checked again: 44, 45. I was flying by runaway truck ramp signs, yellow speed limit signs with curvy arrows that read 20 mph, the guardrail and open valley scenery to my right and the jagged rocky mountain face to my left.

I checked again: 48, 49. The wind was blowing my shirt like I was skydiving now, and it was becoming exceedingly difficult to breathe. I cleared 50. The handlebars were shaking hard. My heart was in my throat. 51, 52. I still didn't touch the brake. 52, 53! That's about as fast as NYC subways travel at their very top speed.

It was a thundering waterfall of adrenaline like no other, but I knew right after, as I slowly pressed on the brake, and as the road began to flatten out, that I could never let myself go that fast again. The bike wasn't built for that kind of speed (it was a touring bike, after all), and a fall or blowout could've killed me. It wouldn't have taken much to pop those skinny tires at that speed. At the very least, a wipeout would've resulted in serious injury, almost certainly ending the trip.

As I coasted into Jackson and my racing heart rate began to recover, I was relieved and on an extreme high. Fleetwood Mac's "Go Your Own Way" played on my iPod, the next song alphabetically after the Eagles' "Get Over It." Three years later, in 2015, I met Eagles vocalist Glenn Frey when I was at a New York Rangers playoff game with my sister Annie at Madison Square Garden. Frey was on the bathroom line behind me and initiated the conversation, saying, "You know when you get to be my age, you're on this line all the time."

As strange as it sounds, one of the biggest rock stars the world has ever seen was talking to me about going to the bathroom when I'm an old man. Yes, he was, no doubt, one of the best ever—the fact that the *Eagles' Greatest Hits* is the best-selling album of all time in the US is proof on its own. Frey wrote or cowrote many of the Eagles' songs, along with Don Henley, and sang the lead vocals on a number of the group's best tracks, including "Take It Easy," "Already Gone," "Peaceful Easy Feeling," "Lyin' Eyes," and "Tequila Sunrise."

At first, I didn't bring up anything Eagles-related. But then I regretted it. *What if I never meet someone from the Eagles again? And who knows, maybe he's never heard of anyone using one of his songs to literally make it over a mountain.* So I approached him again later and told him the story—how I listened to his song "Get Over It," over and over again, until I reached the top of the extremely steep Wyoming mountain—the steepest I'd ever faced. He got a good laugh out of it—especially the part about the 53 mph descent.

"I'm glad we could help," he said, with a smile.

I'm glad I got the chance to tell him. Sadly, Glenn died unexpectedly in a New York City hospital just eight months later, at the age of sixty-seven.

The feeling of relief I had (and the abundance of no-longer-needed adrenaline that was still coursing through my veins) as I coasted into Jackson was only comparable to one feeling I'd ever experienced: the feeling of running with the bulls two years prior, just after the bulls had passed and I knew I'd survived.

***

When Brendan and I arrived in Pamplona, Spain, on July 6, 2010, via bus from Barcelona, the renowned Festival of San Fermín was in full swing. Raucous revelers filled the streets, singing and spraying sangria in the middle of the weeklong festival's first day, eventually rendering our white t-shirts partially purple. Everyone was wearing the same thing. For about 20 euros at a number of shops in town, you could buy the traditional San Fermín uniform: a white t-shirt, white pants, a red bandana to wear around your neck, and a red sash to wear around your waist. I'd first learned about the annual event in Señor Hodum's high school Spanish class. Without technically *recommending* that we participate, Hodum suggested that if we ever *happen to* participate and people ask us why we would ever do such a dumb thing, we simply answer, *Por qué no? Why not?*

After we "slept" on church steps the night before the run, spectators filled the windows of the old buildings along the route in the early morning, spilling into five stories worth of small Juliet balconies to get a prime view; others, below, lined the wooden barricades of the twisting cobblestone course. Shop owners wisely boarded up their windows. Police went through the crowd of runners, picking out anyone that appeared overly inebriated; otherwise, though, there were no rules. No liabilities. No checks and balances. *Run at your own risk.* Hundreds are injured every year and a fatality had occurred just the year before—in 2009.

At around 8:00 a.m., the first firework-like rocket, or *chupinazo*, went off at the starting line where the bulls were corralled. The first one was just the warning rocket. The streets echoed in cheers and the nervous anticipation went up a few notches. My pulse quickened.

With the shrilling whistle and subsequent exploding *boom* of the second *chupinazo* a few minutes later, my trepidation just about maxed out. The bulls were now loose in the streets!

The high barricades lining the course prevented any escape. There was no turning back now—the boats had been burned. People began jumping up and down, facing the distant starting line, trying to get a look at where the bulls were over everyone else's heads. I couldn't see anything yet—just a mass of people jumping at various frequencies, which was an odd sight. Then, the people around me began to slowly drift. I had no choice but to join them.

In an instant, the walking drift turned to a jog. Then the jog turned to a run. Then the run turned to a fast run, nearly a sprint!

As a novice, I had no idea it would all happen so quickly. As we ran, my focus was keeping my feet. I knew if I got tripped up in the madness, the bulls wouldn't go around me. They'd go *through* me.

But all of a sudden, like the parting of the Red Sea, the crowd in front of me dispersed. It was *gone*. There was a blur of red and white on either side of the street, and now plenty of open cobblestone in the middle of the street in front of me, which was *not* a good thing. It was like a school of fish clearing the way for a hungry shark. I was the little rookie fish that didn't get the memo.

Still running, now realizing what was happening and starting to drift to the right, I heard screams and heavy, clinking cowbells. I turned my head to the left to look behind me and saw them. *A freight train of charging bulls!* The terrifying view I suddenly had won't be found in any Pamplona tourism brochure. The rumbling behemoths, just feet away, were brown, white, and black—all with big, sharp horns.

As they stormed right past my left hip, I snapped a photo with my digital camera. In the photo, all the other runners are bunched up on the sides of the street. When the last of the bulls had passed, a feeling of immense relief came over me. *I'd survived.* Unscathed.

The crowd filled in again behind the bulls, and we all ran into the Plaza de Toros, the old bullfighting stadium, filled to capacity with a roaring crowd, pulsing with electricity. Running into the circular arena, with its dirt floor, as the crowd cheered, felt very much like running into a rambunctious Roman Colosseum a couple of thousand years ago, in the era of the gladiator—it was a dream-like trip back in time.

To this day, the two biggest adrenaline rushes I've ever had are running with the bulls in Pamplona and biking down Teton Pass in Wyoming. I imagine they'll be far surpassed by having children someday. Uncle John said that when he first held his child in his arms at the hospital, it was like he was "levitating in the air." Marty Lyons said, "The birth of a child is one of the most beautiful parts of life. It's God's way of saying this world should continue."

***

In Jackson, Wyoming, an hour or so after the thrilling descent, I ate a cheesesteak for dinner at Cutty's Bar and Grill, sitting up at the bar, and talking to the snowboarder bro local sitting next to me about my experience going over Teton Pass that afternoon, and how it was the toughest climb of my trip so far. Proud of his mountains, he was psyched about that, and posted to biket-rip2012.com the next day: *Glad Teton Pass kicked your ass.*

As I scarfed down breakfast the next morning at a renowned restaurant and lodge in the area called The Virginian, fueling up for the much-anticipated ride into Yellowstone National Park, I heard an unexpected rumble of thunder outside. Minutes later, a very severe thunderstorm struck, dumping torrential rain. Still beat up from Teton Pass the day before, I took the storm as a sign and decided to take the day off.

When I checked into The Virginian after breakfast, the lady at the front desk cheerfully said, "Well, you're in luck. It's Wednesday."

I must have sort of given her a blank stare, not understanding.

"It's karaoke night!" she exclaimed, like I should've known.

Picturing a few drunk locals in a dingy, dimly lit bar, sitting around a karaoke machine being screamed into, I pretended to be a little interested, not wanting to insult her. But I didn't think I'd actually show up. Later that night, though, as I watched a show on the Discovery Channel about string theory and asteroids (like a true nerd), sitting on my motel bed, I decided to check it out—at least to grab a beer at the bar.

To my total surprise, the Virginian Saloon & Convention Center was a big, wooden, Old Western bar with a large open room with a bunch of tables—and the place was packed! And *hopping*—unlike any other karaoke night I'd ever seen. *Karaoke must be a big deal in Wyoming.* The singing sounded pretty good too.

After speaking to people at the bar over a couple of beers about being from New York (they had asked about my FDNY hat), I did something I'd never done before—I *signed up* for karaoke, just out of the blue. For the hell of it. I figured that I didn't know anyone for thousands of miles (*If you're ever going to try karaoke, now's the time*), but was still nervous as I took the mic up on stage, because there were so many people.

My song choice was a big hit with the country-loving crowd, though—it was Johnny Cash's "Folsom Prison Blues." I don't have a great voice, but there are certain songs I can at least *sing*, and the baritone "Folsom Prison Blues" is one of them.

After singing the first two verses and barely hitting the very low note on "cry," the song went into an instrumental part and the crowd cheered emphatically—people were whistling, shouting. My nerves were suddenly gone, and I started to have a lot of *fun* up there. Way more fun than I thought karaoke could be.

When the song ended, I got a generous reception from the crowd, one I didn't think I deserved but will never forget, with more loud cheering and whistling—and then some people even getting up for a standing ovation! Sometimes you have to get out of your comfort zone to have a little fun.

I had breakfast at The Virginian again the next morning before an incredibly scenic ride through Grand Teton National Park (and its postcard-worthy, triangular, snow-capped peaks) and into Yellowstone, America's first national park. Because Yellowstone sits on top of a supervolcano, there was a good amount of climbing once I got into the park (to my surprise). The park is kind of like a gigantic green plateau. As a biker, my $12 park pass was good for a week, and good for both Grand Teton and Yellowstone parks, which neighbored each other. I learned that campgrounds in Yellowstone will never turn down bikers or hikers, regardless of vacancy.

The first night in Yellowstone, on July 12, I camped in Grant Village. To me, camping in Yellowstone was like gambling in Vegas—I saw it as the real deal. Going from campground to campground in Yellowstone was about as tech-free as I was the entire trip. I barely looked at my phone and just kind of got off the grid for a few days, camping and biking. It was a reminder that, without technology, the world is a lot bigger. It's a lot more intimidating and formidable. A lot dirtier. More physically cold. But maybe it's a lot warmer too. More invigorating. More memorable. More charming. Less cluttered. Less micromanaged. You feel this way when you bike and when you camp; it's amplified when you do these two things together. And when you rough it a little, you appreciate the small comforts of life that much more—the warmth of a fire, the taste of food, the quench of water, the wonderful feeling of a hot shower.

The elevation of that first campground was up there (about 8,000 feet), so I got ready for the cold, sleeping in sweats and using the rain cover on the tent for extra warmth. I had my bear spray from my sister Cailyn ready to go, right next to me as I slept, but didn't end up seeing a single bear in the entire park, despite its reputation. All I had for dinner was a can of cold Chef Boyardee lasagna (just 260 calories), so I treated myself to a huge hot breakfast in the closest lodge the next morning before crossing the Continental Divide twice in the first fifteen miles of the day.

At the second one, I crossed over to the eastern side of the Divide for good. At the top of that pass resides Isa Lake (it's more like a docile little pond, with green water lilies that make it look very much like a Monet painting). Perplexingly, Isa Lake drains into both the Atlantic and Pacific oceans, with an elevation of 8,300 feet. From there, I cruised down into more open land, and stopped at Old Faithful, the iconic geyser, to watch it erupt at 2:15 p.m.

Old Faithful apparently wasn't as faithful as it used to be, after a relatively recent earthquake, and the eruptions had become a little more unpredictable, a woman from Hawaii told me as we waited for 2:15, sitting under blue skies and the midday July sun. The guide told me and the rest of the crowd of anxious onlookers about how early settlers used to do their *laundry* down in the narrow geyser vent—which is at one point just four inches wide—and that the hot water, which has been measured at over two hundred degrees Fahrenheit at eruption, would shrink their wool.

When Old Faithful finally erupted, it was a sight to see. After a prelude of building white steam, the hot white water began shooting into the air, majestically towering nearly two hundred feet above the ground, and cascading down like a waterfall from the sky.

Biking though Yellowstone was an otherworldly experience. There was something very prehistoric about it—with a slew of unique, strange things to see. There was stuff bubbling up everywhere, boiling mud pits, stinking sulfur that smelled like rotten eggs, bright multicolor ponds painted like rainbows by rare strains of bacteria, hissing steam vents, puzzling orange waterfalls, and exploding geysers. I felt like I should be looking for dinosaurs as I biked through. It was as if I'd used a time machine to go back sixty-five million years, before the asteroid hit, or had found myself on another planet altogether.

When I was a kid, I first learned about the asteroid that killed off the dinosaurs and the Big Bang that started the universe in one fell swoop, in the span of about thirty seconds, at around five years old. Uncle Brian was the one who taught me, before I learned about either event in school. We were sitting at the breakfast table in Nana Mac's kitchen one morning, in the early 1990s. He was sitting at the end of the table next to the fridge, reading the paper, in his late twenties. As I sat next to him, probably eating Nana Mac's famous waffles, he pointed to an artist's rendering of the asteroid strike in the paper, and began the lesson, excitedly, speaking like he was reading me a story. "Hey, John Michael, do you know how the dinosaurs died?"

I had no idea.

"A huge asteroid from space hit the Earth millions of years ago, which blocked out the sun and eventually killed all the plants. Without food, none of the dinosaurs survived. And do you know how the universe started? All the stars and planets and everything in space came from one *big* explosion—it's called the Big Bang. *Isn't that cool*?!"

Imagine hearing both of these concepts in the same breath for the first time in your life, at five years old—it was like he wanted to see how much he could shock me. They were two immense, mind-blowing concepts that were brand new to me, and of course, were difficult to grasp at such a young age. I'll never forget first learning about them, though, in the span of about thirty seconds in Nana Mac's kitchen, and of course, who I learned them *from*.

I left Yellowstone one evening, exiting through the west entrance into Montana, and spent a rest day in West Yellowstone, Montana, seeing a live performance of *Annie Get Your Gun* at a very small theater downtown.

Back in Wyoming in the park, continuing northeast through its central loop toward Canyon Village, after a great breakfast at West Yellowstone's Running Bear Pancake House, I came around one bend and saw a cluster of cars along the roadside. Considering all there was to see in Yellowstone, I wondered intently what they were looking at. Then I spotted it grazing out in the field . . . a bison! An icon of the American West.

I stopped and took a good look, wishing I could get closer. I'd never seen a bison before in person. A few minutes later, the lumbering old brute disappeared into the brush and the crowd dispersed. The tourists got back in their cars, maps in hand, pulled back onto the road and roamed on, in search of the next spectacle. But I kept my eye on that brush. I biked a little farther down the road. And then, low and behold, right where I figured it might emerge again, the old brute rose to the occasion, this time just yards from the road!

I slowly got off my bike. Two other people were right next to me on my left—a man holding his very young daughter in his arms. We gazed at the timeless, woolly figure in wonder, and I noticed a crowd of cars begin to accumulate back by the road behind us. Another spectacle.

The bison just stood there, breathing heavily. Now that I was so close, just yards away, I could fully appreciate just how enormous and incredibly dangerous he was. He was significantly bigger than a Spanish bull.

And then I noticed he was doing something rather peculiar. I figured he must have had an itch on his head, because he kept rubbing it against the tree beside him. Except, rubbing his gargantuan, horned head was much more like *clobbering* it on the poor tree; the ground literally shook beneath our feet as he did it. Then, the monstrous animal looked right at us, itch apparently gone—and, to our shock, began *stampeding directly toward us!*

It was something out of a horrible nightmare, this colossal beast seconds from trampling us . . . but shortly thereafter, before I really knew what was happening, a sigh of relief. It was just a bluff. He had only taken a couple of steps before pulling up—to remind us to keep our distance, perhaps. Or maybe it was just for fun—just to fuck with us.

Whatever the reason, it was more than enough to send the father next to me hastily retreating to his car, his little daughter suddenly wailing in his arms, and me hurrying back to the road. The show was over. Time to get moving, on to the next spectacle—*before* you *become the spectacle.*

Yellowstone's a little more dangerous than many imagine. "The park is not Disneyland, Rocky Mountain version," says Lee Whittlesey, a former park ranger, who wrote a book on the different ways the park can kill you, from its hot springs that can boil you alive to its bison, which I was now fully aware of, that can trample or gore you. The next spectacle down the road was a large wolf—but it was only visible from somewhat of a distance, across a ridge.

Later, I camped at the Canyon Village campground, building a fire for the first time—not so much for warmth, but to keep the mosquitoes away. It was more difficult to start the fire than I figured it'd be, because the wood I used wasn't very dry, but I used some blank pages from my journal notebook as kindling to get it going.

On the way out of Yellowstone, after cruising downhill on wet pavement off the gigantic green plateau, I stayed at the Pahaska Tepee Resort (it's more of a motel than a "resort") just outside the east entrance of the park, arriving *just* in time—another massive thunderstorm came through. I walked into the gift shop there just a couple of minutes before the skies opened up, then watched the pouring rain and impressive lightning show from the gift shop doorway.

The ride from Pahaska Tepee, Wyoming, to Cody, Wyoming, the next day was what Teddy Roosevelt called "the most scenic fifty miles in America." I was skeptical of that claim at first, but the road ended up having some of the most impressive western scenery you'll find, living up to the hype, with dramatic brown rock formations. It was mostly downhill, too, which made the panoramas even better. In Greybull, Wyoming, I ran into four high schoolers biking from Washington State back home to Westchester, New York, before their senior year started. We grabbed a quick dinner together at A&W, eating outside.

They were easily the youngest cyclists I'd met on the trip, and they were traveling light—a little *too* light, I remember thinking, with fairly shabby equipment. They must've not had much money to spend. I gave one of them an old tire I was about to replace, because he needed it badly, along with a new $8 tube and a little advice. He was overwhelmingly grateful when I refused to take his eight dollars. I was impressed with them; they had to be only seventeen. I wondered what *their* parents thought.

After Greybull, I came across an intersection with a sign that read "Route 38½." Thinking it was funny and odd, like the hidden Hogwarts Express train platform, I took a photo of it. The really funny part, though, was that I should've *taken* Route 38½ instead of the road I chose, because the road I chose later turned into a dirt road to the middle of nowhere.

At first, the dirt was packed down, with gravel, and the bike was able to move fairly well on it. But later, it turned to deeper, finer, dried-out, light brown dirt, which had my skinny tires sinking, slipping, and fishtailing all over the place. It was like driving in the snow in a car that can't quite handle it. An unsettling feeling for sure. The tires were constantly losing traction, especially on slight downhills; they were much too thin for this kind of terrain. I almost fell several times. I wasn't sure I'd make it. *How long will this last?* I didn't have much of a clue. And the feeling of desolation had hit an all-time high. The dirt road wound its way through exposed brown rock hills and layered mesas—and nothing else. It was an empty, lonely, eerily quiet place with no wildlife and no people. The road blended in with the light brown landscape, so that the last sign of humanity (the pavement) was completely gone.

I was inundated now by an intolerant nature. An ant crawling on an uninhabited, lifeless desert planet. The situation kind of felt like treading water in an open ocean, with no land in sight. If for some reason you couldn't keep moving, you'd die and nobody would know. My phone didn't have service, of course, so this feeling of total self-reliance came over me. I couldn't break down. I couldn't get hurt. I had to keep moving. I had benefited from a great deal of unexpected help at every stage of the journey thus far—but nobody would help me here.

Every now and then, the road would come to a fence with an opening in it, where I had to get off the bike and lift it over the cattle guard (clunky grates made of large-gapped metal piping laid over a deep ditch, to prohibit cattle from escaping), gingerly walking over them with my slippery metal-bottomed bike shoes like they were Indiana Jones booby traps—being extra careful to make sure I didn't slip and break an ankle. I never saw any cattle, so I'm not sure what purpose they served.

Churning through the dirt with a heavy road bike, not equipped for it, for eighteen miles proved arduous. It was a *long* eighteen miles, especially in such heat, and I quickly became exhausted and drenched in sweat.

The dirt road finally ended in a small town called Ten Sleep, where I'd stay the night. Getting back on pavement felt like taking three weights off of a baseball bat in the on-deck circle. The bike just *glided*. The name of the town comes from the Native American custom of measuring distance by the number of "sleeps," or nights spent after days on horseback. The Sioux called the location "Ten Sleeps" because it was halfway between two of their main camps—ten sleeps in either direction. The location was represented in their written language by two hands (each with five spread fingers) and a tepee.

Still soaked in sweat from the unsparing July sun and the difficult dirt road, I had a satisfying steak dinner in the old, but air-conditioned, Ten Sleep Saloon. Then I checked into the nearby motel, showered, and later went back to the saloon, one of just a few buildings on 2nd Street (the town's main street), for a beer.

I grabbed an open seat at the end of the bar, next to a few truck drivers and construction workers. The trucker next to me, around forty, had a long black mustache and ponytail. After we talked for a bit, he ordered us all a round of Jäger shots. They all thought it was hilarious that I was biking across the country, and got a particular kick out of the *direction* I was going.

"He's heading *east*!" one cackled to another. It was like an inside joke I didn't get.

The trucker next to me explained. "Yer goin' *east*? On a *bicycle*? Oh yeah, you got a *day* ahead of you tomorrow. You'll be *climbin'*. Got some real steep climbs and some bad construction zones right now up there in the Bighorns. Here, have another shot. Might as well."

We all ended up doing shot after shot after shot of Jäger, laughing our asses off about how miserable the next day was going to be for me. They thought I was *insane*.

Emily Corrow, the blonde twenty-something bartender, joined the party, continuing to serve trays of Jäger shots and taking a couple herself. For some reason, the whole thing kept getting funnier and *funnier*. The laughter didn't stop, bouncing off the walls of the Ten Sleep Saloon late into the night.

At closing time, Emily kindly drove me (the very short distance) back to the motel. She must've had a much better grasp than I of just how many shots we'd actually all consumed.

When my alarm went off a few hours later, a thunderclapping sledgehammer pounded at my temples, somehow hitting both of them simultaneously. There was an awful, acidic, metallic taste in my mouth and I felt like I could throw up at any second. I slowly sat up on the bed and lumbered over to the bathroom, its bright light inflicting searing pain into my eyes, and was ready to vomit. But I couldn't. Everything hurt. *I'm never drinking again.* The sledgehammer persisted. Pounding and pounding, unapologetically.

My dad always told us growing up, "If you hoot with the owls, you gotta soar with the eagles." Translation: If you stay out late, you better get your ass up and do what you have to do.

Doing so had never been more difficult—it was by far the worst hangover I'd ever had in my life. The looming Bighorns would have no sympathy for me; in fact, the mountain range seemed kind of psyched that I was in such bad shape. Back on the road, I could barely move the bike forward. I kept thinking I'd have to leap off and run over to the side of the road to puke.

Just when you think you're out of the Rockies, the little-known Bighorn range sprouts up out of nowhere to say, belligerently, *Not out yet, you drunk bastard.* See, it had a bit of a chip on its shoulder, tired of being in the shadow of its famous, heroic, snow-capped Rocky Mountain siblings in Colorado and Utah. Sick of all those nauseating Coors Light commercials. But its climbs packed a punch, to say the least, *for a full thirty miles.*

Right out of the gate, only a few miles into the morning on US-16, the long ascent began. Just a few miles later, the Bighorns' brutal switchbacks already had me drenched, sweating out the alcohol—achingly, yet wonderfully, beginning to evaporate my horrible hangover. It was a wrenching cure for a wretched soul.

I shook my head, cursing myself for laughing about it all the night before at the saloon, with such foolish jauntiness, and wondered if any of the truck drivers or construction workers would pass me with a hearty laugh and honking horn. I didn't notice any. Throughout the miserable morning, I kept thinking about going to the movies that night when I arrived in Buffalo, Wyoming. It would be my reward. The last Christopher Nolan Batman film, titled *The Dark Knight Rises*, starring Christian Bale, was coming out that day—Friday, July 20.

After pounding the pedals for hours in the very low gears, I ran into a series of construction zones near the summit, as advertised. Sometimes throughout the trip, construction zones were only open to one-way traffic; cars would have to wait their turn and then follow the construction crew's pilot car through a narrow, single lane, until the second lane opened up again. Normally, in these situations, I'd go in front of the line of cars and stay directly behind the pilot car. Usually, the pilot car would go 25–30 mph, so I'd have to pedal as fast as I could to keep up (and hope there were no uphills or headwinds).

When I came upon the first one-way traffic zone in the Bighorns, though, in a relatively flat area near the summit, the construction worker at the front of the line of cars said I had to get off the bike and throw it in the back of the pilot car (which was a pickup truck in this case) and hitch a ride through the work area. I hadn't had to do that the entire trip, so of course, I *really* didn't want to. I wanted to bike the entire distance, coast to coast to coast.

After arguing with the construction guy, trying to plead my case, I finally asked, "If I just *went*, would you guys get in trouble?"

In trouble. As a little kid would say.

Dryly, and without missing a beat, he answered, "*You* would get in trouble."

Okay, good answer. I contemplated just taking off anyway, wondering if they'd actually try to physically stop me and whether the road conditions were bikeable, but ultimately decided it wasn't worth it. Getting arrested in Wyoming might've sounded cool to my friends back home, but I didn't *actually* want to get arrested in Wyoming.

So I threw the bike and myself in the back of the pilot car pickup and rode the one or two miles through the work zone, feeling guilty and angry as hell. I felt like I was cheating. It still bothers me that I wasn't able to bike that mile or two.

Late in the day, after cruising down the Bighorns, past runaway truck ramps, into Buffalo, I checked into the legendary Occidental Hotel—one of the country's best known and most traditional Old Western hotels, right in the middle of town. The only room available was the most expensive—it was the hotel's two-bedroom crown jewel—but I wanted to stay there, so I bit the bullet. It was the room Butch Cassidy and the Sundance Kid (the infamous Wild West train and bank robbers who inspired the classic 1969 movie starring Robert Redford and Paul Newman) had actually stayed in, now aptly called the "Outlaw Suite." Other hotel guests have included the likes of Calamity Jane, Buffalo Bill, a young Teddy Roosevelt, Herbert Hoover, and Ernest Hemingway.

Wearing a cowboy hat, the teenage kid who assisted the front desk helped me carry the fully loaded bike up the Occidental's very traditional Old Western wraparound staircase, since there wasn't an elevator. He lifted it from the handlebars and walked backward up the stairs, leaving the rear, and lion's share of the work, to me. I lifted it from the rear rack and we began to ascend. After just a few stairs up, though, the back end of the rack—where the red rear reflector attached—cracked and broke off, cutting the palm of my hand pretty badly.

After we made it up to the Outlaw Suite, and I turned on the shower in its ancient claw foot tub, which sat awkwardly in the middle of the bathroom with a curtain that wrapped all the way around it and water pressure that struggled, I still couldn't stop the bleeding. The white tub had a rusty red stream trickling down its center, as if I'd just committed a horrible murder and was feverishly trying to wash away the evidence. An Outlaw Suite pastime, perhaps. Annoyingly, the blood continued to drip everywhere, refusing to coagulate, as I dried off and got dressed.

I didn't bike over the Bighorns all day to miss that movie, though, and I was running late, so I quickly wrapped my hand with Kleenex tissue and tape, a very improvised bandage of sorts, and bolted over to the theater. I bought buttered popcorn and a Sprite, found a seat, plopped down in the worn-leather, cushioned chair, and exhaled deeply. It was the end of a very long day.

I'd never been to the movies alone before. The situation was a little odd on paper—I was at a movie, by myself, on a Friday night in the middle of Wyoming, and my hand was wrapped in tissues and tape and still bleeding, the blood now showing signs of beginning to overwhelm the Kleenex. But I had a movie, popcorn, and a comfortable bed in the Outlaw Suite all ahead of me. I don't think I could've been happier.

Back at the hotel after the movie, though, I watched news coverage of a horrific mass shooting that had occurred at a screening of the very same Batman movie in Aurora, Colorado, near Denver, directly south of me—just a few hours down I-25. A man dressed as The Joker, with tactical gear, set off tear gas grenades and opened fire, with multiple guns, on a packed theater of helpless moviegoers. Incredibly senseless. Incredibly disturbing. There would be a disquieting string of similar mass shootings in the years to come, reigniting the gun control debate in the US and creating a new genre of American and international heroes—those who rush to stop random shooters, sometimes sacrificing their lives—as sixteen-year-old high school football player Tate Myre did in 2021, at Oxford High School in Michigan. Despite my comfortable Outlaw Suite bed and long day of biking over the Bighorns, I had trouble falling asleep that night.

I had planned a rest day in Buffalo, but there wasn't much to do in the town, and I definitely couldn't afford another night in the Outlaw Suite. So, after sleeping in late and having a leisurely breakfast at The Busy Bee Café adjacent to the Occidental's lobby, I checked out of the hotel and found the log cabin-style Blue Gables Motel on the outskirts of town. The owners, Jim and Karen Henry, generously let me stay for free.

I spent the afternoon just hanging out at the motel with my log cabin neighbors, Lyndon, and his son, Daniel, who were stranded there due to car trouble. We drank beer and grilled up a nice little barbecue dinner with two other long-distance cyclists who were hoping to make it from South Dakota to Oregon.

Lyndon was adopted as a child but reconnected with his parents as an adult; he said he was a "strong believer in nature over nurture" as a result. The five of us made the most of our downtime with long conversations, and the afternoon and evening passed quickly. It felt like a summer night hanging out with friends—"friends" I'd just met—and it helped take my mind off the Colorado movie theater shooting. What I had expected to be a boring rest day alone was anything but, and I retired to my log cabin grateful for the random encounter.

From Buffalo, I could've hopped on I-90 legally, since there's no direct alternative heading east, but I opted to stay off the interstate and take the roundabout Route 14 to the north, even though it was out of the way. I'd mapped it out this way, to avoid interstates as much as possible. Route 14 was extremely desolate. Even by local standards, it was isolation at its most extreme (there's a town just off 14 called Recluse). I was back on the Great Plains.

I stopped for the day in a town called Spotted Horse—where the population was literally 2. The two had names: Coleen and Jerome. The entire town was just one bar—the Spotted Horse Bar, of course, whose motto was "Coldest Beer in Town." *Can't argue with that.* Outside, there was a statue of a bucking bronco, oddly painted like a cow, with black and white spots, and an old free-standing gas station sign with the antiquated blue and red Standard Oil logo on it, faded and chipping away.

A sign above the barred-door entrance to the Spotted Horse Bar advertised the annual pig roast coming up in August. But for *who*? There was nobody around. Not a single person or sign of *any* life, stretching to the 360-degree horizon.

I walked toward the door, in the late afternoon light, and slowly walked in, almost suspiciously. *Could people really live here? Could this really be a functioning bar?* As I walked in, I found that the only person inside was Coleen, behind the bar—and she was *drunk* to *quite* drunk. To *quite, quite* drunk. She was good-natured and friendly though.

I sat down at the bar, and we talked for a while. She had a lot to say, including the story of how *Easy Rider* actor Peter Fonda hit a deer in the area while riding his motorcycle a couple decades back, and would come back to sit at her bar and have a "beer for the deer" from time to time (after that accident, he never rode at dusk or later again). They didn't really have any food there (I guess there was no one to prepare it), but she threw a frozen personal pizza in the microwave for me for dinner. Probably their best (and maybe only) customer of the day, I also bought a burnt orange t-shirt with a drawing of the bar with its fake, cow-spotted horse outside, with "Coldest Beer in Town" printed on it.

Coleen let me stay the night in an empty trailer out back for free. Although it was about as hot as a sauna in the trailer, it was a good thing I had shelter other than just my tent—another big thunderstorm came through that night. I watched it from a distance as it approached from the north, sitting on a picnic table outside the trailer in complete darkness, before I went to sleep, enjoying the encroaching storm very silently light up the sky on the northern horizon a dazzling neon purple, with small angry bolts of white-hot lightning.

After a very late lunch at Subway in Gillette, Wyoming, the next day, I took I-90, the big interstate that stretches from Seattle to Boston, to Moorcroft, Wyoming—the town where the friendly, weed-smoking alien voiced by Seth Rogen crashes his ship in the 2011 movie *Paul*. Unlike other interstates I'd cycled on, this one was clean, smooth, and lightly traveled. I made great time on 90, despite the stifling late-July heat, and happily blasted the AC in my room at the Cozy Motel upon arriving in Moorcroft.

The next morning, elderly local men in cowboy hats gathered around the table next to mine for their daily morning coffee and gossip session as I ate breakfast in the tiny Donna's Diner next to the motel. From there, I took US-16 through Thunder Basin National Grassland toward the South Dakota border, passing through a small town named Upton, whose water tower read, "Upton: Best Town on Earth."

During the Five-Mile Water/Stretch that day, someone pulled over to see if I was okay, exclaiming, "Thought the heat got to ya!"

I guess seeing a biker lying on the ground on the side of the highway might raise a red flag.

ROUTE 212: MILES FROM NOWHERE

SOUTH DAKOTA
JULY 24–30

"Into the Great Wide Open" – Tom Petty

The South Dakota welcome sign had an artist's rendering of Mount Rushmore with the tagline "Great Faces. Great Places." Immediately upon crossing the border, as I got into the beautiful Black Hills, I ran into two brothers biking home to Ohio. They looked alike, and both wore the same exact, unorthodox cycling getup—a gray collared shirt and long pants. They were friendly, offering some ice-cold water from their Camelbaks, and seemed more than thrilled to chat with another cyclist.

That night, I stayed in Custer, South Dakota, at the retro Rocket Motel; it was one of my favorite motels of the trip because, while it was well-maintained, it hadn't really changed since opening in 1950.

At the Rocket, I caught up with Nana Mac on the phone and captured a bolt of lightning with my digital camera from the motel parking lot (after a few tries) as another strong thunderstorm closed in fast, leaving an arching rainbow in its wake. Anytime I'd call Nana Mac, she'd answer her landline phone, not knowing who it was. So I'd surprise her each time. I always loved doing that.

The next day was the shortest day of biking of the trip—just twenty-four miles, to allow time to explore Mount Rushmore. The carved stone faces of Presidents Washington, Jefferson, Roosevelt, and Lincoln—chosen to represent the nation's birth, growth, development, and preservation, respectively[35]— were smaller than I'd imagined, but nevertheless impressive.

From there, I went through Keystone and Rapid City, then went north on I-90 *west* to Sturgis, which was out of the way—but I wanted to cross South Dakota on Route 212.

Sturgis is home to the long-running Sturgis Motorcycle Rally each August, which was only days away. The town was gearing up; you could feel it brimming with anticipation for the big weeklong event. Clearly, it was the week the town lived for. Jan Weimer, the owner of Weimer's Diner & Donuts in the heart of town, kindly treated me to a free lunch and some donuts, and I stopped by the famous Full Throttle Saloon, "the world's largest biker bar" and said hello to Emmett the donkey hanging out under a high table, lying on the floor and enjoying the sun and fresh air that the indoor/outdoor bar allowed. The famous mascot of the bar, Emmett was a staple of the well-known reality TV show that ran from 2009-2013 about the establishment and was rescued from a massive fire that completely destroyed the bar in 2015.

Late in the afternoon, I continued north on a very barren road into Newell, South Dakota, an isolated one-square-mile town with just a few hundred people in it. I spent just $11.01 for a hearty dinner at TJ's Café and Waterin' Hole and just $30 for an upstairs room in an old house that felt like it'd been built over a century prior, perhaps when the town was first laid out in 1910. It felt creaky, haunted—a bit like the Just-Us Inn, way back in Oregon.

The waitress at the Blue Line Diner the next morning had a certain melancholy about her as she poured my coffee. At nineteen or twenty years old, she was pale and pretty, and decidedly down. After she brought out the stack of pancakes I ordered a little later, she started talking more. She told me her parents had recently moved the family up to Newell from somewhere in Arizona—they said they wanted to "get away from people."

"I *like* people," she lamented, with genuine sadness. "I can't wait to go back to college."

Despite the eatery's presence on Google Maps, and its chipped, fading, wooden sign that read BLUE LINE DINER in old blue paint, the place looked nothing like a diner to me. It looked like a plain and simple one-story trailer home on the outskirts of town, with a couple of cars parked in front of it—a far cry from the dressed-up, sprawling, tall, metallic diners with multicolored neon lights back home, throughout New York and New Jersey. It was unequivocally homely—but charming in a way too. From out front, you could see South Dakota's Route 212 stretching endlessly and ominously, straight out to the eastern horizon, well beyond the last couple of buildings of the small town. I knew there wasn't much out there.

Connie, the owner of the Blue Line Diner, saw my bike propped up outside and warned me that there was, in fact, *absolutely nothing* out there. Nowhere to get food. Nowhere to get water. For nearly eighty miles—in other words, all day. She seemed legitimately uneasy.

Generously, she paid for my breakfast and had the kitchen prepare a bag lunch for me, also on the house, but seemed most concerned about *water*.

"I really don't know what you're gonna do about water," she admonished, shaking her head.

She had a point. My five water bottles wouldn't be nearly enough to make it through the entire day, but I figured I'd stop for lunch and refill them in Mud Butte, a blip on Google Maps that was about halfway to Faith, the next real town. If I really conserved water, I knew I could probably scrape by refilling just once.

I'd read about Mud Butte—Barbara Savage wrote about it in her book *Miles from Nowhere*, which was one of the inspirations for my trip. Named after a nearby mud-colored butte (a butte is an isolated hill with steep sides and a flat top, similar to, but narrower than, a mesa), Mud Butte, South Dakota, is also known for being the site of the excavation of a 65-million-year-old *Tyrannosaurus rex* skeleton in 1981—just the sixth *T. rex* ever discovered—after a northwestern South Dakota rancher finally called in some experts to check out large bones he'd seen for years, embedded in a steep cliff in the area.[36]

The Mud Butte vicinity is part of the greater Hell Creek geological formation, an area known for well-preserved dinosaur fossils that spans parts of North Dakota, South Dakota, Wyoming, and Montana. The first *T. rex* ever discovered was found in Hell Creek. Before the fateful asteroid impact, the landscape here contrasted sharply to what it is today. It consisted of humid, subtropical floodplains, along the shores of an inland sea, teeming with life, especially *T. rex*: "One paleontologist estimated that in the Cretaceous period Hell Creek was so thick with *T. rexes* that they were like hyenas on the Serengeti,"[37] according to American journalist Douglas Preston. Some well-preserved Hell Creek excavation sites may be critically important to our understanding of the asteroid impact, as they contain a precise record of the very sixty minutes of the event. This could possibly help prove that dinosaurs weren't already in decline (as some scientists believe), according to Preston.

Other recent research on the asteroid impact claims that if it had landed in the Atlantic or Pacific oceans, or almost *anywhere* other than present-day Mexico's Yucatán Peninsula (then a shallow sea), it wouldn't have had nearly as devastating an effect and almost certainly wouldn't have led to a mass extinction (which led to the rise of mammals, and eventually, humans). The hydrocarbon- and sulfur-rich sedimentary rock in the oil-abundant Yucatán region released much more sulfur and soot than rock in other areas would have, blocking out the sun more severely and for a longer time. The research suggests that just 13% of Earth's surface contains rock of such composition.[38]

***

Barbara Savage's book was the only reason I went out of my way to take Route 212 across South Dakota. I wanted to relive what I'd read, in person. Experience what she experienced in South Dakota on her 23,000-mile, two-year, round-the-world trip with her husband, Larry, in the late 1970s. After biking around the world, Savage dedicated an entire chapter (out of just eighteen) to Route 212. She described in detail how desolate, monotonous, and challenging it was, and how she and Larry had to pedal fast enough (at least 10 mph) so that the mosquitoes wouldn't land on them, as I had to do in the swampland approaching New Orleans early on in my trip.

On the map of the couple's journey around the world, in the first pages of Savage's book, Mud Butte is one of twenty dots that the route connects; some of the others include Los Angeles, Miami, Paris, and New Delhi—you know, slightly bigger places. Before Barbara and Larry tackled Route 212, others had warned them of cycling in South Dakota: "Nothing but flat or rolling empty prairie. You'll die of boredom," said one. "I've never heard of a bicycler catching a tailwind in South Dakota. Everyone has headwinds no matter which direction they're pedaling," said another.[39]

Of Mud Butte in 1978, she writes:

Booming downtown Mud Butte, South Dakota (population two) consisted of a rustic coffee shop on one side of Route 212 and a one-room volunteer fire station on the other; if a fire broke out in the coffee shop, the McGillivrays, the middle-aged couple that ran the coffee shop and lived in the cottage connected to it, would, I suppose, dash across Route 212, jump into the fire engine, drive back across to the coffee shop, and put out the fire. As Larry and I stumbled through the front door of their shop, the McGillivrays took a look at our long faces and heavy bikes and shook their heads knowingly.

"The last bicycler that rolled in here hitchhiked out," Mrs. McGillivray shrugged as she slapped our iced teas onto the counter and straightened her cotton dress. He dragged in here 'round noon a few months ago, and he was a real wreck. That long dry stretch between Newell and here 'bout drove the poor kid to despair. He was a real nice boy, though. Was bicyclin' from somewhere on the West Coast to his home on the East Coast somewhere. Boston, I think it was; somewhere big, anyway. And he had his heart set on bicyclin' the whole way; and up until South Dakota he was farin' just fine."

-*Miles from Nowhere*. Barbara Savage.

After some deliberation (he didn't want to cheat, of course), the kid ends up hitching a ride in a rancher's pickup to Watertown, a town 304 miles east of the coffee shop on the opposite end of the state—almost to the Minnesota border—after the McGillivrays tell him it gets even *more* boring after Mud Butte.

"A month later we got a letter from him," Mrs. McGillivray continued. "He was back home in Boston or wherever it was. Said, after he got to Watertown he cycled the whole rest of the way to the East Coast. Never had to hitchhike again after South Dakota. Guess that says somethin' 'bout this here state. It does in the best of folks."[40]

As tough and tedious and *long* as the book made the road seem, I thought it was intriguing enough to go out of my way a little and experience Route 212 for myself. It was like reading the book and then seeing the movie, but much better. This was reading the book and then *living* the movie. And I didn't even have mosquitoes to deal with. Taking Route 212 was also my personal tribute to Barbara Savage, who was tragically killed in a cycling accident just before her book was published in 1983, for helping to inspire my trip.

I guess, somehow, I hadn't considered the possibility that a coffee shop in a forgotten South Dakota town in the middle of nowhere with no people in it could ever *close* after thirty-four years. I asked Connie and the Blue Line crew about it, and they just laughed, and kind of looked at me like I was crazy.

"Nope. No coffee shop," Connie chuckled. "There's nothin' out there. I mean, *nothin'*."

"But what about the fire stati—"

The confusion and suspicion on their faces convinced me to just immediately drop the whole thing.

I crammed the bag lunch into the last few square inches of my handlebar bag, but there was no way for me to carry additional water. There were no lakes, rivers, or streams along the route, either (I could purify water from sources like these with my iodine pills in an emergency). So I gulped as much water as I could before I left the diner, and steeled myself to conserve as much as I could as I set out.

As soon as I set out, I realized the combination of the hot July sun and the merciless, unexpected headwind I was battling was going to make it very difficult, if not impossible, to conserve water. But the pure *emptiness* of this road was just as disconcerting. I had to agree with Barbara Savage. Route 212 was the most desolate, lonesome road I'd ever seen—and it certainly did seem, as Savage described it in her chapter title, to be "The Endless Road."

It was *so* different from what I was used to back home, that, at first, I kind of enjoyed it, in a way, as I did other isolated stretches of the trip, but it was beginning to push my comfort level as it went on and on . . . and on. The road extended in front of me as a straight line to the horizon. There were a few very slight, rolling hills, which made the asphalt look like a slightly undulating ribbon stretching out to infinity—but other than that, absolutely nothing to see. No people. No buildings. No cars. No rock formations. No trees. No wildlife. The fields weren't even *farms* or anything; they didn't seem to have any purpose whatsoever. No crops. No livestock. Just openness. A vast void. These were the true badlands, I figured—the humdrum desertedness Fritz had worried about a lifetime ago, back at Tower 7 in Wrightsville Beach, North Carolina, the night before I set out. I'd never seen such prolonged desolation on this level, not even in Kansas or Wyoming.

The whole morning was a struggle, and as midday approached, the wind picked up even more and I needed to work really hard to keep moving, which made me need to drink more. I was making terrible time, and was *already* low on water.

But then, something amazing happened.

Just before I got to Mud Butte, a motorcyclist passed me and pulled over to the side of the road in front of me. Seasoned and tough-looking, with short gray hair, the woman hopped off her Harley and took something out of the back compartment of her bike. Then she walked over and handed it to me. *It was a tall, ice-cold bottle of water.*

I couldn't believe it.

"This is from Connie and the crew at the Blue Line Diner. Have a good ride," she said, with a smile.

I was kind of in a state of shock as she revved the motor and peeled off. *What the hell just happened?* I was dangerously low on water, still early in the day . . . and now, there's a large water bottle in my hand, cold and dripping with condensation like it was just pulled from a cooler at a tailgate party. I took a few gulps of the deliciously frigid water, needing it badly. I stopped for a lunch break in Mud Butte a few minutes later, still a bit stunned.

There was just one empty house in Mud Butte, on the right, with a smaller, garage-like shed across the road from it. That was *it.* Now I understood—now the prospect of a coffee shop seemed comical. Just totally ridiculous. I tried to picture it there in 1978, but couldn't. It would just be so out of place. The house had a small circle of grass, with about a five-yard radius, in front of it, that served as a modest front yard. The backyard was a little bigger—it stretched as far as the eye could see, all the way to the horizon. Eerily, the only sound I could hear was the soft clanging of wind chimes coming from the home's front porch, and the whistle of the wind itself. The pensive open plains of South Dakota said nothing else.

I sat cross-legged in the center of the circle of grass and ate my bag lunch in the sun, hoping someone would come out and say hello or something, or at least tell me to get the hell off their property. *Did the McGillivrays still live here? Or were they long gone?* It's amazing how time can change a place—in this case, from a lush, swampy *Tyrannosaurus rex* hunting ground to a friendly, rustic coffee shop to a silent, windy vacuity. Warm in temperature, but cold in every other way.

As I sat there on the grass and ate, listening to the wind chimes and feeling like I was in some rural Edward Hopper painting, overwhelmed with isolation, I came to the following conclusion: Mud Butte, South Dakota, was the loneliest place on Earth.

I finished the bag lunch quickly, anxious to get back on the road.

Luckily, the feeling of loneliness didn't last long. A little later, *another* motorcyclist, traveling in the opposite direction this time, pulled over and handed me an even *bigger, colder* bottle of water, saying it was from the first motorcyclist! I guess he'd run into her at a gas station way down the road.

I couldn't believe it. Somewhere in the middle of barren South Dakota, there was a network of perfect strangers looking out for me, on literally *the* day I needed it most. I was astounded. The *one* day I needed help with water more than *any other* day—and I had it, from people I'd never met or had any connection to whatsoever. The road was derelict and the wind demoralizing, but this unexpected water-bottle exchange—this altruistic badlands relay—was heartwarming and inspiring. Even more than the water itself, such simple, but profound, acts of kindness really gave me a boost that day. As it turned out, there wasn't any water to be found anywhere on this hot July day, not even in Mud Butte, so the help those motorcyclists gave me was critical. North and South Dakota are named after the Dakota, a Sioux tribe that inhabited the area, and the word Dakota means "friend" or "ally" in the Sioux language. On this day, I had many unexpected friends. Unforeseen allies of the road.

The next day, I got up at 5:00 a.m. in Faith, South Dakota, for the first of four consecutive centuries to close out the month of July. Most of the day was more of the same—lonely, fruitless stretches with nothing to see. But toward the end of the day, I ran into another cyclist! I certainly didn't expect it—not *here*. This wasn't Portland or the Pacific Coast Highway.

The guy, probably in his thirties, was named Wes. We spoke for a few minutes, then took a picture of one another—I later found his, of me, posted on his blog. He was cycling from New Jersey to Seattle, and he was out of water. It was extremely hot, and I was running low, but I gave him nearly all of what I had left, paying forward the kindness the Blue Line Diner crew and the motorcyclists showed me. Soon after that, though, another friendly couple gave me a bunch of cold water out of their trunk—about as much as I could drink. Just after that, I crossed the Missouri River (the *only* river or tangible landmark I remember on Route 212) into the Central Time Zone, and the scenery improved significantly.

After passing dream-like fields of beautiful yellow sunflowers and then fields of endless round bales (cylinder-shaped bales of hay that look like randomly dispersed, rolled-up golden carpets), the long, 115-mile day ended in Gettysburg, South Dakota, "Where the battle wasn't," according to the town's welcome sign.

Gettysburg is almost exactly halfway across the country, so I was really making progress now on the return trip back east. I met a friendly family at a drive-in-style BBQ restaurant, eating at one of the outdoor picnic tables. They insisted on buying my dinner. The heat lingered well into the early evening as I ate next to them, happy to have some company, and grateful for yet another random act of kindness.

The father of the family, Mike Schlacter, made a living by continuing the successful family business in town and was proud of where he came from—a trait I've always admired. When I mentioned the welcome sign, he said he wasn't too thrilled about it. He thought it was disrespectful, tacky. I'd think the same thing, if I were from there.

Mike also gave me some good news. "From this point on," he said, "you'll hit a town every ten miles, because the locomotives in the old days needed water about that often."

Me and them both.

As I checked into the tiny, $41-per-night Trail Motel in the middle of "town," the Indian owner asked me questions about where I'd been and where I was going. After everything I said—at each and every pause—all he said was "Ho-ly *shit,*" over and over, more emphatically each time—almost exactly as John Belushi does in *Animal House.* I kept the story going, on purpose, to see how long the streak would go. He must have said "Ho-ly *shit*" at least eight or ten times in a row, without a single other word.

After another century the next day, I stayed at another motel in Doland for only $20, a new record low (for a clean room, that is). A lot of *campgrounds* aren't that cheap. Like that tiny motel in Ashland, Kansas, I had to call the owner to come drop off the key. The room had a TV, so I watched the 2012 London Olympics that night before drifting off to sleep.

After breakfast at the gas station across the street the next day and a free lunch at Perkins in Watertown, South Dakota, courtesy of Megan the waitress, I crossed into Minnesota, continuing on Route 212 into the Land of 10,000 Lakes.

Time Travel

MINNESOTA
JULY 30 – AUGUST 2

"Ramblin' Man" – The Allman Brothers Band

When Barbara Savage crosses into Minnesota on Route 212, she describes a tailwind picking them up right at the border. Mrs. McGillivray describes Minnesota as the beginning of "lots of farms and towns and green grass." For me, Minnesota is where the road work, construction zones, and closures started. I kept on riding right through them, constantly on the lookout for holes and wet concrete. On the first day, nobody was around, because it was after working hours. In the following days, the workers didn't seem to have a problem with my blatant disregard for the closures and their bright orange signs. I spoke to a few of them, and they were friendly.

I stopped that first night in the small town of Dawson, Minnesota, then turned off Route 212 to go south on Route 59 the next day.

I was really psyched to get to Worthington, Minnesota, where I finally had a scheduled rest day. Getting there on time would be a major moral victory, because it would cap ten straight days and 815 miles of biking without rest, including four centuries totaling 430 miles on the last four days. It was the toughest ten-day stretch on paper of the entire trip.

When I mapped out the route in college, I figured we'd be in good shape at this point and could cover 100+ miles a day on flat terrain without a problem—so I was aggressive with the schedule, wanting to get across the badlands in as little time as possible. What I didn't factor in enough, of course, was the *wind*. And century after century on consecutive days is hard on *any* cyclist—no matter what kind of shape you're in and no matter what the wind is doing. Sure, you can do it once, somewhat easily, if you're in reasonably good cycling shape—if you work up to it a little. But *again the next morning*? And *again* the *next* morning? Different story.

On this brutal ten-day stretch, I set the alarm on my stopwatch to go off each morning at 5:00 a.m., placing it well out of arm's reach, to force myself to get up. These were some of the most difficult days to wake up I'd ever experienced in my life—definitely more so than football training camp in high school and college, which had early wake-ups and often two practices a day. Picture the deepest sleep of your life—you're in a pleasant coma-like state, dreaming, maybe of being on a beautiful beach somewhere—as your body gratefully repairs itself from the beating it took the previous day, and then . . . *BEEP, BEEP, BEEP, BEEP*. You have no idea where you are. It's still dark out. Your eyes feel pasted shut. You're in a minuscule motel room, or your tiny tent, or maybe on someone's couch or in an upstairs bedroom of an old creaky house. But *where*? You can't remember at first. Oh, yeah—South Dakota—about as far from the beach as it *gets*.

You reach for the stopwatch, then curse yourself for setting it so far away. Then, it *hits* you. Crippling soreness from head to toe. Moving is like trying to run when you're having one of those nightmares where you *can't* run. But there's no time to waste. If you don't hit the road fairly quickly, you won't finish before dark. And as you knew all too well at this point, riding on the highway in the dark is *never* a situation you want to be in as a cyclist.

These days were a challenge, and there's always intrinsic reward when you truly challenge yourself. But, for the most part, they were *not* fun. If I could've sustained this pace for twenty-five or so days instead of ten, I could've made it across the whole country in under a month, as some cross-country cyclists have done. But I wouldn't recommend it. There just isn't enough time to fully appreciate the journey.

At the same time, I enjoyed riding in the very early morning in such wide-open spaces. It was so tranquil—a daily morning meditation session of sorts. As I made my way into the Corn Belt in eastern South Dakota, there was something spellbinding about watching the sun come up over the infinite corn fields, with the heavy moisture of the cool morning air and the smell of the dew on the stalks, which politely hinted that the end of summer was near. The Corn Belt would continue all the way through Ohio—through Minnesota, Iowa, Wisconsin, Illinois, and Indiana. I'd stretch by the edge of the stalks each morning.

On one particular morning on Route 212, right after the Five-Mile Water/Stretch, I was riding into the rising sun, which was just peeking over the corn fields on the horizon. It was a crisp, lovely morning. Just as the first song of the day—The Allman Brothers' "Ramblin' Man"—started to play, gifting me a little adrenaline and amiably waking me up, I imagined myself, for whatever reason, as an old man in his nineties. Sitting in a nursing home.

It was an unprecedented thought for me. I imagined that man thinking back to this particular sunrise in the eastern South Dakota corn fields, listening to "Ramblin' Man," and being very happy that he did that crazy trip all those years back. Maybe even happier that he did it looking back on it than he was when he was actually *doing* it. But I thought that man might want to go back in time to that very moment, if he could.

Zoning out as the music seemed to fade, I could see and feel the cold fluorescent lighting of the 2080s nursing home. The stuffy, artificial, air-conditioned air. The sleek interiors. The walkers and wheel chairs. The helpful, but pulse-lacking, robots. The loneliness and the silence. The indifference. The intangible sun transcending the high floor-to-ceiling windows. But only its light. Not its warmth.

And then, faster than a flash, I was *back*. For *real*. Back to twenty-four years old. Back to 2012. Feeling the brightening, rising sun beginning to warm my skin, as the music faded back in. Breathing in the pleasant, organic aroma of the dew and the corn. Cruising on a slight downhill through the fresh, early morning air, on Route 212 but *rollin' down Highway 41*. What a pompous trick for the young.

The scheduled rest day in Worthington, Minnesota, was the first since way back in Buffalo, Wyoming—a reward, finally, for all of those impossibly long, lonesome stretches of Route 212 across South Dakota. Throughout the ten days, I kept thinking about making it to Worthington, over and over. Getting there on time was a lofty goal for me, but I was determined to hit it. A new mantra was born, with a new imaginary t-shirt to put it on: *Are you worthy?*

I woke up very late on August 1, in a hotel room in Worthington, sore all over, feeling like I'd been hit by a train. I'd never needed a rest day so badly. But my morale was up.

Since I'd missed breakfast by a long shot, I basically limped over to the Ground Round Grill & Bar next door for a big midday lunch. There wasn't much to do in Worthington, or so it seemed, and I didn't know anybody there, but I was more than happy simply resting and eating that day.

CORN BELT BUCKLE

IOWA & WISCONSIN
AUGUST 2-13

"Hound Dog" - Elvis

I either made a wrong turn, or 59 was closed, but I took the less direct Route 60 down into Iowa, then turned left on US-18 near Sheldon. I'd continue east on 18 across the entire state of Iowa.

For days, there was nothing to see but corn, corn, and more corn. This was the heart of the Corn Belt, as far as I could tell—Iowa is the largest corn producer in America, after all. I spent the early August nights in Spencer, Algona, and then Clear Lake, where I stayed at the home of Tim and Darlene Veach; I was connected with them by a young couple I met eating dinner at a KFC the night before, in Algona.

I arrived at the Veach home, which looked over the actual lake the town is named for, just in time for a wonderful home-cooked dinner that included delicious, local, Iowa sweet corn. I never imagined simple corn could taste so good; it literally tasted like candy. Tim, who made his living managing a Super 8 nearby, said grace before we ate, praying with his eyes closed and hands crossed that I would "stay focused" finishing the trip.

I free camped the next night in a small park in the middle of Fredericksburg, another small Iowa town, then stayed in a motel on the Mississippi River the following night.

First thing the next morning, Monday, August 7, I crossed the Mississippi for the second time, this time into Wisconsin, to start a long day—a 104-mile century to Madison, past Wisconsin dairy farms, with black-and-white-spotted cows, and green rolling hills that were very reminiscent of the state's license plate. The state is known, after all, as "America's Dairyland." I discovered Naked brand "Green Machine" juice at a gas station that day—and found that there's a lot of energy packed into that little bottle; for a cyclist, it was like rocket fuel.

The following day was a rainy one. After getting a little lost in Waukesha, I found my way into Brookfield, Wisconsin, a suburb of Milwaukee, where I stayed with Zim, a Cornell teammate with a built figure and a blond buzz cut, and his kind, soft-spoken parents.

Like many in the area, the Zimmermans were of German descent. When I pulled into their driveway in the rain, I saw Zim's mom waving excitedly through the small kitchen window—I knew his parents pretty well from all of their Ithaca visits over our college years. The four of us had dinner at their kitchen table that night and talked for a long time, telling stories and enjoying Mrs. Zimmerman's famous pistachio torte.

After I dropped off the bike for its last tune-up nearby, to be done by some die-hard Green Bay Packers fans, Zim and I had some more nutritious snacks for breakfast at the Wisconsin State Fair the next morning, including chocolate-covered bacon (served cold with sea salt), cream puffs, hot dogs, and the infamous "Fat Elvis On-a-Stick" (a Reese's peanut butter cup dipped in banana batter, deep-fried and topped with chocolate sauce and bacon sprinkles). Bacon seemed to be a theme. We rode down the carnival-style big slide on potato sacks, racing side by side, like two overgrown third graders.

From the fair, we drove to Chicago O'Hare to pick up my college roommate, Alex, who flew out to visit us in Wisconsin for a couple of days—and to join at least part of the bike trip, after all (a couple of rest days of it, anyway). The three of us had pizza and beers at the original Pizzeria UNO, on the corner of East Ohio and Wabash, in the River North neighborhood of downtown Chicago, sitting in the first old-fashioned, green booth right behind the front door.

The original Pizzeria UNO, which began in 1943 when Ike Sewell invented the now-iconic Chicago deep dish pizza, still has an old school tin ceiling and a green-and-white-checkered tile floor. Surprisingly, it also has significantly better pizza than all its sister satellite franchises; it was fresher, with a harder, almost scone-like deep dish crust. (The recipe at the original location is, in fact, different, the waitress told us.)

That night, we went to a bar called Old German Beer Hall in downtown Milwaukee, where we played a drinking game called *Hammerschlagen* with a big group—the game consisted of hammering large nails into a tree stump. Between the game, the oversized Oktoberfest-style beer steins filled with Munich-brewed beer, and the genuine Old World Bavarian style of the bar (modeled after Munich's *Hofbräuhaus, the most famous beer hall in the world),* the night felt a little like a trip to Europe 400 years ago.

We packed a lot into the next day, Saturday, August 11. First, we went to a shooting range, where I fired a real gun for the first time. Zim was a shooting veteran, bound for army basic training in Georgia a few weeks later, which he was preparing for by sleeping on the floor in his parents' house. We used his handgun, which his parents didn't know he owned, at the range.

After that, I raced Alex and Zim the short distance back from the bike shop (they drove, I biked— they won, albeit narrowly) after I picked up my perfectly tuned-up bike (the fourth and final tune-up was the best work since Kansas, easily edging out the tune-ups of the Vegas and Portland bike shops). We grilled some brats on the deck in the backyard for lunch, then crashed a Finnish wedding that night (well, Alex and I technically were the only ones that "crashed"), and hit the bars on the river in downtown Milwaukee afterward, where I rode and got violently tossed off a mechanical bull for the first time. Yep, it was a full day and a full weekend. We even got the Miller Brewery tour in on the way to the airport the next morning to drop off Alex.

33

REAL-LIFE MARIO KART

ILLINOIS
AUGUST 13–15

"Cherub Rock" – The Smashing Pumpkins

It poured sheets of rain for the entire 104-mile bike ride from Brookfield to Milwaukee to Chicago the following day, completely soaking me and all my gear. It was the rainiest day of riding of the whole trip, by a good margin. Late in the day, the soaring Willis Tower rose and disappeared into dark gray clouds, making it seem never-ending, as I approached downtown Chicago. A gray puddle of rainwater collected around the bike after I wheeled it into Chris Li's apartment in a modern, high-rise building toward the city center.

Despite their yellow rain covers, the panniers had been soaked through. Most of my clothes were very wet (luckily, Chris had a dryer). A tall, Pacific Islander-looking guy with curly hair and an athletic build that made him look like a professional Hawaiian surfer, Chris was a senior when I was a freshman in high school. We played football together that one year, but he was on varsity and I was on JV. While we didn't know each other overly well, he was one of the best leaders and one of the most athletic people I knew from my hometown. A guy I looked up to. And he didn't talk down to the freshmen like some of the other seniors.

He went on to captain the lacrosse team at Ohio State, then lived in Hawaii for a while (where the locals were so sure he was one of them that they'd give him the "local discount" everywhere he went) before moving to Chicago.

I thought Chris would never leave Hawaii. But he posted a message on my Facebook wall on May 17, when I was staying at Bruce's in Los Angeles:

Nitti. U are awesome and nuts at the same time for the biking. Hope ur safe and doin well. Relocated to Chicago from Hawaii for the time being. On ur way back you've def got a place to stay here. Lmk if you come by!

So I took him up on it.

I had a rest day in Chicago, so when Chris got home from work (he was in fintech sales) we went over to North Avenue Beach to play some beach volley-ball, which was quickly becoming my favorite sport now that football was over for me. Chris, who hated going to the gym and was accustomed to doing all of his exercise outdoors (this was *before* his first Chicago winter; he later moved to Austin, Texas), thought beach volleyball was "the best workout you can do." The iconic Chicago skyline served as an epic backdrop for the sand courts, the expressionist 100-story John Hancock Tower, once the second-tallest building in the world after the Empire State Building, looming over them in such proximity that you felt like you could reach out and touch it.

Chris couldn't play because he'd torn his hamstring, but he arranged some two-on-two games for me with the group he normally played with, who were mostly Open-level players (one step below the pro level—in other words, these guys were *good*—definitely better than me). I had trouble keeping up at first, but they taught me some things, and I finally won a game after losing the first three. We played until the sun went down, but I couldn't have gone on much longer anyway. Not being used to that type of anaerobic workout *at all*, I was spent after just four games—and would be sore the next day from it. Before the bike trip, I could easily play the sport for hours and hours on consecutive days; but after six months of biking, my body and stamina had changed—in some ways for the better, but in other ways for the worse.

The next morning, I jumped into a churning river of yellow taxi cabs and scurrying cars at the bottom of The Windy City's soaring steel canyons. It was the heart of a sunny Wednesday morning rush as I biked down Michigan Avenue, the bustling "Main Street" of Chicago. This was an entirely different kind of cycling—it was on the extreme opposite end of the spectrum from Route 212 in South Dakota. A totally different world. A real-life version of *Mario Kart*. (Picture playing *Mario Kart* as a kid, with your friends, blasting "Cherub Rock" by The Smashing Pumpkins. But you're *in* the TV, among the karts but on a bike. On Michigan Avenue in Chicago.)

The cars honked and changed lanes precipitously. A yellow cab cut me off, swerving to the sidewalk into my space to pick up another fare and bumping me into the next lane, into the heart of the rushing river. Pretending to be a car now, I pedaled hard to keep pace—my heart rate escalating a few beats—then tried to stay along the white dotted lines between the two rightmost lanes, narrowly cramming between cars with my wide panniers. Another taxi rubbed up against me as it changed lanes, kissing my right pannier bag and beginning to push me over. No longer a passive novice on the bike at this point in the trip, I slammed the taxi's rear driver-side window with my open right palm, giving it two hard "taps" to let him know I was there. I kept going, enjoying the mayhem of Michigan Avenue, navigating its rush hour rapids.

34

LEG ROOM

INDIANA
AUGUST 15–17

"Fly Over States" – Jason Aldean

I spent the morning leaving Chicago on US-41, which runs along Lake Michigan and crosses into Indiana, then took 12 to 20 to 2, which runs parallel to the Michigan border, into South Bend, Indiana, arriving after dark. I'm not sure how, but the ride to South Bend was about twenty miles more than I'd expected—it was around ninety-seven miles instead of seventy-seven. I also lost an hour crossing back into the Eastern Time Zone, so it wasn't until about 10:00 p.m. that I arrived at Judy Kuhl's home on Appletree Lane, a mini cul-de-sac with a few small houses.

Seventy years old, with a prosthetic leg, Judy was waiting on her front steps when I arrived, smoking a cigarette and talking with her neighbors. Judy lived alone and considered herself to be a very spiritual person. I don't even remember how we were connected. She had a stairlift to bring her upstairs, which is where my bedroom was too.

I took off the next day and biked around the University of Notre Dame campus nearby. I knew immediately it was the most beautiful campus I'd ever been on. As I sat down on a bench near the football stadium, eating a sandwich Judy had made me for lunch, an elder professor named Lee Tavis walked over and sat next to me. We were sitting in front of a building that read "Mendoza College of Business" on its exterior. I knew the name—Mendoza is one of the very best business schools in the country, right up there with UPenn Wharton. We started talking, and sure enough, Lee was a Mendoza professor—he taught finance. He fired off question after question about the trip, showing more interest than I would've expected from an elite finance professor, and put his face in his hands and shook his head back and forth as I said, "Almost 8,500 miles down, around 1,500 to go."

I learned that Judy lost her leg riding on the back of a motorcycle as a young woman—they were sideswiped by a drunk driver. She wasn't bitter about it, though. In fact, she even had a sense of humor about it. When her friend picked us up that night to go out to a little Mexican restaurant for dinner, I offered Judy the front seat of the sedan so she would have extra room. She refused it. "I don't *need* extra room," she reasoned. "I've only got one leg!"

I picked up a tailwind out of South Bend, cruising right past Waterloo, Indiana, on US-6 to the Ohio border. The tailwind made a century seem easy—it felt like cheating, and set me on pace to finish the day with plenty of daylight left.

As soon as I passed the Ohio welcome sign (after taking the obligatory photo, of course), I extended my right hand over my head to wave to a freight train passing on the right, on tracks parallel to the road. At this point, I'd waved to and gotten waves from all sorts of people and vehicles on the road, from people in their yard to other passing bikers and motorcyclists (motorcyclists would give the "low five" and I'd give it back) to farmers on tractors and even people on jet skis. Cars and trucks would honk in support, often with a thumbs-up out the window, and I'd wave back. I'd never waved to a *train*, but I figured what the hell. My spirits were up, as they always were crossing a state line, or when I had a tailwind, and I thought the conductor might see me, since there was hardly any traffic or obstructions on the open, rural road.

Sure enough, the train said hello right back, with two short whistles— *shocking* me. Sane people don't wave to trains in New York, and the trains *certainly* don't wave back. The gesture was a harbinger of the kindness that was to come in Ohio.

"REST" DAYS

OHIO
AUGUST 17–28

"Paradise" – Coldplay

The bag was getting heavy now, and my tattered gray t-shirt and worn blue jeans were fully drenched, to the point that you could easily wring out the shirt. But not from sweat—it was from the corn stalks. A little early morning dew can add up faster than you'd think. I'd tear the ears from the stalks by turning them down, like pulling down a lever, as Marcus had taught me. They'd crack right off with a crisp *snap*.

I'd also learned that you can find better ears in less time by searching for the "honeypots" in the field, as Marcus called them—particularly abundant areas that are usually marked by patches of green grass springing up from the ground beneath the stalks. When you find a honeypot, you don't have to move much. You just pick. Turn and snap. Turn and snap.

After throwing the last couple of light green, stringy, husk-covered ears into my brimming burlap bag, I stopped and listened carefully, in the peaceful shade rendered by the stalks. The faint sound in the distance, determinedly making its way through the rows and rows of dense corn forest, was country music. It was Little Big Town's new song, "Pontoon." It was coming from Marcus's pickup truck, and served as my breadcrumb trail back. Without it, I'd be totally lost, walking in circles in a massive, high, thick corn field labyrinth somewhere in the middle of Ohio.

I hoisted the bulky bag over my head, putting the brunt of its weight on my upper back, and began the long hike back, moving swiftly, and listening for the sound of the music to point me in the right direction. Just getting back to the truck was a workout in itself.

Finally, a clearing. The truck in view, I could feel the August sun again. And *feel* the vibrations of the music. Now it was Coldplay's "Paradise," and it was *blasting*. You didn't have to worry about neighbors out here. There *weren't* any neighbors.

Marcus unloaded his bag into the back of the pickup truck, and then I did. A welcome relief for my back and shoulders. There was a potent sense of accomplishment in making it back to the truck, in delivering the goods. In pulling your weight. The booming music welcomed you back and gave you a little adrenaline, quickly pushing you back into the corn fields, which teemed with timeless mystique. I took another empty burlap bag. The simplicity of a day's work in the fields. Hard work, yes. But simple. *I could get used to this life.* Life on the farm.

But Marcus Hendren was no ordinary farmer. In fact, he was a famous CrossFit champion, a world-class athlete. A modern Roman gladiator. He'd become internationally renowned, a legend in the CrossFit world, with an intimidating and inspiring backstory. He was the farmer from Ohio who looked like The Hulk, outworking his competition and sculpting a stout mental fortitude by baling hay all day. Just the previous month, in July 2012, he'd come in seventh place at the CrossFit Games, whose winner lays claim to the impressive title "World's Fittest Man." Seventh place—that's seventh best in the *world*.

Marcus played running back at Cornell and was an excellent special teams player, graduating in my 2011 class. When football ended, he started getting into CrossFit to "fill the competitive void" it left behind. Marcus had a quiet way about him. He was often reticent and taciturn, with a no-excuses attitude and a dry, often tongue-in-cheek, sense of humor. He was probably the hardest hitter on the team, but as strong as he was physically, he was even stronger *men-*

tally. Without question, he was as mentally tough as anyone I'd ever met. For these reasons, his nickname in college was The Silent Assassin.

Despite his recent success and rapid rise as a world-class CrossFit athlete, his family—especially his parents—were only mildly supportive. At *best.* They didn't really understand it all, steadfastly believing he should be focusing on the farm. Whether they actually said it or not, they felt that CrossFit was a bunch of nonsense. A distraction from the farm. A diversion from their son's *real* future. And a threat to the preservation of the family tradition of running the farm—a major enterprise in the Johnstown, Ohio, area.

I'd stay in Johnstown for four nights. The two nights before I arrived, I was put up by two other Cornell football alums: Pat Potts, who I'd never met, in Kenton, Ohio, on August 19, and Ted Sonnenberg and his wife, Kari, in Holgate, Ohio, on August 18. Since the Sonnenbergs had a large dairy farm, they showed me how to feed their baby calves (with oversized bottles of formula that looked like they were made for baby giants). It was easy to feed the older ones; they knew the drill. But as we went down the line of stalls, it got more and more difficult as they got younger and younger. It was almost impossible to feed the calves that were just a day old—I couldn't get the bottle to stay in their mouths (it was also unfathomable that something that big had been born just the *day* before).

When I got to Johnstown on August 20, the first thing Marcus and I did, of course, was CrossFit. I threw my bike in the garage, and we drove over to the "box" (the CrossFit term for gym) in a rush. Doing a lot of front squats as part of a CrossFit circuit *right* after biking about seventy miles wasn't exactly easy, but it was fun doing it as part of a class; the energy reminded me of Coach Howley's team workouts in college. As regimented as he was, even Marcus said that he hated working out alone. He loved the camaraderie of the classes and the friendships he'd formed there. I could see why. It was a second family to him. A big part of his life. I might have actually *almost* lived up to the members of CrossFit New Albany's expectations of "Marcus's friend" when I was doing all those sets of front squats on the first day after cycling seventy miles—but probably not so much the following afternoon, when I could literally barely walk and *barely* get through the WOD (Workout of the Day—these are often named after military heroes that were killed in action, and there's one named after Uncle Brian). But there were no excuses for Marcus. Skipping the workout wasn't an option—not even for me on my "rest" days.

***

Marcus and I had once gone head-to-head in a CrossFit-like competition in college, in front of the entire football team. One offseason, Coach Howley organized team competitions after lifts to change things up a bit. The group was divided into eight or so teams (different each time) and would compete in things like pushups, tug of war, power cleans, conditioning, wall sits, etc. Each player on the winning team earned points, and individual standings were posted on the locker room door for everyone to see. The top ten players (out of over eighty) at the end of the semester were supposed to win a steak dinner with the head coach, but it was more about pride and perception. It was a good look to make the Top 10, of course, so everyone took it seriously.

On one particular day, the competition wasn't physical at all—oddly, it was a series of trivia questions. A key question my team answered incorrectly was "How many living species of sea turtles are there in the world?" My team said eight, but the correct answer was ten. Still thinking about the question the next day, and our disappointing third-place finish, I googled it back at my castle closet dorm room, and found that the real answer was seven (but *eight* if you count the East Pacific subpopulation of the green turtle). So I emailed Coach Howley, with a supporting link, to ask for a points recalculation.

I got a classic Howley response:

John

Thanks for the link. In light of this new "evidence" regarding yesterday's event, the competition committee held an emergency meeting this afternoon and decided (unanimously) that your research regarding sea turtles is indeed valid! After many hours of heated debate, thoughtful contemplation and numerous secret ballots, a single point was taken away from the first and second place teams and your team was awarded an extra point. The conclusion of the committee is that a revision of the final score is the only equitable and legally binding means of handling such disputes. With the revised points now fairly distributed, your team finished in third place.

See you Monday!

TH

On the midwinter afternoon that Marcus and I faced each other, the competition of the day was the flex arm hang. A flex arm hang is like a pullup, but instead of going up and down, you hold yourself up over the pullup bar, chin above it, with your hands gripping it from opposite directions (one hand over the bar, the other under)—for as long as you can.

On flex arm hang day, my team made it to the finals. The other team chose their champion wisely. They sent out the best overall athlete, the hardest hitter on the team. The running back and special teams MVP. The hulking, strong-as-oak, shredded farmer from Ohio, who gained forty-five pounds of muscle by making 50,000 bales of hay and straw one summer. The future CrossFit champion. The Silent Assassin. The great Marcus Hendren. My team sent out me—the walk-on, reserve quarterback, who could hang on a bar for an unusually long period of time. I was no match for Hendren, and everyone knew it. Marcus had his determined, locked-in look in his eyes. Without saying a word, he said he was going to embarrass me and make my team regret its choice.

The whistle blew and we pulled ourselves up over the bars, high above the rest of the team. Adrenaline was pumping. In the first few seconds, I tried to control my breathing and think about *anything* besides my already-tired arms. It was the end of a long offseason workout, after all, and yet *another* round of flex arm hang. The whole football team was vehemently cheering us on, imploring us to hang on. Points were on the line, and everyone wanted to move up in the standings. But those without a vested interest cheered loudly too.

After about a minute, we were both rock solid, hanging on strong. Then the lactic acid started building up immensely, cascading into my forearms and turning them to rubber, swiftly sapping their strength. I figured Marcus felt nothing.

At around a minute and a half, I turned my head to the left to look over at my opponent and could see slight pain in his face, surprising me. I knew at that moment that I could win. My forearms were screaming for mercy, too, and I knew I only had seconds left—but I wasn't on empty just yet. His arms started to shake a little, as did mine.

Approaching two minutes, we were both on our last legs, in a state of all-out fiery agony, but I sure as hell wasn't going to *show* it. So I looked over my left shoulder at Marcus again and smiled. A big, wide, stupid smile. His narrowed eyes rolled toward me, but he didn't return the gesture. Actually, he looked like he wanted to kill me.

Head Coach Jim Knowles took notice and pointed up at me, laughing, and excitedly shouting out to the other coaches and the team, "Look at that! He's *smiling*!"

Just after that, Marcus dropped off the bar, and the weight room erupted. If it were any other physical competition, he would've beaten me. But I had his number in the flex arm hang, for whatever reason. It was the only time we ever went head-to-head like that. I didn't bring it up, of course, during my stay on the farm.

I spent three "rest" days in Johnstown, but of course, there wasn't much rest involved at all. Not with Marcus Hendren at the helm. He even posted to biketrip2012.com (which showed REST DAY on the schedule at the top of the page for those following back home), "I just want everyone to know that John is not resting in Johnstown. He's being put to work in the fields." He smiled as he typed those words.

Nevertheless, our daily routine was a welcome respite from biking all day, and it was fun to live a different life for a few days. Our agreement was that I would receive a bed to sleep in and free, very healthy meals (Marcus had an impeccable diet) for the entirety of my stay, in exchange for working in the fields and helping out on the farm.

After three days, I'd become very accustomed to our daily routine. I liked it, mostly because it was vastly different from any routine I'd ever known. We'd get up early, around sunrise, get dressed in our weather-worn gray t-shirts and jeans, strap on our boots, and have breakfast, which consisted of Cascadian Farm Organic dark chocolate almond granola cereal topped with fresh strawberries and blueberries, with scrambled eggs on the side. Then we'd go out into the fields and pick corn for a couple of hours, filling the bags and loading them on the truck. Then we'd shower back at the house and make lunch (and have a cup of green tea), pack up the truck, go sell the sweet corn and some other vegetables (tomatoes, green beans, onions, and potatoes) on the side of the road until around 4:00 p.m., then go to CrossFit New Albany for Marcus's favorite part of the day.

As with breakfast, we had the same thing for lunch every day, sitting under umbrellas at the roadside stand, always at 1:00 p.m.: a delicious salad consisting of romaine, spinach, grilled chicken (seasoned with chili powder, garlic powder, basil, and crushed red pepper), craisins, almonds, applewood smoked cheddar, extra sharp cheddar, and ranch dressing. Marcus only ate organic foods, barely ate bread or any starchy carbs, never drank alcohol, only drank whole milk (as opposed to skim or 2%), and tried to eat farm-to-table as much as possible. He told me, "I feel really good all the time now. I wish everyone could feel this good." There wasn't a hint of ostentatiousness or narcissism in his voice when he said that. He was just being honest. He had basically perfected the integral, but complicated, science of nutrition and exercise, and was reaping the benefits—especially in the way that he *felt*.

After not lifting weights for six months, I was *extremely sore* from the daily afternoon CrossFit workouts. And after not eating healthy for six months, I was pretty *sick* from Marcus's diet. My stomach just didn't agree with all this healthy food. I'd been eating crap for six months straight—cheeseburgers, pancakes, giant cinnamon rolls, greasy fast-food fries, milkshakes, low-quality pizza, whatever I could find. My body had become acclimated to using cheap, carb-heavy food as fuel. All these organic salads and such were delivering a complete shock to my digestive system. To this day, however, I still have the Cascadian Farm Organic dark chocolate almond granola cereal with blueberries and strawberries for breakfast—almost every day. It's delicious.

At our roadside vegetable stand, on the southwest corner of Old Dublin Granville Road and Hamilton Road, on the outskirts of Columbus, the sunny hours passed slowly. I'd write in my journal, trying to catch up to the present, and Marcus would read.

After zero sales in the first half hour of the first day, Marcus broke a long silence. "Well, we're off to a terrible start, John."

When customers finally came, we turned into attentive salesmen. I'd help gather and bag the vegetables, and Marcus would calculate the fee and collect payment. We each had our own chairs and umbrellas. Marcus sat up in the flatbed of the pickup, and I was below, on street level, in the dirt. One day, we drove into Amish country on the way to the stand, to pick up the vegetables other than sweet corn to resell. (The Amish man Marcus bought from didn't own a cell phone, so he'd borrow other people's to get in touch with him—this made it pretty difficult to get back to him, of course.)

On the first day at the stand, some of the ears I'd picked that morning were definitely too small for Marcus's standards, and he wasn't shy about letting me know it, but one of our first customers that day *preferred* small ears. I grinned from ear to ear as I proudly doled out some from one of my bags, delighted to meet the exact specifications of our customers on my first day.

Marcus just shook his head, with the slightest hint of an infinitesimal half-smile. "Few and far between, John."

As the hours passed, I'd eat the fresh sweet corn we'd picked that morning; it was a delectable, addicting snack, but Marcus wasn't thrilled.

"You're eating the inventory, John," he said dryly. He was ultimately fine with it, though, acknowledging that it was "good marketing."

When we pulled up to CrossFit New Albany each afternoon, Marcus left the keys to his truck in the ignition when we went inside—on purpose. When I asked why he would do such a (stupid) thing, he just shrugged. "I don't know, everybody does that around here."

I imagined trying to do that in the Bronx, wondering how long it would take for your car to disappear. Not surprisingly, Marcus was the celebrity of the box. Inside, there was a plastic bucket with a slit cut into its cover—a piggy bank. The members of the box had saved up to cover Marcus's expenses to send him to the CrossFit Games in Los Angeles, and they were planning on doing the same the following year, when the goal would be to win it all.

It was inspiring that Marcus could be so committed to both CrossFit and farming. Often getting up at 4:30 in the morning to train for three hours before working until 9:30 at night on the farm, he was living proof that you could successfully pursue a wild dream without quitting a grueling day job—if you were tough enough to make some sacrifices. I believed CrossFit could lead to endorsement deals and be a potential career for him, and I was rooting for it.

A year later, I opened up *ESPN The Magazine* and the first thing I saw was Marcus, alone, deadlifting in a full-page ad for a muscle-building supplement. Maybe the farm could wait a bit.

On Friday, August 24, I said goodbye to Marcus and the farm life, the CrossFit and the corn. I'd miss him. He was a good friend, but I wondered when, or if, I'd see him again. I couldn't really picture keeping in touch in any meaningful or consistent way—neither of us was really that type. College was over.

We texted a little in the following months, but after that, I didn't hear from him again until five years later. The correspondence was a short, to-the-point, six-word comment on a photo I posted of my sister Annie and me, holding our turquoise and white All-City bikes, which matched the colors of the rolling waves behind us, on a sunny May 2017 day on the pier in Manhattan Beach, California. She had recently moved from New York to LA, and I was visiting, riding a bike again for just the second or third time in nearly five years. In classic Hendrenesque sarcasm and brevity, he commented, "You ride your bike there again?" I could *hear* him saying the words, with the slightest hint of a smile on his face, as I read it, which made me laugh out loud to myself. In a succinct way I knew he'd appreciate, I replied with just four words. "This time I flew."

***

With my legs as sore as they'd ever been (thanks to Marcus's CrossFit workouts), getting on the road again was painful. The ride from Johnstown to Wooster through sunny Ohio farmland was the hilliest I'd had in a long time. I plodded along, slowly and achingly. Somewhere else in Ohio, in a hospital just north of Cincinnati, astronaut Neil Armstrong was living his final day on Earth. He died the next day—Saturday, August 25, 2012, at age eighty-two, of complications from heart surgery two weeks prior.

Also in August 2012, the *Voyager 1* spacecraft officially left the solar system, becoming the first human-made object to reach interstellar space. Launched in 1977 to explore the outer planets, the *Voyager 1* has remained operational for far longer than expected. On the off-chance it's ever found by other intelligent life, the spacecraft was equipped with a kind of time capsule that included a record album, named "The Sounds of Earth," with sounds from our planet— including the human heartbeat; the songs of birds and whales; the sounds of surf and thunder; the sounds of different languages and laughter; and music from around the world, including Bach and Beethoven, a Navajo chant, pan-pipes from the Solomon Islands, and Chuck Berry's iconic rock and roll song "Johnny B. Goode." Every time I hear that song, I think about it hurtling across the cosmos, traveling farther than any human-made object from Earth ever has. And I try to imagine what aliens would think of it if they heard it. The craft also includes a signed letter from US President Jimmy Carter accompanying the re-cord—it's the only letter in history to travel beyond the solar system:

This is a present from a small, distant world, a token of our sounds, our science, our images, our music, our thoughts and our feelings. We are attempting to survive our time so we may live into yours. We hope someday, having solved the problems we face, to join a community of galactic civilizations. This record represents our hope and our determi-nation, and our good will in a vast and awesome universe.[41]

The ride from Wooster to Cleveland on August 25 was easier. Trying to continue the healthy eating trend Marcus had instilled in me over the previous few days, I ordered a strawberry chicken salad for lunch at the Main Street Café in the charming downtown of Medina, Ohio—and sent a photo of it to Marcus for approval.

Later that afternoon, I found out that none of the hotels in downtown Cleveland, where I was planning on staying, had any vacancy. I called literally every single one. I tried to book online. Not a single room was available. So I started branching out into the suburbs, where finally—at a La Quinta in North Olmsted, Ohio—I found a room. After biking around downtown Cleveland for what seemed like hours, making call after call, I had to go backward at the very end of the day and basically retrace my route to get to North Olmsted.

I spent the next day, a hot and sunny Sunday afternoon, at Progressive Field with the pretty blonde stranger I'd met on spring break in Panama City Beach, watching Derek Jeter and the New York Yankees in their road grays defeat the hometown Cleveland Indians 4-2. Then I spent a third night at the La Quinta, because Monday was a total washout. It poured all day, leaving me cooped up and bored in the hotel room. I liked Cleveland, though. It was a nice little city, despite the apparent lack of hotel rooms (I think the Yankees being in town had something to do with that).

After the rainout day, feeling rested and restless and wanting to get back on schedule, I set out early, with the lofty goal of reaching Erie, Pennsylvania, combining two days into one, for a total of 113 miles. The day started out going back through downtown Cleveland (again), where I spoke to a guy commuting to work on his bike, who later posted to biketrip2012.com. Then, I got into a groove and started making great time, stopping for two lunches (one at about forty miles and the next at eighty miles, as was customary on long days), and cruising past Geneva-on-the-Lake and into Pennsylvania. 113 miles made that Tuesday the third-longest ride of the entire trip, and it was a great one—until the last half-mile.

THE CRASH

PENNSYLVANIA
AUGUST 28-30

"Hurt" – Nine Inch Nails

On mile 113, with just 0.4 miles to the Flamingo Motel on Route 5 in Erie, Pennsylvania, I was cruising down an overpass on Peninsula Drive, coasting fast into the setting sun, excited to finish the day and be back on schedule. But then, out of nowhere, a red car suddenly pulled into my path, from a small side street on the right.

BOOM!

I was on the ground.

Out of it. But immediately in pain. Unlike the crash in Alabama, this time, I didn't pop back up.

I was conscious but hadn't fully processed what had just happened. I stayed down on the pavement, dazed, and not sure yet if I was okay or seriously injured. In a strange kind of slow motion, I could hear my empty water bottle—the one I kept in the handlebar bag—bouncing haphazardly down the street, far away from me. People were stopping and getting out of their cars; I could hear the opening and closing of car doors. I began to realize that I'd gone straight into the rear driver's side door of the car, *hard*.

Someone got out of their car and shouted "I saw that!" across the street.

Still sprawled on the pavement, I looked over at the man. "You saw it?" I confirmed, thinking it was a good thing that there was a witness.

Others rushed over.

"Should I call an ambulance?" someone asked.

Slowly, I rolled over and began to stand up. I was cut up and bruised, and my left elbow and left hip were especially banged up, and bleeding, but I didn't have any broken bones or serious injuries, somehow. I knew I didn't need an ambulance.

The car didn't fare as well. The entire driver's side rear door was dented in. It shocked me to think that a bike could do so much damage. The driver was completely fine, but she seemed just as rattled and perplexed as I was. The car took me so much by surprise that I didn't have a chance to even touch the brake. In Alabama, I was able to brake for a good second or two, and I wasn't going as fast. But this time, I'd hit it at full speed, going *downhill*. It was a brutal, vicious collision, and my whole body hurt. Luckily, I didn't flip right over the car and go airborne—the weight of my pannier bags was enough to keep me anchored to the ground.

The driver of the car said the light had just turned green for her. Someone else who stopped backed that up, saying that his light had just changed to red. What surprised me about what they were saying is that they kept talking about a *light*. With the glare of the setting sun, not only was I unable to see the *color* of the light—I didn't even notice that there was a light there *at all*. So, to make matters even worse—and unlike the Alabama collision—this accident was *my fault*.

I exchanged contact information with the driver, not having a clue of how insurance would handle the situation, and looked for a bike shop on Google Maps—somehow, the bike had fared better than the car, but it still had significant damage. Luckily, there was a bike shop within walking distance. They closed at 7:00, though, and it was already 6:45. I didn't have much time.

I walked over to check into the Flamingo Motel and quickly drop my bags in the motel office, then continued along the busy Route 5 toward the bike shop. I limped along the sidewalk, my leg throbbing and blood dripping down my arm. The bike limped too. The front fork was severely twisted, so the front wheel was all crooked and rubbing against the brake pads when I tried to wheel the bike forward. It wouldn't go unless it was really forced. The two of us had a great 112 miles together that day, and a very rough 113th mile.

The two guys behind the counter at the Competitive Gear bike shop were friendly, but somewhat bewildered that I was still upright after taking a look at the bike.

"Whoa . . . you know, you're extremely lucky. You're lucky to be alive," one of them said, handing me a cold beer out of their fridge. "No joke. The amount of force it takes to twist steel like that . . . I've never seen anything like it, and I've been working here a long time."

Pointing to the front fork, the other guy said, "We could try twisting it back into place, but I'm not sure that would work—and even if it did, it wouldn't be safe to ride with it like that. We need to order the part and replace it." Looking at his computer screen, he continued, "It doesn't look like it'll get here 'til Thursday. We'll call as soon as it arrives."

It was only Tuesday evening, so I'd have to take the next day off. I figured I'd probably need to anyway. Surprisingly, the front wheel was completely fine, and barely needed to be trued up.

I walked back to the Flamingo, still limping. As I cooled down, the pain and stiffness were getting worse. The manager of the motel gave me a discount because of what had happened, and his son helped me carry my bags to my room, recommending a few places to eat along the way. "You gotta get the shark at the Japanese place across the street," he said, excitedly. "Trust me."

So before even showering, I limped across the road and sat at the bar in a room by myself, away from the hibachis, and ordered the shark platter. I felt down. Exhausted. Guilty. In pain. I noticed I had a voicemail, so I listened to it as I ate. It was from the ornery attorney representing the twenty-something woman who'd been driving the car (I later found out they were married).

I called him back right away, and later paid their insurance deductible. I iced and took a lot of Advil that night as I watched TV at the Flamingo. After I spoke to my parents about the crash—who had become more and more reassured as the trip progressed but now sounded as worried as they were in the early days—I went to bed early.

I slept well, but as expected, I woke up the next morning stiffer and in more pain than the night before. It was like waking up the morning after a football game times ten. I took it easy that day.

As I sat out on my motel room porch and scrolled through Facebook, I saw some alarming posts from someone I went to high school with—the kind that made you wonder about his mental well-being. He wasn't a close friend, but I scrolled through my phone and had his number, unexpectedly, so I gave him a call, just for the hell of it, to check in. He had heard about my trip—probably from the local newspaper back home, so we talked about it for a while—after not speaking at all in years. He said he was fine, but appreciated the call. I think many of us want to do stuff like that, but we don't. I know I often don't. It's easier to pretend we didn't see the posts. But I was glad I called. A few years later, a different high school classmate of mine died by suicide. The starting shortstop on the baseball team, who I'd known since Little League, he was a kid everyone liked and wanted to be like, including myself. I told his father that as he stood next to his casket at the wake—but I never got the chance to tell Tom.

I had brunch at a little breakfast place by the motel and dinner at Five Guys, right by the scene of the accident. The next day I felt a little better—definitely good enough to ride, and I was anxious to get back on the road—so I picked up the bike (with its new black Surly fork, which stood out from the rest of the pewter Trek frame) as soon as it was ready and hit the road immediately.

The bike was ready midday on Thursday, August 30, so I only made it about fifty miles before the sun went down when I was near Dunkirk, New York. Riding that day, I'd never felt more self-reliant. I knew I could depend on myself to finish the trip, no matter what. It was a good feeling. It was pleasantly strange, too, to bike along the Pennsylvania coast that day—you normally don't associate Pennsylvania with coastline, but the northwest corner of the Keystone State kisses Lake Erie. The ride that afternoon was scenic, with wineries. With all the vineyards up by the road and the long blue coastline below, it curiously felt like *California*, of all states.

37

Suspicious Toothbrushing

NEW YORK PART 1
AUGUST 30 – SEPTEMBER 12

"Carousel" – Blink-182

Crossing into New York was bizarre, because I still felt so far from home; the southwest corner of the state was one of the few parts of it still foreign to me. Nevertheless, it was comforting to be back in my home state again. My family was excited when I texted the photo of the bike leaning up against the New York welcome sign.

I found a park near Dunkirk, right on the Lake Erie shore, and free camped by the little beach there. The Great Lakes are so big they sometimes look like oceans. After setting up the tent, I stared at a stunning sunset; the bright orange star dipped gracefully into the calm, glassy ocean of a lake, quietly and carefully. There was nobody around, and the tranquility felt otherworldly. The serenity wouldn't last, though.

I'd set up the tent in the most inconspicuous spot I could find, away from the road, and out of view, but after the sun went down, a cop noticed me with his searchlight. He was looking for people who had ventured away from their parked car, and the park closed at sunset. Knowing I'd been spotted, I went over to talk with him. He decided to let me stay the night, saying, "I didn't see you, and this conversation never happened."

I slept fairly well that night, despite the timeless sound of a few train whistles in the distance periodically waking me up. The peaceful melody of the small waves lapping on the shore always lulled me back to sleep.

But then, a tap on the tent! It was still completely dark out—as I opened my eyes, I couldn't see anything. But then, a bright, powerful light blasted right through the tent and straight into my eyes. A deep voice bellowed.

"*Police!*"

I forgot where I was for a second or two.

Startled, I jumped up. But I was confined by my sleeping bag and the very low roof of my extremely small tent. Rushing, and foggily thinking in the first seconds of consciousness that I'd have to come out with my hands up as quickly as possible before they started shooting, I reached for the zipper of the tent and fumbled with it. The stupid thing wouldn't open!

Finally, I got the zipper to move so that the tent was partially open and I kind of jumped through the small opening, my legs still confined by my sleeping bag . . . and fell right out of the tent like an uncoordinated kid in a potato sack race. It must have been a hell of a sight for the two officers.

As I collected myself and stood up, they looked at me with narrowed eyes and concerned expressions on their faces.

After a moment or two of silence, one of them spoke. "You have to leave. The park is opening soon, and we don't want anyone to see someone camping in a tent. That's not allowed here."

Opening soon? It felt like two in the morning. But I was happy to see, when I looked at my watch, that it was 5:41; my alarm was about to go off in nineteen minutes anyway. It might've been the most terrifying wake-up call I'll ever have, but it ensured an early start—and that was always a good thing (sometimes it was hard to get up right away when I was camping, when I normally didn't sleep straight through the night). I packed up my gear in the darkness and hit the road with the first pre-dawn traces of light showing the way.

I biked into downtown Dunkirk and had a big breakfast at a restaurant on the water by the marina, Demetri's On the Lake, taking my time and charging my phone and iPod. Being the last day of August, it was getting a little cold in the mornings now, and after a night camping out, it was very satisfying to sit inside and warm up with hot coffee and a big breakfast.

Biking along Lake Erie that day, approaching Buffalo, I had the strongest tailwind of the trip. I sailed along at a whirring 25 mph for much of the time, which allowed me to get to Andy Wade's house in East Aurora, New York, a suburb of Buffalo, well before lunchtime. Andy, who at one point was going to be on the bike trip, took me to East Aurora's Main Street for some delicious Buffalo wings and beef on weck (two local specialties) for lunch. Then we drove to Niagara Falls—the last major landmark on the things-to-see list of the trip. Simply seeing the sheer *volume* of water pouring over the falls up close was surprisingly hypnotizing. The water was faster and louder and *bigger* than I'd imagined, exploding on the rocks below to create a ceaseless mist that towered even higher than the falls themselves. In a kind of trance, I just kept staring.

Then Andy and I went back to the house, ordered pizza, and chatted with his parents, Tim and Leslie, about the trip, college, and football. Andy had been a talented defensive back and special teams player at Cornell. One of the most memorable plays of our entire four years of college (one of the few individual plays I can remember, in fact) was when Andy returned a blocked field goal sixty-nine yards for a touchdown, sophomore year, against Dartmouth. His dad, Tim, had coached him in high school. When I visited, Tim was preparing for his first high school game of the season the next day. The Buffalo Bills played basically right down the block, in Orchard Park. So football was a big deal in their family, as it was in mine.

I left the next morning, September 1, for a hot and hilly eighty-mile ride to Canandaigua. When Andy's mom voiced concerns about the hills as I was getting ready to leave, Coach Wade retorted, "Come on, he went over the damn Continental Divide."

It *was* hilly, though, on US-20, and I hadn't been conditioned to any real climbing in recent weeks. I Couchsurfed that night for the first time in a while at the home of a seasoned Couchsurfer named Mike Atwood. Mike was a good guy, and he even paid for my dinner at a small bar and restaurant right on

Canandaigua Lake. I was surprised when he'd already paid. When I objected, he answered, "I always treat."

I was officially back in the Finger Lakes at this point, and the ride the next day to Ithaca—the unofficial capital of the Finger Lakes region and home to Cornell and Ithaca College—was partially familiar. The Ithaca area is beautiful; there are seemingly endless gorges, waterfalls, and cliffs everywhere you turn. The area's popular slogan, which you're guaranteed to see on a t-shirt or bumper sticker if you visit, is "Ithaca is Gorges." But from the perspective of a bicycle, I think I appreciated the natural allure of the Finger Lakes region more that day than I ever did my entire four years of college.

I rode across the narrow strip of land between Seneca Lake and Cayuga Lake, and then down scenic Route 89 along Cayuga Lake, past an unconventionally dried-up Taughannock Falls, past Glenwood Pines (our favorite burger place in college), and past The Boatyard Grill (where we'd go when my parents came to visit). Taughannock Falls, which is taller than Niagara Falls, was normally one of the most picturesque waterfalls in the country. There's a legend that the waterfall was named after Chief Taughannock after he was thrown from the top, to his death, after leading his tribe to invade the local Cayuga people. (There's another, more peaceful, story that ends with the Cayuga tribe leader marrying Chief Taughannock's beautiful daughter beside the falls.) Or, the name could originate from the Delaware word taghkanic, which translates to "great fall in the woods."

From Route 89, there's a hiking trail to Taughannock Falls—as seniors in college, five or six of us finally did the hike for the first time. The setting at the end of the trail was idyllic—a tall, narrow, resplendent waterfall cascading over a canyon surrounded by woodland, and no other people. We thought it'd be a crime not to swim in the small pool at the base of the falls—despite the sign warning that swimming wasn't allowed. There was nobody around to stop us.

Just as we were looking up at the falls deciding what to do, a large chunk of rock—at least the size of three or four Chevy Suburbans, and probably bigger—broke off from the top of the falls, just to the right of the stream of white water, with a loud *crack*, and fell silently for a second or two. We looked up, in awe.

Then, it crashed against the side of the canyon with a deafening, earth-shaking thunder, breaking into smaller boulders that fell precisely in the area we were going to swim! We decided, at that point, to skip the swim. Nobody else saw the monstrous display of erosion, but some locals we ran into on the hike back told us they'd heard it—and that it was louder than they could ever remember.

After I passed The Boatyard Grill, I could see the Cornell clocktower and campus high up on the hill. "Far above Cayuga's waters," as the alma mater goes. Soon I was at the bottom of Buffalo Street, one of notoriously hilly Ithaca's steepest streets and the inspiration for the name of Coach Howley's most difficult stationary bike workout, which I'd used in training: "Buffalo Street . . . in 3 Feet of Snow!" The top of the infamous street reached a 20% grade—about *double* that of Teton Pass. With all the gear I was carrying (again, amounting to a gross weight of over 300 pounds between myself, the bike, and all the gear), I wasn't sure if it would be possible to bike it. There was only one way to find out.

As I stared up at the wall in front of me that was Buffalo Street, I decided that, because it inspired the name of the most difficult training workout I did, back in that little yellow room in the strip mall in what seemed like eons ago, I would not only attempt to bike it—I'd attempt to bike it *without stopping*. I thought it'd be a real test. *The* real test. *There's only one shot at Buffalo Street, and this is it.*

I took a deep breath and began pedaling. The grade wasn't bad at first, but like an exponential curve, it got steeper, and steeper. And *steeper*. As I got toward the top for the 20% grade final push, still seated, I was grinding along slowly, crawling up in my lowest gear, just trying with all my might to stay upright. My heart was beating out of my chest, to what felt to be a dangerous level. It felt like it was going to explode.

A student, who'd watched the last couple of excruciating pedal strokes, stopped walking on the street and stared at me, smiling a little. "Dude, are you okay?"

I nodded "yes," gasping for breath and dripping sweat in the hot afternoon sun. Buffalo Street had lived up to the hype. When I caught my breath after a few minutes, I continued biking up through Collegetown toward 200 Miller Street, where Ty Siam lived as a grad student. Ty's family had generously hosted me for nearly an entire week back in Kansas, but I hadn't seen Ty himself since graduation over a year prior.

It was the Sunday afternoon of Labor Day weekend, and when I got to the house, it was buzzing with activity. There was a big Beer Olympics going on, so there were people everywhere. I was meeting people and shaking hands, drenched in sweat and still a little out of breath. But other than that, it felt like I was back in college again.

I spent the next two days in Ithaca, staying at Ty's and hanging out with him and his grad school friends, eating at Souvlaki House and seeing my friend Debbie, the waitress (who'd lent me her family's condo in Myrtle Beach, where I stayed the first two nights of the trip) and Peter, the owner, and stopping by the Friedman Center in Bartels Hall to say hello to the strength coaches—Coach Howley and Coach Andress—and JC Tretter, who was working out.

JC had put on a ton of mass since I graduated, transitioning from tight end to offensive line, and would go on to have a long and successful NFL career (more so than any other Cornell grad, ever) with the Green Bay Packers and Cleveland Browns, playing center for quarterback Aaron Rodgers and serving as President of the NFL Players Association. When I first met JC when he was an incoming freshman tight end at mini camp, I knew he was going to be highly successful right away, as a player *and* a person. That feeling was confirmed when he, still in high school, proactively sent me a Facebook message after the weekend. "I just wanted to thank you for all the help this weekend in teaching me what I had to do each play. You were truly a big help. Hopefully we can hang out at the July mini camp too," he wrote. No one else had ever done that.

JC had gotten much bigger and stronger since I'd seen him. I, on the other hand, had *lost* a ton of weight. Coach Howley looked at the two of us as we spoke, barely recognizing me. He looked at me, and then JC, and then back at me—and the three of us joked that my weight had been transferred to JC by some miracle. Howley told me to step on the scale. Once a coach, always a coach. It read 186 pounds—exactly 35 pounds less than I was at the beginning of my senior year and about 25 pounds less than I was at the start of 2012.

***

I left Ithaca on Wednesday, September 5, for a short half-day of riding on Route 79 to Whitney Point, New York. About halfway, I saw two hitchhikers sitting by the train tracks playing guitar on the roadside. I asked them how long they'd been on the road. They answered, "Twenty years." I wondered what the tourists that surrounded me in Monument Valley, who asked me the same question, would think of *that* answer.

When I got to Whitney Point, I went into the Italian restaurant there, Aiello's, planning to have dinner and hoping to stay at the inn upstairs. I used to call Aiello's the "hidden gem," because its Italian food was oddly good for upstate New York. I'd stopped there a few times on the drive up to school, so I'd spoken to the owner, Charlie Aiello—who was born in Sicily.

He didn't remember me, but he decided he wanted to help me out after I explained that I'd stopped there before on the way to school and that I knew Ben Lomanto (Ben owned Spuntino, the pizzeria I worked at right after college). He didn't have any rooms available (the inn had become exclusively residential), but he let me sleep in the office upstairs. It was extremely hot up there at first, but it cooled off after I borrowed a resident's fan and opened up the door to the outdoor balcony. I used my sleeping pad for cushion. Charlie said, "No problem," upon showing me the accommodation, as long as I "come down and have a nice meal, and spend some money," in his thick Italian accent. He texted Ben: *John Nitti is staying at my place. The bill is on you.* He laughed heartily as he showed me the text on his phone.

I showered and went down for an early dinner, sitting at the bar in the restaurant's little enclave nearest Route 79, enjoying the good company of a bunch of friendly strangers, all around my parents' age or older, who fired off question after question about the trip. One man generously gave me a $40 gift certificate to use for my dinner. (I ended up eating so much, over such a long period, that the certificate only covered about half the meal.)

After a bunch of laughs and hours sitting at the bar with my new stranger friends, I went back upstairs to sleep in the office and had a full pancake breakfast the next morning for only about $4 at a little place across the road.

The ride that morning was hilly, then escalated into some serious climbing as I got into the Catskills, making the seventy-five-mile ride from Whitney Point to Roscoe, New York, along Route 206 a tough one. The Catskills were the first mountains I had to tackle since the Bighorns—all the way back in Wyoming, a month and a half prior. To say the least, I was no longer conditioned to mountain climbing, and wasn't used to humidity; it was a hot and oppressively muggy day, and I was sweating more than ever—in September!

At one point on 206, the grade reached 10% for a short stretch, tying Teton Pass. I'd had a big chicken marsala lunch at Rosa's Restaurant on Main Street in Bainbridge, which was needed because the latter part of the day brought two mountains to climb: Bear Spring and Cat Hollow. Bear Spring rises somewhat abruptly out of the town of Walton, and proved to be the tougher test. Cat Hollow wasn't as steep, but I was exhausted by the time I got to it. Climbing slowly over it as it got dark (the days were getting noticeably shorter now), a man in a pickup truck pulled over to see if I needed help. He was from Nassau County on Long Island; hearing his familiar accent reminded me I was getting close to home. I told him I was alright—I'd gotten so used to adverse situations by this point that I wasn't even slightly worried, but being out of energy on a mountain in the dark is never an ideal spot for a cyclist to be in.

Feeling sleepy in the Catskills was reminiscent of the old, vaguely familiar tall tale of Rip Van Winkle. If you travel through the Catskills, especially the eastern parts closer to the Hudson River, you're likely to see references to the fabled American character—in the names of parks, campgrounds, businesses, hotels, a lake, a brewery, a bridge, and even golf and mini-golf courses. The guy's a local celebrity. There's even a statue of him, with his signature long beard.

Published in 1819, the short story "Rip Van Winkle," by American author Washington Irving tells the tale of a Dutch-American villager in pre-revolutionary colonial America. Although he wasn't very good at keeping his farm in order, and would "rather starve on a penny than work for a pound," to the chagrin of his nagging wife, Dame Van Winkle, Rip was a well-liked member of his village at the foot of the Catskills. One day, Rip goes for a walk up the Catskill Mountains with his dog and runs into a strange, short man with a gray beard, wearing old Dutch clothes. The short man tells Rip to follow him, and they come upon a group of other strange people in Dutch clothes, deeper in the woodland, playing ninepins and drinking a kind of liquor from a keg. Rip tries the drink and eventually drifts off into a deep sleep. When he wakes up, everyone is gone, including his dog. Even his gun is gone; he finds an old, rusted gun next to him instead.

On the way back to his village, he realizes his beard has grown a foot long, and when he arrives, he doesn't know anyone, and nobody knows him. The buildings look a little different, and the pub has changed names from "King George the Third" to "General Washington." When he thought he'd been sleeping for just one night, he then figures out he'd been asleep for twenty years! In the meantime, the American Revolutionary War had been won, and his nagging wife had died—both to his relief. Otherwise, not much has changed, and he more or less goes back to his old life before his long nap.

This little Catskills story is known to be the most quintessential homegrown American fairy tale.

I finally coasted down the last of Cat Hollow through the dark and into the very small town of Roscoe. I had dinner at the Roscoe Diner—a classic, famous roadside diner along Route 17, decorated with hundreds of college pennants on its walls. I'd stopped there many times before. It was almost exactly halfway between home and school, so I'd eaten there with my parents and friends.

I slept in the overpriced motel next door, went back to the Roscoe for a pancake breakfast the next morning, and then biked along Route 52 through Liberty into Ellenville. I was finally feeling 100% again that morning, fully recovered from the Pennsylvania crash ten days prior, biking *fast* and feeling unstoppable and strong as ever as Blink-182's "Carousel" played on my iPod.

Near Ellenville, a middle-aged Black woman rolled down her window as she passed me and shouted, "I saw you in Liberty! That's amazing!"

The two towns were only about twenty miles apart, but I smiled and waved, grateful for the encouragement. From there, I hopped on US-209 and took it up to Hurley, a small town near Kingston.

Just after Hurley, where 209 runs into Route 28, Maura and Joe Pennachio, part of my extended family (Maura is Nana Mac's younger cousin) picked me up on the side of the busy highway and drove me down to their home in Fishkill, about an hour away, to spend the night. When I came down for dinner after showering, there was a wonderful surprise waiting for me. Aunt Maureen, Uncle Tony, and their three girls—Annalisa, Sophia, and Gianna—drove all the way up from New Jersey to surprise me! Maura and Joe's children, Danielle and Joey, and Danielle's husband, Brian, also came to visit. A big family dinner felt so warm and foreign to me; it was a welcome change of pace. After dinner, they all wanted to see the bike.

We had an early breakfast the next morning at 6:00 a.m., then Maura and Joe drove me back to the exact spot I'd left off at, at the 28/209 junction. As they helped me get the bags out of the car and put them on the bike, I realized I'd forgotten to brush my teeth—so I did it right there, on the shoulder of the busy highway. As I did that, a state trooper pulled over behind the car to investigate, flashing his lights. Joe went over to the trooper's window to explain the situation. We must've looked strange with the bike and all, especially with me brushing my teeth.

As Joe leaned in, saying, "He's come all the way across the country, and we're just dropping him . . ." I walked over, still brushing, and acknowledged the strangeness of the moment.

"You probably don't see this every day," I said to the trooper, a clean-cut Black man wearing the trademark New York State Trooper Smokey Bear hat, as he sat at the wheel of his yellow and blue squad car with a slightly suspicious look on his face.

"No, I don't," he agreed, smiling now. "I just wanted to check it out. You never know when someone's brushing their teeth."

You never know when someone's brushing their teeth. I kind of laughed to myself—somehow I knew that that's exactly what I would've said.

I said goodbye to Maura and Joe with big hugs after the trooper merged back onto the highway. I continued north, going a little out of the way to bike through Woodstock, the town that the epic 1969 music festival was named after, which drew about half a million people (including Maura) and comprised thirty-two acts over four days. (The actual festival was held on a farm in Bethel, New York, about forty miles away, and not in Woodstock itself.) Artists that performed included CCR, The Grateful Dead, The Who, The Band, Santana, Jefferson Airplane, CSNY, Jimi Hendrix, and many more. Anyone who declined the invitation—including The Rolling Stones, Led Zeppelin, Jethro Tull, Simon & Garfunkel, Bob Dylan, Chicago, and The Doors—later regretted it, of course. They didn't know it would go down as the most renowned music festival of all time.

In Woodstock, I saw a car completely covered in green "Ithaca is Gorges" stickers. When I asked about it, the driver told me her dad was the one who came up with the famous slogan. After that, I made a quick pit stop at a bike shop in Saugerties to buy new pedals, then started making good time as I rode toward Albany, with the help of a tailwind and some pressure provided by the threat of a storm hitting that afternoon.

When I was just blocks away from my friend Paul Murphy's apartment (Paul, Brendan's younger brother, was attending Siena College just outside Albany), the storm rolled in, quickly and menacingly. The sky turned a dark gray and thunder rumbled, louder and louder. I took off at a full sprint and *just* before I coasted up to Paul's apartment, the rain came down in torrents and lightning lit up the sky.

Paul didn't tell his roommates I was coming, so when I walked in with all my gear and bike, dripping from the storm, and Paul casually said, "Yeah, he biked here from Oregon," they looked at me like I was insane.

IT'S AN EXPERIENCE . . .

MASSACHUSETTS
SEPTEMBER 12–24

"Exodus" – Bob Marley

From Albany, after a couple of rest days staying with my college roommate Mango and his dog Tucker at his apartment, I crossed into Massachusetts and stayed the night near the border, at the empty Country Inn at the base of Jiminy Peak. Normally packed with families in the winter ski season, the hotel hallways were as quiet as a library, and the landscape outside was barren and green. I walked partway up the mountain to take photos of the empty trails. It was astonishing to me, for some reason, to see how different they looked in the summer. I walked beside a trickling brook over to Powder Hounds, a hospitable little restaurant by the ski resort entrance, to have dinner, as we always did as a family growing up—often as snow fell.

Following Route 9 the next day, I rode through the Berkshires (which were challenging, but not as much as the Catskills) to Amherst, where I slept on the couch of Jenney Shamash, who I was connected with by another Jenny I'd met in Idaho as she drove across the country.

From Amherst, I rode Route 9 to Worcester, hearing my first "wicked" when I stopped for lunch in Ware, Massachusetts. The next stop was Holy Cross, where I'd visit my childhood friend, Conor Prior (Chris and Michelle

Prior's son—Chris was the one who had partially inspired my trip) and spend a couple of rest days over a mid-September weekend. Conor and his older brother, Dylan, who'd just graduated from Holy Cross a few months before, had visited me at Cornell my senior year; this was my chance to return the favor.

Conor and his group of friends had just been kicked out of their house by the Holy Cross administration because they were under twenty-one and had a party. Yeah, *that's it*. They had a party. Nothing more to it. In fact, there's quite a bit *less* to it, because calling it a "party" was a stretch by college standards—it was more like they had a few people over. The administration wanted to make an example out of them, though, so it came down on them with a ridiculously harsh and unfair punishment. The group wasn't only kicked out of their house—they were forced to split up and live with random roommates in on-campus dorms. Conor was forced to live in a "substance-free" dorm. (When I asked him if you had to take a breathalyzer test to enter it, he answered, "No, but that's probably coming.")

His roommate was a strange, squeamish little kid who lacked the slightest trace of any social skills and looked like he was about thirteen years old. All he did was study and didn't even look at me when I walked into the tiny cell of a room, which allowed just a few feet of space between the two beds. I tried to say hello but was ignored.

On Conor's side of the room, he had a fridge full of Bud Light (so much for "substance-free"), while the awkward kid had a teddy bear and a few other stuffed animals. I felt bad for Conor—the two were nothing alike and had to live in close quarters all year. This was only week two. Conor summed it up when he remarked, "We have no relationship."

I'd arrived on a Friday, so that night and the next day was a marathon of partying with Conor and his group of friends—from tailgating at the football game against Brown in the morning to outdoor house parties in the afternoon to heading to the bars late into the night. On Sunday, we all just sat around watching football, drinking Sprites. Nobody wanted to even *look* at a beer.

Sleeping arrangements for the weekend worked out for me—I ended up having a comfortable mattress and the entire house they were thrown out of to myself at 25 Caro Street, an address that had become infamous on campus. Conor pulled an almost-all-nighter to catch up on schoolwork Sunday night, then the two of us went out to breakfast the next morning at Culpeppers Bakery & Café before my ride into Boston. I got my usual breakfast, of course (stack of pancakes, giant cinnamon roll, and coffee). Conor looked baffled. I guess he thought I'd developed some kind of healthy eating routine by now.

"Of all pre-biking foods," he said, "I would've thought, No, no, and no," as he made his way around my plate pointing out each abomination. But you can't argue with carbs and caffeine.

After that weekend, it felt good to get moving again. I felt like I needed the exercise; I'd come to *depend* on getting copious amounts of cardio nearly every day. It was a healthy addiction, I suppose, but I wondered how I would adjust to normal life again. And to a new normal of sitting at a desk all day. *I should probably change my diet*, I thought. *Cutting down on the stacks of pancakes is probably a good place to start.*

The ride into Boston was dangerous at times along Route 9, which had fast, heavy traffic and a very narrow shoulder, but it was a quick and easy forty-mile day, and I pulled up to The Squealing Pig bar, next to the Harvard Medical School, in time for lunch. My high school friend, Matt O'Donnell, was still on his shift, and when I walked in, he gave me a big, congratulatory hug and a drink on the house, loudly announcing my feat to his coworkers. He thought I was ending the trip right then and there, at The Squealing Pig. It kind of made sense, I guess, because I was officially back on the East Coast for the first time, but I explained that I still had a week and a half to go—through Cape Cod, Rhode Island, and Connecticut—and that I was ending the trip in New York City.

"Oh . . . well—*still*, congrats, man!" Matt said, as we clinked glasses over the bar.

Matt and I played football together and sat right next to each other in Mr. Voska's high school physics class, where I'd scribble notes and he'd scribble his memoir, *The Life and Times of Matt O'Donnell*. But I knew him long before high school, since our elementary school principal, Mr. Carolan, gave us the important job of taking down the American flag that flew over the school each afternoon—that's how we met. We'd fold it properly into a blue star-studded triangle and deliver it to Mr. Dozier, the head custodian who'd served in the army in Vietnam. We did this job very diligently, making sure no red was showing when we delivered it to Mr. Dozier in the custodians' office each afternoon—and he was always proud of us, greeting us with a handshake and a big smile. Except for one day.

One day, we were running late and were going to miss the bus home. To a kid, missing the bus is like the End of Days. So, instead of folding the flag, we bunched it together and sprinted it over to the custodians' office. This was clearly the wrong thing to do—even as ten-year-old kids, we should've known that. But it's what we did. The look of disappointment and anger on Mr. Dozier's face was enough to tell us we'd messed up . . . big time. There was actually pain in his eyes as he shook his head and said, "No, man . . . *no*. You don't do that. You *never* do that." I was so embarrassed. I'll never forget that one day. That day completed my education on what it means to respect the flag.

Ranley walked into The Squealing Pig a few minutes after I arrived, after a bus ride up from New York (I made fun of him for beating him there on a bike), and the three of us went out that night, starting with the most expensive dinner of the trip at Durgin-Park, a famous Boston establishment in the heart of the city, by Faneuil Hall and City Hall. Back in the day, the restaurant was known for two things: its overtly rude service and its delicious cornbread. We didn't experience the rude service, unfortunately, but we enjoyed the cornbread, plus a bevy of appetizers, Ipswich clams, and shots, running up a pretty hefty tab.

From there, we went to some of the city's best-known Irish pubs, then ended the Monday night at a Chinese karaoke bar. The next day, the three of us rode bikes around Boston, stopping at a good fish taco place near Fenway Park for lunch. Then Matt went back to The Squealing Pig for his shift, and Ranley and I met him there for a long, delicious dinner, sitting at the bar for about seven hours.

The next day Ranley left, and Matt took me to a sandwich shop on the corner of Tremont and Burney streets, in the Mission Hill neighborhood near his apartment, for dinner. There, I'd meet one of the most memorable people of the whole bike trip.

The name of the sandwich shop was Al's Deli at Wan's Convenience. It looked like a little bodega from the outside, with a green awning with yellow letters. Al Niles, the owner, was the first to greet you as you walked through the front door of his corner store, standing at his grill right by the door ("Wan" was an acronym for his full name—Winston Albert Niles). Al was a big, tall, clean-shaven man of Jamaican descent with short hair; a deep, booming, very intense voice; and a gregarious, charismatic personality. He was a presence, to say the least, and made a point to establish a relationship with every person that walked through his door.

The menu behind the counter comprised individual placards for each sandwich with its name, ingredients, and a large photo of it. The placards took up the entire wall. There was room for nothing else. With all these sandwich choices, I didn't know where to start. I started reading the menu. There was the "The Deathwich," "Richard Pryor," "Jessica Alba," "Heaven Is Here," "Bob Marley," "Three-Way," "Witch Doctor," "The Orgasm," "Bizzy Bone," "David Ortiz," "Nina Caliente," "Jerry Springer," and "The Balboa," to name a few. The photo of "Hush" was blurred and the ingredients a question mark since it was a secret and he's "never tellin.'"

Al entered into the culinary world by happenstance. When he got tired of working for a big industrial company, "mixing chemicals" in a factory setting, he took over a bodega and took a chance at running his own business. About a year into it, he started the sandwich side of it, after college kids from Northeastern kept coming in, asking for something to eat. He started losing grocery business around that time, too, to a new Stop & Shop that had opened nearby. So he started mixing and matching ingredients, and throwing sandwiches together for the students, at very reasonable prices. Mixing ingredients was more fun than mixing chemicals, and the kids kept coming back for more. Some of those college kids helped him with suggestions, and with photographing the growing list of sandwiches to create the placards.[42]

The legend of Al Niles grew from there, and his business took off via word of mouth. Soon, he had a cult following, and was eventually featured in magazines and TV shows, including the Travel Channel's *Man Finds Food*. In 2014, after he opened a new location upon closing the original Mission Hill store at the end of 2013, he told *Boston* magazine, "Anyone can buy a ham and cheese or turkey and cheese; that's bland. I want my food, which is *my* creative art form, to have tons of flavor and a nice presentation. Every bite should make you want to come back."[43]

Still perusing the long, intimidating menu in the original Mission Hill location, I figured maybe I should just ask Al what to get.

"What do you recommend?" I asked.

Intense, and loud enough for everyone in the store to hear, in his Jamaican accent, he clamored, "Go Heaven. You're gonna like it. You're gonna like it *a lot*. All hits here, no misses. If you have a miss, it means that I slipped. *And I don't slip*. It doesn't matter what you have, it's gonna be really fuckin' good."

Another guy in line was also a first-timer. To him, Al said, "So you're a *virgin*."

Then he turned to the rest of the crowd and said, "I'll take it easy on him . . . I'm not gonna hurt him tonight."

Al continued to serenade his store—not speaking to any one person in particular, but the entire group as a whole, as he worked behind the counter, carefully crafting his sandwiches.

"Once you get your sandwich, you're gonna *devour* it. There's gonna be a *feeeeding frenzyyyy*."

Then, a few moments of silence as Al worked his magic. I looked around the store, reading the elaborate sandwich descriptions, noticing a large painting of Yoda on the opposite wall.

Then Al broke the silence by suddenly shouting, "*I got a Pryor!*" startling his patrons.

A high-pitched Jamaican voice responded from the back of the store, sounding far away. "Oh yesss!! Right over here, mon!"

It was a long wait for my sandwich, "Heaven Is Here," but it lived up to the hype and then some. The generous baguette was stuffed with Buffalo chicken, turkey, bacon, roast beef, mozzarella, green peppers, pickles, onions, vinaigrette, lettuce, tomato, and Al's proprietary blend of herbs and spices. It was absolutely delicious—with tons of unique flavor. It had to be the most exceptional, one-of-a-kind sandwich I'd ever had in my life.

Actually, it was so good that I delayed my start and went out of my way to bike to the store the next morning to grab an early lunch before hitting the road—and even waited about fifteen minutes for Al to arrive to open up the store.

"It's a pleasure to have you back, mon," he said as he walked up to the door in the late morning sunshine.

When he saw my loaded bike leaning up against the brick wall of his store, he was immediately intrigued. His eyes lit up, and he started firing questions. Before he even put the key in the door, we spoke for about fifteen minutes about the trip. He handed me his business card. Under "Al's Deli," it read "It's an experience . . . " I don't think I've ever seen a truer slogan. When he was finished asking questions, he paused, smiled, shook his head, and looked down.

"You're a fuckin' monster."

This time, I got the "Bob Marley," enjoying the equally savory, equally un-common concoction in the park across the street. Fall had definitely arrived. It was a blue-skied, sunny day, but there was a very noticeable chill in the air. It was September 20—I had nine days to go. Summer had retired, and the bike trip would soon follow it. But unlike the summer, the bike trip wouldn't make a triumphant return nine months later.

After I ate, I rode past the deli and waved. Al waved back through the win-dow from behind the counter, a big smile on his face. I liked Al. His intensity. His genuineness. The way he took so much pride in his job. A job he was great at. I hoped his business would continue to thrive. I still think of him sometimes, as I'm making a "bland" ham or turkey and cheese sandwich. For some reason, the image of Al waving to me through his store window would be locked in my mind forever. I knew it'd be at that very moment, too, right as it was happening. Somehow, it was already nostalgic.

***

From Boston, I rode down 3A into Duxbury, Massachusetts, where I stayed with the parents of Bobby Murphy, a younger Cornell teammate who was still at school, at their beautiful New England home. I'd met his parents once before—they took me, Alex, and Zim to dinner at Joe's, an old Ithaca Italian restaurant as a thank you "for looking out for Bobby" when he was a freshman playing football. We didn't treat Bobby any differently than any of the other freshmen, and I don't remember why they singled us out, but it was a very kind gesture that I wouldn't forget. The Murphys were far from boring, and it was a fun dinner, so I didn't hesitate to let them know I'd be biking through Duxbury. And they didn't hesitate to invite me for dinner and to stay the night. Bobby's dad, Bob, and his good buddy, Perry, even drove down to Cape Cod the next night to meet me there—so I'd have company again and *another* place to stay (at their second house, in Chatham).

Just off 3A on the way to the Cape, I stopped at Plymouth Rock, the landing site of the Mayflower. It sat in sand a few feet below a fence that enclosed it, the year "1620" engraved on it. It was smaller than I'd imagined, but worth stopping for. There was a line of people there, snapping photos, as you would expect.

A short while later, to get onto the Cape, I had to cross the exceedingly dangerous Sagamore Bridge. With four narrow lanes and absolutely zero shoulder, bikes were illegal on it. I rode it anyway, without incident, but there was no getting used to bridges like that. Even at this point in the trip, on Day 208, crossing it was acutely nerve-wracking—just as much so as Cape Fear Memorial Bridge in Wilmington on Day 1.

After some on and off rain, the gray sky broke into bouts of sunshine on that late Friday afternoon as I rode past old seafood restaurants with lobsters painted on their signs—and crowded parking lots, making me long for company and a nice dinner out.

The company would soon come. When I arrived at the Murphy house—a small, classic Cape Cod-style home—in Chatham, Bob and Perry were already there. It was good to hang out with them—the popular vacation destination of presidents and New England affluency is more fun when you're not alone,

I learned. I had a rest day there the next day, so we had plenty of time to eat some superb fish and chips at The Red Nun (the best of the trip other than The Crazy Norwegian in Oregon), grab some beers both nights at The Squire (a legendary bar in Chatham, where they bought me a purple t-shirt to add to my collection), and do some sightseeing. After a free haircut the next morning (the woman refused to charge me), I rode 28 out to the western part of the Cape, near Falmouth, and exited over the Sagamore Bridge's treacherous twin, the Bourne Bridge, to get back onto the mainland. I shacked up at a motel near East Wareham that night.

The next day, I rode through Mattapoisett and New Bedford along US-6, stopping in Seekonk—at the Massachusetts/Rhode Island border, just outside Providence, for the night. I stayed at the Comfort Inn there and had dinner at TGI Fridays, which was nostalgic because, as kids, we always chose to go to Fridays to celebrate good report cards at the end of each quarter. Dad let us choose any restaurant we wanted, and we always chose Fridays. I'd go there with teammates, sometimes, too, the night before high school football games.

Eating at that Fridays, alone, it kind of hit me. School was over. There were no more report cards. No more football games. It was time to accept that a phase of life was ending, and a new one was beginning. It's not always easy to make a transition like that. I wasn't sure if I was ready. But I was definitely more ready than I was senior year of college. *Much* more, and it was only because of the bike trip. Maybe long journeys are about more than just adventure, proving something to yourself, doing it before it's too late, tuning into humanity's no-madic nature, escaping the routine to slow down time, and smelling the roses. Maybe long journeys are about moving on, too.

WORN OUT

RHODE ISLAND & CONNECTICUT
SEPTEMBER 24–29

"I'm So Tired" – The Beatles

The morning of Monday, September 24, I crossed into Rhode Island, "The Ocean State," (the smallest and second-most densely populated state in the country, behind New Jersey), cycled through Brown University and downtown Providence, and then got on US-1, also known as Boston Post Road or just Post Road, which I'd follow more or less all the way to New York City.

The headwinds were harsh that afternoon, and I crossed into Connecticut, "The Constitution State," late in the day, making it to Mystic, Connecticut, a coastal town known for its seaport museum of centuries-old tall ships.

I didn't get into town until after dark. I had dinner that night at Mango's Pizza Company, the only other one in the country other than the one Mango, Alex, and I had started out of our college apartment (confirmed by Google). At the time, the place had a skeleton logo and a pirate theme, played Jimmy Buffett on Radio Margaritaville, and served pretty decent pizza.

The next morning, I had Friendly's for breakfast, including a Reese's Pieces Sundae. As I sat there, I imagined asking for this moment as a kid. Here it was. It was finally happening. *Ice cream for breakfast.* Mom would never buy us

Cookie Crisp or Lucky Charms or Froot Loops or Count Chocula or Reese's Puffs or any of those other sugary cereals, no matter how much we asked for them, and she certainly wouldn't have allowed ice cream. The stomachache I already had as I climbed on the bike was a robust reminder to never have ice cream for breakfast again.

My knees ached that morning too. I was beginning to feel a little like an old man on the bike by the time I'd reached Connecticut. My sore and creaky knees, perhaps, were my body's way of telling me that it had finally had enough. But it wasn't just my knees. My whole *body* seemed enduringly exhausted, including my mind. The biked squeaked and squawked, whining like a toddler that missed a nap and sounding like it needed a tune-up. The hills I encountered in Connecticut that morning weren't even mildly challenging compared to what I'd faced. But they *seemed* to be. All of a sudden, I didn't feel like the cyclist I used to be, even just weeks before. I felt worn out and burned out.

I rode from Mystic to New Haven, occasionally hopping on the legendary I-95, the United States' most used highway in terms of vehicle miles traveled, according to the Department of Transportation (it's also the country's longest north–south highway and main thoroughfare of the East Coast, stretching from Miami to Maine). The country's busiest highway was intimidating, even for the toughened and seasoned cyclist I had become, and it got the adrenaline going again. The shoulder was wide, luckily, but the traffic was heavy, fast, and large. The skies were a dystopian smokestack plume gray, with a polluting urban landscape below them to match, and the shoulder was littered with broken glass and other debris. Crossing over exits was tricky and dangerous; this was true on all interstates and major highways, but I'd never been on one as busy as 95. There were plenty of other options in this part of Connecticut, so riding on 95 was technically illegal, and of course I knew it, but I wanted to bike 95 before the trip was over, and the ride from Mystic to New Haven was my best chance.

New Haven is a mostly unappealing city, with a high crime rate, but it's also home to beautiful Yale University, my dad's alma mater. I stopped by Yorkside

Pizza, a favorite student eatery on campus and my dad's favorite place to eat at Yale, for a couple of slices and to say hello to the owner, Tony. Tony grew up in poverty in Aigio, Greece, on his family's olive farm. They had no hot water or electricity, and slept on the floor. When he tells you the story of his family, he'll say, "You grew up in a rich country. You don't know poverty." He'll sit down with you, hold your hand as he speaks to you. To escape Greece's Civil War of 1947–48, Tony and his family came over to the US. He started out washing dishes, then selling ice cream. He finally opened his first pizzeria in 1968, then Yorkside Pizza in 1976.

When you sit down for a delicious meal at Yorkside (which, for us, usually consisted of Greek salad, garlic bread topped with melted mozzarella and paprika, and, of course, pizza), Tony will tell you, "This is my house and you are my guests."

He'd hosted all kinds of guests over the years, including the Rolling Stones—in the back room of the pizzeria, the night they played Toad's next door. If you paid three bucks to get into Toad's Place to hear a local band named the Sons of Bob on August 12, 1989, you were in for a surprise. The Sons of Bob *did* play, for about thirty minutes. But then the crowd of a few hundred heard, "Ladies and gentlemen, please welcome the Rolling Stones!" . . . followed by the classic opening riff of "Start Me Up." The Stones hadn't played in front of a live audience in eight years, so they used the secret gig as a warmup before going on tour.

From Yorkside, I rode up to Lloyd and Cathy Suttle's home in the suburbs of New Haven. Lloyd Suttle was one of my dad's professors at Yale. He was also a mentor to him, taking him under his wing. Dad said he "felt at home at Yale" for the first time because of Lloyd. He and Cathy were incredibly kind people. They took me out to a nice Italian restaurant for dinner and some enjoyable conversation, and hosted me that night. They had a very nice, very old home that had been recently broken into, and ferrets as pets. They were the first and only people I've ever met who had ferrets as pets.

From New Haven, I followed Post Road to Westport, and then jutted in-land to the wooded hills of Wilton, where I'd spend my last rest day and final two nights of the trip staying with my mom's cousin, Andrew Gillespie, his wife, Julie, and their two girls, Maddy and Ally. Late in the day on that last rest day, I started to get eager and excited for the final day of the trip—Day 216—the next day. That night, Friday, September 28, we went out for pizza with a group of Andy and Julie's friends, walked through a Stew Leonard's (a cultural staple of the region), and got ice cream. Maddy, the younger sister, handed me a dollar "for the road." I thought that was really cute, so I took it.

On the morning of Day 216, I woke up refreshed. I'd slept very well—not waking up even once. And once I realized where I was and what day it was, I was excited, to say the least. I knew I'd remember this day for the rest of my life. Saturday, September 29, 2012, had been circled on the calendar for a long time, and I was exactly where I was supposed to be—in Wilton, Connecticut. As long as everything went well that day, I'd finish the trip on time and get to celebrate that night in Manhattan, with a big group of family and friends. But unlike any other day on the trip, there was no margin for error. I had a full day of biking ahead of me, and it had to go relatively smoothly for me to hit my goal.

After breakfast with Julie, I rode down their long driveway and turned left onto their street, where I was stopped by Andy and Maddy in the car on their way back from a Saturday morning soccer game (Andy was the coach). After I said goodbye to them and turned off their street, it was back into the hilly woodland I'd rode through the day before. Manhattan seemed thousands of miles away. But I rode with adrenaline, and with purpose.

When I stopped for the final Five-Mile Water/Stretch, my excitement turned to sadness. I realized that a chapter of my life was coming to a close. Not just a phase of life, but a specific chapter. And it wasn't just any chapter; I thought, perhaps, that it was one of the most unique and interesting ones. This trip that had been ahead of me for so long—a big, exciting departure from regular life—was about to no longer be. What was once a far-off, distant, fuzzy dream when I was a college freshman was about to become . . . a *memory*. And maybe, eventually—a far-off, distant, fuzzy memory. As it all was coming to an abrupt close, I realized that, in many ways, I didn't want the journey to end.

After that final Five-Mile Water/Stretch on Day 216, I turned the music on like it was any other day and continued biking south on Boston Post Road. I rode right through downtown Stamford, Connecticut, then somehow made a wrong turn (and got lost for a few minutes), then stopped at a deli for lunch. They didn't take credit cards, so I emptied my wallet with all the cash I had to pay for it. I had exact change. If it wasn't for the dollar five-year-old Maddy had given me the night before, I wouldn't have had enough! If there had been an ATM around, it wouldn't have helped me much anyways. My bank account was just about at zero. I thought it was ironic that the last meal I paid for on the trip literally emptied my wallet.

HOME

NEW YORK PART 2
SEPTEMBER 29

"Salt of the Earth" – The Rolling Stones

I crossed back into New York again, past Port Chester and New Rochelle and into the Bronx, where the streets were crowded and chaotic. From the Bronx, I could see Manhattan's brand-new skyline, with One World Trade Center nearly complete. It was significantly taller than when I had left New York seven months earlier, when it was just beginning to rise over its Financial District neighbors. While I was gone, it had surpassed the Empire State Building's height of 1,250 feet to become New York City's tallest building, and would later top out at 1,776 feet in 2013, as the tallest building in the Western Hemisphere. Lower Manhattan once again had a formidable, soaring skyline; the World Trade Center was *back*. It was immediately apparent that the tower would fit into its new home quite perfectly—a bold, sleek, valiant structure that seemed to embrace the New York attitude, defiantly stretching high and wide into the sky, much like its twin predecessors. It would surely become an unwavering symbol that good prevails over evil in the end. We'd rebuilt—bigger, taller, and stronger than before. Literally rising from the ashes. I didn't know it at the time, but I'd soon be starting my first corporate job in that very World Trade Center complex, all the way up on the fiftieth floor of 7 WTC—the first tower to be completed in the new complex, at 226 meters tall. A new phase of life would start along with it.

I crossed the Harlem River into Manhattan and went down the Upper East Side and into Central Park, where I was one of many cyclists, and went by a long line of people waiting to get into a concert (Neil Young, Foo Fighters, and The Black Keys). While the sections of the Bronx I biked through were new and felt foreign to me, Central Park was welcoming and very familiar. I exited the park at Columbus Circle and biked down Broadway and into Times Square, staying in the green bike lane. New York City felt bigger and busier than I remembered it.

Now, for some reason, I felt a bit like a tourist, awed by the bright lights and towering skyscrapers. I'd always appreciated the irreplaceable energy of New York City's streets, but never quite like this—it took its absence to fully value its presence. I'd missed the less obvious parts of New York too. The neighborhoods away from the walking tours. You could live in New York City, where as many as 800 languages are spoken, for decades and still uncover foreign places within its boroughs—if you're willing to venture out to find the little streets, the unassuming restaurants, the hidden dive bars. And their storytelling people. Perhaps most cities have these things, to a degree; as the urbanist and activist Jane Jacobs said, "By its nature, the metropolis provides what otherwise could be given only by traveling; namely, the strange." But nowhere is it truer than New York.

Right in the middle of Times Square, the music stopped. My iPod died. The song playing was Jay-Z and Alicia Keys' "Empire State of Mind," ironically. After Times Square, I went over to Fifth Avenue and headed south past the Empire State Building, then hopped on Second Avenue.

So many places I'd encountered on the trip had left an imprint on me, and had communicated with me in one way or another throughout the journey. Many challenged me, others accepted me. Most provoked thought. There was the condescending Red Hill in Louisiana. The furious Beast in Texas. The perceptive Peñasco Amarillo in New Mexico. The all-knowing redwoods in California. The belittling Bighorns in Wyoming. The contemplative open plains in South Dakota. They all *spoke* to me, in one way or another. I was waiting for New York, for my hometown, to say something...

And then, on Second Avenue, with only a little over a mile to go, as I was waiting at a red light next to another cyclist, New York City finally spoke to me. It welcomed me home. I'd been waiting for a proper welcome.

"Outta the way, asshole!"

And then, a loud, long, obnoxious honk of the belligerent SUV's horn. Then another one.

I turned around to see an angry, overweight brute with a bright red face and a thick New York accent. He kept *laying* on the horn, the bulging veins in his neck begging for mercy as he continued to scream his head off. Apparently, the other cyclist and I were a little in his way as he tried to make a right on red (rights on red are generally illegal in NYC, allowed only where posted). I couldn't believe it—I only had a mile to go! I'd literally never had an incident like this the whole trip.

"Sorry, I can't hear you," I finally responded, pointing to my ear. That *really* pissed him off.

At that point, the color of his face upgraded from bright red to dark purple and he went full-on ballistic.

"Oh yeah? *OH YEAH? YOU CAN'T HEAR ME? HOW 'BOUT I RUN YA OVAH, YOU (EXPLETIVE) (EXPLETIVE) (EXPLETIVE)."*

He started revving the engine and lurching the SUV forward, in quick, short bursts, just a few feet from me, like he was actually going to run me over. *Not with a goddamn mile left.* In no mood to put up with any bullshit, I backed up to the driver's side window to get right in his face and barked right back at him. A little surprised, he drove away in a huff.

Pulling up to the light again, I looked at the cyclist next to me—a guy around my age with scruffy hair and glasses, who looked a bit like a grown-up Harry Potter, and shook my head. "You believe that guy?" I asked, but he was unfazed.

In a completely monotone voice, like the deadbeat high school economics teacher from *Ferris Bueller's Day Off*, he said, "Just another hot head in an SUV." The light changed to green and we went our separate ways.

I thought about how far I'd come since Day 1, when that guy in South Carolina screamed, "Use the sidewalk!" at me and I just followed orders without saying a word, intimidated.

Minutes later, I made it to my sister Annie's Lower East Side apartment at the end of Second Avenue, on the corner of Stanton and Chrystie. Her two favorite bars were directly below her apartment, conveniently: Bonnie Vee and Rochelle's. When I saw her on the street, she ran over, and I gave her a big hug. It was *so* great to see her. It felt like it had been years! She looked at me with my bike and my gear and seemed to be in disbelief.

"What?" I asked.

"No, it's just . . . this is just *so cool*. I can't believe you went to California and back with just . . . *that*."

I lugged the bike up two flights of stairs to her apartment, got yelled at for stepping on her throw rug with my bike shoes, showered, and changed into fresh clothes. She went ahead of me to walk over to Little Italy, just a few blocks away. After I changed and packed up the bike one last time, I walked it over one block to Bowery. The red t-shirt I changed into was red in the front but had turned pink in the back, faded from seven months of riding under the sun.

It had just gotten dark, and New York City transformed into a different world. Illuminated and alive, but peaceful and tranquil in this part. The pandemonium of Grand Concourse in the Bronx and the tumult of Times Square were distant memories now.

A few people sat outside on Bowery, eating dinner on the street by candlelight. There was a stillness in the air, accompanied by the chill of fall now that the sun had set. It was astonishingly quiet, even on busier Bowery, save for a few distant honks of the horn, soft screeches of brakes, and a gentle rumble of the subway underground—the instruments of that perpetual after-dark Manhattan soundtrack. It was all a confirmation of something I'd always known but before this trip hardly tested: there's *no* place in the world like New York City.

After pausing for a minute or two to listen to this soundtrack, and just appreciate the moment, I got back on the bike. One last time. I rode a few blocks down Bowery, made a right on Broome, went past Elizabeth and Mott, and made a left onto Mulberry. If you look north from this stretch of Mulberry Street, there's a perfect view of the Empire State Building, shining its signature white lights this night; it falls right between the tenements on either side of the street. As I made that left, I nearly got hit by a car!

Right after that turn, I heard someone shout out.

"There he is!"

I knew that voice.

The voice was Uncle John's, unmistakably.

From that moment, the short ride down Mulberry was like floating on air.

I could see La Mela, with its illuminated signs proudly displaying its trademark red apple. That was the finish line I'd imagined for so long. Outside the restaurant, a large crowd had gathered in the street—much bigger than I had envisioned—and as I approached it, a silver ribbon stretched across the street in front me, out of nowhere. It was a finish line. An *actual* finish line. I didn't think there'd be one. And who were the two that unfurled it, just in time, holding each end on opposite sides of Mulberry Street? Uncle John and Uncle Kevin. Uncle Brian would've been there too—right there with them, unfurling the finish line and welcoming me home. While he wasn't there physically, he'd become more a part of the journey than I ever could have imagined, in countless thoughts and conversations.

Maybe, too, he was with me and his best friend Fritz when we raised a glass to him in McFritz's Pub, and when we set out to begin the journey in Wilmington seven months earlier. Maybe I wasn't alone for that encounter with the herd of elk in New Mexico, the storm in Louisiana, the excruciating climb and terrifying descent of Teton Pass, or those crushing crashes in Alabama and Pennsylvania. Or when I knocked on that firehouse door in Mississippi. Or on that day in South Dakota when the motorcyclists helped me out with some desperately needed water. Or as hundreds of thousands of cars and trucks passed right by me, a few feet away. I don't know. But the more time that passes since the trip, the more I realize how lucky I was to come back unscathed. In so many ways, I felt Uncle Brian, the "salt of the Earth," as our family had thought of him in all those years since 9/11, was with me the whole time. Maybe we always carry parts of those who have gone before us. They live on, through us.

* * *

Time seemed to slow down for a few moments on Mulberry Street as I took off my helmet and crossed the finish line, looking around me. After seven months of being almost constantly alone, I was surrounded by family and friends . . . the people in the world most important to me. Everyone was cheering. Even strangers stopped to clap on the sidewalk—even though they didn't know what they were clapping for. That's the kind of thing that only happens in New York.

When you cross the finish line and you're greeted by your family and closest lifelong friends, there's no better ending. It was one of the happiest moments of my life. My life could have taken any number of positive or negative turns in the years to come, but nothing could ever take away that moment. And isn't that what life is, in many ways? A grand collection of moments?

I got off the bike and immediately started hugging everyone around me. The mosaic of familiar faces around me was surreal. My parents, brother, sisters, aunts, uncles, cousins—plus other family, friends, and family friends. Alex and Mango were there. Marty Lyons himself was there. Even Patrick McAleese was there, all the way from Seattle—he'd kept his word.

There was one person that came up to me I didn't personally know. He put out his hand and said, "Tom Mendoza. Let's get to know each other."

I shook his hand and hugged him, even though we'd never met. Of course, I knew who he was. This was *the* Tom Mendoza, the one that the Notre Dame business school was named after. He was a legend, and an important supporter of the foundation.

I could almost feel Uncle Brian's presence there on that final night, too, as if he were looking on from the sidewalk, behind the crowd and onlookers. The World Trade Center was only about fifteen blocks away, after all; we were on the outer fringes of its hallowed ground. I pictured looking up and seeing him back behind the crowd, in the distance. Inconspicuously wearing that FDNY

Yankee hat, he nodded with a very slight smile and took a step back. But then my eyes darted away for just a second, to greet someone I hadn't seen in so long. When I looked back, he was gone.

***

The odometer on the bike read 9,969 miles. I subtracted the 107 miles that were already on it from the training runs before the trip started (the sixty-mile ride to Port Jeff and back plus a few other shorter rides). The result was 9,862 miles. When I graduated college, I had been to thirteen US states. Now, that tally had risen to forty-one.

The group on the street made its way into La Mela, funneling into a private room of the sprawling Italian restaurant. In the front of the room, Dad displayed his large, now-completed map he'd been charting my course and progress on since I'd left—first in pencil, and then in Sharpie. Next to that, there was a board for everyone to write a message on. My favorite note might have been from Patrick McAleese's cousin, Johnny, who I'd just met that night. He simply wrote, "Johnny from Belfast. That was quite the cycle. Well done."

As we sat down to eat, I looked around the room and was grateful for the moment. La Mela's never-changing, family-style courses were as familiar as they were delicious—the abundant five-course meal included large slabs of tomato and mozzarella drizzled with olive oil as a first course; a hot antipasto tray with stuffed mushrooms, roasted red peppers, Asparagus Parmigiana, and delectable mozzarella layered squares called Spiedini Alla Romana as a second course; a heaping pasta tray with gnocchi, tortellini, and Rigatoni Pomodoro as a third course; a meat and seafood tray with Veal Francaise, Chicken Scarpariello, and Shrimp Marinara as a fourth course; and a dessert tray with tartufo, Italian cheesecake, tiramisu, homemade cannoli, and zabaglione with fresh fruit as a fifth course. It was a meal fit for kings and queens. If I were on death row, I'd choose this five-course meal as my last. True to his word, my dad paid for it all. I'd arrived on time, on the evening of September 29, and had won our bet. My dad was always a man of his word.

The room buzzed with conversation as everyone ate. Dad silenced it, though, when he got up to make a very good speech (he'd always been an excellent public speaker). Then Marty Lyons spoke. Marty was a mountain of a man—not only physically (he was six-foot-five and 270 pounds when he played), but charismatically and morally.

When Marty speaks about his foundation and the children it benefits, it's truly moving. He's often brought to tears, along with his audience. In his opinion, he explained, the money we raised was "great"—but the awareness we raised was immeasurable. And he was most grateful for that. Marty spoke with a kind voice. He didn't sound like the man that used to break furniture before NFL games, or the "New York Sack Exchange" member that was penalized for punching Buffalo Bills quarterback Jim Kelly on the ground after sacking him, "giving him the business down there," as NFL referee Ben Dreith famously called as he improvised a gesture of holding someone in a headlock and punching them repeatedly in the gut. Marty called me up and handed me a large lion-shaped trophy that he called "The Heisman" because it was so heavy. He said, "Be careful. It's heavy. It's The Heisman."

I wasn't expecting a trophy, of course, and hadn't prepared anything to say, but as I explained to the group that we were getting close to our fundraising goal of $20,000 and that we'd accept donations until Thanksgiving to try to get the last couple of thousand dollars, Tom Mendoza stood up in the back of the room and pledged another $5,000, on the spot. The room erupted in wild cheers—and then a loud, rhythmic chant of "Tom Men-do-za," over and over, for a good minute or two, as if we were in the bleachers of the old Yankee Stadium. He started to tear up. There was a big reason to celebrate. We'd hit our goal on the trip's final night, exceeding $20,000, and ended up raising about $26,000 when it was all said and done, which was enough for at least six or seven children's wishes at the time.

The inscription on the trophy Marty handed me read:

COAST TO COAST BIKE RIDE
FEBRUARY 27, 2012 – SEPTEMBER 29, 2012

10,000 MILES 216 DAYS
"TO TRUST YOURSELF TO TEST YOUR LIMITS,
THAT IS THE COURAGE TO SUCCEED."
THE CHILDREN OF THE MARTY LYONS FOUNDATION

***

My takeaways from the trip:

1.   The vast majority of people in the world are inherently good, and can be surprisingly generous—even to perfect strangers. Generosity has absolutely nothing to do with wealth.
2.   The country is more physically beautiful than I ever could have imagined; there are still plenty of pristine, unspoiled places out there if you're willing to go out and find them.
3.   Highways are dangerous places.
4.   The Rocky Mountains are steep and cold.
5.   The Grand Canyon lives up to the hype.
6.   Idaho might be the most beautiful state in the US.
7.   Never try to turn a bicycle in the middle of a puddle.
8.   Changing a flat tire never gets less frustrating, but you can get pretty good at it with practice.
9.   Wind is a force to be reckoned with.

I also learned a lot about myself. I learned that, sometimes, the biggest obstacle to overcome is your own self-doubt. I learned that being alone, traveling alone, is okay. Even great, sometimes. And that walking into a bar or restaurant on your own isn't so bad—it can be *empowering*, in fact. Before the trip, I feared being alone. Now, I'll even go to a Yankee game or a concert on my own every once in a while and just hang out with the people in my row—and it doesn't feel weird. There's no longer that fear.

I learned to live in the present and appreciate the little moments in front of your very eyes, as the man on the edge of the cliff in Utah. I learned that some swamps smell like cotton candy. That cycling is the most immersive form of travel. That karaoke is a big deal in Wyoming. I learned that the hard days are sometimes the most memorable; the storm often becomes the most fun part of the journey. I learned the value of getting out of your comfort zone. I learned the importance of searching for awe every day, both in the natural world and in humanity. Of searching for things every day that make us feel *alive*.

But more than anything, I think, I learned this: Don't be afraid. Don't be afraid to take risks and chase your dreams, no matter how formidable their obstacles. You might just receive some unexpected help along the way—help you could have never foreseen. Help that could make all the difference. It may have been a solo trip, but I certainly didn't do it alone.

Since the bike trip, I've found myself striking up far more conversations with perfect strangers than I used to. Traveling alone will change you in that way. Sure, those interactions don't typically render deep, meaningful conversations. They're menial. But I still think they're important. They give you a sense of community. Of humanity. And they're always a nice reminder that the person on the street, in the elevator, or on line in front of you has more in common with you than it may seem at first, regardless of their appearance or culture.

I also learned that long journeys of any kind are respected and admired— and to take one yourself is to be about as fundamentally human as it gets. It's one of the core values of humanity that unites cultures—across states, across continents, and across millennia—similar to how different religions commonly value the welfare of others. If exploration and long journeys are valued today, and are valued as far back in recorded human history as we can go, we can assume that they'll be valued and celebrated far into the future, as well, when humanity has spread to other worlds beyond our solar system. Even if those worlds diverge so much, and are separated by so much space and time that virtually all elements of common culture are lost, we can assume that the core values of humanity will remain—including the need to explore and travel long distances.

As Michio Kaku writes in *The Future of Humanity*, "Various forms of the Golden Rule are found in numerous civilizations . . . The other core characteristic is focused not inward, but outward. This includes curiosity, innovation, creativity, and the urge to explore and discover. All the cultures of the world have myths and legends about great explorers and pathfinders. Thus, the caveman principle recognizes that our core personalities have not changed much in two hundred thousand years, so even as we spread out among the stars, we will most likely retain our values and personal characteristics."[44]

***

The bike still hangs from the wall of my parents' garage on Long Island, collecting dust. The bike that was almost named Talulah. Are there more adventures in its future? Maybe it has other long journeys ahead of it, across other continents. Maybe it will see Europe one day. Or South America. Or Asia.

Maybe. But probably not.

The bike trip was full of surprises. As is life. It wasn't at all what I originally envisioned it to be—with Alex, Mango, Ranley, and Tucker the Jack Russell Terrier, touring the country as a group. It was more difficult and more dangerous than I'd imagined, but also *better*. Actually, it was the best experience of my life so far. Life doesn't always stick to the script—in fact, it almost never does. But that's part of what keeps it so interesting, I think.

On the trip, I found myself enjoying hitting the road more and more as I went, and enjoying meeting people along it more and more as I went. Every day. I knew I'd miss it. That it couldn't last. If we could travel every day of our lives, wandering as nomads across the globe as our ancestors did for the vast majority of human history, *would it be better?* Maybe. But probably not. As Neil Armstrong said on the way back from the moon, "No matter where you travel, it's always nice to get home." It's always nice to sleep in your own bed again.

But, in some ways, moving from place to place every day hardly seemed like *enough* travel to me, somehow. In some ways, the road had become another home for me. I guess I'd learned to just appreciate it *all*. The loneliness and the new friendships. The soreness and the deep sleeps. The trucks and the fresh air. The deserts and the forests. The elk and the stars. The mountain climbs and their panoramic views. The lonesome highways and their little roadside oases. The crashes and the thumbs-ups held out windows. The storms and the scenery. The obstacles and the unexpected help. The headwinds and the strangers. The strangers that shared the road.

***

A couple of days after the La Mela celebration, I went for a bike ride—the old nine-mile loop through Dix Hills—the one I'd imagined as I was battling those headwinds in Kansas. I guess I wasn't sure what else to do just yet.

A few days after that, I realized I'd almost forgotten. It seemed like a lifetime ago, but I had a promise to keep. So I called up the Johnsons, the first strangers to help me on the journey all the way back in South Carolina seven months prior, to tell them I was home.

ENDNOTES

1   *The Future of Humanity*. Michio Kaku.

2   George, Cassidy. "The ancient origins of the new nomads." BBC. August 1, 2021. https://www.bbc.com/culture/article/20210730-the-ancient-origins-of-the-new-nomads.

3   "Gen Z started building wealth earlier than millennials, and an expert says 9/11 is the main event that divided the 2 generations and their views on money" Hillary Hoffower. *Insider*. Sept 11, 2019.

4   Vasarhelyi, Elizabeth Chai, and Jimmy Chin. 2018. Free Solo. United States: National Geographic Documentary Films.

5   Chinchar, Allison. "Here's Why the US Has More Tornadoes than Any Other Country." CNN. Cable News Network, March 7, 2021. https://www.cnn.com/2021/03/07/weather/us-leads-tornado-numbers-tornado-alley/index.html.

6   "Music Can Charm Beasts and Plants into Higher Productivity." Office for Science and Society, May 29, 2018. https://www.mcgill.ca/oss/article/controversial-science-health-quirky-science/music-can-charm-beasts-and-plants-higher-productivity.

7   "Beaufort Scale." National Geographic Society. Accessed July 7, 2022. https://education.nationalgeographic.org/resource/beaufort-scale.

8   Media, NHTSA. "Newly Released Estimates Show Traffic Fatalities Reached a 16-Year High in 2021." NHTSA. NHTSA, May 17, 2022. https://www.nhtsa.gov/press-releases/early-estimate-2021-traffic-fatalities.

9   Jaipuria, Tanay. "Self-Driving Cars and the Trolley Problem." Medium. Medium, May 26, 2015. https://medium.com/@tanayj/self-driving-cars-and-the-trolley-problem-5363b86cb82d.

10 Salge, Christoph. "Asimov's Laws Won't Stop Robots from Harming Humans, so We've Developed a Better Solution." Scientific American. Scientific American, July 11, 2017. https://www.scientificamerican.com/article/asimovs-laws-wont-stop-robots-from-harming-humans-so-weve-developed-a-better-solution/.

11 "Theodore Roosevelt Quotes." TR Center - TR Quotes - Leave it as it is You can not improve on it The ages have been at work on it. Accessed July 7, 2022. https://www.theodorerooseveltcenter.org/Learn-About-TR/TR-Quotes/Leave%20it%20as%20it%20is%20%20You%20can%20not%20improve%20on%20it%20%20The%20ages%20have%20been%20at%20work%20on%20it.

12 *The Language of Humor, An Introduction*, by Don L. F. Nilsen, Alleen Pace Nilsen

13 Turteltaub, Jon. 1993. Cool Runnings. United States: Buena Vista Pictures Distribution.

14 Centers for Disease Control and Prevention

15 "Redwood Facts." Sempervirens Fund, February 25, 2022. https://sempervirens.org/learn/redwood-facts/.

16 "New York's Great Fire of 1835," by Robert McNamara.

17 "Renan Ozturk - LIVECHAT Today with @Gatherfilm &..." Facebook. Accessed July 7, 2022. https://m.facebook.com/renanozturkmedia/photos/a.489137514460452/4394761127231385.

18 CalMatters, Julie Cart and, Thadeus Greenson, Collin Yeo, Jennifer Fumiko Cahill, Meg Wall-Wild, Kenny Priest, Barry Evans, et al. "Humboldt County." North Coast Journal. Accessed July 7, 2022. https://www.northcoastjournal.com/.

19 "Immerse Yourself in a Forest for Better Health." Immerse Yourself in a Forest for Better Health - NYS Dept. of Environmental Conservation. Accessed July 7, 2022. https://www.dec.ny.gov/lands/90720.html.

20 Wiemin Chu, National Geographic.

21 US Department of Commerce, National Oceanic and Atmospheric Administration. "How Much of the Ocean Have We Explored?" NOAA's National Ocean Service, January 1, 2009. https://oceanservice.noaa.gov/facts/exploration.html.

22 US Energy Information Administration. "US electricity generation from renewables surpassed coal in April." June 26, 2019.

23 *The Future of Humanity*. Michio Kaku.

24 *The Future of Humanity*. Michio Kaku.

25 *The Cosmic Perspective, Fifth Edition*. Bennett, Donahue, Schneider, Voit.

26   *The Cosmic Perspective, Fifth Edition*. Bennett, Donahue, Schneider, Voit.

27   *The Cosmic Perspective, Fifth Edition*. Bennett, Donahue, Schneider, Voit.

28   *Brief Answers to the Big Questions*. Stephen Hawking.

29   *The Cosmic Perspective, Fifth Edition*. Bennett, Donahue, Schneider, Voit.

30   *Astrophysics for People in a Hurry*. Neil deGrasse Tyson.

31   *The Cosmic Perspective, Ninth Edition*. Bennett, Donahue, Schneider, Voit.

32   *Astrophysics for People in a Hurry*. Neil deGrasse Tyson.

33   Gray, Melissa. "Hubble Telescope Spots Azure Blue Planet Where It Rains Glass." CNN. Cable News Network, July 14, 2013. https://www.cnn.com/2013/07/11/world/space-blue-planet/index.html.

34   *The Future of Humanity*. Michio Kaku.

35   "Why These Four Presidents?" *nps.gov*. National Park Service.

36   "Dinosaur Skeleton Excavated." *Toledo Blade*. December 27, 1981.

37   "The Day the Dinosaurs Died." Douglas Preston, *The New Yorker*. March 29, 2019.

38   "Site of asteroid impact changed the history of life on Earth: the low probability of mass extinction." Scientific Reports. Kunio Kaiho & Naga Oshima.

39   *Miles from Nowhere*. Barbara Savage.

40   *Miles from Nowhere*. Barbara Savage.

41   "Voyager Spacecraft Statement by the President." Voyager Spacecraft Statement by the President. | The American Presidency Project, July 29, 1977. https://www.presidency.ucsb.edu/documents/voyager-spacecraft-statement-the-president.

42   Hughes, Christopher. "The Old Charm Is Back at Wan's New Location in Allston." *Boston Magazine*. February 8, 2016. https://www.bostonmagazine.com/restaurants/2014/07/29/wans-deli-allston-al-niles

43   Hughes, Christopher. "The Old Charm Is Back at Wan's New Location in Allston." *Boston Magazine*. February 8, 2016. https://www.bostonmagazine.com/restaurants/2014/07/29/wans-deli-allston-al-niles

44   *The Future of Humanity*. Michio Kaku.

Acknowledgements

I'd like to extend big thank yous to my parents, my family, and a few close friends for reading chapters as I wrote them and providing feedback and encouragement over the last few years; my agent Esther Fedorkevich for answering my cold email and taking a chance on a first-time author; my editors Tori Thacher and Katelyn Harger for their guidance and feedback, and for being receptive to my vision for this book (and constant revisions); Brittney Bossow and the rest of the team at Fedd Books; and to all the people that appear in the pages, some of whom I've known my whole life and many of whom I randomly encountered as I rode, for inspiring me to write them. Special thanks to Tommy Casatelli, John McAleese, Kevin McAleese, Greg Fix, and my dad, John J. Nitti, for contributing to this book by sharing their stories over the years.